Contesting Neoliberal Education

Routledge Studies in Education and Neoliberalism

EDITED BY DAVE HILL, *University of Northampton, UK*

Contesting Neoliberal Education

Public Resistance and Collective Advance

Edited by Dave Hill

Routledge
Taylor & Francis Group
New York   London

First published 2009
by Routledge
711 Third Avenue, New York, NY 10017

Simultaneously published in the UK
by Routledge
2 Park Square, Milton Park, Abingdon, Oxon OX14 4RN

Routledge is an imprint of the Taylor & Francis Group, an informa business

First issued in paperback 2011

© 2009 Taylor & Francis

Typeset in Sabon by IBT Global.

Library of Congress Cataloging in Publication Data

Contesting neoliberal education : public resistance and collective advance / edited by
    Dave Hill.
        p. cm. — (Routledge studies in education and neoliberalism ; 2)
    Includes index.
    ISBN 978-0-415-95777-9
    1. Education and state   2. Neoliberalism.   3. Socialism.   I. Hill, Dave, 1945–
    LC71.C66 2008
    379 — dc22
    2008004329

ISBN13: 978-0-415-50710-3 (pbk)
ISBN13: 978-0-415-95777-9 (hbk)
ISBN13: 978-0-203-89306-7 (ebk)

Contents

Tables

Foreword

Peter McLaren

Thanks to the efforts of Dave Hill, Britain's relentless, white-knuckled scourge and leading teacher educator, Marxist educational critique is racking up some considerable achievements in the United Kingdom. Along with comrades Mike Cole, Paula Allman and Glenn Rikowksi, Hill has, with impressive frequency, been pounding away at capital's viscera for decades, specializing in freeing teacher education from the thrall of the forces of marketization and privatization. In the landmark volume, *Contesting Neoliberal Education: Public Resistance and Collective Advance,* Hill has brought together radical/left academics and trade union/labor organization activists in a text that is as uncompromising as it is protagonist. Hill is not content to be merely an editor or a contributor to leftist journals, or the author of leftist tomes; he is a Marxist scholar/activist with unflinching intent. That intent is directed not only at promoting resistance to the globalization of capitalism in general and neoliberalism as policy and practice in particular, but at charting out the promises and possibilities for a postcapitalist society.

Descended from a sturdy workingman lineage whose forebears would just as soon have punched scabs trying to cross the picket line as the time clock on the shop floor, Hill carries socialism in his bone marrow and is ever zealous to do battle with those whose indurate programs and policies confabulated by the highest echelons of education ministries and government agencies tend to derail by the force of inertia interventions into the structural determinations of capital. He is a working-class fighter who is torn between rage at the effrontery of the ruling class' war on the poor and powerless and a desire to manumit all those held in bondage to capital. (See Hill, 2003; Wikipedia, 2008.)

David Harvey argues that the ascendancy of neoliberalism, usually attributed to Thatcher and Reagan in the 1980s, had to be accomplished by popular democratic consent. He writes that "a shift of this magnitude to occur required the prior construction of political consent across a sufficiently large spectrum of the population to win elections" (2005, p. 39). The mobilization and political support for neoliberal economic policies by the transnational capitalist class was accompanied by an assault on Keynesian-inspired state intervention and trade union power; it was followed by the

steady erosion of democratic means for popular participation in the workings of state power and a malignant attempt to contain spaces of resistance
within the public sphere. While much of the educational establishment has
truckled to right wing ideology and the draconian programs that dictate
the social interests of the neoliberal elite (programs that have become so
successful at mulcting the public and that accept the vast and unbridgeable
gap between classes and the scale of suffering produced by such a gap), leftist educationalists have assumed contrarian positions animated by a spectrum of political attitudes often of unmoored vagueness. Yes, exponents of
the educational left want social justice and the empowerment of the working class, but what does that mean, after all?

Unlike the fraternal solidarity of working-class boys sharing a Penny
Dreadful after their fourteen-hour shift in a cotton factory during the days
of industrial capitalism, today's working-class youth are kept fragmented
by internet culture and the politics of conspicuous consumption. So, many
"social justice" leftists have, quite unimpeded, opted to give these youth
more consumer options according to the political contingencies available
in the marketplace. Is this liberation? Some of these same "radical" educators feel that since neoliberalism demands so many unpredictable company
layoffs, that distance learning is a way to empower students suddenly made
maladroit by an unstable economy. Hence, they dedicate themselves to
helping students get re-trained in a competitive and insecure marketplace.
Is this liberation? Accordingly, some of these selfsame educators want students to resist or "decenter" or "trouble" the hegemonic discourses and
discursive orthodoxies that marry them ideologically to the apparatuses
of the state and that naturalize global institutional apparatuses such as
the World Bank and the World Monetary Fund. This is of signal importance, indeed, but without addressing the social causes and deep-seated
structural determinations at the roots of capitalist exploitation, can we
describe it as liberation? As neoliberalism creates conditions that exacerbate racialized forms of exploitation, both in terms of the social relations
of production and the creation of standards based and high stakes testing
regimes, some educators are calling for racially sensitive curricula and
school policies and practices that will help promote an equality of educational outcomes? This is a fundamentally important step, but by itself will
it lead to liberation?

All of the above initiatives are well-intentioned goals, but as *Contesting
Neoliberal Education* makes clear, if not conjugated with the struggle for
a socialist alternative to capitalism, they become fraught with contractions
and in some cases turn into their opposites. For instance, as Mike Cole
points out in this volume, the phenomena of globalization has produced
important new opportunities for more in-depth and nuanced discussions
of ecology and global poverty, but few opportunities are provided in the
public sphere for discussions of world democratic socialism. This amounts,
in effect, to a tacit endorsement of neoliberal capitalism as the best of all

possible economic systems available to humanity. It confers legitimacy upon—or "naturalizes"—a very robust system of exploitation by making it seem necessary and inevitable for world peace and prosperity. In actual fact, it is the root of the problem disguised as its antidote.

In the face of the current assault on the welfare state (the "nanny state" with its "culture of dependency"), the freeing of private enterprise from state restrictions and regulations, the increasing pressure on international trade and investment while ratcheting up the assault on unions and workers' rights, the elimination of price controls, the greater mobility of capital, the reduction of spending on social services, the evisceration of social safety nets, and the withdrawal of investment in the social infrastructure, the seamless transition to another form of imperialist political objectives during elections in key democratic states, regardless of the elected party, the abandoning of anticapitalist agendas in even the most dominant prolabor parties, and the demonization of socialism by the transnational capitalist class, the struggle for an equitable and democratic society seems a ungraspable phantom.

In order to understand what is at stake here, it is important to identify two sharply contrasting types of neoliberalism. The first type of neoliberalism is what John D. Holst calls the "strong version" of globalization and the second type he describes as the "longer version" globalization. According to Holst (2007)

> strong versions of globalization argue that we have witnessed a qualitative transformation of capitalism beginning in the post-World War II era and accelerating in the last three decades. This transformation is the result of an explosion in information-based technology and automation that have pushed manufacturing and productive capital to the margins of capitalist relations. Today's economy is technology- and information-based, characterized most typically by the billions of dollars of financial capital that effortlessly and continuously circulate across the planet conflating space and time, creating a truly globalized economy. In this new economy, the nation-state is nearly powerless. . . . Since productive capital is now marginal in this globalized, financial economy, the producing or working classes are equally marginal as significant actors for social change. In short, then, strong versions of globalization posit that we have a globalized and ever-expanding information economy where productive capital, the nation-state, and the working class are becoming increasingly irrelevant. The political implications of this argument are clear: with virtually no working class and no nation-state, the traditional socialist paradigm is obsolete.(9)

Within the parameters of this "strong version" of globalization, "the agent of the working class and its traditional socialist goals now seen as no longer viable or even desirable"(10) and as a result activists embrace what Holst calls a "civil societarian perspective"; in other words, they have turned to nongovernmental organizations (NGOs) and new social movements operating in civil society (a social sphere generally seen, to varying degrees, as relatively autonomous from the state and the market) "as the agents best situated to protect and perhaps expand this social realm of civil society in the face of increasing "colonization" from new economy forces" (Holst, 2007, 10). According to Holst (2007), this political strategy at times feeds off of and facilitates the privatization of former state-run services in housing, education, and community development and essentially represents "a turn to the local, often couched in a global/local dialectic where low-income people, along with professional adult and community educators, seek private or public funds for local social service projects as a response to globalization forces."(10) Holst (2007) describes the "longer version" globalization as follows:

> Longer versions of globalization, drawing explicitly from Marxist political economy, begin with the premise that capitalism from its beginning over 500 years ago has been based on international or global economic relations. . . . Therefore, one must be immediately skeptical of talk of a qualitative transformation to a "new" global economy. In other words we have not seen a qualitative rupture or transformation of capitalism from the beginnings of the twentieth century. Long versions of globalization are also skeptical of claims of a post-industrial era. This argument is largely based on the idea that the North, through capital flight to the low-wage South, has been reindustrialized . . . foreign direct investment (FDI) reveals that it is almost exclusively controlled by the economies of the North. . . . The fact that Northern economies still dominate FDI and invest it largely among themselves sheds light on the fact that the nation-states attached to these economies are still strong and in fact vital to the continuation of the historical expansion of capitalist relations.(11)

This "longer view" globalization contradicts neoliberal claims that we have arrived at the end of the nation–state and the working-class made by advocates of strong globalization theories, since the nation–state is simply taking on other tasks, such as capitalist expansion and it still works in conjunction with international institutions to brutally implement neoliberal policies. This view of globalization puts the working class and peasants squarely at the forefront of current anti-neoliberal struggles. Holst (2007) correctly notes that

> The fundamental contradictions within capitalism are not external relations (global/local), but contradictory relations internal to the process of capitalism itself that manifest themselves through the long history of the vertical (creating market relations where none existed previously)

and horizontal (territorial) expansions of capitalism that today are commonly placed under the label of globalization.(15)

Drawing upon the work of Paula Allman, Holst maintains that we need to understand critically and struggle against the internal relations of capitalism from which its contradictions emerge and this entails "moving from a limited/reproductive praxis where one merely tries to better one's position within a dialectical relation to a critical/revolutionary praxis where one understands the internal relations and struggles to overcome them."(15) Holst recognizes that we are facing qualitative changes at the level of the economic, and we need new strategies to contest the neoliberal onslaught that follows in its wake.

Holst makes a convincing case that the political goals of "small utopias" engaged by the civil societarians needlessly abandon what is considered the "dead dream" of socialism. Here, Marxist analyses

> should provide the tools to understand that the subjective experience of the enormity of the task of fundamental social change today that pushes the civil societarians to call for its abandonment is dialectically related to the growing objective conditions for precisely such transformation.(31)

Marxists need to acknowledge the qualitative changes of globalization and move beyond merely trying to rebuild traditional left institutions. Capitalism and wage labor cannot solve the day-to-day survival issues of a growing sector of humanity and more than ever we need cooperative sociopolitical economic relationships or what Holst calls the "big utopia" of socialism. This clearly stipulates new forms of organization and struggle.

This is essentially the position taken in *Contesting Neoliberal Education,* where we can discern implicitly the tensions among civil societarian positions and Marxist positions. Hill believes there is value to both positions, but as a Marxist, he pushes readers to consider questions and issues rarely addressed in liberal and left-liberal discussions of neoliberalism and education.

Contesting neoliberalism is a daunting challenge, as Hill's text makes abundantly clear. *Contesting Neoliberal Education* challenges the social norms produced in mainstream classrooms in various geopolitical settings and asks how these norms serve the needs of the corporate–state–military–media complex (or simply, the "power complex"). Youth in contemporary capitalist countries are born into societies intractably marked by asymmetrical relations of power and privilege, irredeemably hierarchicized on the basis of social class.

Hill's book raises the fundamental question: What does it mean when so-called democratic states refuse to let teachers challenge the economic systems that underpin them? The separation between social justice and economic justice is one of the hallmarks of our global capitalist society. Economic justice is, for many politicians here in the United States, just another word for socialism. And given the history of the Cold War here in the United States, socialism is just a substitute word for the evils of totalitarian communism. Inroads to teaching youth about socialism have always been difficult to create, but post September 11, 2001, they have been well nigh impossible. As Naomi Klein (2007) tells us, we were informed in no uncertain terms by the Bush administration that after September 11, 2001 (which was designated as Year Zero), history had to begin over again. Whatever happened prior to this date did not matter and that history has to be re-booted like a computer, with all the files prior to September 11 erased as irrelevant to the immediate goal of the United States: fighting terrorist evil-doers and creating a war economy in order to be able increase corporate wealth. All of the work by social movements that had been gaining momentum before 9/11 was immediately halted. This especially concerns us as researchers who work with contemporary youth, since one of the projects that animates our work is to develop postcapitalist possibilities of living on our deeply endangered planet. Klein (2007) reminds us of another September 11, this time, in 1973, when Chile's president Salvador Allende was killed during a U.S.-sponsored coup led by General Augusto Pinochet. Publicly, the United States maintained that Allende and his party were going to install a totalitarian communist regime in Chile. Privately, however, National Security Advisor, Henry Kissinger, told President Richard Nixon:

> The example of a successful elected Marxist government in Chile would surely have an impact on—and even precedent value for—other parts of the world . . . The imitative spread of similar phenomenon elsewhere would in turn significantly affect the world balance and our own position in it. (as cited in Klein, 2007, 28)

Thus, Allende had to be destroyed. Since that time, the United States has made sure no socialist government would prevail anywhere in the world such that it could serve as a shining alternative to capitalism. I have revisited this moment in the history of Chile as a way of underscoring how political statecraft very much reflects the prevailing assumptions about the nature of the society in which we live. As numerous authors in *Contesting Neoliberal Education* have pointed out the assumption among neoliberal educational reformers is that a capitalist society (because it supposedly facilitates democracy) is desirable whereas a socialist society (which supposedly leads to totalitarianism and fascism) is to be avoided at all costs—even if it means destroying a democratically elected socialist government through violent means.

Capitalism is the backdrop against which everyday life in the United States plays itself out in all myriads of complex and contradictory ways.

It permeates the whole cloth of familial, cultural, social, and institutional life. And it is very much present in the cultural life of the academy and research institutions where we work. But the preservation of capital goes beyond the reproduction of the principal Western powers. Capital must continue to be self-renewing worldwide since it remains the systematic controller of our social metabolic reproduction as a human species, and the forced readjustment of the interstate relation of forces must produce the required cohesion for capital to thrive by any means necessary. The forced reconstitution of modern state—which produces the totalizing command structure of capital—that is compatible with capital's normality is the means by which capitalism is reproduced as a world system, even though such "forced normality" demands that we suffer endless wars, deprivation, famine, the dissolution of international law, the rewriting of constitutional rights, "humanitarian" military intervention, preemptive military strikes, and possibly nuclear annihilation (Meszaros, 2006).

Contesting Neoliberal Education does offer strategies against neoliberalism's "forced normality" we have come to know as the age of barbarism. In the pages that follow the reader will find discussions, analyses and strategies of possibility for continuing struggle and transformation on a number of fronts, from campaigning against neoliberal education in Britain (including campaigning against the SATs), to efforts by NGOs such as the Pubic Services International, public sector workers, activist organizations such as the Socialist Teachers Alliance in Britain, the Rouge Forum in the United States, teacher unions in Latin America, Chavista activists in Venezuela, teachers armed with new pedagogical and curricular approaches ("open architectures of learning"), to global struggles challenging the World Trade Organization (WTO) and the General Agreement on Trade in Services (GATS), to teacher praxis stressing learner initiative and collaboration, to struggles in Porto Alegre for participatory democracy. In this sense, Hill's text is one of promise and hope, while at one and the same time refusing to ignore the seriousness and scope of the obstacles that face us as an international community. His manifesto for revolutionary educational transformation included in this volume, the culmination of years of dialogue with international educational activists and scholars and a protracted struggle against Thatcherite and Blarite educational reforms, is a jeremiad against corporate globalists whose ignoble insinuation into the world of teaching and learning has played havoc with public education worldwide and brings us face-to-face with the most important educational challenges of our times. *Contesting Neoliberal Education* will repay a close reading with new answers to and reformulations of the age old question coined by Lenin, "what must be done"? Most important, Hill's book can help us in our efforts to reclaim the democratic socialist project from the claws of capitalist power.

REFERENCES

Harvey, D. (2005). *A brief history of neoliberalism*. Oxford: Oxford University Press.

Hill, D. (2003). *Brief Autobiography of a Bolshie Dismissed*. Institute for Education Policy Studies. Retrieved March 18, 2008, from: http://www.ieps.org.uk.cwc.net/bolsharticle.pdf

Holst, J. D. (2007, May). The politics and economics of globalization and social change in radical adult education: A critical view of recent literature. *Journal for Critical Education Policy Studies, 5*(1). Retrieved March 18, 2008, from: http://www.jceps.com/index.php?pageID=article&articleID=91

Klein, N. (2007, October 16). *An interview with Amy Goodman of Democracy Now*. Retrieved March 18, 2008, from: http://www.alterinfos.org/spip.php?article1578

Meszaros, I. (2006, September). The structural crisis of politics. *Monthly Review, 58*(4). Retrieved March 18, 2008, from: http://www.monthlyreview.org/0906meszaros.htm

Wikipedia (2008) *Dave Hill*. Wikipedia. Retrieved March 18, 2008, from: http://en.wikipedia.org/wikipedia.org/wiki/Dave_Hill_(Professor)

Acknowledgments

With thanks to my daughter Naomi Hill for her proofing and help and smiles and sunniness in Brighton, England, and to Eleanor Chan of IBT Global in Troy, New York for her proofing and efficiency and greatness to work with, and to Benjamin Holtzman at Routledge in New York for his support and encouragement and patience.

Thanks also to the radical academics, labour movement activists, and leftists and all those exposing and challenging the dominant neoliberal capitalist hegemony, and pointing the way to resistance to national and global economic, social and political injustices and oppression. Not all the writers by any means share my own democratic socialist/Marxist beliefs and activism—writers in this book come from a variety of left and radical political and ideological traditions and perspectives. But we, in this book, unite in our criticisms of neoliberal Capital, and in our belief at its replacement.

Dave Hill

1 Introduction

Gustavo Fischman

No matter how important, contentious or debated an idea may appear to scholars, when a concept becomes a buzzword and is used to describe phenomena as varied as political processes, musical rhythms, economic styles, educational programs and culinary approaches; something akin to a process of willful ignorance begins. Based on the huge number of articles and books using the word in their title, and its ubiquitous presence in casual explanations, I suspect that *globalization* must be one of the most abused buzzwords in contemporary times. In some academic buzzing circles, globalization is so powerful and so pervasive that it appears to explain everything and, thus, any further effort to theorize the phenomenon appears to be a waste of time.

Fortunately, the contributors of this book consistently demonstrate there is an important difference between polysemic concepts and abused clichés. The editor of this volume, Dave Hill, has gathered an impressive group of scholars who, using a variety of critical lenses, engage in the very timely and needed analysis of globalization and neoliberalism as manifested in the economic, educational, political and social dynamics affecting educational institutions.

Globalization is often equated with a vaguely-defined notion of modernization and is conceptualized as a technologically determined process, unavoidable and unstoppable (Friedman, 2005). From this *top down* perspective, globalization is a seemingly complex yet "natural" phenomenon and related phenomena, from the intensification of the use of information and communication technologies, unregulated growth of transnational capital, the supranational character of the management of productive processes, implementation of new worldwide trade and tariffs agreements, to increasing trends pressuring in the direction of internationalization of a culture of consumerism, are also equally naturalized (Bauman, 1998; Harvey, 2003).

Within this top-down perspective (Ball, 2003), there are at least two distinct phenomena. First, globalization implies that political, economic, cultural and social actions are reaching a worldwide scale. Second, it suggests that this worldwide scale is being achieved through an increasing homogenization of patterns of production, consumption and cultural understanding (e.g., human rights, etc.) among states, international corporations and societies. Further, worldwide homogenization is forcing local communities to compete not only in pure economic terms, but also politically and culturally by accommodating their cultural and social particularities to the demands of corporate-defined and standardized indicators of economic efficiency and success.

Doubtless, globalization has resulted in increased levels of capital accumulation, information dissemination and technological discoveries, but it has also intensified disparities and inequalities between and within nations (Hill, 2005; Hill and Kumar, 2009a, 2009b). These gains, disparities and inequalities are reflected in differences in the top and bottom perspectives of globalization (Tabb, 2006). In financial terms, the benefits of globalization have disproportionately gone to the top of society. The income share of the richest 20 percent compared to the poorest 20 percent of the world's population has increased from 30:1 to 61:1 in the last 30 years (Brown & Lauder, 2003). The wealth of the world's 358 billionaires equals or surpasses the combined annual income of 45 percent of the world's population. At the same time, the United Nations Development Program (1996) reports that 1.3 billion people still earn an average of $1 US per day and almost 60 percent (3.3 billion) of the world's population continues to survive on less than $750 US per year. The consequences of globalization have increased the sense of economic precariousness felt among the working and middle classes (Klein, 2007; Stiglitz, 2002; Tabb, 2002).

Given this scenario, it is not surprising then, that the United Nations report on the world social situation concluded that: "Surveys conducted in Africa, East Asia, Europe and Latin America indicate that a growing majority of individuals feel they have no control or influence over the economic, political and social factors that affect their lives. Economic and security concerns are causing a great deal of anxiety, and there is little confidence in the ability or commitment of State institutions to manage these growing problems" (UN, 2005: 113) Undoubtedly, for the majority of the poor working class and unemployed as well as the increasingly impoverished middle classes, their analysis of globalization is much more skeptical, and full of contradictions:

> On one hand, globalization unfolds a process of standardization in which a globalized mass culture circulates the globe creating sameness and homogeneity everywhere. But globalized culture makes possible unique appropriations and developments all over the world, thus proliferating hybridity, difference, and heterogeneity proliferating difference, otherness, diversity, and variety (Meyer, 2007). Grasping that globalization embodies these contradictory tendencies at once, that it can be both a force of homogenization and heterogeneity, is crucial for students to be able to articulate the contradictions of globalization and avoid one-sided and reductive conceptions (Kellner, 2005: 35).

Kellner's suggestion of avoiding reductionism is an underlying premise of this work, and it explains the focus on neoliberal globalization, framed as a complex and worldwide combination of forces and dynamics promoting simultaneously the expansion of loosely regulated market economic exchanges, Anglo-American-like "democratic" forms of government, the use of intensive information technology in all areas of human life, the internationalization of exchanges of goods, services and people and the re-configuration of the meaning, size and functions of the public sector.

The contributors of this book are well aware that neoliberalism is another concept that runs the risk of becoming a catch-all buzzword; that is why while rejecting easy definitions, they expose the ideological bases of key arguments of the neoliberal rationale. The many advocates of the neoliberal reforms in education articulate their discourses around the core belief in the self-correcting qualities of the free market but take pains in depicting their positions as part of a self-proclaimed ideologically neutral discourse of efficiency and accountability (Fischman et al.2003; Giroux, 2008).

Within the neoliberal discourse, institutions associated with the market and loosely-defined notions such as private sector, choice and business like, are sanitized and romanticized. Market failings as well as corrupt operations (such as Enron and WorldCom) and potentially disastrous policies (such as ignoring global warming or neglecting to implement adequate "public policies" as demonstrated during the Hurricane Katrina evacuation) are minimized or erased while the "perfections" of competition are set over and against the "inefficiencies" of state bureaucracies. The role of the State in regulating the corporate sector and in implementing policies aimed at promoting basic social fairness or even timidly redistributing forms of social capital (such as education, health and retirement benefits) are glossed over as the "nanny state" in the enthusiasm for neoliberal politics (Cato *Handbook,* 2005; Huntington, 2005). In this sense, the world is facing what the late Pierre Bourdieu referred to as the "'gospel' of neo-liberalism, a conservative ideology which thinks itself opposed to all ideology" (1998: 126). This gospel is one that serves as a clarion call to combat "by every means, including the destruction of the environment and human sacrifice, against any obstacle to the maximization of profit" (1998: 126).

This ideology without ideology is set over and against the "failures" of social democracy, and the inability of welfare systems to meet the needs of all citizens. Neoliberalism gathers discursive strength and political influence from both its promises of a new kind of non-ideological freedom and a telling critique of democratic failures. It represents, in its own terms, a move beyond politics and back to a state of nature, back to the "natural" impulses of individualism and competition.

At the beginning of the 21st century, there are plenty of "democracies" that have failed to secure minimum standards of fairness and justice. As Brenkman (2000) notes:

> While liberal democracy offers an important discourse around issues of rights, freedoms, participation, self-rule, and citizenship, it has been mediated historically through the damaged and burdened tradition of racial and gender exclusions, economic injustice, and a formalistic, ritualized democracy, which substituted the swindle for the promise of democratic participation. (123)

Despite the problems noted by Brenkman and others (Baudrillard, 2003), the liberal and republican traditions of democratic thought have had enormous influence on the development of extensive systems of public education and a related ethos about the role of education as one of the most effective tools for societies to attempt to address social inequalities emphasizing the principles of fairness, common good and citizenship rights (Anyon, 2005; Lipman, 2003). Granted, the enunciation of these principles was not enough to overcome all the forces that opposed the implementation of truly fair educational systems. Moreover, as the contributors of this book demonstrate in their sharp analyses, it is important not to present the pre-neoliberal educational system as a "golden age of public education." In fact, public schools have never worked as autonomous institutions but as state agencies in a system of controlled democratic institutionalism and increasingly de-regulated capitalism (Carnoy & Levin, 1985). In that regard, schools today always take part in the process of securing the reproduction of the contradictions of the larger social systems.

It is important to emphasize that the criticisms presented in this book are not a nostalgic longing for better times, where supposedly a truly democratic public school system existed, but in the assessment of the poor educational results of neoliberal educational reforms. As David Hursh (2006) comments:

> Contrary to the prevalent view that urban education has been in decline, education achievement has increased for most of the decades following World War II, as measured by the percentages of high school and college graduates and by a decreasing gap in test scores between White students and students of color. It is only within the last few years, under the current high-stakes reforms, such as in Chicago, New York (Hursh, 2004), and Texas (Haney, 2000), that the dropout rate has increased and the test score gap widened. However, even with the increase in overall educational achievement, students have not benefited with better-paying jobs. (19)

Even if the measures of educational achievement do not produce the expected good results, it is undeniable that neoliberalism as an educational discourse has been very influential, not only in changing school practices but also in defining the educational common sense, what can be thought or imagined about schools. The contemporary common sense of the restructured neoliberal global economy is that any society that wants to remain competitive needs to implement educational reforms emphasizing the development of a flexible, entrepreneurial teaching workforce (i.e., broadly educated, specifically trained and without tenure) and a teacher-proof, standards-based and market-oriented curriculum (Peters, 2005; Fischman & McLaren, 2005). Schools and universities must be held responsible, their efficiency and quality measured, their status and outputs ranked, all based on a reductionist logic that equates educational worth with supposedly ideologically free and technically superior perspectives (Altbach, 2007).

The hegemonic position of this rationale was not the product of "natural causes" but part of a long struggle in which the neoliberal defenders were very effective to

> hide public concerns while foregrounding private interests–to encourage people to think of themselves as taxpayers and homeowners rather than as citizens and workers, to depict private property interests and the accumulated advantages accorded to white men as universal while condemning demands for redistributive justice by women, racial and sexual minorities, and by other aggrieved social groups as the complaints of special interests. (Lipsitz, 2000: 84)

Similarly, in most schools, it is nearly impossible to find discourses that emphasize the need for greater democracy or improving quality of life in ways that cannot be measured in economic terms. There is a hegemonic inevitability about the logic of neoliberal reforms, particularly because these reforms are presented as simply rational-technical solutions to the problems of underachievement, separated from their ideological and philosophical origins (Almonacid, Luzon and Torres, 2008; Fischman et al., 2003).

For many educators, the neoliberal emphasis on individualism, measurement and technical solutions can fit well with a commonly accepted (and also carefully and constantly monitored) characterization of schooling within the parameters of a redemptive function: Teaching and learning are individual acts that when properly performed, will solve most problems associated with the lack of formal education (poverty, productivity, morality and many more social ills).

The neoliberal educational discourse is also articulated as a redeeming narrative, and thus, schools should be apolitical institutions, implementing scientifically verified "best practices" which will be assessed through standardized testing (e.g., Elmore, 1996). Taken against public school's constant challenges, mixed record of success and failure and the strong associations between notions of the "public" with authoritarianism, bureaucracy, inefficiency and the paucity of truly democratic schools, neoliberal perspectives reinforce educators' common sense about their individual roles and the need for politics to be kept out of the classroom.

Most of the criticisms briefly presented in this introduction, are carefully considered and analyzed, and pedagogical and political alternatives are presented by this diverse and politically engaged group of educators and scholars gathered around the emblematic figure of Dave Hill.

Mike Waghorne from the Trade Services International offers a sharp analysis of the structure and operations of the General Agreement on Trade in Services (GATS), and the concerns that public sector workers and their unions have about the many ways that GATS undermines democratic processes and institutions in sovereign states. Equally oriented by the need to denounce oppression and offering an alternative, in "Critical Education for

Economic and Social and Environmental Justice," Dave Hill and Simon Boxley present a series of progressive egalitarian policy principles and pro-posals that constitute a democratic Marxist manifesto for schooling and teacher education for economic and social justice.

Terry Wrigley from Edinburgh University, Scotland, presents a bleak yet realistic assessment in his "Rethinking Education in the Era of Globaliza-tion." For Wrigley, humanity is simultaneously facing three kinds of global crises: poverty and debt, a collapse of the planet's ecosystem, and war. What is more, all of them connect back to global capitalism. For this reason, capi-talism now has an even greater need to close down the discursive spaces where connections between these crises and capitalism might be made and where an active critical understanding could be developed. Wrigley concludes that current educational reforms are as much an attempt to prevent people from making sense of the world as a search for greater "effectiveness."

Bernard Regan from the Socialist Teachers Alliance, England, brings his activist experience to his thorough account of the complex and dynamic processes of resistance elaborated by teachers and their unions in "Cam-paigning Against Neoliberal Education in Britain." The next chapter, by Rich Gibson, Greg Queen, E. Wayne Ross and Kevin Vinson, recalls the process of development of the Rouge Forum in its struggles to seek the answers to questions of social justice in schools and out. The Rouge Forum is one among many groups of committed activists who are contributing to the construction of a K-16 movement for progressive change in education and society, but it is the only one that takes on the system of capital publicly and that stresses: Justice demands organization and sacrifice. Being both research and action oriented, the Rouge Forum seeks to critique and engage in a reasoned struggle against standards-based education and high-stakes tests—lynchpins in the continued corporate hegemony of school.

John Lavin brings, in "Solidarity Building Dominican–Haitian Cross Cultural Education," a series of historical and literary definitions for guer-rilla pedagogy as an educational ethic. This chapter ends by presenting a Caribbean community whose educational program is driven by a discourse of radical listening for the purpose of collaborative advocacy that provides a voice to the voiceless.

Luís Armando Gandin's chapter describes and analyzes the experience of the Citizen School in Porto Alegre, Brazil, a progressive citywide edu-cational reform created as a viable alternative to the market-based reforms being implemented worldwide. The article examines how the city adminis-tration—the "Popular Administration" led by the Workers' Party—imple-mented radical changes in the way schools build their curriculum and also discusses some of the successes and potential problems of the proposal and its implementation.

Antoni Verger and Xavier Bonal take the reader again to the analysis of the conflicts between the World Trade Organization and the General Agreement on Trade in Services (GATS) and a broad variety of actors (social movements, trade unions, development NGOs, local governments, public universities, etc.). This chapter contemplates the causes and motives of the reactions against the GATS (specifically, its main effects on the education field), distinguishing three key dimensions: substantive, procedural and symbolic.

Dalila Andrade Oliveira discusses teachers' resistance to the educational policies established by national governments in Latin America. These conflicts are part of a much broader modern crisis of change in the traditional organization of work and society.

Mike Cole follows French Marxist Louis Althusser and examines the roles of the Repressive State Apparatuses (RSAs), and the Ideological State Apparatuses (ISAs) in forging consensus to capitalist norms and values. As a contrast to the political and economic "consensus" which has been engineered in the United Kingdom, Cole introduces the reader to the current developments in Venezuela—at social democracy in action and socialism in embryo.

In the last chapter, Juha Suoranta and Peter McLaren assume the position that socialism and pedagogical socialist principles are not dead letters, but open pages in the book of social and economic justice yet to be written or rewritten by people struggling to build a truly egalitarian social order outside of capitalism's law of value.

To conclude, I want to highlight that each chapter goes beyond declaring a concern with equality and fairness in schools and universities, and simply pointing accusatory fingers to the predatory practices stimulated by neoliberal globalization. All of them cautiously help us better understand the impact of neoliberalism on education and propose strategies aimed at challenging and transforming schools, universities and ultimately societies. In times where most scholars and educators choose to be politically detached, Dave Hill's book offers not only serious scholarship and intellectual courage, but also an unflinching commitment to fairness, justice and social transformation. And that is not a small offering.

REFERENCES

Almonacid, C., Luzón, A., & Torres, M. (2008). Cuasi mercado educacional en Chile; el discurso de los tomadores de decisión. Archivos Analíticos de Políticas Educativas, 16(8). retrieved [6/24/2008] de http://epaa.asu.edu/epaa/v16n8/

Altbach, Philip G. (2007) "Introduction: The underlying realities of Higher Education in the 21st Century" in Altbach, Philip G., & McGill Peterson, Patti (eds) *Higher Education in the New Century: Global Challenges and Innovative Ideas*, Rotterdam Sense Publishers. xv–xxx.

Anyon, J. (2005). *Radical possibilities: Public policy, urban education, and a new social movement*. New York: Routledge.

Ball, S. J. (2003). *Class strategies and the education market*. London: Routledge-Falmer.

Baudrillard, J. (2003). *The spirit of terrorism and other essays*. London: Verso.

Bauman, Z. (1998). *Globalization: The human consequences*. New York: Columbia University Press.

Bourdieu, P. (1998). *Acts of resistance: Against the tyranny of the market*. New York: New Press.

Brenkman, J. (2000). Extreme criticism. In J. Butler, J. Guillary, & K. Thomas (Eds.), *What's left of theory* (pp. 114–137). New York: Routledge.

Brown, P., & Lauder, H. (2003). *Globalization and the knowledge economy: Some observations on recent trends in employment, education and the labour market.* Cardiff, Wales: University of Cardiff.

Carnoy, M., & Levin, H. M. (1985). *Schooling and work in the democratic state.* Stanford, CA: Stanford University Press.

Cato, I. (2005). *Handbook on policy* (6th ed.). Washington, DC: Cato Institute.

Elmore, R. (1996). Getting to scale with good educational practice. *Harvard Educational Review, 66*(1), 1–26.

Fischman, G., & McLaren, P. (2005). Rethinking critical pedagogy and the Gramscian legacy: From organic to committed intellectuals. *Cultural Studies Critical Methodologies, 5,* 425–447.

Fischman, G. E., Ball, S., & Gewirtz, S. (2003). Towards a neo-liberal education? Tension and change in Latin America. In *Education, Crisis and Hope: Tension and Change in Latin-America* (pp. 1–19). New York: Routledge Falmer.

Friedman, T. L. (2005). *The world is flat: A brief history of the twenty-first century.* New York: Farrar, Straus and Giroux.

Giroux, H. (2008). *Against the terror of neoliberalism: Politics beyond the age of greed.* Boulder, CO: Paradigm Publishers.

Harvey, D. (2003). *The new imperialism.* New York: Oxford University Press.

Hill, D. (2005). Globalisation and its educational discontents: Neoliberalisation and its impacts on education workers' rights, pay and conditions. *International Studies in Sociology of Education, 15,* 256–288

Hill, D. and Kumar, R. (eds.) (2009a). *Global neoliberalism and education and its consequences.* New York: Routledge.

———. (eds.) (2009b). Global Neo-Liberalism, the Deformation of Education and Resistance. In Hill, D. and Kumar, R. (eds.) (2009) *Global neoliberalism and education and its consequences.* New York: Routledge.

Huntington, R. (2005). *The nanny state: How new labor stealthed us.* London: Artnik.

Hursh, D. (2006). The crisis in urban education: Resisting neoliberal policies and forging democratic possibilities. *Educational Researcher, 35*(4), 19–25.

Kellner, D. (2005). The conflicts of globalization and restructuring of education. In M. Peters (Ed.), *Education, globalization, and the state in the age of terrorism* (pp. 31–70). Boulder, CO: Paradigm.

Klein, N. (2007). Rise of Disaster Capitalism. New York: Owl Books.

Lipman, P. (2003). *High stakes education: Inequality, globalization, and urban school reform.* New York: Routledge.

Lipsitz, G. (2000). Academic politics and social change. in J. Dean (Ed.), *Cultural studies and political theory* (pp. 80-93). Ithaca, NY: Cornell University Press.

Meyer, J. (2007). "Globalization." *International Journal of Comparative Sociology, 4* 261–273.

Peters, M. (Ed.). (2005). *Education, globalization, and the state in the age of terrorism.* Boulder, CO: Paradigm.

Stiglitz, J. E. (2002). *Globalization and its discontents.* New York: Norton.

Tabb, W. K. (2002). *Unequal partners: A primer on globalization.* New York: New Press.

Tabb, W. K. (2006). Trouble, trouble, debt, and bubble. *The Monthly Review, 58*(1). Retrieved August 15, 2007 from http://www.monthlyreview.org/0506tabb.htm

United Nations Development Program (U.N.D.P.). (1996). *Human development report.* New York: UNDP

United Nations (2005). *The Inequality Predicament: Report of the World Social Situation.* New York: United Nations.

2 The Public Services International

Mike Waghorne

BACKGROUND

In this chapter, I address the issues of globalization, trade and GATS from the perspective of trade union follow-up (especially from the perspective of Public Services International; PSI[1]) to the 6th World Trade Organization (WTO) Ministerial Conference held in Hong Kong in December 2005.

GATS—the WTO's General Agreement on Trade in Services—has had little impact on services trade liberalization to date. Few governments in their first set of GATS commitments, used GATS to liberalize any of their services markets beyond the level of opening that applied at the time GATS was finalized at the end of the Uruguay Round.

Why then do critics suggest that GATS is a new monster threatening the existence of a range of services provided by governments for the public good?

Can both of these claims be true?

GATS critics are not usually talking about what GATS *has done;* rather, their concern is its *potential*. PSI and EI (Education International) fall into this category. We are both concerned with the potential impact of GATS negotiations on services such as education, audio-visual/cultural services, health services, energy, water, waste treatment and so forth. Now, this is a potential only: As we will see later, a number of services were put on the 2006 negotiating table but whether developing countries especially will respond "positively" to these is guess-work.

What do we mean by "potential dangers"? Basically, there are two issues: The future of services for the public good in public hands and of governments' ability to regulate them; and the ability of developing countries to make public service decisions and develop public services in future years. Let's start with a quick overview of these two issues before moving into a general look at the WTO and then a specific look at the GATS details.

PUBLIC SERVICES AND GOVERNMENTS' REGULATORY POWERS

The GATS preamble gives governments a vague right to maintain control over public services but this is a record of an oral "understanding" at Marrakech, with no enforcement rights. GATS Article I 3 (c) (World Trade Organization, 1994) talks of services "supplied in the exercise of governmental authority" and is claimed to protect what we all call public services. However, it has no definitions of two key terms, to which we will come back below, and a WTO Disputes Panel could rule in such a way that it has no real protective standing.

Article VI (World Trade Organization, 1994) specifies a number of conditions—mainly qualifications, licensing and technical matters—where governments can set domestic regulations for services. But the regulatory rights of governments are limited to only the "least trade restrictive" measures—itself open to dispute panel challenges. Governments cannot regulate with certainty for public services.

Article XIV (World Trade Organization, 1994) sets out some general but very restrictive exceptions which governments can use to defend public services.

THE SOVEREIGNTY OF DEVELOPING COUNTRIES

In theory, all governments are equal at the WTO. In reality, many developing country governments admit that they are pressured by the major WTO powers to concede key strategic issues. Worse is the overlap between the GATS and World Bank/International Monetary Fund (IMF) policies. These latter often force a government to privatize/liberalize/deregulate public services or to establish any new public services under private sector ownership or control and/or with private sector participation. But if national development ever happens, WTO rules make it virtually impossible to revert to public ownership/control if a GATS commitment for that sector has been made. This could cut off for many countries the political choice in favor of public services that developed countries have made and can maintain.

In Pakistan, a May 2001 Country Assistance Strategy (CAS) Progress Report prepared by the World Bank expresses approval of the military government's intentions to proceed with rapid privatization and deregulation of sectors such as power and telecommunication. This is despite the potential for abuse in privatizing natural monopolies, especially given the lack of democratic control, and the refusal of the authorities to negotiate with unions affected by the privatization program. The World Bank's report admits that a risk exists and that Pakistan's economic reform and devolution plan "could be hastily implemented and captured by powerful interest groups."[2] Such pressured privatization is often followed by pressure from the international financial institutions, powerful northern governments and the WTO to commit these sectors under the GATS.

And do not think that multinational enterprises (MNEs)—some of the "powerful interest groups"—just sit around waiting for the cherries to fall. MNEs actively lobby the World Bank and the IMF to promote or impose privatization of public services. They actively solicit World Bank projects for privatization, which governments have to accept. The World Bank and the International Monetary Fund often require trade and services liberalization of client governments and, to close the circle, the MNEs are often part of government delegations at the WTO which push for GATS policies and negotiating agendas which cement all these things together.

In Chile, the administrative expenses of the privatized pension system absorb nearly one-quarter of contributions (several times higher than the public system it replaced). So, net rates of return have been severely limited. The United Nations Development Project estimates that because of this 40% of Chileans who participated in these schemes require State assistance to stay out of poverty. The proportion is even higher among women, who are particularly disadvantaged by the privatized scheme.

Pension services are covered by GATS. Some public sector unions used to think that globalization and international trade policy didn't mean anything for public services. They don't think so anymore.

GLOBAL UNIONS AND HONG KONG

Hopes that the 4th WTO Ministerial Conference in Doha, Qatar had set the agenda for a genuine Development Round are being disappointed as one WTO deadline after another has been missed. Developing country concerns are being set to one side on an almost daily basis at the WTO, even if, on paper, there are technical assistance programs. It will be no surprise to workers that no progress is being made on the ability of the WTO to override or undermine core labor standards. The rights to food security and to adequate health care in developing countries are increasingly far from being realized, particularly for the world's poorest, with the worst impact on women. These may not be public services but they are important public policy issues for trade unions.

If the current WTO negotiations are to produce an outcome that could benefit working people, particularly in developing countries, the broken promises from Doha must be resolved and developing countries' concerns dealt with first, before negotiations proceed further to complete the Doha Round. In preparation for our participation at the 6th WTO Ministerial Conference, global unions met to set our policy approaches. The full statement emerging from this meeting, as well as global union analyses of the

Hong Kong Ministerial, are available from Svend.Robinson@world-psi. org and on the www.icftu.org, the former International Confederation of Free Trade Unions (ICFTU) website, which is still live. The website for the newly formed International Trade Union Confederation (ITUC) is www. ituc-csi.org but both sites are accessible for this kind of material, with the ICFTU site holding pre-2007 material.

At all of the WTO Ministerial Conferences there has been a fairly consistent list of issues of concern to unions and allied non-government organizations (NGOs), on the campaign agenda (apart from the trade and labor standards issue already mentioned). The Global Unions' position paper for the Hong Kong Ministerial covered the following issues:

- Transparency, coherence, democracy and consultation at the WTO
- Advancing development and decent work for a decent life
- The non-agricultural market access (NAMA) negotiations
- Services
- Agriculture and food security
- Trade facilitation and the other "Singapore issues"
- Environmentally sustainable development at the WTO. (ICFTU, 2005)

From PSI's perspective, the outcome was predictably disastrous: The services negotiations agenda of the European Union (EU) was nearly totally endorsed, putting many developing countries at risk of significant forced permanent liberalization of their services industries/sectors in return for paltry uncertain gains in agriculture.

SHRINK OR SINK!

As part of its preparations for the 2001 Doha Ministerial in Qatar, PSI began working very closely with a group of NGOs who support the development agenda and whose message is *Our World is Not For Sale!* (OWINFS). In pursuing this, these groups, including PSI, signed a statement called *WTO—Sink or Shrink!,* which is aimed at saying that the WTO should not expand its powers and mandates; that it should fix what many in civil society see as its basic deficits and that, if it does not do these things, then it should be dismantled or de-legitimized. The revised elaboration of that statement for the Hong Kong ministerial is on the OWINFS website (www. ourworldisnotforsale.org) as noted earlier.

Not all trade unions are certain about this PSI–NGO linkage but there has been general agreement among the ICFTU–GUFs (Global Union Federations) that PSI is serving as a useful bridge between the union and NGO worlds and that we should continue this work. It has certainly led to more recognition among NGOs that they cannot achieve their goals if they do not have labor on board.

GATS IN THE BUILT-IN AGENDA FOR 2006

For public sector unions, the GATS is the most significant component of the WTO's built-in agenda. In sharp contrast to the agriculture negotiations, there has been a higher degree of government consensus on the desirability of broader and deeper liberalization of services through the GATS. This unity is most evident among the old Quad countries—the EU, the United States, Japan and Canada. It is only in the last year that, among developing countries, there is a growing opposition to the GATS agenda because of both the lack of balance between the services negotiations and those in agriculture and non-agricultural products and also because of a change in services tactics by developed countries in mid-2005.

Essentially, the developed countries claimed in early 2005 to be frustrated at the lack of progress in the services negotiations, on two grounds. First, they felt that the negotiations were going far too slow. Second, they believed that developing countries were not serious about services market liberalization. What many countries were doing with one-on-one requests from the North was making "offers," if at all, that merely committed themselves to a level of liberalization that was equal to or less than their actual current practice. In other words, people were not opening markets to more foreign trade in services.

So, the North changed tack and the result of the negotiations in Hong Kong was a legitimization of plurilateral requests. That meant that a group of (usually) northern countries would get together and identify a critical mass of countries, service by service, that would make negotiations worth it in terms of genuinely new market access. They would then approach those non-requesting critical mass countries and "invite" them to plurilateral negotiations on a service-by-service basis.

There was a round of plurilateral negotiations with a 2006 timetable, as agreed in Hong Kong. Governments who wished, as a group, to ask other members to open up specific services had until the end of February to make those requests. These did not have to be lodged with the WTO. The governments requested to liberalize had until the end of July to make an offer and, at that stage, begin real negotiations so that governments would have their "new" commitments lodged with the WTO in October. Do not forget that a government that responds "positively" to any one request must liberalize that service for all other member states.

None of these requests or reciprocal offers needs to be made public. Most governments seem to be indicating that they have no intention of revealing what they have asked from others or what they will be offering others. In fact, even identifying which countries have been targeted with these requests has been a matter of leaks and sleuthing around Geneva. That means formally many citizens who elected a government to protect their interests and on a particular policy platform, are being told that what happens at the WTO to their public services is none of their business—they will find out when the negotiations finish.

What services are up for grabs? By late March 2006, we knew of the following: agricultural services; air transport services; architectural and engineering services; audiovisual services; computer-related services; construction services; distribution services; energy services; environmental services (including some water and waste services); legal services; logistical services; maritime transport; postal, courier and express delivery services; private education services; telecommunication services; as well as horizontal requests across all four modes of services and general most-favored nation exemptions.

Now, there will be governments that will say that this information is now all out in the public domain. It is important to recognize that none of the official releases of the requests and offers has been voluntary. All of them have been forced by leaks of the information, leaks that have then seen governments scrambling to make a show of openness and consultation. There is not a shred of evidence that any government had any initial intention of being open with their people or of consulting with their people.

I do not need to say how contemptuous that is of democracy. Our demands to open up the process are not, as some governments claim, undermining their negotiating position, and Pascal Lamy, when he was the European Commission Trade Commissioner and not yet WTO Director General, agreed with us on this when we met with him in early 2003[3], although this contradicted his own first responses to the leaks from the initial bilateral request-offer process. If the process is open, governments can see what their electors say and then frame their (properly confidential) bottom line as they get close to the finish line. But we have the right to know what our representatives are planning to do with our services, and what they are trying to force developing countries to do to theirs.

The problem with what has been said in the last few paragraphs is that this whole process was suddenly put on hold in mid-2006 when it appeared that the whole Doha Round had collapsed. Rather than declaring a failure, the WTO simply decided to "suspend" negotiations to allow for a period of "reflection." All serious negotiating stopped in all sectors, although some technical work continued—in services, on the domestic regulations front, to which we will return. Certainly, the plurilateral negotiations had got nowhere by the time of the suspension, although indications were that the North was beginning to realize that by turning up the heat on the South, it had actually stiffened resistance in the South and created a negotiating environment in which countries could work together to block requests. They were talking of going back to the old system.

During the reflection period and since the official resumption of talks in early 2007, there have been ongoing negotiations on domestic regulations, under Article VI (4) of the GATS (World Trade Organization,

1994). These negotiations aim to develop rules that would permit challenges to general, nondiscriminatory regulations on the basis that they are, in the view of a WTO panel, "unnecessary" or "anticompetitive." The regulations concerned are those relating to qualification requirements and procedures, technical standards and licensing requirements.

The WTO does not have the right to contest the content of such regulations, only to query whether they are as least trade restrictive as is possible. There is much public debate on whether this is a substantial threat to the right of governments to regulate. Our reading of the GATS is that governments retain the right to regulate but lose the security of knowing that regulations (which can be any kind of official measure) democratically adopted are secure: They can be challenged and effectively overturned at the WTO. There is an argument that some aspects of labor market regulation may fall foul of such rules. Certainly, in an EU context, this was an issue several years ago in a transport strike that affected transborder traffic and, therefore, trade. We come back to this again below.

GATS AND PUBLIC SECTOR WORKERS

I now turn to public sector union concerns about GATS. There are many civil society concerns about the WTO's GATS. Many developing countries used to say that they saw the GATS as the most development friendly of all the WTO treaties, although, as noted above, that verdict seems to be changing. For public sector and education unions, however, the five most significant concerns relate to:

1. Threats to the security of existing public services (see for example, Hill, 2006; Rosskam, 2006; Navarro, 2007).
2. The needs of developing countries wanting to develop public services (see for example Devidal, 2008; Leher 2008; Verger and Bonal, 2008).
3. The potential undermining of governments' ability to regulate with certainty;
4. The mobility of labor and
5. The need for there to be a full assessment of GATS before negotiations proceed.

I am going to start by describing the four modes of trade under GATS as they might affect public services. I will pass on through the concerns about developing countries and the regulatory issues fairly quickly, not because they are unimportant but because many other civil society bodies share our views on these matters and they are well known. I will then move on to concerns we have about the movement of labor since that is less often dealt with by people concerned about GATS. Finally, I will cover the assessment concern.

GATS does not operate in isolation. The WTO works in close policy cohesion with the World Bank and the IMF. In fact, a proposal at Doha to have wider policy cohesion with other international and intergovernmental organizations, including UN agencies, was rejected by trade ministers. The World Bank and the IMF act as the butchers, who inspect, slaughter and dress the meat. The WTO then puts it into permanent refrigeration until MNEs want a cut.

Governments in developing countries (but not only those) are told by the World Bank and the IMF what to do to their government services—cutting them back, sacking staff, privatizing the services or contracting them out—and urges them, under Quad and MNE pressure, to liberalize their services under GATS. Then the GATS disciplines keep you on the treadmill of further liberalization. Unless you are prepared to trade away something else you value, you cannot go back on a commitment you made with one arm up behind your back: GATS is a one-way street.

Under GATS there are four forms of trade in services—"modes" in WTO jargon. Note that some of the examples I give here are things that we as public sector unions would not necessarily oppose. The last three of these are conceptually different from the traditional concept of cross-border trade in goods.

A point here about the GATS negotiations as they stood at mid-2008: no progress had been made in negotiating any agreed text on services, beyond what had been agreed in Hong Kong—indeed, on whether any new text was even required; on the domestic regulations negotiations, fresh texts appear from time to time, with some reported progress, but each such text still contains many disputed paragraphs. Readers can only follow progress on the WTO website.

Mode 1: Cross-Border Supply

This is the supply of services from the territory of one member country to the territory of another member country. It corresponds most readily with normal trade in goods. Examples include banking, data processing, architectural services and medical consultations transmitted via telecommunications or mail. Currently there is a lot of telemedical servicing from the United States to Arab Gulf states, telediagnostic servicing from China to several Asian countries and from Mexico to Central American countries. Virtual universities are providing university courses across national borders. The potential for growth here lies in the development of Internet and telecommunications access.

Mode 2: Consumption Abroad

This refers to situations whereby consumers of a service go to another member's territory to get the service. Examples include tourism, ship and aircraft maintenance. Students travel to study in foreign countries and patients travel from one country to another to get treatment. The treatment may be of higher quality, cheaper, faster or simply not obtainable in the patient's country. This also includes the practice of people seeking exotic therapies in poorer countries. Developing countries may have price advantages in surgical procedures. India and Cuba are both cited by the WTO as having significant price advantages in this area.

A key question is whether you can use such services and have your home country pay for them on social security/insurance. This can be a major policy issue, although it seems to have been settled positively in the EU.

In my part of the world, it certainly used to be the case that Fiji, which could not afford to provide a full range of high-tech or highly specialized services for its people would, on an approved basis, send patients to Australia or New Zealand for some heart treatments, for example. However, people travelling from developed countries to developing countries for such purposes on a heavily commercialized basis can distort training and treatment priorities in the host country, as we will come back to shortly.

Mode 3: Commercial Presence

This is the setting up of a branch of a foreign service supplier in another member country. Examples include hotel chains, insurance companies and foreign banks. Health service examples include the U.S. Sun Health System clinics in Europe and the Singapore Parkway hospitals and dental surgeries throughout South-East Asia. In education, particularly in the higher education sector, universities are exporting their services by establishing university campuses in foreign countries. Degrees or diplomas are then granted from the country of origin of the university. The current services negotiations have made clear what many GATS critics have maintained for a long time: GATS has become essentially an investment treaty, a tool by which multinational capital can prize open developing markets. Many of the current GATS requests, either on a service basis or in the Mode 3 horizontal requests, are demanding that northern companies get the right to majority equity ownership of services in host countries. Go back and look at that list of service requests and it becomes clear that strategic areas of developing country economies are being re-colonized.

Insurance is a dangerous example under Mode 3. Many governments did not realize, when they committed themselves to liberalize financial services that they were liberalizing health insurance as well—allowing foreign health insurance companies access to their markets. This is a real Trojan horse, as companies get access to this "innocuous" part of the health system and then use it as a base from which to infiltrate and take over the service delivery itself.

Dr. Suwit Wibulpolprasert, Deputy Permanent Secretary in the Thai Ministry of Health (suwit@health.moph.go.th) is a potential source of data on what happens under health service liberalization—not necessarily GATS driven. He describes both the foreign and internal brain drain in the Thai health services as a result of liberalization. He saw what was an improving doctor/hospital provision in rural areas turned into an urban drift. In turn, this transmuted into an urban provision of services for the wealthy and foreign tourists until the 1997 financial crisis stopped and reversed foreign investment in hospital facilities. He also saw how Thai medical training started to be redirected into meeting the needs of westerners, not those of Thais. The financial crisis outcome saw health workers returning to the rural areas as the short-term horizon investors pulled out. "Long may the crisis continue," says Suwit.[4]

Mode 4: Individual Presence

In WTO jargon this is called *presence of natural persons*. It means services provided in a host country by people who are nationals of another member country. This includes, for example, the services of teachers, accountants, nurses or doctors. The temporary employment of health professionals is particularly common in the Arab/Gulf states. The GATS agreement is quite specific about how this relates only to *temporary* entry by people. It does not at all cover the permanent migration of people. The main problems with this mode are that temporary is not defined and can last from a few months up to five years; there is no definition of which workers are covered. In theory, the original signatories to GATS thought they meant only top level professional and managers such as architects and senior Mechanical and Nuclear Engineering staff working in a foreign subsidiary for a project. It is this Mode 4 to which I am going to return later.

GOVERNMENT SERVICES ARE VULNERABLE

While GATS specifically excludes the coverage of services *"in the exercise of governmental authority"*[5] under two explicit conditions it remains unclear and untested as to what this actually means. The two terms, which are basic to the asserted protection for public services, are not defined in the GATS or anywhere else in the WTO texts. So we do not know—nobody knows until there is a dispute panel ruling, which there has not been so far—what the GATS means by services delivered "on a commercial basis" nor do we know what is meant by a service delivered "in competition with another service provider." No serious commentator that I know of, including senior WTO staff, disputes this. Anyone who tells you otherwise is a fool or a liar.

The WTO Secretariat does not give legal interpretations. It says this can only happen following the outcome of dispute hearings. It does, however, give advice or explanations. We have sought such advice that I have made available in the Appendix[6] to this chapter but let me quickly summarize it here. Essentially, David Hartridge, former Director of the WTO Services Division acknowledges—and his successors and colleagues at the WTO concur—that it is not clear as to when money "charged" for a service (university student fees, for example) counts as a commercial operation: Is it enough that some fee is charged or does it have to represent some concept of a market price, such as when a university system charges different fees for different kinds of courses? Similarly, it is not agreed as to when a government service is in competition with a private provider. If the public university system has to accept all students who have qualified for admission while a private university will admit only students who can pay, then are they really "competing" for the same market? The latter question is important also for other parts of the GATS because if the public university system is receiving grants/subsidies from the state, then the national treatment rules of the WTO could mean that, where a government has made a GATS commitment for university education system, it might have to provide the same subsidies/grants to the private system. Given that we also do not know what the GATS means by subsidies, it is not clear what other support that the state provides to its public university might have to be extended to private competitors.

GATS dispute panels in other WTO areas have traditionally ruled in very narrow hard interpretation terms that suggests that trade generally really does trump all other concerns and there is good reason for defenders of education, health and other public services to fear that their services are not finally protected by the GATS texts. All we can rely on is that ministers agreed informally in Marrakech not to include public services under GATS. But George Bush was not there at that time and if he can treat written treaties and agreements the way he has so far, why should we trust him (and others) with an informal agreement which he was not party to?

When one considers the scope of privatization and commercialization possible—including prison systems (in parts of Australia and the United States), hospitals, health care and health insurance, tertiary education, energy, water and aspects of social welfare—any reassurance about the safety of public services under GATS is misleading.

In health services, for example, rising costs associated with ageing populations, more expensive treatments, over-servicing and the rise of widespread epidemics have coincided with falling taxation revenues. Pressures to commercialize more and more of our health services have meant more private hospitals, private insurance and private medicine. Governments are under pressure to accept reality and the ground is laid for GATS commitments. GATS can apply to health services. GATS applies to any service.

Another question that public sector GATS critics overlook, especially those concerned about health and education, is that when governments make health or education commitments under the GATS, they are generally doing so only for the professional/clinical services of teaching, nursing, doctoring and so forth. Because of the way that the WTO classifies services, many other services commitments made by governments may include significant parts of their health and education systems: insurance, catering, cleaning, building maintenance, IT services, library and research services/ facilities and so forth. If governments have not excluded the health and/ or education elements of these services when they made commitments in those support/peripheral services, then it is possible to find that the teachers, nurses and doctors are the only parts of the system that are supposedly protected under GATS. Once the multinational companies have surrounded these professional services with liberalized service sectors inside the system, it is a simple step for them to say: "You have given us the rest of your health/education system. Why not just hand over the rest and let us run the whole show?"

DEVELOPING COUNTRIES

These next comments elaborate on those concerns for developing countries caught in the World Bank–IMF trap I talked about earlier. They are forced into privatizing their public services by the World Bank or IMF. They are then threatened by Quad countries or MNEs that they won't get loans, aid, and investment if they don't liberalize under GATS. I have spoken with national delegations that cannot afford to have a mission in Geneva and they tell me that they don't need bulldozers in their countries—the World Bank–IMF–WTO–Quad–MNE process does the same job. If you doubt the brutality of the WTO negotiating culture, go to the Focus on the Global South website (www.focusweb.org) and read Aileen Kwa's publication *Power and Politics in the WTO*.

Having privatized, liberalized and committed their services under pressure, if these developing countries later want to develop public services as people have done in Europe, they find that they cannot realistically go back on their GATS commitments. To try to do so would force them to lose something else of value under the GATS rules. The unholy bullyboy becomes a way of depriving developing countries from developing public services that people in Europe take for granted.

Of course, one of the best examples of this at present is the huge number of countries which the EU is currently urging to open up their non-drinking water services for EU multinationals, even though the EU has made it clear that it will refuse to open up its own water services—an action which would be politically suicidal.

REGULATIONS

The GATS does not prevent governments from regulating, including in sectors where they have made commitments. But that is too simple a summary. Apart from general horizontal GATS rules, GATS allows governments to regulate in areas not committed. It allows regulations for a variety of reasonable reasons even in areas where they have made commitments. However, when it comes to "qualification requirements or procedures, technical standards or licensing requirements" in the area of services, governments must not take measures (not just regulations) which are unnecessary barriers to trade in services. How do you know when any of your measures are "unnecessary barriers"? When someone lodges a dispute claim against you and you may then find too late that your action must be rescinded or you will face financial penalties from the successful complainant member states. This takes away certainty from governments and becomes an incentive to do nothing to protect standards and so forth.

One particular group that tends to get agitated about the GATS impacts on services regulations is the municipal sector. Many public services, most in some countries, are delivered at (and owned by) municipalities or state/provincial governments. Even conservative councils/states get angry when they hear that their national government is negotiating on these issues without consulting them. This has resulted in hundreds of municipal, regional and state/provincial governments passing resolutions declaring themselves GATS free and saying to their national governments that they will not consider themselves bound by GATS commitments made in their areas. This movement has been especially strong in Europe, Canada, the United States, Australia and New Zealand. Depending on the national constitution, such resolutions may have only political repercussions for the central government but in some countries this has a legal consequence as well.

MODE 4

Unions are concerned at the implications of Mode 4 trade—the temporary movement of natural persons to provide services—in all services covered by the GATS. However, the reality is that many services are not yet typified by a large movement of temporary persons to provide services as envisioned under Mode 4. When the GATS was first negotiated, it was agreed that Mode 4 would cover the movement of professionals such as architects and engineers or others working on major projects under a contract that a foreign firm had won—to build a harbor, a bridge or a roadway system. These people would be on site to supervise the project but would be heading back home once their part of job was done. It would also cover intracompany transferees, where a multinational company with a commercial presence in a host country would station some of its senior people in the foreign subsidiary/branch for one or two years. And there was also provision for "business visitors"—people who worked for a company that was providing cross-border services of one kind or another under Mode 1, and who were visiting their customers in the host country.

Unions were not especially concerned at these developments. These people tended not to be union members and/or they were not a threat to the local labor market. However, in the current round of services nego-tiations, developing countries have made it clear that they want this old understanding changed. For them, the competitive advantage that their workers have in terms of a willingness to work for low wages offers the possibility of many other groups of workers to move to a host country to provide services on a temporary service contract. For the sending country this offers a way of solving acute unemployment problems, of generating foreign exchange as these workers remit their earnings back home and of getting the skills of its workforce upgraded abroad.

Unions fear a number of things. The potential brain drain caused by hav-ing a permanent pool of skilled workers outside the country can be critical in health and education systems (even if there is a possible brain gain effect in some cases). There is a fear that a large enough pool of such workers (remember, they are not supposed to be entering the labor market properly) can lower the wage and conditions floors for local workers who earn local wages and have local working conditions. There is also a fear, based on real experience in many European countries, that such temporary service con-tracts are ritually and massively abused, such that many "temporary service providers" simply move from one project to the next, effectively becoming a part of the labor market in numbers large enough to make a negative impact. The construction labor market in Germany is one such example.

In such circumstances, unions have insisted that such workers must have equity with local workers: equal pay rates, access to union membership, equal protection under antidiscrimination legislation/policies and so forth. Several developing countries have explicitly rejected the notion that their exported labor must have such equitable treatment. In fact, countries such as India have proposed that such workers would not be governed by the law and entitlements of the host country but by those of the sending country. This certainly happens already, before the GATS negotiations have started, and has led to gross abuse of such migrant workers—abuse that goes beyond the denial of trade union and worker rights and extends into physical and sexual abuse that is expertly hidden. It has certainly seen many nurses and doctors being ripped off in their host country as their skills are ripped off by employers who use these skills but pay such people as nurse assistants rather than as registered nurses. I have spoken with a former labor attaché of one South Asian country (now a trade negotiator in Geneva) who saw the abuse that his people were subject to in one of the Gulf States. He asked his government whether he should protest: *You just keep quiet*, was the response, *or else our people will be tossed out of the country and that gov-ernment will simply bring in people from X instead.*[7] In another context, we might call this human trafficking.

In response, unions and many NGOs have argued that because it is not possible to handle temporary workers without impacting on labor and migration policies, the WTO has no mandate to deal with these issues and that therefore, Mode 4 should be taken out of the GATS.

One further issue, Mode 4 activists tend to focus on mass movements of workers. It should be kept in mind that in some small island nations, even the loss of one anesthetist could close the country's only intensive care unit. Ethical recruitment strategies are not just fine words: They can save lives.

ASSESSMENT

The GATS text requires the Council on Trade in Services (CTS) to carry out a full assessment of the impacts of services trade liberalization under GATS before a round of negotiations. No such assessment has been done and many developing countries have complained about this, arguing that it is both ridiculous and unfair to ask them to make new commitments when there is no available evidence on the impacts of services trade liberalization. The CTS has attempted to "bury" this complaint by "agreeing" to have assessment as a standing item on its meeting agendas but this does not produce the evidence which people seek. Yet again, the WTO stands aside from international trends that demand that policy be evidence based. Not at the WTO.

PITY ABOUT THE DEMOCRACY

As the above indicates, the GATS has the potential to impact on public services of many kinds. When proposals are made to get member states to make further GATS commitments, the whole process is carried out in secret, away from the eyes and ears of the people who own, pay for, run, provide and use these services. Many of the GATS rules have the potential to impact on the security with which governments can operate in terms of policy setting and rule making. It may well be that some of this does not come to pass, that critics land up with egg on their faces. But egg on your face is a better option than no egg at all. The WTO may be a trading body but we must not let them trade away our democracy.

APPENDIX: EXCERPT FROM REPLY OF DAVID HARTRIDGE, FORMER DIRECTOR OF THE WTO TRADE IN SERVICES DIVISION, TO PSI ON 31 MAY 2000.[8]

1. *What GATS protection is there for a government which wishes to declare the whole of one service a public service and /or a public monopoly?*

    Article I of the GATS makes it clear that there is a complete exemption from the GATS for all services supplied "in the exercise of governmental authority," which means any service which is supplied neither on a commercial basis nor in competition with one or more service suppliers. Such services are not subject to any GATS disciplines—they are simply outside its scope. A government which maintains a given service as a public service or a public monopoly would not need to declare it as such: There is no obligation to notify governmental services.

Not all monopolies, of course, are "public monopolies" in the sense that they provide services supplied in the exercise of governmental authority, which I take to be the sense of your question. There are monopolies which operate commercially and have nothing to do with government, even if they have been granted monopoly rights by the government, and in dealing with these the government is bound by the normal GATS obligations, notably the Most Favored Nation principle. Article VIII of the GATS, which deals with monopolies and exclusive service suppliers, also contains certain disciplines intended to ensure that such monopolies do not act in a way that would undermine the country's non-discrimination and market access obligations on other services which the monopoly may be in a position to influence. But nothing in Article VIII overrides the basic point that services supplied in the exercise of governmental authority, as defined in Article I, are outside the scope of the Agreement. . . .

2. *What protection is there for a government which allows both a private services provision and a public provision but wants to ring-fence the public component?*

The basic answer is the same: If the public component, as you put it, consists of services supplied in the exercise of governmental authority, it is outside the scope of the GATS, by virtue of Article I. It is perfectly possible for governmental services to co-exist in the same jurisdiction with private services. In the health and education sectors, for example, it is so common for public and private sectors to co-exist that I would regard it virtually as the norm. It was in order to preserve the non-commercial nature of such governmental services and to put the right to maintain them beyond question that the governments negotiating the GATS agreed on the exclusion in Article I. Again, there is no need for a government to take any specific action to "ring-fence" the public component. The status of the public component could only ever become an issue if some measure taken by the government concerned were to be questioned by another WTO Member.

3. *Is there any prohibition on a government subsidizing the public provision of a service, in a context where there is a commercially viable private service which does not receive such subsidies?*

At present there are no specific rules in the GATS on the subsidization of services. Article XV recognizes that in some circumstances subsidies may have distortive effects on services trade and mandates negotiations "with a view to developing the necessary multilateral disciplines to avoid such trade-distortive effects." These negotiations are now under way but it is impossible as yet to predict what their outcome will be. It is certain, however, that whatever disciplines were agreed they would not apply to governmental services as defined in Article I, because these simply are not covered by the GATS. There could be thus no prohibition on subsidies to the public sector which were not extended to private service providers—even if financial transfers within the public sector could be regarded as subsidies. I would expect such transfers to fall outside any ordinary definition of subsidies. In answering this question I have again taken your "public provision of a service" as meaning governmental services as defined in Article I. It would not be sufficient to meet this definition for the government simply to own a service provider operating in competition with the private sector.

Since I have said above that at present there are no rules in the GATS on subsidies, I should make it clear that there is one exception to this. If a government wants to subsidize national suppliers of a service on which it has made a market access and national treatment commitment, but not to extend the subsidy to foreign suppliers of the same service, it should make that clear as a national treatment limitation in its national schedule; otherwise a national treatment commitment without limitations would be understood to mean that the subsidy was available to national and foreign suppliers alike. But once more I should emphasize, with apologies for insisting on the point, that subsidies to governmental services would not have to be scheduled—they are not covered.

4. *Are there any limits on the kinds of conditions which a government can impose on foreign and domestic providers when it comes to universal access provisions? (Obviously, there are negotiating limits, if you want anybody to invest at all but that is a different matter.)*

There is nothing in the GATS which would limit the universal service obligations which a government might impose on foreign and domestic providers. For example, it would be possible to require that banks wishing to establish in the country should set up branches in every village. It would even be possible to impose such a requirement on foreign banks alone, as a limitation on national treatment. As you suggest, that would no doubt ensure that no banks came in, but there is nothing in the GATS to prevent such a requirement.

5. *More specifically, as an extension of Question 4, would it be accept-able for a government to say, in the water services sector, for example, that all investors (foreign and domestic) who wish to enter the market, must pay a development levy of X% to finance water services in less attractive parts of the country?*

Again, there is nothing in the GATS which would make such a requirement inadmissible. Furthermore, it would be possible to make it applicable to foreign investors only, by means of a national treat-ment limitation. Perhaps I should make it clear what I mean when talking about "limitations" in this sense. When governments make commitments to allow foreign suppliers to provide a service in their country, they set out the conditions attached to the commitment in their national schedule of commitments. In each case, they indicate any limitations on market access or national treatment which they wish to maintain: the entry "none" in the market access column means that there are no limitations on access and the same entry in the national treatment column means that foreign suppliers will be treated in the same way as national suppliers. If a government wanted to apply a universal service obligation to all providers, national and foreign, it would not need to indicate this in the schedule; the nego-tiators were agreed that universal service obligations were not to be regarded as market access limitations. However, if the condition were applied only to foreign suppliers it would need to be inscribed in the national treatment column, because it would obviously represent a substantial differentiation between national and foreign suppliers.

NOTES

1. Public Services International (PSI) is the global trade union federation for public sector trade unions, with 651 affiliated unions in 154 countries, orga-nizing some 20 million members. PSI works in conjunction with another nine global union federations covering other sectors of the economy and with the International Trade Union Confederation (the former International Confed-eration of Free Trade Unions) and the Trade Union Advisory Committee at the OECD—the Global Unions group. PSI also works closely with a number of NGOs on a range of WTO issues, especially on GATS and on development issues.
2. This is based on the ICFTU, ITS, TUAC paper, Global Unions' Statement: The Role of the IMF & World Bank, Ottawa, 17-18 November 2001 (pages 3-4). The short quote within the passage comes, as identified, from the May 2001 WB CAS for Pakistan.

3. Personal Communication
4. Personal Communication
5. GATS Article I, s.3(c) (World Trade Organization, 1994)
6. Personal Communication
7. Personal Communication
8. In this Appendix, all questions in italics are from PSI; the rest of the text are the replies of David Hartidge

REFERENCES

Devidal, P. (2008). Trading away human rights? The GATS and the right to education: A Legal Perspective. In Hill, D. and Kumar, R. (eds.) (2009) *Global neoliberalism and education and its consequences*, pp. 71–99. New York: Routledge.
Hill, D. (2006). Education Services Liberalization. In E. Rosskam (ed.) *Winners or Losers? Liberalizing public service*, pp. 3–54. Geneva: ILO.
International Confederation of Free Trade Unions. (2001). A paper entitled *Global unions' statement: The role of the IMF & World Bank*. Ottawa, 17-18 November 2001. Canada Retrieved August 27, 2007, from http://www.icftu.org/displaydocument.asp?Index=991214325&Language=EN.
International Confederation of Free Trade Unions. (2005). *Final trade union statement on the agenda for the 6th ministerial conference of the World Trade Organisation (WTO)—Hong Kong, 13–18 December 2005*. Retrieved August 27, 2007, from http://www.icftu.org/displaydocument.asp?Index=991221675&Language=EN.
International Confederation of Free Trade Unions. (2006). *Summary of trade union priorities for the 30 April 2006 deadlines in the WTO trade negotiations*. Retrieved August 27, 2007, from http://www.icftu.org/displaydocument.asp?Index=991223590&Language=EN.
Leher, R. (2008). Brazilian Education, Dependent Capitalism, and the World Bank In Hill, D. and Kumar, R. (eds.) (2009). *Global neoliberalism and education and its consequences*, pp. 125–148. New York: Routledge.
Kwa, A. (2003). *Power and politics in the WTO, focus on the global south* (2nd ed.) Retrieved August 27, 2007, from http://www.focusweb.org/publications/Books/power-politics-in-the-WTO.pdf.
Navarro, V. (2007). *Neoliberalism, globalization, and inequalities: Consequences for health and quality of life*. Amityville, NY: Baywood.
Our World Is Not For Sale. (2006). *Stop corporate globalisation: Another world is possible. A statement of unity from the Our World Is Not For Sale network*. Retrieved August 27, 2007, from http://www.ourworldisnotforsale.org/about.asp?about=signon&lang=english.
Rosskam, E. (ed.) *Winners or Losers? Liberalizing public services*. Geneva: ILO.
Verger, A. and Bonal, X. (2008). Resistance to the GATS. In D. Hill (Ed.) *Contesting neoliberal education: Public resistance and collective advance*, pp. 181–201. London: New York: Routledge.
World Trade Organization (1994). Final Act embodying the results of The Uruguay Round of Multilateral Trade Negotiations, available at http:/www.wto.org/english/docs_e/legal_e/03-fa_e.htm in which all references to the GATS can be found in the Annex 1B General Agreement on Trade in Services (GATS), the full text of which can be found at http://www.wto.org/english/docs_e/legal_e/26-gats_01_e.htm.

3 Critical Teacher Education for Economic, Environmental and Social Justice
An Ecosocialist Manifesto

Dave Hill and Simon Boxley

PART ONE: THE RESTRUCTURING OF TEACHER EDUCATION

Critical Teacher Education

On the relation of radical egalitarian teacher education to securing economic and social justice in society, Paula Allmann (2000) suggests that

> education has the potential to fuel the flames of resistance to global capitalism as well as the passion for socialist transformation—indeed, the potential to provide a spark that can ignite the desire for revolutionary democratic social transformation throughout the world. To carry the metaphor even further, it does so at a time when critical/radical education, almost everywhere, is in danger of terminal "burn-out." (p. 10)

How far this transformative potential can be realized is the subject of considerable debate, for contemporary theory as well as practice. The autonomy and agency available to individual teachers, teacher educators, schools and departments of education has been brutally curtailed—though not obliterated—in the face of the structures of capital and its current neoliberal project for education (Hill, 2001d, 2004a, 2004b, 2005b, 2007a). It is necessary to highlight the phrase "potential to fuel the flames of resistance" in Allman's quote above. One of the greatest structural blocks on the development of cadres of "teacher-intellectuals" willing and able to develop and ultimately lead counterhegemonic action is the political neutralization of potentially resistant professionals at the earliest stages of their induction into the mechanisms of schooling and teaching as governmentally proscribed ritual. Hence the main focus of what follows represents an attack on the ideological functioning of bourgeois initial teacher education/"teacher training."

As noted elsewhere[1] the neoliberal project for education is part of the bigger picture of the neoliberal project of global capitalism.[2] Markets in education worldwide, combined with so-called "parental choice" of a diverse range of schools, are only one small part of the education strategy of the capitalist class, with its Business Agenda *for* Education (what it requires education to do) and its Business Agenda *in* Education (how it plans to make money out of education).[3]

The bigger picture, seen both globally and across national policy spectra, enables an overall understanding of how the move towards markets in education relates to the overall intentions and project of transnational multinational capital, and to the policies that governments try to put into practice on their behalf. This big picture shows that schools are continuing their role, *inter alia,* as a disciplinary force of the capitalist class through the corporate managerialization of teacher education. For McLaren (2000) "the major purpose of education is to make the world safe for global capitalism" (p. 196) and:

> What teachers are witnessing at the end of the century is the consolidation of control over the process of schooling and particularly over the certification of teachers in order to realign education to the need of the globalized economy. (McLaren & Baltodano, 2000, p. 35)

The scarcely contested success of this project has rendered the social democratic (and the sometimes contradictory liberal progressive) content and objectives of initial teacher education in England and Wales, for example, almost unrecognizable, compared with those of the 1960s and 1970s. Then there was, in many schools and teacher education institutions, and, indeed, in some local education authority/school districts in the 1970s and early mid-1980s (such as the Inner London Education Authority) a real commitment and curriculum content and objectives relating to issues of equality and to the social and political (if not economic) contexts of education policy.

Detheorized Teacher Education in England and Wales Under the Conservatives and New Labour

One key characteristic of this restructuring is the detheorization of initial teacher education (ITE). In England and Wales, under Conservative and New Labour Governments, this has entailed the virtual removal of issues of equity and social justice, let alone economic justice, from the ITE curriculum. Study of the social, political and economic contexts of schooling and education has similarly been hidden and expunged. In England and Wales and elsewhere, ITE is now rigorously policed and its critics sidelined or, in some cases, dismissed (Hill, 1997a, b, e; Rikowski, 2001f). Since the Conservative Government introduced new regulations for teacher training and education in 1992/1993 (Department for Education [DfE], 1992, 1993) "how to" has replaced "why to" in a technicist curriculum based on "delivery" of a quietist and overwhelmingly conservative set of "standards"—for student teachers.[4] This has, of course, had a major impact on the teaching force, and thereby on schooling. Teachers are now, by and large, trained in skills rather than educated to examine the "whys and the why nots" and the contexts of curriculum, pedagogy, educational purposes and structures and the effects these have on reproducing capitalist economy, society and politics.

New Labour has (for example through its regulations of 1998; Department of Education and Employment [DfEE], 1998) *to an overwhelming extent,* accepted the Radical Right revolution in ITE, as it has in schooling, the Conservative legacy has scarcely been amended in terms of routes into teaching, the changing nature of teachers' work, and curriculum and assessment (Hill, 1999a, 2000). For millions of working class children, in particular, education has become uncritical basic skills training.

When set in the context of what could have been done to promote critical reflection and a more egalitarian curriculum for ITE, the New Labour changes from Conservative policy here are very modest indeed. Consequently, the Conservative government policy and proposals for ITE are being sustained *almost in toto,* based as they are on a neo-Conservative cultural nationalism and authoritarianism and a neoliberal competitive, individualist anti-egalitarianism.

Education policy effecting this detheorization of teacher education is a symptom of the project of capital, which requires the suppression of oppositional, critical and autonomous thought. Needless to say, government in the United Kingdom, as elsewhere never presents its technicist agenda for ITE as repressive, but makes it quite clear that the ongoing focus on the Standards Agenda requires a workforce who is not prone to the ideological waywardness of the 1970s and 80s! Government's policing of "standards" has been consistently represented as "neutral." "To them it is the *teachers* who have suffered from ideology. . . . The government's firm standpoint on the other hand, represents a drive for 'common sense.'" (Jeffrey & Woods, 1998, p. 57; emphasis added). As McMurtry (1991) has noted, the suppression of critical voices is particularly iniquitous in education since

> Freedom in the market is the enjoyment of whatever one is able to buy from others with no questions asked, and profit from whatever one is able to sell to others with no requirement to answer to anyone else. Freedom in the place of education, on the other hand, is precisely the freedom to question, and to seek answers, whether it offends people's self-gratification or not. (p. 213)[5]

This occurs with the "systematic reduction of the historically hard won social institution of education to a commodity for private purchase and sale" (McMurtry, 1991, p. 216), where the "commodification of education rules out the very critical freedom and academic rigour which education requires to be more than indoctrination" (McMurtry, 1991, p. 215).

Strategic Considerations: Resistance in the Here and Now and the Environmental Question

For the great majority of student teachers in England and Wales, Radical Left groups, ideas and educators have negligible impact upon their lives either within or out of schools and universities. The voices of socialists and Marxists are rarely if ever heard presenting the case for a wholescale revolutionary transformation of values and praxis in ITE and schooling (for a fuller discussion of the role of ideology in effectively marginalizing socialist consciousness among teachers and students in England and Wales, see Cole, 2008). Furthermore, almost all "big-P" Political positions are effectively withheld from ITE students during their "professional studies," lending educational discourses a dull patina of neutrality—the currency of the *traditional intellectual* (Gramsci, 1971). As coordinated political action among students and more widely among the population as a whole has tended to fracture into a series of specific issue-orientated campaigns, a kind of pedagogical economism, those few political engagements with which ITE students will be faced are largely of the "how should we teach about the War in Iraq" kind. Of course, the importance of such issues should not be diminished: On the contrary, many of the questions raised by single issues and campaign groups go to the heart of the neoliberal project for education which the manifesto sketched in this chapter take on in a frontal assault. We argue that the mix of specifically politically orientated campaigning over, for instance privatization issues alongside more traditional bread-and-butter teacher trade union type campaign work, can and should become *stimuli* and *subject matter* for ITE and school staff workplace discussions. Clearly, the role of the teacher unions is crucial in this respect, and the efforts of individuals and groups in relation to both local and global issues are very often most effectively articulated within and through trade union channels and structures. It is no surprise then that Radical Left groups in the United Kingdom have made the teaching unions, and, in particular the largest of these, the National Union of Teachers (NUT) the major conduit through which to argue for change.

The great stalwart of the NUT left, Bernard Regan, recalls the battles conducted by the Union and Socialist Teachers Alliance (STA) elsewhere in this volume (Regan, 2008). Though, as has often been remarked, it "punches above its weight," the organized left within the NUT remains relatively small and its presence and influence is not evenly felt, especially outside the capital. As in British politics more widely, the STA reflects a range of positions and includes within it or works alongside members of most of the small (some *very* small) parties and groups on the Marxist Radical Left. In order to offer examples of some of the organizations from which this chapter draws its research and to map the wider political territory within which the authors are to be located, it is relevant to very briefly mention some of the U.K. parties (associated, in educational terms, with the STA) with which some common ground is shared on the question of radical educational resistance to neoliberal hegemony. Similar groups, sometimes larger, sometimes smaller, exist in most developed countries and some developing countries. Such parties or groups, or grouplets/groupuscules, collaborate together in various Internationals.

In the United Kingdom, alongside non-affiliated and ex-Labour activists, and a few remaining Marxists and socialists within the Labour Party, the STA includes or has recently included teachers who are organized and have published educational pamphlets or periodicals as members of the following organizations:

1. The Socialist Workers Party (SWP): the SWP's status as the largest avowedly Marxist group in Britain is reflected in their numerical presence in the NUT. Whereas the SWP previously organized separately and published *The Class Issue* newspaper aimed at education workers, it has over recent years worked within the STA, and where it has organized teachers' meetings independently, such as at NUT conference, has done so largely under the auspices of its electoral alliance, Respect.
2. The International Socialist Group, the British section of the Fourth International are also active within the STA, and (currently) are members, albeit with increasing unease, in the SWP's Respect project, and publish conference bulletins. Their presence is stronger in Birmingham than London.
3. The Alliance for Workers' Liberty operates within the STA and have an organizational presence in Leeds and Nottingham. They publish the annual *Workers' Liberty Teachers* magazine.

Other than the SWP, all of these groups are small. Two other groups are visibly present within the NUT. The Socialist Party (formerly Militant, then Militant Labour) has had a consistent commitment to union work over many years and has successfully won places on the Union's Executive. Its relationship with the STA is generally cooperative, but was strained by its launch of a bid for the General Secretaryship in 2004 in opposition to the STA's backing for the left Campaign for a Democratic Fighting Union candidate. The Socialist Party (SP) have the most organized faction of any single left party within the NUT, with a web presence (http://socialistteachers.org.uk/) and bulletin publication, *Socialist Party Teachers,* and relative influence within their electoral strongholds of Coventry and Lewisham. The SP has also organized education workers under the banner of its Campaign for a New Workers Party (CNWP). The tiny Workers Power (British section of the League for the Fifth International) backed the SP's leadership effort as well as joining the CNWP. They published a teachers' newssheet entitled *Class Matters*.

In total, STA members and those education workers organized within or on the periphery of these Radical Left groups, along with the smattering of teacher members of other socialist groups in the United Kingdom such as Alliance for Green Socialism, Socialist Alliance, A World to Win and Permanent Revolution, can be counted in the (low) hundreds, rather than the thousands across the whole of England and Wales. (The total membership of all Radical Left/Marxist groups in England and Wales is probably between 5,000 and 8,000). It is thus unsurprising that, even given the relative strength of the NUT with its membership of 265,000, very few student teachers are ever exposed to proposals of the kind offered by these organizations and in this and similar articles.

The National Union of Teachers, in cooperation with the National Union of Students has recently begun to establish campus NUT student societies, with the first launched in the University of Winchester, University of Central England, Manchester Metropolitan and Canterbury Christchurch in late 2007. Though limited in scope such a development can only be welcomed as a means by which ITE students might be introduced to principled positions which run counter to "Third Way" and neoliberal hegemony in educational discourses. Student teacher trade union meetings might at least open up some democratic space within which the possibility exists for critical discourses and consciousness to arise. It is hard to overestimate the overwhelming passivity inculcated by anticritical, technically-orientated ITE curricula, and even such small interstitial opportunities for the articulation of counterhegemonic ideas should be welcomed as a means to offer students the chance to consider the kinds of arguments presented by the labour and trades union movement and the Radical Left.

We have already referred to the importance of "single issue campaigning" and its apparent supersession in the new politics of "the Big ideas" of the past. Of course, socialists have not historically failed to recognize the relevance of such work for galvanizing and mobilizing student support for broader antineoliberalcapitalist agendas. It is therefore probably inevitable that those such as the left in the NUT seeking to build opposition to broad swathes of government policy will need to continue to engage with the iconic issues of the day—the occupation of Iraq, the Palestinian question and global climate change *as educational questions*.

Let us take the last of these as an example. Debate within Radical Left political formations will continue to build around responses to the social, economic and environmental impact of ecological crisis for years to come, and with the Respect project, which was an attempt to mobilize on the back of the momentum created by the anti-war groundswell, appearing to run out of steam, this focus for campaigning may be increasingly prioritized. Currently, across both the Radical Left, and the labor and trades union movements, socialists are enthusiastic to demonstrate their green credentials. There are parallels and historical precendents for this in Australia, see for example, Burgman and Burgman (1998) *Green Bans, Red Union* and Mallory (2005) *Unchartered Waters*.

The Turn to Ecosocialism

The International Socialst Group (ISG), along with, to a greater or lesser extent the SWP, SP and the rest have organized and published materials (e.g., Kelly & Malone, 2006; Cole & Wade, 2007). The ISG support-ing Socialist Resistance has recently (September 2007) published *Savage Capitalism—The Ecosocialist Alternative* (Socialist Resistance, 2007; from the ISG, see also, Wilkes, 2007a, 2007b) on capitalism and cli-mate change, representing a major "turn" to ecosocialism by the ISG.[6] The Radical Left rightly recognizes that discussions concerning extreme weather and peak oil resonate widely within the United Kingdom, even when fundamental questions over the commodification of nature and the crises of capitalism do not. This may be particularly true within educational settings where youthful green sentiment sometimes runs strong. It is thus imperative to make the connection between opposition to "climate chaos" and neoliberal policies—indeed, to the capitalist sys-tem itself—unfettered growth and an education system which feeds, sup-ports and reproduces both the production and consumption sides of an unsustainable economic system. This chapter is not the place to draw out these connections,[7] let it suffice to say that, in his last days Paolo Freire (2004) recognized that "[e]cology has gained tremendous importance at the end of this century. It must be present in any educational practice of a radical, critical, and liberating nature" (p. 47).

The strategic efforts of the Left in aiming to transform ITE also need to reflect the increasing significance of the environmental–ecological–jus-tice struggle. Recent developments in critical ecopedagogy emphasize an education within a "dialectics of justice" (McLaren & Houston, 2005b, p. 169), the two sides of this dialectic being *environmental justice*—the question of the unequal distribution of harmful environments between people—and *ecological justice*—the justice of the relationship between humans and the rest of the world. McLaren and Houston aim to "map out what a dialectics of environmental and ecological justice might look like for critical and revolutionary educators by examining how justice toward those exploited under the capitalist class system is increasingly shaped by environmental concerns" (pp. 169–170). Fundamentally, what this means for those working with ITE and other students is a drawing out of the complex web of relations between (a) local, place-based environmental injustices; (b) historical injustices arising out of the circuits of capitalist social, political and ultimately economic relations (including racism and colonialism); (c) the impacts of industrial and neoliberal processes on the planet's ecosystems and (d) the ideological production of nature under capitalism. The exploration of this web of relations operates to allow stu-dent teachers to develop critique of educational and social practice at All-man's different levels of truth (Allman, 1999). Understanding the material and ideological production of nature (and indeed environmental crisis) as a social and historical process highlights how our ideas of what matters in nature is never fixed, uniform or stable. What an ecosocialist project for ITE and education, as McLaren and Houston suggest, "broadly illuminates is precisely how the present state of nature is neither inevitable nor desirable—and that ecologically and socially just alternatives exist." (p. 173).

PART TWO: RADICAL LEFT PRINCIPLES FOR EDUCATION AND FOR ITE

The Radical Left and Education

In the face of the Conservative and New Labour restructuring of initial teacher education, Marxist, socialist and Radical Green-Left teacher educators share principles and policies for counterhegemonic theory and practice in teacher education. We now proceed to define a set of Radical Left principles for re-theorized egalitarian *education as a whole* in Tables 3.1 and 3.2, then in Table 3.3 and Table 3.4 a set of principles and proposals for the ITE curriculum.

There is some debate within the Radical Left over the specific policies suggested, notably over questions of the degree of student-based pedagogy and course development. The following four principles for education as a whole are, however, widely accepted by the Radical Left.

In the recent period, several groups on the Radical Left in the United Kingdom and Europe have also begun to recognize the shortcomings of some features of well-established Marxist educational theory in relation to the environmental crisis, identifying Promethean elements in established Marxist educational principles.[8] Thus the four overarching Radical Left principles for education as a whole are expressed through the following twenty principles,[9] which include some recognition of the emerging debate both in Europe and the United States over what McLaren and Houston (2005b) term "critical ecopedagogy." [10]

Table 3.1   List of Four Overarching Radical Left Principles for Education

- Vastly increased equality (of outcome)

- Comprehensive provision (i.e., no private or selective provision of schooling)

- Democratic community control over education

- Use of the local and national state to achieve a socially just (defined as egalitarian), anti-discriminatory society, rather than simply an inegalitarian meritocratic focus on equal opportunities to get to very unequal outcomes

Table 3.2 Radical Left (and Green-Left) Principles for Education

1. Vastly increased funding for education, resulting in, for example, smaller class sizes, better resources and hugely improved, low environmental impact school buildings set in grounds conducive to children's development of a love of nature as well as of their communities

2. A complete end to selection and the development of fully comprehensive schooling, further and higher education

3. A complete ban on private education

4. Schools and colleges on a "human scale" within or as local to communities as possible

5. Greatly increased provision of free school transportation, including, where possible "walking buses"

6. Free nutritious school food, prepared onsite with the use of locally sourced organic produce where possible

7. Cooperation between schools and local authorities, rather than competitive markets

8. Greatly increased local community democratic accountability in schooling and further education, rather than illusory "parental choice"

9. Increased powers for democratically elected and accountable local government to redistribute resources, control quality and engage in the development of anti-racist, anti-sexist, anti-homophobic policies and practices

10. The enactment of egalitarian policies aimed at achieving greatly more equal educational outcomes, irrespective of factors such as social class, gender, "race," sexuality or disability, while recognizing that what education can achieve is limited unless part of a thoroughgoing social transformation to eliminate poverty and discrimination

11. An anti-elitist, anti-racist, flexible common curriculum that seeks to support the transition from current social relations to those based on socialist cooperation and ecological justice, to be negotiated by local and national governments in cooperation with workers' representatives and communities

12. The curriculum to be rich and varied, allowing themes, natural and human processes to be explored in a range of ways—artistically, musically, scientifically, politically, ecologically

13. Place-based learning, concerned with the meaning of everyday life: Critical studies of environmental impacts of capital on local scales alongside historical injustices arising out of the circuits of capitalist social, political and ultimately economic relations

14. Teaching and learning to foster critical awareness, sensitivity towards and confidence and ability to challenge ecological and social injustice, a planetary consciousness rooted in an internationalist global citizenship, and empowerment to act in defense of the oppressed, of other species and ecosystems

15. The abolition of punitive testing regimes and the exploration and establishment of alternative creative assessment practices

(continued)

Table 3.2 Radical Left (and Green-Left) Principles for Education (continued)

16. Teachers educated to exercise authority in democratic and anti-authoritarian ways, engaging in critical ecopedagogy, with a commitment to developing their school and community as sites of ecological and political awareness and activism

17. A breaking down of boundaries fixed within educational systems for example, between childhood dependency and adult responsibility and between subject specialisms

18. Teachers and administrators who act as role models of integrity, care and thoughtfulness in institutions capable of embodying ideals in all of their operations, avoiding hypocrisy in a separation of academic and theoretical ideals from reality

19. A recognition on the part of teachers and officials that all knowledge acquired in schools and Further Education (FE) and Higher Education (HE) institutions such as universities carries with it the responsibility to see that it is well used in the world

20. A fostering of cultures within classrooms and schools and FE and HE institutions which is democratic, egalitarian, collaborative and collegiate promoting an educational system the aim of which is the flourishing of society, collectives, communities and ecosystems

Radical Left Principles for ITE

The similarity between the Radical Right and New Labour in the United Kingdom is remarkable [11]. The lack of congruence between the Radical Left and the Radical Right/New Labour axis is less remarkable: Both the Radical Right and New Labour have identified themselves substantially in terms of their anti-socialism.[12]

We now want to detail principles for economic, environmental and social justice within teacher education. These, we suggest, should form the basis of the review and development of current policy, theory and not least, practice in ITE. In the table below, we set out those principles, together with New Labour, social democratic (e.g., much of "Old Labour"—the Labour Party prior to Tony Blair's assumption of leadership in 1994), and Radical Right positions on these principles.

Radical Left Proposals for a Core Curriculum for ITE

These proposals do more than return to the status quo *ante* the Thatcherite election victory of 1979, or the (Labour Prime Minister) James Callaghan Ruskin speech of 1976 (Callaghan, 1976) that presaged the end of both liberal-progressive and social democratic ends in teacher education and schooling (with its call in "the Ruskin Speech" for prioritizing economic and vocational ends of schooling). Instead, they should be regarded as arising in a landscape

Table 3.3   Fifteen Radical Left Principles for the Initial Teacher Education Curriculum

	Radical Left	New Labour	Social Democratic	Radical Right
1. The development of classroom skills and competencies	√√	√√	√√	√√
2. The development of subject knowledge	√√	√√	√√	√√
3. The development of intellectual critical skills	√√	√√	√	XX
4. Commitment to ethical/moral/environmental "critical reflection" and its egalitarianism	√√	XX	√	XX
5. Inclusion of data on equality issues organized both as core units and as permeation	√√	XX	√	XX
6. A holistic approach to social, economic and environmental justice in the curriculum	√√	XX	X	XX
7. Skills in dealing with discrimination, harassment and labeling within classrooms and institutions	√√	√?	√	XX
8. The development within institutions of open *fora* on social and ecological justice and equality where students and staff in institutions can meet in a supportive environment	√√	XX?	√?	XX
9. Development of critiques of competing social and economic theories and ideologies in schooling and society	√√	XX	?	XX
10. Development of knowledge and skills to critically examine the ideological nature of teaching and the nature of teachers' work	√√	XX	?	XX

(continued)

Table 3.3   Fifteen Radical Left Principles for the Initial Teacher Education
Curriculum (continued)

	Radical Left	New Labour	Social Democratic	Radical Right
11. Knowledge and skills to critically examine the ideological nature and effects of education policy and its relationship to broader economic, environmental, social and political developments	√√	XX	?	XX
12. The concurrent development of critical reflection, throughout and from the beginning of the ITE course	√√	XX	?	XX
13. Primarily, but not totally predetermined rather than primarily negotiated curriculum objectives	√√	XX	?	√
14. Support for a major role for higher education institutions in ITE; opposition to totally/primarily school-based routes	√√	O	√√	XX
15. Acceptance of different routes into teaching concordant with graduate teacher status and the above principles	√√	XX	?	XX

Key:
√√ = strong agreement; √ = agreement; X = disagreement; XX = strong disagreement; ? = not clear/arguably so; ?? = not at all clear/very arguably so; O= equanimity.

dominated by neoliberalisms and subject not only to the social and economic insecurities inherent to the capitalist mode of production, but also environmental insecurities of the most pressing kind arising from the same material bases. They pursue the four overarching principles for education as a whole by requiring a core curriculum for ITE that is described in Table 3.4.

Of the following proposals, the first three are common across different ideological positions, and because of their near universality in Britain, we do not develop them here. The next two are also widely shared, although they assume different degrees of salience within different rhetorics. The final ten propositions are more specifically Radical Left-Green.

Table 3.4   List of Radical Left Proposals for the ITE Core Curriculum

- Include macro- and micro-theory regarding teaching and learning, in which the sociopolitical, economic and environmental contexts of schooling and education are made explicit; this refers to not only classroom skills and competencies, but also theoretical understanding of children, schooling, society and nature, their inter-relationships, and alternative views and methods of, for example, classroom organization, schooling, and the economic and political relationship to society and nature.

- Embrace and develop equal opportunities so that children do not suffer from labeling, under-expectation, stereotyping or prejudice from their teachers, or indeed, from their peers.

- Enable student teachers to develop as critical, reflective teachers, able, for example, to decode media, ministerial (and indeed, Radical Left) distortion, bias, and propaganda on, for example, falling standards in schools and institutions of teacher education; this encourages the development of effective classroom-skilled teachers, able to interrelate and critique theory and practice (their own and that of others).

- Include not only technical and situational reflection, but also critical reflection, so as to question a particular policy, a particular theory, or a particular level of reflection, and to ask such critical questions as "Whose interests are served?"; "Who wins?" (if only by legitimating the status quo); "Who loses?" (who has to deny identity in order to join the winners, if this is at all possible?); "Who is likely to have to continue accepting a subordinate and exploited position in society (by virtue of their membership of oppressed groups)?"

- Enable student teachers to examine and understand the social, economic and environmental inequalities and injustices present in their specific places of work and residence, and to critically engage with ways in which these inequalities might be challenged.

The ITE curriculum should include:

1. Classroom skills and competencies: In addition to a deep knowledge of core subjects, student teachers need to develop reflective skills on pupil/student learning and on teaching and classroom management, and on stimulating all the children in their classes to learn.
2. Subject knowledge: Clearly, teachers need to know what they are talking about and what they wish students/pupils to learn.
3. The development of higher education level, analytical and intellectual skills: This demands that teachers are capable of acting and thinking at graduate level.
4. Support for a major role for higher education institutions in ITE and opposition to totally/primarily school-based routes: Higher education institutions are better able to develop the theoretical perspectives outlined above, to enable student teachers to interrelate theory and practice so that they inform each other.

5. Welcoming of different routes into teaching concordant with graduate teacher status and the above principles: As long as the above principles are upheld—including the requirement of graduate status for teachers—then there is scope for a variety of routes into teaching. The routes into teaching are tactical matters, subject to these principled considerations. The provision of more "flexible" routes into teaching should not result in a compromising of other principles, for instance, in relation to the roles and responsibilities of class teachers, of adult–child ratios and teacher supervision, and should not translate into a "flexibilization" or fractionalizing of the mass-teaching force, such as the inclusion within the ranks of "teachers" of a second class of "paraprofessional" cadres.

6. A commitment to the development of the ethical/moral dimension of critical reflection and the Radical Left and ecosocialist egalitarian concern with working for economic, social and environmental justice, and recognition of the interconnection between the three: If equal opportunities policies stop at celebrating subcultural diversity and establishing positive and nonstereotypical role models, and do not see themselves as a development of a metanarrative of social egalitarianism and justice, then they can be viewed as, in essence, conservative, for failing to challenge the economic, political and social status quo, based as it is on social class, "racial" and sexual and disability stratifications and exploitation including environmental exploitation and injustice which intersects with class and racial stratification in complex and structured ways (Bullard, 2005). Hence, a Radical Left perspective calls for teacher education (and schooling) to be socially egalitarian, ecologically sustainable, anti-racist, anti-sexist, and also to challenge other forms of structural inequality and discrimination, such as those based on sexuality and disability.[13] It also highlights the partial and therefore illusory nature of economic and social justice within the anti-egalitarian capitalist economic system. Economic justice, of course, is scarcely referred to within capitalist systems, it being one of the *desiderata* and a *sine qua non* of capitalism.

7. Research evidence on equality issues: on racism, sexism, social class inequality, homophobia, and discrimination/prejudice regarding disability and special needs, and the intersection if these factors with economic and environmental inequalities: Many teachers and ITE students are simply not aware of the existence of such research in education and society or the impact of individual labeling, and of structural discriminations on the lives, and educational and life opportunities of the children in their classes, schools and society. This is particularly true of teachers trained/educated under the Conservative Party regulations of 1992 and 1993 and (to an extent only slightly diminished) also by the current New Labour regulations.

Core units on equality and equal opportunities are required.[14] Weaknesses of the permeation model limit effectiveness and, as Gaine (1995) notes, such issues must be put firmly on the agenda, not just slipped into myriad spaces within other sessions. Equality and Equal Opportunities need to be dealt with holistically in two senses. First, they must be approached *conceptually,* as part of a holistic and egalitarian program interlinking different forms of oppression. Second, *organizationally,* as part of teacher education/training courses with units of study focusing on data, theory and policy in general. As Kincheloe, Slattery and Steinberg (2000) note, radical teachers move beyond white, Anglo-Saxon, middle-class and heterosexual educational norms, and explore the subjugated knowledges of women, minority groups and indigenous groups.

8. A holistic and social class-based approach to social, economic and environmental justice in the curriculum: Race, gender, social class, sexuality and disability, and special needs should be considered as part of an overall understanding of economic, social and environmental ecological justice within teacher education courses. Inequalities in practice can be multidimensional and their effects impact one upon the other. The desirability of maintaining their separateness needs to be questioned (although this is not to ignore the fact that inequalities and forms of oppression can clearly be unidimensional—as for example with "gay-bashing" or "Paki-bashing"). However, links should be drawn between, for example, anti-racism and anti-working class discrimination, so that anti-racism and multiculturalism can lead to, and be informed by, "anti-classism" and anti-sexism.

Similarly, just as it is possible to look at the different amount of time and types of response given by teachers to boys and girls in the same class, the same observation techniques can be applied to race, social class, disability and youth sexuality. This is not to declare, *ab initio,* that all children should receive totally equal amounts of teacher time. Equality of treatment ignores the greater resources required by children with greater needs. It is antithetical to policies of equal opportunities and to a policy for equality. Table 3.5 below indicates a possible content/objectives outline that could develop a number of these proposals.

Within this developing awareness of inequalities, the essentially and pre-eminently class-based nature of exploitation within the capitalist economic system and its educational and legal and other apparatuses needs to be understood. Class is the salient form of structural oppression within capitalist society; it is the inevitable and defining feature of capitalist exploitation, whereas the various other forms of oppression are not essential to its nature and continuation, however much they are commonly functional to this. However, student teachers should be made aware that the lexicon of "class" in current common usage rarely maps neatly onto the economic categories of classical Marxist critique, tending instead to be a reflection of stratified commodified relations defined by levels and patterns of consumption, and largely of use to bourgeois social theorists, marketers and economists. Within the ITE curriculum (and, indeed, where teachers can find spaces within the school, further education, adult education, prison education and other curricula) the existence of various and multiple forms of oppression and the similarity of their effects on individuals and communities should not disguise nor weaken an analysis (and consequent political and social action) that recognizes the structural centrality of social class exploitation and conflict.[15]

McLaren and Farahmandpur (2001) note that "recognizing the 'class character' of education in capitalist schooling, and advocating a 'socialist re-organization of capitalist society' (Krupskaya, 1985) are two fundamental principles of a revolutionary critical pedagogy" (p. 299). (See also McLaren and Jaramillo, 2007)

Table 3.5 Curriculum Detail for Student and In-Service Teacher Education Courses

	Social Class	Race and Religion	Sex	Sexuality	Special Needs
What's the problem?					
Evidence/data on inequality					
Quantitative statistical					
Qualitative student's life histories children's life histories					
in					
• Classrooms					
• School institutions					
• The education system					
• ITE					
• Societal structures and environments (e.g., housing, employment, politics, media)					
Why is it happening and why it should or should not					
Theoretical analyses explaining, justifying, critiquing/attacking such inequality, including, for example:					
• Biological models					
• Conservative structural functionalism					

(continued)

Table 3.5 Curriculum Detail for Student and In-Service Teacher Education
           Courses (continued)

	Social Class	Race and Religion	Sex	Sexuality	Special Needs
• Liberal democratic pluralism					
• Structuralist neo-Marxism					
• Culturalist neo-Marxism					
Anti-egalitarianism policy developments which seek, or have the effect of, increasing inequality in:					
• Classrooms					
• School institutions					
• The education system/ITE					
• Society and societal structures					
• Local and global environments					
Egalitarian policy developments that seek, or have the effect of increasing, egalitarianism in:					
• Classrooms					
• School institutions					
• The education system/ITE					
• Society and societal structures					
• Local and global environments					

We are aware here of different *levels* of truth (without lapsing into a disabling and uncritical modernist or postmodernist liberal ultra-pluralist relativism. See Hill and Cole, 1995, 1996a, b; Cole and Hill, 1995; Cole, Hill and Rikowski 1997; McLaren, Hill, Cole and Rikowski, 1999, 2001). As Allman (1999) notes, there are meta-transhistorical truths which hold across "the entirety of human history"

(p. 136), and it is difficult to hold that they could be otherwise. Then there are transhistorical truths, which have held good to date but could possibly be invalidated in the future. Finally, there are truths historically specific to a particular historical formation—such as capitalism. These were the sorts of truths Marx was primarily interested in when analyzing capitalist society. Finally, there are conjuncturally specific truths—propositions that attain validity within specific developmental phases of a social formation, such as current data and specific issues, which are transient to a greater or lesser degree, even though the mode of their analysis may not be so.

From a Marxist or ecosocialist perspective, it is essential to accept as fundamental to the effective operation of a dialectical methodology the epistemological liberty to abstract conceptual particularities in a flexible manner with regard to their generality. It would be of no use to abstract a singular phenomenon such as a sudden shift in government education policy without the capacity to identify the event not only locally and in policy-specific context, but also within the context of economic growth imperatives derived from structural features of capitalist accumulation. A failure to recognize the importance of expanding the parameters of a process can result in a tendency to abstract end results as self-referencing and requiring only internal reorientation. A re-emphasis of the pupil testing regime, for instance might be understood largely in terms of "correcting" or "rebalancing" results, requiring technical or working practice solutions, rather than raising questions about real, radical change in terms of patterns of teaching and learning, knowledge production consumption and exchange.

Ollman (2003) formalizes this capacity to abstract by means of imposing a framework of levels of generality within which abstractive acts may occur. For instance, the abstractive lens at Ollman's "level two" de-focuses those attributes which are particular to individuals and brings into sharp relief "what is general to people, their activities, and products *because they exist and function within modern capitalism*" (p. 88; emphases added). Clearly, a dialogical and dialectical relationship between critical educator and teachers would result in a degree of negotiated curriculum detail to bring into focus different levels of analysis and critique.

9. Skills in dealing with the incidence of classist, homophobic, racist, and sexist remarks and harassment at various levels, such as within the classroom and throughout the institution: It is important here to address other types of harassment, such as labeling and bullying based on body shape, and their corrosive effects on children's learning, lives and happiness. (There is, however, a danger that generic anti-bullying policies can individualize the problem and deny any structural aspects such as racism, sexism, social class and sexuality).

10. The development within institutions of open fora on social and eco-
    logical justice where students and staff in institutions can meet in a
    supportive environment: This is an additional form of learning, where
    individual self-development comes through sharing experience and
    ideas. Teachers contribute their knowledge not only by transmission
    (though this frequently might be part of a teacher's repertoire of teach-
    ing methods), but also through interlocution where individual contri-
    butions are valued and respected. The culture of such a forum can
    foster a climate where individual "voices," levels of consciousness and
    experiences, and levels of critique are legitimated. Such voices however
    should be subject to critical interrogation, not accepted uncritically.[16]

11. Critiques of competing approaches and ideologies of schooling,
    teacher education and social and economic organization: This should
    include skills to examine critically the nature of the curricula, hid-
    den curricula and pedagogy, schooling, education and society. This
    enables student teachers to consider and challenge the ideologies that
    underpin the selection of knowledge that they are being asked to
    acquire and teach through the whole curriculum, as well as challeng-
    ing the prioritized model of the teacher and critical mode of reflec-
    tion. Ultimately, as McLaren and Baltodano (2000) observe, ITE
    courses should "locate the schooling process in both local and global
    socio-economic and political contexts, while exploring the relations
    between them" (p. 43).

    This should include a consideration of the different current major
    ideologies of education (socialism/Marxism, social democracy, lib-
    eral-progressivism, neo-Conservatism, neoliberalism and New
    Labourism and their policy expressions). In relation to these it should
    also include understanding and evaluation of anti-racism as well as
    multiculturalism and assimilationism; Marxist analysis of social class
    and the concept of a classless society, as well as meritocratic social
    mobility or elitist stratification and reproduction; anti-sexism as well
    as non-sexism, and, indeed, sexism. In addition, different models
    of disability and lesbian-gay-bisexual-transgender issues should be
    addressed.[17]

12. The development of knowledge and skills to critically examine the
    ideological nature of teaching and the nature of teachers' work: Here,
    student teachers should develop an understanding of the potential
    role of teachers in transforming society. This is, as Harris (1994) sug-
    gests, so that, while teachers retain some critical agency in the area of
    the transmission of knowledge

    > it remains possible for teachers to adopt the function of intellec-
    > tuals . . . and . . . to resist becoming mere managers of day-to-
    > day activities imposed from beyond the school, and to redefine
    > their role within counter hegemonic practice. They can, through
    > their discourse and interventionary practice in the ideological

and political determinants of schooling, promote empowerment, autonomy and democracy. (p. 115)

13. The concurrent rather than the consecutive development of critical
reflection, throughout and from the beginning of the ITE course:
Teacher educators differ in their views of which levels, or "arena"
of reflection, offer an appropriate starting point for reflection in the
learning-to-teach process. Commentators as diverse as Calderhead
and Gates (1993), and the DfE Circular 9/92 (DfE, 1992) all assume
or argue that the three levels of reflection need to be developed in
sequential order, that is that contextual-situational, and indeed, critical reflection are more appropriate for teachers who have attained
technical and practical skills and skills of reflection.

   Our view is that a three- or four-year undergraduate teacher education course provides a sufficient period of time. Furthermore, with
appropriate support (as set out in the next proposal), some increase
in the school-centered and school-based component of undergraduate
student teacher courses may well provide a more appropriate immer-
sion into the practices of teaching, learning and schooling and facilitate, organize and encourage the application of theory to practice and
practice to theory.

   If "learning theory," "critical theory" or issues of the social context of schooling are left until "postinitial training," many newly
qualified teachers will not actually get any postinitial training other
than "inset days"—the school-based in-service education for teachers, and these in-service training days appear to be overwhelmingly
instrumental, and technical—in particular, to be concerned with how
to "deliver" results from recent policy initiatives such as the revamped
Primary Strategies, or requirements arising from *Every Child Matters*. If contextual, theoretical and social/economic justice and equality issues are not studied during ITE, they may never be.

14. Substantially predetermined rather than primarily negotiated curriculum objectives:
   Calderhead and Gates (1993) raise the key questions of whether
"a truly reflective teaching program [should have] predefined content
or . . . be negotiated, [and how to] reconcile the aim of developing
particular areas of knowledge, skill and attitudes with the aim of
encouraging autonomy and professional responsibility" (p. 3). These
are crucial issues in various postmodernist, postmodern feminist and
liberal pluralist critiques of the concept of teachers as critical transformative intellectuals. They are also key elements of postmodernist
critiques of Marxist class-based transformativist, solidaristic analysis
and policy proposals in education. They refer to the tension between
developing student teacher autonomy on the one hand and seeking
to develop a particular ideology on the other. Zeichner and Liston
(1990) observe the significant historical shift of emphasis within the

Radical Left (See also Liston and Zeichner, 1987; Zeichner and Liston, 1996).

At various times the focus has been on the content of programmes, the skill of critical analysis and curriculum development, the nature of the pedagogic relationships between teachers and pupils, and between teacher educators and their students, or on the connections between teacher educators and other political projects which seek to address the many instances of suffering and injustice in our society. (p. 22)

The debate centers on whether "democratic participative pedagogy" should typify a course. Arguably, a heavy use of discussion based and "own-experience based" small group collaborative work, typical of much primary schooling and primary teacher education in Britain in the 1970s and 1980s, militates against the development of the broad span of critical theoretical insights argued for in this chapter. In accordance with the Radical Left principles outlined here, course objectives, if not the content-based means to their attainment, should—following national debate and taking into account particular student needs at any particular historical juncture—be substantially predetermined in such a way as to allow critique to be brought to bear at the different levels of analysis referred to above.

This proposal is for a curriculum which is organic in the sense Gramsci (1971) intends when referring to the formation of intellectuals. As Rikowski (2001c) notes for

> organic intellectuals, the goal is not "to tell the people what to think" but to enable them to think clearly—to provide them with the tools (critical literacy in the first instance) to engage in cultural action incorporating the exercise of critical (dialectical) consciousness aimed at social transformation. (p. 63)

Moreover, transformative intellectuals must engage in self-criticism. This is especially in relation to forming a dialectical unity with the student groups/teachers that is non-antagonistic, in order to assist in moving people from their "concrete conceptions of the world (their limited praxis) . . . [towards] . . . a critical, scientific or, in other words, dialectical conceptualization" (Allman, 1999, p. 115).

15. The application of critical evaluation to school-based practice and experience: Theory can provide the analytic and conceptual apparatus for thinking about practice in schools and classrooms, within the formal and within the hidden curriculum, while practice can provide the opportunity for the testing and assimilation of theory.

Since the Conservative government's 1992/93 regulations for teacher training and education (DfE, 1992, 1993) demanded more school basing in ITE courses and the continued development of school-based ITE programs, the detheorization of teacher education through an emphasis on untheorized practice is a major problem in the development of effective teaching, in the development of critical transformatory skills, awareness and teaching, and in the development of a revolutionary transformative critical pedagogy.

16. Environmental justice pedagogy: Environmental justice pedagogy also entails active engagement between students, communities and the environment—activities and projects might include urban food production/gardening (particularly in economically disadvantaged areas); water catchment monitoring, public open space issues, green energy, sustainable transport, local impacts of climate change, such as flooding and so forth in addition to the more traditional "ecosustainability" activities such as recycling and visiting national parks. Environmental justice pedagogy enlarges the field of environmental education to address complex social, economic and environmental issues at multiple-geographical scales so that students can empirically locate themselves within them and develop critical, historical and transformative knowledge. It also breaks down unproductive dualisms between nature and society, urban and wilderness and so forth. This is important for students and teachers living and working in economically disadvantaged urban communities—because it can reorient the curriculum to deal with specific environmental justice issues that these communities face (Houston, 2007).

CONCLUSION: THE POLITICS OF EDUCATIONAL TRANSFORMATION

Arguments that we live in a postcapitalist, postindustrial, or postmodern era can be contested, as can the Radical Right argument set out in only slightly different ways by Conservative and New Labour governments, that the only future for humankind is the application of free market economics to the societies of the world. Yet a Radical Left re-organization of global and national societies, and of their educational apparatuses, committed to egalitarianism and economic and social justice, remains viable (see e.g., McLaren, 2000, 2001).

Radical Right models, even with the social democrat gloss applied by New Labour in the UK, are of little relevance in this endeavor. Practices in schooling and in teacher education and training need to be changed, rather than accepted and reproduced, therefore the emphasis should be on challenging the dominant neoliberal and neoconservative cultures, rather than reproducing and reinforcing them. Radical Right and Centrist ideology on schooling, training and ITE serves a society aiming only for the hegemony of the few and the entrenchment of privilege, not the promotion of equality and economic and social justice.

Teacher educators and cultural workers from various other ideological and political perspectives may well agree with a number of the recommendations we make. They may not agree with the explicit emancipatory, critical and transformatory role of teacher educators, education, and schooling in the interests of social and environmental justice and egalitarianism. Yet this role and the role of teacher educators and teachers as intellectuals instead of mechanics or technicians are necessary for the development of a critical, active, interrogating, citizenry—thoughtful, questioning, perceptive as well as skilled—pursuing a democratic, anti-authoritarian, socially responsible and socially and economically just society.

Much of the Left has vacated the ideological battlefield during neoliberal media offensives and government attempts at strengthening control and hegemony over the schooling and teacher education ideological state apparatuses. As McLaren (2001) notes, "part of the problem faced by the educational left today is that even among progressive educators there exists an ominous resignation produced by the seeming inevitability of capital" (p. 28). This is true of the caution of erstwhile Left writers, educationalists and ideologues in Britain in their retreat from the cultural and educational advances of the 1970s and 1980s (see for example, Farahmandpur, 2004; Kelsh & Hill, 2006; Rikowski, 2006; Hill, 2007a, 2007b). It is a feature of education policy and analysis and other policy areas (typified by the rightward Labour party shift) that has culminated in the New Labour Party of Gordon Brown.

We recognize and do not underestimate the limitations on the agency and autonomy of teachers, teacher educators, cultural workers and indeed, the very limited autonomy of the educational sphere of the state from the economic. McLaren and Baltodano (2000) note (with respect to California in particular, but with a wider global resonance) the "greater restrictions on the ability of teachers to use their pedagogical spaces for emancipatory purposes" (p. 34). Hence, we give rather less credence than Ball (1994a, 1994b) and Smyth and Shatlock (1998) to the notion that teachers, and teacher educators, are able to "co-write" texts such as curriculum and assessment circulars (see Hill, 2001d; Evans, Davies and Penney, 1994).

The repressive cards within the ideological state apparatuses are stacked against the possibilities of transformative change through ITE and through schooling. But historically and internationally, this often has been the case. Spaces do exist for counter-hegemonic struggle—sometimes (as now) narrower, sometimes (as in the 1960s and 1970s) broader. Having recognized the limitations, though, and having recognized that there is some potential for transformative change, we maintain that whatever space does exist should be exploited.

By itself, divorced from other arenas of progressive struggle, its success will be limited. This necessitates the development of pro-active debate both by, and within Radical Left organizations and parties, and education worker trade unions. But it necessitates more than that. It calls for direct engagement with liberal pluralist (modernist or postmodernist) and with Radical Right ideologies and programs, in all the areas of the state and of civil society, in and through all the ideological and repressive state apparatuses.

As intellectual workers educating teachers, the ideological intervention of teacher educators is likely to have more impact than that of sections of the workforce less saliently engaged in ideological production and reproduction. But, by itself, the activity of transformative intellectual teacher educators, however skilful and committed, can have only an extremely limited impact on an egalitarian transformation of society. Unless linked to a grammar of resistance, such resistant and counter-hegemonic activity is likely to fall on relatively stony ground. As McLaren and Baltodano (2000) suggest (see also, Rikowski, 2001c; McLaren & Farahmandpur, 2002; McLaren and Jaramillo, 2007; Rikowski & McLaren, 2001),

> Reclaiming schools and teacher education as arenas of cultural struggle and education in general as a vehicle for social transformation in conservative/capitalist times is premised upon a clear commitment to organize parents, students and communities. It stipulates that society needs to develop critical educators, community activists, organic intellectuals, and teachers whose advocacy of social justice will illuminate their pedagogical practices. (p. 41)

In keeping aloft ideals of plurality of thought, of economic, social and environmental justice and of dissent, teachers, teacher educators and the community must resist the ideological hijacking of our past, present and future. Teachers and teacher educators are too strategically valuable in children's and students' education to have slick media panaceas and slanted ministerial programs attempting to dragoon them into being uncritical functionaries of a conservative state and of the fundamentally and essentially inegalitarian and immoral society and education system reproduced by the capitalist state and its apparatuses.

The particular perspectives defined in this chapter, from a Radical Left position, are based on a belief that teachers must not only be skilled, competent, classroom technicians. They must also be critical and reflective and transformative and intellectual, that is to say, they should operate at the critical level of reflection. They should enable and encourage their students, not only to gain basic and advanced knowledge and skills: They should enable and encourage their students to question, critique, judge and evaluate "what is," "what effects it has," and "why?" and to be concerned and informed about equality and economic, environmental and social justice—in life beyond the classroom door and within the classroom walls. Rikowski (2007) describes such radical educators as those "advocating education as an aspect of anti-capitalist social transformation."

As McLaren (2001) puts it

Do we, as radical educators, help capital find its way out of crisis, or do we help students find their way out of capital? The success of the former challenge will only buy further time for the capitalists to adapt both its victims and its critics, the success of the latter will determine the future of civilization, or whether or not we have one. (p. 31)

ACKNOWLEDGMENT

We would like to thank Donna Houston and Richard Kahn for their comments on this paper.

NOTES

1. See e.g., Cole, 1998; Hill, 2001b, 2001e; Rikowski, 2001b, 2001d, 2001e, 2002a, 2002b; McLaren, 2000; Rees, 2001, 2007c.
2. See also Cole, 1998; Smyth and Shatlock, 1998; Ainley, 1999, 2000; McMurtry, 1999; McLaren, 2000; Rikowski, 2000, 2001a, 2001b, 2002a, 2002b; Hatcher and Hirtt, 1999; Hatcher, 2001.
3. Hatcher, 2001; Molnar, 1999, 2001; Hill, 2001b; Rikowski, 2001b, 2001d, 2001e, 2002a.
4. Hill, 1994a, 1994b, 1997c, 1997d, 2005a, 2007a.
5. See also McMurtry, 1998; Grace, 1994; Winch, 1998.
6. This document lists the flowing policies/demands: Ecosocialists have to start from a class analysis, an analysis that can unite the largest possible number of people to make the rich, not the poor, pay. We support the building of a mass movement, nationally and internationally to impose the types of demand below.
   - For a unilateral reduction of greenhouse gas emissions in Britain of 90% by 2030, with similar reductions in other developed countries
   - For an international treaty to cap global carbon emissions, not because we think this is an easy option, or even likely to be achieved (this depends on the balance of forces), but because it is necessary and can unite the movements internationally against the failures of the capitalist system
   - For international rationing of air travel, any market in rations to be made illegal
   - Opposition to nuclear energy and the building of any new nuclear power stations
   - For a massive expansion of renewable energy
   - For subsidies from national and local government
     - to replace the use of cars by providing cheap, accessible and frequent public transport
     - to ensure all new buildings are zero-carbon
     - to provide insulation, energy conservation, and so forth for all homes to make them energy efficient

On climate change we should campaign around the following transitional and immediate demands which are designed to halt and reverse the global warming process and thus prevent climate chaos and rising sea levels. These should include a 90% reduction in fossil fuel use by 2050, based on a 6%

annual target, monitored by independent scrutiny. The industrialized countries, who have caused the problem, must take the lead in this. The most impoverished people are paying the highest price for the actions of the advanced countries. There is no point in asking them to take measures not being taken in the industrialized countries. This means:

- Cancellation of the third-world debt: There is no point on calling on impoverished counties to tackle climate change if they are saddled with debt.
- A massive increase in investment in renewable energy including solar, wind wave, tidal and hydro power (with the exception of destructive mega-dam projects). These should be monitored for anti-social consequences; no nuclear power.
- End the productivist throwaway society: production for use and not for profit.
- Tough action against industrial and corporate polluters.
- Free, or cheap, integrated publicly owned transport systems to provide and alternative to the car.
- Nationalization of rail, road freight and bus companies.
- Halt airport expansion, restrict flights and end binge flying; nationalize the airlines.
- Redesign cities to eliminate unnecessary journeys and conserve energy
- Scrap weapons of mass destruction and use the resources for sustainable development and renewable energy.
- Massive investment to make homes more energy efficient. Move toward the collectivization of living spaces.
- Nationalization of the supermarkets, localized food production and a big reduction in food miles.
- No GM crops for food or fuel.
- End the destruction of the rain forests.
- Defend the rights of climate change refugees and migrants. Protect those hit by drought, desertization, floods, crop failure and extreme weather conditions.
- Renationalize water and protect water reserves. End the pollution of the rivers and the water ways.

7. See McLaren and Houston, 2005b.
8. Foremost among the U.K. groups advocating recognition of the importance of ecosocialist solutions to educational questions are the Alliance for Green Socialism and the International Socialist Group and its linked group, Socialist Resistance. See, for example, Socialist Resistance, 2007.
9. For Radical Left discussion of these principles, see the citations in note 1 (above) together with Cole, 2000; Cole, Hill and Shan, 1997; Cole, Hill, McLaren and Rikowski, 2001; Cole, Hill, Soudien and Pease, 1997; Hill, 1990, 1991b; Hill, Cole and Williams, 1997; Hillcole Group, 1991, 1997; McLaren, Cole, Hill and Rikowski, 2001. In Australia this tradition is exemplified in the work of Kevin Harris (1979, 1982, 1984, 1994), and in the United States, most recently, by Peter McLaren and his associates, for example: Aguirre, 2001; McLaren, 2000, 2001; McLaren and Farahmandpur, 2001, 2001b, 2005; McLaren and Jaramillo, 2007; McLaren and Rikowski, 2001, 2002.
10. This is an emerging field: This article is not the place to map it. See for instance, Gadotti, 2003; Kahn 2003a, 2003b, 2005; McLaren and Houston, 2005a.
11. Hill, 1999a, 2000, 2001a, 2001c.
12. See Cliff and Gluckstein, 1996; Driver and Martell, 1998; Giddens, 1998, 2000; Cole et al., 2001; McLaren et al., 2001.

13. See Hill, 1991a, 1994b, 1997d.
14. See Hill, 1989, which sets out two such courses of the late 1980s from two different institutions; these were West Sussex Institute of Higher Education, where the courses were (co-)developed by Dave Hill, and Brighton Polytechnic, where the course was developed by Mike Cole.
15. See e.g., Hill, 1999b, 2001c, 2001d, 2002; Sanders, Hill and Hankin, 1999; Aguirre, 2001; Cole and Hill, 2001; Cole et al., 2001, Rikowski, 2001a, 2001b, 2001e; Hill, Sanders and Hankin, 2002; McLaren and Farahmandpur, 2002; McLaren and Rikowski, 2001; Rikowski and McLaren, 2001.
16. See Cole, Clay and Hill, 1990; Cole and Hill, 1999, 2002; Sanders et al., 1999; Kincheloe et al., 2000; McLaren and Farahmandpur, 2001b, 2002a; Hill et al., 2002.
17. See the Institute for Education Policy Studies website www.ieps.org.uk for details of three such undergraduate modules with a potential for developing critical education. These were (co-)developed by Dave Hill at University College, Northampton, United Kingdom. The module aims, content, assessment procedures and bibliographies are set out.

REFERENCES

Aguirre, L. C. (2001). The role of critical pedagogy in the globalisation era and the aftermath of September 11, 2001. Interview with Peter McLaren. *Revista Electronica de Investigacion Educativa, (3)* 2. Available at www.redie.ens.uabc.mx/vol3no2/contenido-coral.html

Ainley, P. (1999). Left in a right state: Towards a new alternative. *Education and Social Justice, 2*(1), 74–78.

Ainley, P. (2000). *From earning to learning: What is happening to education and the welfare state?* London: Tufnell.

Allman, P. (1999). *Revolutionary social transformation: Democratic hopes, political possibilities and critical education.* Westport, CT: Bergin and Garvey.

Allman, P. (2000). *Critical education against global capital: Karl Marx and revolutionary critical education.* Westport, CT: Bergin and Garvey.

Ball, S. (1994a). *Education reform: A critical and post-structural approach.* London: Open University Press.

Ball, S. (1994b). Some reflections on policy theory: A brief response to Hatcher and Troyna. *Journal of Education Policy, 9,* 171–182.

Bullard, R. (2005). Environmental justice in the twenty-first century. In R. Bullard (Ed.), *The quest for environmental justice: Human rights and the politics of pollution.* San Francisco: Sierra Club Books.

Burgman, M., & Burgman, V. (1998). *Green bans, red union.* Sydney, Australia: UNSW Press.

Calderhead, J., & Gates, P. (1993). *Conceptualising reflection in teacher development.* London: Falmer.

Callaghan, J. (1976) The Ruskin Speech.

Cliff, T., & Gluckstein, D. (1996) *The labour party: A Marxist history.* London: Bookmarks.

Cole, M. (1998). Globalisation, modernisation and competitiveness: A critique of the new labour project in education. *International Studies in the Sociology of Education, 8,* 315–332.

Cole, M. (Ed.). (2000). *Education, equality and human rights: Issues of gender, "race," sexuality, special needs, and social class.* London: Routledge Falmer.

Cole, M. (2008). The state apparatuses and the working class: Experiences from the United Kingdom: Educational lessons from Venezuela. In D. Hill (Ed.), *Contesting neoliberal education: Public resistance and collective advance* (pp. 218–240). New York: Routledge.

Cole, M., Clay, J., & Hill, D. (1990). The citizen as individual and nationalist or as social and internationalist? What is the role of education? *Critical Social Policy, 10*(30), 68–87.

Cole, M., & Hill, D. (1995). Games of despair and rhetorics of resistance: Postmodernism, education and reaction. *British Journal of Sociology of Education, 16,* 165–182.

Cole, M., & Hill, D. (1999). Into the hands of capital: The deluge of postmodernism and the delusions of resistance postmodernism. In D. Hill, P. McLaren, M. Cole, & G. Rikowski (Eds.), *Postmodernism and educational theory: Education and the politics of human resistance* (pp. 31–49). London: Tufnell.

Cole, M., & Hill, D. (2002). Resistance postmodernism: Progressive politics or rhetorical left posturing? In D. Hill, P. McLaren, M. Cole, & G. Rikowski (Eds.), *Marxism against postmodernism in educational theory* (pp. 91–111). Lanham, MD: Lexington.

Cole, M., Hill, D., & Rikowski, G. (1997). Between postmodernism and nowhere: The predicament of the postmodernist. *British Journal of Education Studies, 45,* 187–200.

Cole, M., Hill, D., McLaren, P., & Rikowski, G. (2001). *Red chalk: On schooling, capitalism and politics.* Brighton, England: Institute for Education Policy Studies. Available at http://www.ieps.org.uk.cwc.net/redchalk.pdf

Cole, M. Hill, D. and Shan, S. (Eds.) (1997) *Promoting equality in primary schools.* London: Cassell.

Cole, M., Hill, D., Soudien, C., & Pease, J. (1997). Critical transformative teacher education: A model for the new South Africa. In J. Lynch, S. Modgil, & C. Modgil (Eds.), *Education and development: Tradition and innovation, Vol. 3: Innovations in developing primary education* (pp. 97–121). London: Cassell.

Cole, P., & Wade, P. (2007). *Running a temperature: An action plan for the eco-crisis.* London: Lupus Books.

Department for Education (DfE). (1992). *Circular 9/92. Initial teacher training (secondary phase).* London: Author.

Department for Education (DfE). (1993). *Circular 14/93: The initial training of primary school teachers.* London: Author.

Department for Education and Employment (DfEE). (1998). *DfEE circular 4/98: Teaching: High status, high standards-requirements for courses of initial teacher training.* London: Author.

Driver, S., & Martell, L. (1998). *New labour: Politics after Thatcherism.* Cambridge, England: Polity.

Evans, J., Davies, B., & Penney, D. (1994). Whatever happened to the subject and the state? *Discourse, 14*(2), 57–65.

Farahmandpur, R. (2004) Essay review: A Marxist critique of Michael Apple's neo-Marxist approach to education reform. *Journal of Critical Education Policy Studies, 2*(1). Available at http://www.jceps.com/index.php?pageID=article&articleID=24

Freire, P. (2004). *Pedagogy of indignation.* Boulder CO: Paradigm.

Gadotti, M. (2003, October). *Pedagogy of the earth and culture of sustainability.* Paper presented at the international conference Lifelong Citizenship Learning, Participatory Democracy and Social Change, Toronto, Ontario, Canada.

Gaine, C. (1995). *Still no problem here*. Stoke-on-Trent, England: Trentham Books.

Giddens, A. (1998) *The third way: The renewal of social democracy*. Cambridge, England: Polity.

Giddens, A. (2000). *The third way and its critics*. Cambridge, England: Polity.

Grace, G. (1994). Education as a public good: On the need to resist the domination of economic science. In D. Bridges & T. McLaughlin (Eds.), *Education and the market place*. London: Falmer.

Gramsci, A. (1971). *Selections from the prison notebooks*. London: Lawrence and Wishart.

Harris, K. (1979). *Education and knowledge*. London: RKP.

Harris, K. (1982). *Teachers and classes: A Marxist analysis*. London: Routledge and Kegan Paul.

Harris, K. (1984). Two contrasting theories. *Education With Production, 3*(1), 13–33.

Harris, K. (1994). *Teachers: Constructing the future*. London: Falmer.

Hatcher, R. (2001). Getting down to the business: Schooling in the globalised economy. *Education and Social Justice, 3*(2), 45–59.

Hatcher, R., & Hirtt, N. (1999). The business agenda behind labour's education policy. In M. Allen, Benn, C., Chitty, C., Cole, M., Hatcher, R., Hirtt, N., and Rikowski, G., *New labour's education policy*. London: Tufnell.

Hill, D. (1989). *Charge of the right brigade: The radical right's assault on teacher education*. Brighton, England: Institute for Education Policy Studies. Avilable at http://www.ieps.org.uk.cwc.net/hill1989.pdf.

Hill, D. (1990). *Something old, something new, something borrowed, something blue: Teacher education, schooling and the radical right in Britain and the USA*. London: Tufnell.

Hill, D. (1991a). Seven ideological perspectives on teacher education today and the development of a radical left discourse. *Australian Journal of Teacher Education, 16*(2), 5–29.

Hill, D. (1991b). *What's left in teacher education: Teacher education, the radical left and policy proposals*. London: Tufnell.

Hill, D. (1994a). A radical left policy for teacher education. *Socialist Teacher, 56*, 23–24.

Hill, D. (1994b). Teacher education and ethnic diversity. In G. Verma & P. Pumfrey (Eds.), *Cultural diversity and the curriculum, Vol. 4: Cross-curricular contexts, themes and dimensions in primary schools* (pp. 218–241). London: Falmer.

Hill, D. (1997a). Brief autobiography of a bolshie dismissed. *General Educator, 44*, 15–17.

Hill, D. (1997b). Critical research and the dismissal of dissent. *Research Intelligence, 59*, 25–26.

Hill, D. (1997c). Equality and primary schooling: The policy context intentions and effects of the conservative "reforms." In M. Cole, D. Hill, & S. Shan (Eds.), *Promoting equality in primary schools* (pp. 15–47). London: Cassell.

Hill, D. (1997d). Reflection in initial teacher education. In K. Watson, S. Modgil, & C. Modgil (Eds.), *Educational dilemmas: Debate and diversity, Vol.1: Teacher education and training* (pp. 193–208). London: Cassell.

Hill, D. (1997e). In white chalk . . . on a white board: The writing's on the wall for radicals in British education. *Education Australia, 35*, 51–53.

Hill, D. (1999a). *New labour and education: Policy, ideology and the third way*. London: Tufnell.

Hill, D. (1999b). Social class and education. In D. Matheson & I. Grosvenor (Eds.), *An introduction to the study of education* (pp. 84–102). London: Fulton.

Hill, D. (2000). The third way ideology of new labour's educational policy in England and Wales. In G. Walraven, C. Parsons, D. van Deen, & C. Day (Eds.), *Combating social exclusion through education: Laissez faire, authoritarianism or third way?* (pp. 51–67). Leuven-Apeldoon, The Netherlands: Garant.

Hill, D. (2001a). Equality, ideology and education policy. In D. Hill & M. Cole (Eds.), *Schooling and equality: Fact, concept and policy* (pp. 7–34). London: Kogan Page.

Hill, D. (2001b). Global capital, neo-liberalism, and privatisation: The growth of educational inequality. In D. Hill & M. Cole (Eds.), *Schooling and equality: Fact, concept and policy* (pp. 35–54). London: Kogan Page.

Hill, D. (2001c). The national curriculum, the hidden curriculum and equality. In D. Hill & M. Cole (Eds.), *Schooling and equality: Fact, concept and policy* (pp. 95–116). London: Kogan Page.

Hill, D. (2001d). State theory and the neo-liberal reconstruction of teacher education: A structuralist neo-Marxist critique of postmodernist, quasi-postmodernist, and culturalist neo-Marxist theory. *British Journal of Sociology of Education, 22*(1), 137–157.

Hill, D. (2001e, September) *The third way in Britain: New labour's neo-liberal education policy.* Paper presented at the conference Marx 111, Paris.

Hill, D. (2002). Global capital, neo-liberalism and the growth of educational inequality. *The School Field: International Journal of Theory and Research in Education, 13*(1/2), 81–107.

Hill, D. (2004a). Books, banks and bullets: Controlling our minds—The global project of imperialistic and militaristic neo-liberalism and its effect on education policy. *Policy Futures in Education,* 2(3/4). Available at http://www.wwwords.co.uk/pdf/viewpdf.asp/j=pfie&vol=2&issue=3&year=2004&article=6_Hill_PFIE_2_3-4_web&id=81.158.104.245

Hill, D. (2004b). Educational perversion and global neo-liberalism: A Marxist critique. *Cultural Logic: An Electronic Journal of Marxist Theory and Practice.* Available at http://eserver.org/clogic/2004/2004.html

Hill, D. (2005a). Critical education for economic and social justice. In M. Pruyn and L. Huerta-Charles (Eds.), *Teaching Peter McLaren: Paths of dissent.* New York: Lang.

Hill, D. (2005b). State theory and the neoliberal reconstruction of schooling and teacher education. In G. Fischman, P. McLaren, H. Sünker, and C. Lankshear (Eds.), *Critical theories, radical pedagogies and global conflicts.* Boulder, CO: Rowman and Littlefield.

Hill, D. (2007a). Critical teacher education, New Labour in Britain, and the global project of neoliberal capital. *Policy Futures,* 5(2). Available at http://www.wwwords.co.uk/pfie/content/pdfs/5/issue5_2.asp

Hill, D. (2007b). Education, class and capital in the epoch of neo-liberal globalisation. In A. Green & G. Rikowski (Eds.), *Marxism and education: Renewing dialogues: Vol. 1—Opening the dialogue,* (pp. 71). London: Palgrave Macmillan

Hill, D. (2007c) Socialist Educators and Capitalist Education. *Socialist Outlook, 13.* Online at http://www.isg-fi.org.uk/spip.php?article576

Hill, D. (2008). "Race," class and neoliberal capital in urban contexts: Resistance and egalitarian education. In C. Mallot, & B. Porfilio (Eds.), *An international examination of urban education: The destructive path of neoliberalism.* Rotterdam, The Netherlands: Sense.

Hill, D., & Cole, M. (1993). *Postmodernism, education and the road to nowhere: A materialist critique.* Paper presented at the annual association for Teacher Education in Europe. Lisbon University, Portugal.

Hill, D., & Cole, M. (1996a). Materialism and the postmodern fallacy: The case of education. In J. V. Fernandes (Ed.), *Proceedings, of the second international conference of sociology of education* (pp. 475–594). Faro, Portugal: Escola Superior de Educacao da Universidade do Algarve.

Hill, D., & Cole, M. (1996b). Postmodernism, educational contemporary capitalism: a materialist critique. In M. O. Valente, A Barrios, A Gaspar, & V. Teodoro (Eds.), *Teacher training and values education* (pp. 27–89). Lisbon, Portugal: Association for Teacher Education in Europe in association with Departamento de Educacao da Faculdade de Ciencias da Universidade de Lisboa.

Hill, D. and Cole, M. (2001) *Schooling and Equality: Fact, Concept and Policy*. London: Routledge.

Hill, D., Cole, M., & Williams, C. (1997). Teacher education and equality in the primary school. In M. Cole, D. Hill, & S. Shan (Eds.), *Promoting equality in primary schools* (pp. 91–114). London: Cassell.

Hill, D., McLaren, P., Cole, M., & Rikowski, G. (Eds.). (1999). *Postmodernism in educational theory: Education and the politics of human resistance*. London: Tufnell.

Hill, D., McLaren, P., Cole, M., & Rikowski, G. (Eds.). (2002). *Marxism against postmodernism in educational theory*. Lanham, MD: Lexington.

Hill, D., Sanders, M., & Hankin, T. (2002). Marxism, class analysis and postmodernism. In D. Hill, P. McLaren, M. Cole, & G. Rikowski (Eds.), *Marxism against postmodernism in educational theory* (pp. 167–206). Lanham, MD: Lexington.

Hillcole Group. (1991). *Changing the future: Redprint for education*. London: Tufnell.

Hillcole Group. (1997). *Rethinking education and democracy: A socialist alternative for the twenty-first century*. London: Tufnell.

Jeffrey, B. and Woods, R. (1998). *Testing Teachers: The Effect of School Inspections on Primary Teachers*. London: Falmer Press.

Kahn, R. (2003a) Paulo Freire and eco-justice: Updating pedagogy of the oppressed for the age of ecological calamity. *Freire Online, A Journal of the Paulo Freire Institute/UCLA, 1*(1). Available at http://www.paulofreireinstitute.org/freireonline/volume1/1kahn1.html

Kahn, R. (2003b). Towards ecopedagogy: Weaving a broad-based pedagogy of liberation for animals, nature, and the oppressed people of the earth. *Animal Liberation Philosophy and Policy Journal, 1*(1). Available at http://www.cala-online.org/Journal/Issue_1/Towards%20Ecopedagogy.htm

Kahn, R. (2005). From Herbert Marcuse to the earth liberation front: Considerations for revolutionary ecopedagogy. *Green Theory and Praxis: A Journal of Ecological Politics, 1*. Available at http://greentheoryandpraxis.csufresno.edu/pdfs/kahn.pdf

Kelly, J., & Malone, S. (2006). *Ecosocialism or barbarism*. London: Socialist Resistance.

Kelsh, D., & Hill, D. (2006). The culturalization of class and the occluding of class consciousness: The knowledge industry in/of education. *Journal for Critical Education Policy Studies, 4*(1). Available at http://www.jceps.com/index.php?pageID=article&articleID=59

Kincheloe, J., Slattery, P., & Steinberg, S. (2000). *Contextualising teaching: Introduction to education and educational foundations*. Boulder, CO: Westview.

Krupskaya, N. (1985). *On labour-oriented education and instruction*. Moscow: Progressive.

Liston, D., & Zeichner, K. (1987). *Critical pedagogy and teacher education. Journal of Education, 169*, 117–137.

Mallory, G. (2005). *Unchartered waters: Social responsibility in Australian trade unions*. Brisbane, Australia: Author.

McLaren P. (2000). *Che Guevara, Paolo Freire and the pedagogy of revolution*. Lanham, MD: Rowman and Littlefield.

McLaren, P. (2001). Marxist revolutionary praxis: A curriculum of transgression. *Journal of Critical Inquiry Into Curriculum and Instruction, 3*(3), 27–32.

McLaren, P., & Baltodano, M. (2000). The future of teacher education and the politics of resistance. *Teacher Education, 11*(1), 31–44.

McLaren P., Cole, M., Hill, D., & Rikowski, G. (2001). An interview with three UK Marxist educational theorists—Mike Cole, Dave Hill and Glenn Rikowski. *International Journal of Educational Reform, 10,* 145–162.

McLaren, P., & Farahmandpur, R. (2001). The globalization of capitalism and the new imperialism: Notes towards a revolutionary critical pedagogy. *The Review of Education, Pedagogy and Cultural Studies, 2,* 271–315.

McLaren, P., & Farahmandpur, R. (2002). Recentering class: Wither postmodernism? Toward a contraband pedagogy. In D. Hill, P. McLaren, M. Cole, & G. Rikowski (Eds.). *Marxism against postmodernism in educational theory.* Lanham, MD: Lexington.

McLaren, P., & Farahmandpur, R. (2005) *Teaching Against Global Capitalism and the New Imperialism: A Critical Pedagogy.* Lanham, MD.: Rowman & Littlefield.

McLaren, P., & Houston, D. (2005a). Response to Bowers. The "nature" of political amnesia: A response to C. A. "Chet" Bowers. *Educational Studies: A Journal of the American Education Studies Association, 37,* 196–206.

McLaren, P., & Houston, D. (2005b). Revolutionary ecologies: Ecosocialism and critical pedagogy. In P. McLaren (Ed.), *Capitalists & conquerors: A critical pedagogy against empire* (pp. 166-185). Oxford: Rowman & Littlefield.

McLaren, P. and Jaramillo, N. (2007). Pedagogy and Praxis in the Age of Empire. Rotterdam, The Netherlands: Sense Publications.

McLaren, P., & Rikowski, G. (2001). Pedagogy for revolution against education for capital: An e-dialogue on education in capitalism today. *Cultural Logic: An Electronic Journal of Marxist Theory and Practice, 4*(1). Available at www.eserver.org/clogic.

McLaren, P., & Rikowski, G. (2002). Pedagogy against capital today: An e-interview: Peter McLaren interviewed by Glenn Rikowski. *The Hobgoblin: A Journal of Marxist Humanism, 4,* 31–38.

McMurtry, J. (1991). Education and the market model. *Journal of the Philosophy of Education, 25,* 209–217.

McMurtry, J. (1998). *Unequal freedoms: The global market as an ethical system.* West Hartford, CT: Kumarian.

McMurtry, J. (1999). *The cancer stage of capitalism.* London: Pluto.

Molnar, A. (1999). *Cashing in on kids: The second annual report on trends in schoolhouse commercialism, 1997–98—1998–99.* Milwaukee: University of Wisconsin, Centre for Analysis of Commercialism in Education, School of Education.

Molnar, A. (2001). *Giving kids the business: The commercialisation of America's schools* (2nd ed.) . Boulder, CO: Westview Press.

Ollman, B. (2003). *Dance of the dialectic: Steps in Marx's method.* Chicago: University of Illinois Press.

Rees, J. (2001). Imperialism, globalisation, the state and war. *International Socialism, 93,* 3–30.

Regan, B. (2008). *Campaigning against neo-liberal education in Britain.* In D. Hill (Ed.), *Contesting neoliberal education: Public resistance and collective advance. (pp. 83-109)* New York: Routledge.

Rikowski, G. (2000). Marxist educational theory transformed, a review article on P. Allman: Revolutionary social transformation: Democratic hopes, political possibilities and critical education. *Education and Social Justice, 2*(3), 60–64.

Rikowski, G. (2001a, June). *After the manuscript broke off: Thoughts on Marx, social class and education.* Paper presented at the British Sociological Association Education Study Group Meeting, London. Available at http://www.flow-ideas.co.uk/?page=pub&sub=Online%20Publications%20Glenn%Rikowski.

Rikowski, G. (2001b). *The Battle in Seattle.* London: Tufnell.

Rikowski, G. (2001c). Fuel for the living fire: Labour-power! In A. Dinerstein & M. Neary (Eds.), *The labour debate: An investigation into the theory and reality of capitalist work.* Aldershot, England: Ashgate.

Rikowski, G. (2001d). New Labour and the business take-over of education. *Socialist Future: Quarterly Magazine of the Movement for a Socialist Future, 9*(4), 14–17.

Rikowski, G. (2001e, May/June). Schools: Building for business. *Post-16 Educator, 3*, 10–11.

Rikowski, G. (2001f). *The importance of being a radical educator in capitalism today.* Available at http://www.ieps.org.uk.cwc.net/rikowski2005a.pdf.

Rikowski, G. (2002a). *Globalisation and education.* Paper prepared for the House of Lords Select Committee on Economic Affairs, Inquiry into the Global Economy. Available at www.ieps.org.uk or rikowski.uk@tinyworld.co.uk

Rikowski, G. (2002b). Transfiguration: Globalisation, the World Trade Organisation and the national faces of the GATS. *Information for Social Change, 14*, 8–17.

Rikowski, G. (2006). In retro glide. *Journal for Critical Education Policy Studies, 5*(1). Available at: http://www.jceps.com/index.php?pageID=article&articleID=81

Rikowski, G., (2007) Critical Pedagogy and the Constitution of Capitalist Society. *The Flow of Ideas*, 9 September. Available at http://www.flowofideas.co.uk/?page=article&sub=Critical20%Pedagogy/20%and20%Captialism

Rikowski, G., & McLaren, P. (2001). Pedagogy against capital today: An e-interview with Peter McLaren. *The Hobgoblin: Journal of Marxist-Humanism, 4.* Available at www.members.aol.com/thehobgoblin/index.html

Sanders, M., Hill, D., & Hankin, T. (1999). Education theory and the return to class analysis. In D. Hill, P. McLaren, M. Cole, & G. Rikowski (Eds.), *Postmodernism in educational theory: Education and the politics of human resistance* (pp. 98–130). London: Tufnell.

Smyth, J., & Shatlock, G. (1998). *Re-making teaching: Ideology, policy and practice.* London: Routledge.

Socialist Resistance. (2007, September). Savage capitalism—The ecosocialist alternative. *IV Online Magazine: IV392.* Available at http://www.internationalviewpoint.org/spip.php?article1311

Wilkes, R. (2007a). Building a movement against climate change. *Socialist Resistance, 46.* Available at http://www.isg-fi.org.uk/spip.php?article518&var_recherche=climate

Wilkes, R. (2007b). The dialectics of climate change. *Socialist Outlook, 12.* Available at http://www.isg-fi.org.uk/spip.php?article498&var_recherche=climate

Winch, C. (1998). Markets, educational opportunities and education: Reply to Tooley. *Journal of Philosophy of Education, 32*, 429–436.

Zeichner, K. and Liston, D. (1996) *Reflective Teaching: an introduction.* Mahwah, NJ: Lawrence Erlbaum.

Zeichner, K.M. and Liston, D.P. (1990) *Traditions of Reform in U.S. Teacher Education.* Michigan: National Centre for Research in Teacher Education, Michigan State University.

4   Rethinking Education in the Era of Globalization

Terry Wrigley

INTRODUCTION

Capitalism has always had a problem with education. Since the Industrial Revolution, and the early days of mass schooling for working-class children,[1] the ruling class has needed to increase the skills of future workers but was afraid they might become articulate, knowledgeable and rebellious.

The response to this contradiction has taken many forms over two centuries of capitalist development and working-class struggle (see for example Simon, 1960 and subsequent volumes; Lawton and Silver, 1973). Early in the 19th century, Hannah Moore justified the founding of Sunday Schools for children who were at work the rest of the week; reading was important, so that her association's pious tracts could be read, but writing was dangerous, since workers might frame and disseminate their own experiences and ideas:

> They learn, on weekdays, such coarse works as may fit them for servants. I allow of no writing for the poor. My object is . . . to train up the lower classes in habits of industry and piety . . . Beautiful is the order of society when each, according to his place, pays willing honour to his superiors. (cited in Simon, 1960, p. 133)

Perhaps that is why reactionaries still prefer children to complete meaningless exercises than to express their feelings and ideas.

Throughout the 19th century, English policy documents stated bluntly that working class children should not be educated beyond their station in life. The aim of elementary schools was to teach basic literacy and numeracy, discipline children into the rhythms of factory life and instill pride in the British Empire. Some teachers, of course, always struggled to overcome these constraints.

Often the British ruling class's fears of over-educating workers endangered their own competitiveness. For example, at the start of the 20th century, local School Boards were forbidden from providing secondary education, thus delaying the spread of scientific and technical education. Since Germany and other European countries were rapidly catching up with Britain in industrial production and productivity, this represents, in Marxist terminology, a contradiction between education: a) responding to *relations* of production, and b) developing the *means* of production. The relations of production acted as a brake on development of the means of production. For most of the 20th century, technical courses in schools were restricted to woodwork and metalwork (needlework for girls), although the economy had moved on. These subjects must largely have served a disciplinary function since they were largely archaic in terms of industrial production. It took until about 1990 for the widespread introduction of design and technology in its various forms.

Times have changed, but the basic principle remains: Capitalism needs workers who are *clever enough to be profitable, but not wise enough to know what's really going on*. This appears stark, but is fundamental to understanding the dynamics. There are however two factors which complicate the basic contradiction, so that we cannot simply map curricular formation onto socioeconomic analysis in a crude base-superstructure manner. First, employers have different views of what they need: Some insist on "back to basics"—more spelling practice and multiplication tables—while others, more forward looking, would like communication skills and initiative—though not *too* much of these! Second, there have always been many teachers, individually and organized in curriculum associations and trade unions, who persist in believing that schools should do more than prepare young people for work and their subordinate role in a social hierarchy—a more democratic and responsible vision.

What is particularly interesting, and critical, about the age we live in is that the contradictions are now exacerbated by globalization, including the neoliberal project to recreate a purer form of market capitalism and the sheer finality of looming environmental crisis. Humanity is faced simultaneously with three kinds of global crisis: poverty and debt; a collapse of the planet's ecosystem; and war. What is more, all of them connect back to global capitalism. For this reason, capitalism now has an even greater need to close down the discursive spaces where such a connection might be made, and where an active critical understanding could be developed. Current educational reforms are as much an attempt to prevent people making sense of the world as a search for greater "effectiveness."

THATCHERITE AND BLAIRITE EDUCATION REFORMS: A MODEL FOR NEOLIBERAL SCHOOLING

After a relatively progressive period from the 1960s to the mid-1980s, including more pupil-centered pedagogies in primary schools and the establishment of comprehensive secondary schooling, teachers in Britain were faced with a barrage of demands for restoring traditional practices. Key events in reversing the progressive trend were:

- Publication of the "Black Papers on Education" between 1969 and 1971 (book edition Cox and Dyson, 1971);
- Callaghan's speech calling for a "great debate" in 1976 (Callaghan, 1976);
- Thatcher's 1988 Education Reform Act (OPSI, 1988).

This is no place for a detailed history, but it is worthwhile summarizing some basic features. A sense of crisis had to be manufactured, which took the form of a moral panic about "low standards." This is not to say that there wasn't a real economic and political crisis involving (internationally) a falling rate of profit and (nationally) resurgent trade-union militancy, but the ideological work consisted in constructing this as a crisis of schooling and educational standards, and laying the blame on teachers and schools.[2] The panic generated by politicians and the right-wing press involved fears of economic decline, but also social chaos—a collapse of moral standards. Spurious links were made between curriculum and social order:

> If you allow standards to slip to the stage where good English is no better than bad English, where people can turn up filthy and nobody takes any notice of them at school—just as well as turning up clean—all those thing tend to cause people to have no standards at all, and once you lose your standards then there's no imperative to stay out of crime. (Norman Tebbit,[3] 1985; as cited in Marshall, 1998).

After about 10 years of ideological preparation, Thatcher felt able to introduce her far-reaching Education Reform Act (OPSI, 1988). This fulfilled a number of purposes.

1. It marketized the governance of public education, by disconnecting schools from their geographical communities and establishing a quasi-market of parental choice.
2. Head teachers were won over with offers of more power and freedom from local authority control. This "devolved management" gained them control of the accounts but simultaneously control of the curriculum was centralized through the National Curriculum and its associated test regime (see Point 4 below).
3. Schools were subjected to pervasive and often draconian structures of surveillance, under the guise of improving quality. These included national testing, the publication of "league tables," a threatening new system of inspection and performance pay. Private capitalism found new means of involvement (and profit-making) through the contracting out of testing and inspection. All of these created major difficulties for schools in the most challenging areas—those already suffering massively as a result of neoliberal economic policies and de-industrialization.

4. Thatcher's National Curriculum was simultaneously a technological modernization and an ideological retrenchment. Mathematics, science, design and technology and IT expanded to half the curriculum time. On the other hand, the space for creativity and self-expression was reduced, and for understanding the social world: The arts had a marginal role; there was no place for contemporary social studies; history had a nationalistic emphasis and events from the past 25 years were excluded. In many ways, the National Curriculum was a fusion between neoliberal and neoconservative elements (see also Apple, 1996).

Blair's reforms are, in many respects, far worse than Thatcher's government achieved, though largely built on those foundations.

1. There has been no slackening in the centralized surveillance and control. Indeed, in many respects it is worse. For example, teachers' salary progression from the moment of initial qualification is subject to decisions about "performance."
2. The Conservatives once argued that they would determine *what* should be taught but not *how*, which would remain a professional matter; whereas New Labour have closely regulated lesson structures and pedagogies through their various "Strategies" (see discussion in Jones, 2001).
3. Whereas Thatcher's National Curriculum made common provision to the age of 16, based on a "broad and balanced" curriculum, Blair's new Education and Inspection Act decrees two separate tracks from age 14: academic and vocational. The 2006 Education and Inspection Act (OPSI, 2006) explicitly prevents those pursuing the vocational route from studying drama, music, media studies, languages, history, geography; these pupils will even have a functionalist version of the subject English, stripped bare of personal writing, debate and literature.
4. This legislation pursues a policy of accelerating privatization, such that local education authorities become "commissioners" not "providers" of education. First the "academies" (secondary schools serving poorer urban areas) then "trust schools" (primary or secondary, with no restriction of location) are publicly funded but privately managed, albeit (for the moment at least) not-for-profit. Like many other New Labour reforms, it flies under the flag of "social justice." (See Ball, 2007 and 2008; Lister 2007.) That, of course, is Blair's Third Way; the wolf in sheep's clothing, neoliberalism disguised and mystified.

THE CHANGING NATURE OF THE STATE

As David Harvey (2005) has demonstrated, neoliberalism by no means entails a diminution of state power. On the contrary, a strong state is needed to regulate the market, to combat any class resistance to it, and to eliminate/commodify any nonmarket spaces. Similarly, in the field of education, Stephen Ball (2007) has powerfully demonstrated the complex ways in which the state is used to open up public services to the private sector.

Sears argues that we must see privatization not simply as schools under new ownership or management, but as a reorientation of education towards the needs and interests of capitalism.

> Privatization should not be seen as simply a reduction in the breadth of state activity, but rather as an active policy of extending market discipline. . . . The decommodified spaces of education are being eroded as part of the elimination of any spaces outside of market relations. (Sears, 2003, pp. 18, 21)

This radical commodification affects all areas of life. Pleasures which were once free (play in open spaces, the countryside, interpersonal communications) are replaced by those which are bought and sold. We are living through a cultural equivalent of the economic dispossession brought about by the enclosure of the common land (England) and the highland clearances (Scotland).

Parents were promised a greater say over their children's education through "accountability" and "choice." In reality, the development of parental participation and community schools has been held back, and parents given the surrogate involvement of a commodity relationship: Schools as an item of consumer choice. (The choice is often spurious; only a minority of London children gain a place in their parents' first-choice school.)

Some outrageous measures have been designed to drive schools towards privatization, including making inspection tougher so that more schools would fail. The 2005 White Paper[4] decreed that the local education authority should then take drastic measures, dismissing the head teacher and other senior teachers, removing the governors, seizing control of the budget, to compel "improvement" within a year. This was followed by specific threads of closure issued to nearly a fifth of English secondary schools, in which a baseline for acceptable exam success was set regardless of the the extent of social deprivation (http://news.bbc.co.uk/1/hi/education/7444822.stm, June 2008). Such draconian measures are more likely to destroy schools which are already fragile; this is the cure of the leech doctor who bleeds the patient dry. Local authorities must be "commissioners not providers" of education, and are only allowed to run newly opened or re-organized schools if they receive permission to tender for them in an open market. It seems unlikely that the increased diversity of school types which is destroying community-based comprehensive schools will extend to permit the political or pedagogical diversity existing in Denmark or The Netherlands.[5]

There has been considerable debate on the left about the purpose of Blair's latest reform. Schools Minister Ruth Kelly insisted that it was not privatization since the companies running schools are not allowed to make a profit. However, indirect profits can be made by contracting the provision of services to other capitalists, including those with close associations to the sponsor. It has also been argued that quasi-privatized schools in England will serve as a shop window for full privatization elsewhere in the world, leading to a rich seam of profits for the emergent edubusinesses. It is impossible to fully write off the economic argument, given the Confederation of British Industry's paper "The Business of School Improvement" (2005), which demanded that a larger and larger share of the national school budget should pass through the hands of profit-making businesses.

It is important to appreciate the political as well as economic dimension to this reform. In a sense, we face a return to 19th century systems of governance whereby each school was beholden to a representative of capitalist class power such as the local farmer or the vicar's wife. Although they often also raided the school for cheap labor, as maids or to collect in the harvest, the essential function of these individuals was to exercise control on behalf of their class in general, rather than themselves in particular. They ensured, for example, that rituals of loyalty such as Empire Day were enthusiastically observed, that religious teaching was orthodox, that teachers maintained strict discipline and did not express radical views.

The switch to a more vocational curriculum is a crucial part of Blairite reforms. I have referred above to the division of pupils, under new English legislation, into two distinct tracks. Jones and Duceux (2006) draw important parallels with similar reforms in other parts of the European Union. However, to believe that only those in the vocational track are deprived of important social and environment knowledge is to underestimate the problem. The academic track may well learn history and geography and literature but are likely to do so in such a high-pressured and disengaged way, as a succession of testable facts, that they will find it hard to develop a critical sense of the world. I am reminded of Camus's description in The Plague (1948) of life under fascist occupation as *frenetic and absent*.

A traditional academic curriculum and a vocational curriculum are often constructed as opposites, without recognizing their similarities. Kemmis et al. (1983) argue that both serve to place young people in a hierarchical society as it exists, without seeing the need for social change; the only difference is their intended place in the social order. Whereas vocational courses prepare some young people for specific manual trades, young people pursuing more academic studies receive a less clearly defined and broader preparation for the more flexible challenges they will face in white-collar and professional employment.

We might extend this argument in various ways. First, for the most part, the products of both tracks within the public system will end up within the working class, in a classic Marxist sense—those who sell their labor power. They will not be capitalists, nor become a middle *class* as an independent historic force.[6] Second, as Sears (2003) sees with considerable clarity, their preparation for the world of work is as much ideological as it is technical—the development of habitus and identity for work under fast capitalism.

It is not difficult to find manifestations of this. One clear example is the insistence on *enterprise* as a curricular value and activity, even for classes of very young children.[7] Another is the exaggerated emphasis on assessment, which Sally Tomlinson argues has become a means of initiating young people into a culture of vicious and relentless competition:

> Market states must maximise opportunities by encouraging competition between individuals and promote those with merit, but also threaten penalties—poor education and low-level jobs or unemployment for those deemed without merit. Market states encourage meritocracies where "ruthless assessment" is the norm, and "choices" are in fact strategies in a competitive marketplace. Market states are not places where mutual assistance thrives and are largely indifferent to social justice. (Tomlinson, 2006, p. 52)

Sears (2003) argues that just as 19th century England capitalism "had to destroy the old moral economy that included a particular structure of entitlements and expectations" (2003, p. 12), so today's young people have to be "prepared for life without a net, or at least for a world with an Internet rather than a social safety net." (ibid, p. 20).

> Students are encouraged to think about the market throughout their educational career—for example, they are encouraged to keep a portfolio from the earliest grades that relates their educational experience to their career goals. (ibid, p. 21)

> Educational reform is replacing the embrace of the state with a harsher market model of inclusion, marked by insecurity, user pay and increased opportunity to fail. The aim may be less to drive students out than to challenge them to survive in this new environment, hardening them for the lean world that awaits them after graduation. (ibid, p. 57)

Despite the moral panic about education not producing the quality of skills the economy needs, the rhetoric of "post-industrial knowledge economies" and the supposed need for everyone to become "highly skilled problem solvers," most young people entering the labor market are confronted with a demand deficit rather than a skills deficit—there simply is not enough demand for their labor irrespective of skills levels (ibid: 69, drawing on Morisette et al.).

At the same time, young people are confronted with an increasingly abusive tirade from politicians, inculcating a sense of worthlessness if they do not concur with this culture of instrumentalism. Young people growing up in the poorer areas of Britain are increasingly being criminalized, in the double sense of facing incarceration and of being labelled as criminally deviant. (The parallel to this, of course, is the Islamophobic campaign of

Blair's government, which led the neofascist British Nationalist Party[8] to claim that "New Labour ministers are scrambling over one another . . . leaving BNP spokesmen trailing!")

A further component of neoliberal "citizenship" is the denial of essential knowledge. History and geography are in rapid decline as school subjects, and English is being redefined through new qualifications as a narrowly instrumental "functional literacy." The creative and performing arts are being squeezed out of the curriculum, while having to fight for their place in the curriculum through arguments about their economic value.

VOICE AND AGENCY

Two major discourses are available at present for thinking about school reform. One is the body of School Effectiveness, Improvement and Leadership texts, with their hollowed-out sense of the future; for all their talk of "vision," they are largely silent on the big issues of our time such as poverty, environmental collapse and imperialism. The other is a literature on critical pedagogy which is generally too abstract and remote to be of much practical value. The important task for socialists working in education is to find practical ways of involving young people in a critical and engaged study of the world.

The recent interest in "student voice" has sought to provide both a heuristic and a banner for challenging current practices theoretically and practically, but we need to add to the notion of *voice*, a concern for *agency*. Both voice and agency are systematically denied in traditional practices of schooling on three levels:

1. The organization and disciplining of relationships in the school institution;
2. The curriculum, as a selection of content;
3. The preferred modes of teaching and learning.

This is particularly the case for young people from poorer and ethnic minority communities. It was Freire's lasting contribution (e.g. 1998, 2005) to imagine and mount a challenge to all three forms of oppression: disciplinary, curricular and pedagogical.

Disciplinary

Disciplining young people no longer takes the form of physical beatings but current practices are equally deserving of the term "discipline": long period of immobility, the strict regulation of time and space, a disconnection from activities which are valued by adults and exclusion of those who break the rules. All of these have been increased by the intensification of instruction resulting from high-stakes testing and government regulation of teaching methods. To some extent control of behavior and relationships is made necessary by the compression of young bodies in the classroom, and learning cannot take place in too chaotic or hostile an environment, but it has ideological consequences nonetheless.

Disciplinary measures are more likely to meet resistance in areas of deprivation for a number of reasons which are connected to teachers' social and cultural distance from the local community, adolescents confronted with too many different subject specialists for a secure trust to be established, and the washing over into school of domestic and neighborhood problems. Teacher actions which are simply accepted as "normal" in other schools take on the cultural significance of the disciplining of workers by a boss, or of ethnic minorities by a White majority, in such schools.

There has been considerable emphasis in government guidelines of the term "orderly" but the keyword I have found most significant and positively used in successful inner-city schools is "respect." This is important, as it points to the importance of establishing less oppressive relationships. (There is also an interesting cultural resonance here with the use of the term within Afro-Caribbean communities in Britain.) This emerges in many ways in school culture:

- The display of children's photographs and their work;
- The quality of interpersonal relationships;
- A reaching out to parents, even when they haven't turned up to consultation evenings;
- A respect for heritage and youth cultures;
- The creation of social spaces.

It is important to question seemingly "natural" structures, both those internal to the school and the boundary between school and the wider world. Given the turmoil of life under globalized late capitalism, and particularly for the most oppressed, it is essential to create a safe and nurturing environment for young people. Paradoxically, this safe space is a necessary foundation from which they can reach out to the complex world outside. The phrase "school as a home for learning"[9] encapsulates this idea; schools should be nurturing social communities as well as learning communities.

There are many alternatives to the current organization of secondary schools in Britain, or to the large urban high schools in the United States which have been dubbed "shopping mall schools." It is far too easy for disturbed young people to get lost in these anonymous spaces while wandering from room to room every hour. Scandinavian schools are generally much smaller, and often divided up into smaller communities.

In Norway, for example, a year of 60 to 100 pupils is looked after by a team of 5 to 6 teachers, who teach the curriculum, provide pastoral care and guidance, and liaise with parents. They include expertise in learning support, and as a team have the power to reorganize their own timetable, making special projects and learning out of school easy to organize. The result is a much better quality of relationships and very little disruption; school exclusions are very rare. Many smaller schools and schools-within-schools are being established in the United States, with extremely positive results,[10] and the movement is supported from across the political spectrum, from communitarian radicals to the Gates Foundation.[11]

Curricula

Since Thatcher's 1988 reform, it has become common to take for granted the centralized control of the curriculum, the teacher's role being to "deliver" it. Schools are now being offered only one alternative to a traditional academic curriculum: vocational preparation. This is particularly the case in more deprived or troubled areas, where job training is seen as the answer to apathy and alienation. Although there are still some remnants of a "multicultural" or even "antiracist" curriculum, we no longer even have a word to indicate a curricular alternative which might meet the particular needs of poor urban communities.[12] One lesson from the past is that the curriculum should connect up with pupils' lives and experiences, but also open up new opportunities and horizons. It is important to ground learning in community experience and a local culture, but at the same time education involves opening new horizons and opportunities and developing a critical vision.

Socialist teachers need a critical understanding of curriculum issues, in order not to accept too easily the neoliberal alternative of vocationalism. There are many possibilities for a community- and activity-based curriculum which is more socially critical. For example, a design and technology project might involve investigation of the play facilities in the area, and then the construction of a new playground based on children's needs and wishes. In the process, much would be learned about social inequalities and political structures.

A reformed curriculum needs to be critical and theoretical as well as practical. Philip Wexler argued that the following aspects of critical understanding are typically silenced in school texts:

1. "The location of human activity in *history*"
2. "The ability to situate the individual and the immediate within a larger frame, to have a view of the social *totality*"
3. *Conflict* rooted in opposing interests'—and particularly exploitation (not just "differences as cultural pluralism")

4. *Work,* that is, "collective human labour as the continuing source of what we are and of what we have, the human social making of relations and products." (summarised, including quotations, from Wexler, 1982, pp. 287-8)

Furthermore, he pointed out that the authoritative tone of school textbooks—and we might add, its reinforcement by teacher voice—conceals from the learner the bias or inadequacies of the text's construction, disabling the learning from further enquiry and action (ibid, pp. 289–290).

Here we might take issue with progressives who focus on process to the neglect of content. How, for example, could someone take a stand on the Israeli government's oppression of Palestinians without some key factual knowledge, for instance:

- The *historical* fact that Jews returned to their "homeland" after an absence of 2,000 years;
- That the Palestinian territories have a tenuous and marginal position within a wider *totality,* including a third generation of refugees in Lebanon;
- That they are largely denied the means to develop the land and engage in productive *work;*
- And that the Israeli state is able to deploy overwhelming force supported by $100 million of U.S. aid each day (i.e., knowledge of *conflict* and unequal power relationships).

These facts, along with knowledge of the horrors of the Holocaust which gave impetus to the Zionist solution, are necessary for a critical and responsible understanding. For example, the final point illustrates the important difference between an emphasis on conflict and structural inequalities and a liberal-pluralist emphasis on *diversity* alone. Without such key knowledge, we remain trapped in a limited "two tribes" understanding of Israeli–Palestinian relations and a vague sense of "isn't it terrible but what can you do?"

Particular subject paradigms may have a limiting effect on learning, such as the "great men and battles" version of history, or a language curriculum crammed with technical detail about grammar. Sometimes teachers may subvert the state's attempt to impose a conservative version of a subject; for example, when Shakespeare was made compulsory for 14 year olds in England, the curriculum policy clearly intended "iconic Shakespeare" but many teachers seized the opportunity to develop socially critical responses—the Shakespeare who calls into question kingship, filial obedience and racial prejudice. In other cases a full challenge is needed; for example we should insist on the central importance of media education for the education of democratic citizens in the 21st century.

Tim Brighouse (2002), on his retirement as the highly successful director of England's largest local education authority, asserted that the national curriculum is now more tightly regulated than in Stalinist Russia! We need to argue for a degree of "authorship" on the part of the learners:

> How can we reconceptualise and reconstruct the curriculum in such a way that pupils, at least for part of the time, have an opportunity for fashioning some time for themselves so that they can pursue their own ideas and studies? (Davies & Edwards, 2001, p. 104)

It was a shock and welcome surprise to discover the Danish education ministry advising teachers against writing a precise plan for the year for social studies as this could undermine *negotiations* with the learners (Undervisningminsteriet, 1995).

Pedagogical

There is ample research from the 1970s and 1980s to show the typical asymmetry of language use in the classroom. The teacher's voice dominates, with the teacher speaking more than everyone else put together. The teacher asks all the questions, including many phony questions to which s/he already knows the answers. The frequency of test questions undermines a real dialogue, as discussion becomes examination. Pupil contributions are normally very brief, and real discussion is rare.

Alongside this denial of voice, the denial of agency is part of the deep grammar of traditional schooling. There are rare examples of real problem-solving, such as I found in a German manual for social studies (Weissenau & Kuhn, 2000)—the town hall or hospital comes to school with a problem which students are asked to help solve; they discuss and research it before presenting their answers to the local policy makers. Students are constantly told "you'll use this knowledge when you're older" or "you'll need this for your exam," with little sense of engagement in the here and now.

School learning is often a kind of alienated labor, with the exchange value of extrinsic rewards (grades, merit certificates, etc.) compensating for the lack of a sense of use value. The regular pattern of this economic exchange is:

- Teacher tells pupils what to produce, and how long they must work at the task
- Pupils hand it to teacher, who looks hastily at the product
- Teacher hands it back defaced with a small token of its worth
- The product is of no earthly use to anybody.

This really is a lesson in selling your labor power. There are alternatives, where learners become genuinely engaged in working at a task, work in groups and then present back to the class or a wider audience.

ABSTRACT AND EXPERIENTIAL KNOWLEDGE: IN SEARCH OF INCLUSIVE PEDAGOGIES[13]

The relationship between symbolic representations and lived experience is a complex one, and seriously problematic when the abstract and decontextualized forms privileged by schools jar with more experiential and narrative cultures rooted in manual labor.

The identification of a general and innate intelligence (IQ) through tests of decontextualized abstract reasoning inevitably positions many students as *lacking* in intelligence per se. Similarly, Bernstein's (1971) loaded use of the term *restricted code* has been criticized for portraying working-class (i.e., manual worker) families as linguistically deficient (see Wrigley, 2003, pp. 76–83; Rosen, 1972). A more productive understanding of different forms of knowledge can help us overcome the barriers to learning faced by many young people.

It is useful to recognize a broad spectrum of forms of representation, from concrete to abstract. In broad terms, and omitting some important types (e.g., musical notation), the spectrum would run from physical models to virtual models, from narrative to academic language and finally through arithmetic to algebra. My argument is that improving access for marginalized young people requires grounding theoretical knowledge in lived experience, but as a road towards theoretical understanding, not its avoidance. For many learners the best pathway to $C = 2\pi r$ could be guided experimentation with different sizes of bicycle wheels, comparing the lengths of the spoke and the rim, but once properly acquired, the abstract language of algebra is very powerful in its ability to comprehend general relationships. Similarly, narrative styles can be more accessible than abstract academic language, and hold together affective and cognitive dimensions, but there are advantages to consolidating and critiquing the knowledge gained via narrative by using more formal academic discourses. Both examples illustrate the importance of moving up and down the experience-abstraction scale.

Models and simulations are forms of representations which come nearest to lived experience. Along with works of art, drama, novels, they are a kind of "microworld." They are multisensory and multidimensional mappings of lived experience, but they are also "offline" in the sense that they have no direct practical consequences (see Wartofsky, 1973). This provides the opportunity to play with alternatives—to explore different relationships and outcomes. Play provides a means of exploring alternative futures.

Unfortunately, in dealing with a gulf between the colloquial language of young people, particularly those from manual-worker backgrounds, and the abstract language of academic learning, teachers often fall back on a traditional diet of decontextualized exercises. Jim Cummins (www.iteachilearn.com/cummins/bicscalp.html) has identified a similar tendency in the case of bilingual pupils whose home language is not the school language. He represents this as a quadrant:

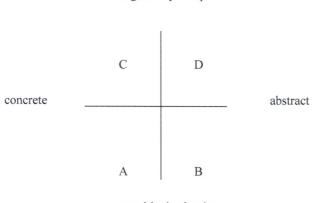

A represents everyday conversational and transactional language, while D represents the academic language of school learning. He argues that schools tend to trap learners who are struggling with abstract learning to Zone B, which is abstract but cognitively simple, instead of developing Zone C activities which root challenging ideas in experiences and richer forms of representation. C is the route to D, whereas B is a cul-de-sac.[14] Zone C activities provide opportunities for teachers to scaffold the learner's language from descriptive/narrative to more abstract theoretical discourses, and from colloquial to formal registers. Cummins model is, I believe, equally applicable to large numbers of monolingual learners from manual-worker families.[15]

OPEN ARCHITECTURES OF LEARNING

New Labour's curriculum "strategies" have been highly scripted and prescriptive, though there is now some greater freedom and diversity. Teachers have been encouraged to "deliver" tightly planned but fragmentary lessons, such as stereotypical "four-part lessons" which divide each 50 to 60 minute lesson into a starter activity, a plenary explanation, a group based activity, and a final plenary. Strange, the starter often has no connection to the main lesson, as it consists generally of skills practice such as spelling; and the group activity and final plenary are far too short to enable a real construction of knowledge. One such example allows each group of pupils a mere 20 minutes to struggle with a difficult 19th century poem, identifying the main theme and unusual language, followed by a 10 minute plenary for the six groups to share their understandings of the six different poems and decide on the poet's main issues and beliefs. This fast-paced fulfillment of curricular objectives is not pedagogy of engaged and interactive learning; indeed, it is almost a parody.

An alternative can be found in methods such as project, storyline and design challenges (see Wrigley, 2006a, pp. 105–109; Wrigley, 2007). I have called these "open architectures" because they provide a structure while leaving scope for learner initiative and collaboration. They have many advantages: They are language rich, collaborative, connect with learners' prior experience, and give a sense of achievement through a final product or real audience. Each of these architectures has its characteristic structure and benefits, though they can also be hybridized.

Project method begins with a topic suggested by the teacher or the learners, perhaps a significant current event. The next stage, also plenary, consists of discussion to problematize this topic, during which specific questions and directions of enquiry are identified. This stage also involves the teacher bringing in insights from academic disciplines. Stage 3 involves individuals and groups of learners researching sub-topics and questions of their choice. The fourth stage, again a plenary, allows groups to share their knowledge and engage the class in further debate, while a fifth stage can be added involving some kind of action in the wider community.

I have used this approach with student teachers to help them understand the situation of refugees, beginning with a simulation exercise. In Stage 2 it becomes clear that some know more than others, and students differentiate themselves (in response to prior knowledge, not "ability") through Stage 3 research topics. For example, some will find out where refugees come from and why, whereas others choose to explore complex issues such as national identity and xenophobia.

Storyline is based on a narrative[16] in which each event stimulates a learning activity (research, writing, drama, painting, discussion, etc.) It begins with a visual representation of the setting (e.g. a mural), then each participant invents and identifies as a character. Storyline was first devised in Scotland as a form of thematic work appropriate to lower primary children, but is now used extensively in Scandinavia in secondary schools as well. (Bell et al. eds., 2007)

Design challenges[17] work by the teacher proposing a final product in response to an initial problem or problem-posing situation. Usually groups work collaboratively and have a strict deadline for preparing and presenting.

Such approaches to learning, along with other collaborative problem-based pedagogies, provide a means of generating a community of common concern as a basis for learning, rather than the competitive individualism of test preparation and the accumulation of dead facts.

LITERACY

The teaching of "literacy" has been a particular target of educational reform; indeed, in the English-speaking world, the shift in terminology from English, Language or Reading to Literacy has betoken the introduction of a highly regulated and fragmented approach.

Mirroring the dominance of test questions in teacher-pupil interchanges, reading beyond the initial stages is often characterized by "comprehensions" or reading-as-test. It would be foolish to write them off altogether, as skilful questioning can focus readers' attentions on rhetorical features, ambiguities and ill-founded assertations, and can help to develop skills of critical literacy, but comprehensions rarely invite engagement.

Alternatives include the invitation to readers actively to "do something" with the text, for example,

- Predicting how the story will continue
- Disputing a statement from someone else's point of view
- Comparing two texts on a similar subject. (Simons, c.1986)

Converting textual information into diagrammatic form requires a more proactive struggle to find the holistic meaning offered and can help to highlight flaws in the logic.

Critical literacy can be brought to life through dramatic techniques such as hot-seating, thus helping to reveal the dialogic nature concealed within apparently monologic texts. This was developed by drama teachers (the actor playing Lady Macbeth is in the hotseat, facing questions from other actors or the audience). It could be extended to political situations, for example:

- Ask somebody to represent the author of a newspaper article, and subject them to questions about their intentions, motives and evidence;
- Role play Tony Blair or George Bush to ask them to justify their decision to occupy Iraq;
- Hotseat an abstract concept such as Imperialism, or more specifically the British Empire or the American Empire.

Supplying some key quotations can heighten this. We could use Madeleine Albright's infamous television comment that the death of half a million Iraqi children through the sanctions was "worth it" (Albright, 1996)[18] or Bishop Tutu's summary of colonization:

> When the missionaries first came to Africa, they had bibles and we had the land. They said, "Let us pray." We closed our eyes. When we opened them, we had the bibles and they had the land. (Peterson, as cited in Darder et al., p. 379)

In an era of globalization, it should be a central part of education to learn to question its dark side, particularly imperialist war and the racism that accompanies it. At the time of writing, Blair's ministers are falling over themselves to generate anti-Muslim prejudice.

Critical literacy can also extend to studying the graphical techniques of tabloid journalism and advertising, including classic illustrations of subversive art—Herzfeld's photomontage, or the wonderful moment when the *Daily Mirror* (20.12.2002) subverted G. W. Bush's own rhetoric through parody, turning it against himself:

> There is a lunatic with weapons of mass destruction "ramping up" for a war that will threaten the whole world. Stop him!

> [A picture of the President appeared below this headline.]

One of the best developed examples of education for critical understanding comes from New York's Central Park East Secondary School, where the teachers worked out a code for evaluating new texts and ideas:

- *Viewpoint:* From whose viewpoint are we hearing this? to whose speaking? Would this look different if she or he were in another place or time?
- *Evidence:* How do we know what we know? What evidence will we accept? How credible will such evidence appear to others? What rules of evidence are appropriate to different tasks?
- *Connections and patterns:* How are things connected together? Have we ever encountered this before? Is there a discernable pattern here? What came first? Is there a clear cause and effect? Is this a "law" or causality, a probability, or a mere correlation?
- *Conjecture:* What if things had been different? Suppose King George had been a very different personality? Suppose Napoleon or Martin Luther King, Jr. or Hitler had not been born? Suppose King's assassin had missed? (Our fourth habit encompassed our belief that a well-educated person saw alternatives, other possibilities, and assumed that choices mattered. They could make a difference. The future wasn't, perhaps, inevitable.)
- And finally—who, after all, cares? Does it *matter?* And to whom? Is it of mere "academic" interest, or might it lead to significant changes in the way we see the world and the world sees us? (from Meier, 1998, pp. 607–608)

A DIFFERENT FUTURE

Schools have rarely been future orientated, but now, in our neoliberal "postmodern" world, they are in danger of losing sight of the past as well. It is crucial that we defend history from marginalization in a new "lean" curriculum which is only concerned with providing skills for a capitalist economy (albeit an economy which has no idea how to use them). As Howard Zinn expressed it:

If you don't know history, it's as if you were born yesterday. And if you were born yesterday, anybody up there in a position of power can tell you anything, and you have no way of checking up on it.[19]

We also need to develop a sense of openness towards the future—a sense that life can be different. Many of the pedagogies in this article have done this implicitly, but let us finally consider two ideas which focus explicitly on the future: a futures website, and a futures timeline.

The former can be generalized (the global future), localized (Imagine Scotland, Imagine London), or thematized (environment, peace, etc.) It provides a structured but open opportunity for young people to combine text and images, their own voices and others, and relate knowledge of past and present to hopes for a different future.

A futures timeline is rather like those we use for history, but since we don't know how the future will turn out, it divides into three: from the current year, one line slants upwards (the future we dream of), one downwards (the future we fear), and one is horizontal (the probable future). Of course, drawing the timeline is not an end in itself but should serve as the focus and trigger for discussion and action.

SCHOOLS FOR A FUTURE

It is a cliché that we are living in an era of unprecedented change. It is a reasonable conclusion that schools must also change, but an absurd non sequitur to believe that this can be limited to buying more computers, more "effective" instruction or better management techniques.

In the last 20 years, government-favored versions of "school improvement" and "leadership" have led to little more than intensification—a speeding up of the old structures and processes rather than genuine transformation. We are expected to believe that this theory of school improvement is universal, a kind of global common sense, and indeed agencies such as the World Bank seek to make it so. Despite this, there are many alternatives which result from teachers' courageous attempts to do education differently. These bold attempts to change direction involve a challenge to current norms at the different levels referred to earlier: disciplinary, curricular and pedagogical. They offer learners a chance to develop both voice and agency so that they can create a more democratic and just world.

Because of the weight and force of what we are opposing, this involves us in working together in new ways. A powerful model is Rethinking Schools, a teachers' network in the United States, which simultaneously campaigns against government policy and develops practical resources and methods for critical pedagogy. My recent book *Another School Is Possible*, and the U.K.-based network Rethinking Education (albeit at an early stage of development), seek to open up new possibilities, particularly for a generation of young teachers who have been narrowly "trained" to think that *this is all there is*.

We are at a critical point in educational history. We face, to a heightened degree, the enduring contradiction of a dynamic economic system which needs its workers to acquire knowledge and skills, but is terrified lest they become truly educated. Overlaid onto this is another deep contradiction: That today's young people are saturated in consumer culture and changed by it, but the very same corporate forces which pour out commodified excitement are imposing a pedagogy which is regimented and dull (see, Kenway & Bullen, 2001).

We are confronted with the challenge of developing new forms of curriculum and new pedagogies in the face of heavy opposition. The road ahead is unclear, but a quotation from novelist Philip Pullman (2005) may shed some light on our task:

True education flowers when delight falls in love with responsibility.[20]

NOTES

1. The principal reference here is to the first Western European countries to industrialize and particularly England. As a result of religious Reformations, some countries such as Scotland and Sweden had an earlier development of mass education and literacy.
2. Bethan Marshall's (1998) illustrations of how a moral panic about standards in English was fostered. See also Alan Sears (2003) for evidence that a media panic was deliberately engineered by Canadian politicians.
3. Tebbit was a leading minister in Margaret Thatcher's conservative government and also the Conservative Party's chairman. This quotation and others can be found in Marshall (1998).
4. *Higher Standards, Better Schools for All* (2005), subtitled 'More Choice for Parents and Pupils'. London: HM Government, Cm 6677.
5. An outline summary can be found in Justesen (2002), with useful references to sources, though I do not agree with the lessons drawn by this report on behalf of the Adam Smith Institute.
6. This is not to deny, of course, the constant reconstruction and positioning of professional families as agents competing for their children's relative advantage within a marketized school system, see Power, Edwards and Wigfall (2003).
7. I have yet to hear of a school running "enterprise projects" which are not sanitized—ones in which participants in the role of employers pay minimal wages, sack workers, face industrial disputes or go bankrupt.
8. Cited, within a broader argument, in http://laboursfightback.blogspot.com/2007/07/secularism-of-fools.html (accessed 23.3.08)
9. The phrase derives from a conference which took place in Germany in the mid 1990s, see Wrigley (2003, pp. 5, 141–152).
10. A good starting point for research and further information is www.school-redesign.net
11. It should be noted that, unlike the "sponsors" of the privatized city academies in England, the Gates Foundation has taken a deliberately hands-off approach, encouraging a diversity of models which can then be evaluated.
12. The term *urban education* is frequently used in the United States but rarely in the United Kingdom.

13. This section provides a reworking of the issues which led Howard Gardner (1983) to his concept of "multiple intelligences." The arguments presented here can be found at greater length in Wrigley (2006b).
14. Many successful learning activities can be found in Wrigley (2000), a set of case studies of successful multi-ethnic schools.
15. Further explanations can be found at www.iteachilearn.com/cummins/bicscalp. html and www.naldic.org.uk/ITTSEAL2/resource/readings/KS6Cummins.htm. Many illustrations of how this works in practice appear in Wrigley (2000).
16. Storyline can be based on a novel or short story, but usually it is based on a skeletal plot which is fleshed out by participants. Further information and examples can be found at www.acskive.dk/storyline/index.htm
17. For further information, see www.criticalskills.co.uk
18. The many critical commentaries on this interview which are to be found on the internet provide a provocative resource for critical literacy, eg John Pilger on the impact of sanctions (www.johnpilger.com/page.asp?partid=11), Rahul Mahajan on the lack of mainstream media interest (www.fair.org/index.php?page=1084), and Alexander Cockburn and Jeffrey St Clair in the context of 9/11 (www. counterpunch.org/theprice.html). Madeleine Allbright's own apologia in her memoir *Madam Secretary* (2003) is also of interest (cited in counter-comment by Sheldon Richman in www.fff.org/comment/com0311c.asp, 7 Nov 2003) The original interview is on www.youtube.com/watch?v=1k_Qsh52EW8.
19. This quotation can be found in an interview on the American new program Democracy Now, broadcast 27.4.05. www.democracynow.org/article. pl?sid=05/04/27/1350240.
20. *The Guardian,* (2005, January 22).

REFERENCES

Albright, M. (1996). Interview on Sixty Minutes (CBS news broadcast) 5.12.1996.
Apple, M. (1996). *Cultural politics and education.* New York: Teachers College Press.
Ball, S. (2007). *Education plc: Understanding private sector participation in public sector education.* Abingdon, England: Routledge.
Ball, S. (2008). *The education debate.* Bristol: Policy Press.
Bell, S., Harkness, S. and White, G. (2007). *Storyline past, present and future.* Glasglow: University of Strathclyde.
Bernstein, B. (1971). *Class, codes and control, vol. 1.* London: Routledge and Kegan Paul.
Brighouse, T. (2002). *Education chief attacks test regime.* Available at: http://news. bbc.co.uk/1/hi/education/1924203.stm
Callaghan, J. (1976). *Towards a national debate.* Speech at Ruskin College, Oxford on Oct 18. Reproduced http://education.guardian.co.uk/thegreatdebate/story/0,9860,574645,00.html. (accessed 23.3.08).
Camus, A. (1948). *The Plague.* London: Hamish Hamilton. Translated from the French by S Gilbert.
Confederation of British Industry. (2005). The business of education improvement: raising LEA performance through competition. London: CBI Publications. Available at: www.cbi.org.uk/pdf/businessagenda05.pdf.
Cox, C.B., and Dyson, A.E. (1971). *The Black Papers on education.* London: Davis-Poynter.
Cummins, J. (1981). The role of primary language development in promoting educational success for language minority students. In California State Department

of Education (Ed.), *Schooling and language minority students: A theoretical framework*. Los Angeles: Evaluation, Dissemination and Assessment Center, California State University, Los Angeles.

Daily Mirror (20.12.2002) Front page reproduced at http://www.mydailymirror.com/newspapersview.php?view=37244&day=20&month=12&year=2002. (Accessed 23.3.07)

Darder, A., Baltodano, M., and Torres, R. (Eds.). (2003). *The critical pedagogy reader*. London: RoutledgeFalmer.

Davies, M., & Edwards, G. (2001). Will the curriculum caterpillar ever learn to fly? In M. Fielding (Ed.), *Taking education really seriously: Four years hard Labour* (pp. 96–107). London: RoutledgeFalmer.

Freire, P. (1998). *Pedagogy of freedom: ethics, democracy and civic courage*. Oxford: Rowman and Littlefield

Freire, P. (2005). *Teachers as cultural workers: letters to those who dare teach*. (expanded edition) Boulder, Colorado: Westview.

Gardner, H. (1983) *Frames of mind: the theory of multiple intelligences*. New York: Basic Books.

Harvey, D. (2005). *A brief history of neoliberalism*. Oxford: Oxford University Press.

Jones, K. (2001). Responding to the themes of the collection. In C. Chitty, & B. Simon (Eds.), *Promoting comprehensive education in the 21st century* (pp. 87-91). Stoke, England: Trentham.

Jones, K., & Duceux, N. (2006). Neo-liberalism in the schools of Western Europe. *Our Schools/Our Selves* (pp. 93-112) (special issue: 'Education's iron cage and its dismantling in the new global order'). Ottawa: Canadian Centre for Policy Alternatives.

Justesen, M. (2002). Learning from Europe: The Dutch and Danish school systems. London: Adam Smith Institute. Available at www.adamsmith.org/images/uploads/publications/learning-from-europe.pdf

Kemmis, S., Cole, P., & Suggett, D. (1983). *Orientations to curriculum and transition: towards the socially-critical school*. Melbourne, Australia: Victorian Institute of Secondary Education.

Kenway, J., & Bullen, E. (2001). *Consuming children: Education-entertainment-advertising*. Buckingham, England: Open University Press

Lawton, J., and Silver, H. (1973) *A social history of education in England*. London: Methuen

Lister, T. (2007). The real egalitarianism? Social justice after Blair. In G. Hassan (Ed.), *After Blair: politics after the New Labour decade*. London: Lawrence and Wisthart.

Marshall, B. (1998). English teachers and the third way. In B. Cox (Ed.), *Literacy is not enough (pp. 109-115)*. Manchester, England: Manchester University Press.

Meier, D. (1998). Authenticity and educational change. In A. Hargreaves et al. (Eds.), *International handbook of educational change* (pp. 596-615). Dordrecht, The Netherlands: Kluwer.

Ministry of Education, Denmark. (1995). *Samfundsfag* [Curriculum guidelines for citizenship education]. Copenhagen: Ministry of Defence.

Pilger, J. (1998, December 14). Killing Iraq. *The Nation*.

OPSI. (1988). Education Reform Act. Reproduced in https://www.opsi.gov.uk/acts/acts1988/ukpga_19880040_en_1 (accessed 23.3.08).

OPSI. (2006). Education and Inspections Act. Reproduced in http://www.opsi.gov.uk/acts/acts2006/ukpga_20060040_en_1 (accessed 23.3.08).

Power, S., Edwards, T., & Wigfall, V. (2003). *Education and the middle class*. Buckingham, England: Open University Press.

Rosen, H. (1972). *Language and class: a critical look at the theories of Basil Bernstein*. Bristol: Falling Wall Press.

Sears, A. (2003). *Retooling the mind factory: Education in a lean state*. Aurora, Ontario, Canada: Garamond.

Simon, B. (1960). *Studies in the history of education 1780–1870*. London: Lawrence and Wishart.

Simons, M. (with E. Plackett). (Eds.). (c.1986). *The English curriculum: Reading 1. comprehension*. London: English and Media Centre.

Tomlinson, S. (2006). Another day, another white paper. *Forum, 48*(1), 52.

Undervisningsministeriet - Folkeskoleafdelingen (1995) *Samfundsfag* (Faghæfte 5). Copenhagen: Undervisningsministeriet forlag. [Danish education ministry's curriculum guidelines for secondary Social Studies].

Wartofsky, M. (1973). *Models*. Dordrecht, The Netherlands: Reide.

Weissenau, G., & Kuhn, H.-W. (2000). *Lexikon der Politischen Bildung Band 3*. [Dictionary of political education, vol.3] Schwalbach: Wochenschauverlag

Wexler, P. (1982). Structure, text and subject: A critical sociology of school knowledge. In M. Apple (Ed.), *Cultural and economic reproduction in education* (pp. 275-303). London: Routledge and Kegan Paul.

Wrigley, T. (2000). *The power to learn: Stories of success in the education of Asian and other bilingual pupils*. Stoke-on-Trent, England: Trentham Books.

Wrigley, T. (2003). *Schools of hope: A new agenda for school improvement*. Stoke-on-Trent, England: Trentham Books.

Wrigley, T. (2006a). *Another school is possible*. London: Bookmarks.

Wrigley, T. (2006b). In search of inclusive pedagogies: The role of experience and symbolic representation in cognition. *International Journal of Pedagogies and Learning, 2*(1) 114-128.

Wrigley, T. (2007). Project, stories and challenges: More open architectures for school learning. In S. Bell, S. Harkness and G. White, *Storyline past, present, and future*. Glasglow: University of Strathclyde.

5   Campaigning Against Neoliberal Education in Britain

Bernard Regan

INTRODUCTION: NEW LABOUR AND EDUCATION

The election of the Labour Government headed by Prime Minister Tony Blair, on the first of May in 1997 presaged changes to the world of education in England and Wales,[1] which few working inside education had anticipated. Blair, describing himself and the politics he represented as "New Labour," declared that the priority for the incoming government would be "Education, Education, Education." However his policies represented a radical departure from the traditional notions of education as a public service, publicly funded and locally administered which had dominated Labour Party thinking since its foundation at the beginning of the 20th century and more especially since the 1940s.

CONSERVATIVES, THATCHER AND EDUCATION

The changes to education, and to other areas of public services such as the health service, embraced and built on policies introduced during the previous Conservative (Tory) administrations of Prime Ministers Margaret Thatcher (1979 to 1990) and John Major (1990 to 1997). Central to the strategy of Thatcher's government had been the policy of "Privatization"—the wholesale selling off to private companies of nationalized or publicly-owned industries and utilities, coupled with the dismemberment of sections of the public services. Private companies invited to run these newly acquired services would shift the emphasis from concerns for public welfare to the imperatives of finance, management and profitability. Although this was driven largely by the ideologically motivated neoliberal monetarist policies of economists like Milton Friedman, their successful introduction into Britain required the political defeat of the longstanding adherence to "welfarism" and the "Welfare State"—a concept that certain fields of economic and social activity should be informed by a desire to address people's needs rather than notions of profitability and efficiency defined in narrow capitalist economic terms. This was especially true in the arena of education.

The Tory blueprint for this offensive which ranged from nationalized industries like water, coal, gas, steel, electricity, rail industry, telephones and others through to public housing, education and health was drawn up by Nicholas Ridley, one of Thatcher's aides, later to hold a variety of ministerial posts in her government. The "Ridley Plan"[2] was put together in 1974 and spelt out a detailed strategy to achieve the objective of privatization focusing principally on the coal industry.[3] Thatcher understood that in order to achieve her goals, the destruction of the "Welfare State" and the denationalization of sections of the economy, it would be necessary to take on and defeat those who were the staunchest defenders of the public services, the trade unions and especially those who organized the workers in the fields she saw as her prime targets for transformation.

The objective of the Thatcher era was the introduction of "popular capitalism" based on individual consumerism and the commodification of all social provision. Margaret Thatcher once said, "There is no such thing as society: there are individual men and women, and there are families."[4] Any collective view of the world or a sense that there could be socialised provision of welfare was anathema[5]. Blair too exhibited a similar almost visceral hatred for the public sector, those who worked in it and the trade union organizations to which many of them belonged.[6]

In a politically astute ideological offensive Margaret Thatcher called for greater individual choice, arguing that the free market would improve quality through competition. Competition had in the economic world, she argued, increased choice, pushed down the prices of commodities and resulted in improvements in the qualities of products and the services to the individual consumer. She extended this argument to the operations of core areas of the Welfare State putting forward the view that in the public service sector the introduction of marketization would in addition to providing choice lead to an improvement in quality and standards of service. By opening up sections of provision to competitive bidding those who won contracts would contribute to driving up the quality of provision through their introduction of management systems; systems based on models of individualized performance management derived from the world of business and commerce. At the same time those who worked in these sectors, especially the trade unions, were presented as the opponents of choice, denying the consumer their "rights" and the improvements they claimed would result from these innovations. The trade unions in particular were subjected to a relentless offensive, accused of being preoccupied with narrow self-interests to the detriment of the users of the services thereby denying the public the opportunities and advantages which privatization would bring.

In education the teacher trade unions were described as part of an "Educational Establishment" opposed to change, professionally complacent, unaccountable and indifferent to the concerns of parents who wanted to see their children receiving a "better" education which could only be guaranteed by creating greater choice in the system.[7] The teacher unions and especially the largest, the National Union of Teachers, were targeted as an adversary which had to be subjugated. Before addressing her ideas to the world of education she well understood that there were politically and industrially stronger opponents who stood in her way. The changes she wished to introduce could not have been achieved without simultaneously introducing legislation that reduced the capacity of trade unions to mount effective forms of actions to defend those services and their members. The anti-trade union legislation introduced by the Thatcher Government which attacked the ability of unions to respond swiftly to threats to jobs, poor pay or the worsening of employment conditions, was a prerequisite to pushing through her agenda.[8]

The most significant confrontation that took place during the Thatcher years was with the National Union of Miners (NUM) whose union members had won the campaign after many years to nationalize the coal industry in the late 1940s. The NUM had the reputation of being one of the best organized and most effective unions at defending the employment, terms and conditions of employment of its members. Through their successful strike actions in 1972 and 1974 the NUM had had a major influence on the downfall of the Conservative Government of Edward Heath, which she had been a minister. To her they epitomized the problem. Thatcher viewed the NUM as the most dangerous opponent in the trade union field. Inflicting a defeat on them would send a message to every trade union, their members and anyone who might oppose the denationalization program and the dissecting of the Welfare State.

The changes that the Conservative Government, elected in 1979 and re-elected in 1983, sought to bring in to education accelerated rapidly after the 1984/85 miners strike and the defeat of the NUM. The National Union of Teachers (NUT) embarked on a pay campaign in 1985 which lasted around two years but petered out when the union leadership accepted promises of a pay review. Some in the union saw this dispute as a defining moment which would have a major impact on the balance of influence between the neoliberalists and their opponents which would shape the educational landscape of the future. Within the NUT there was opposition. The Socialist Teachers Alliance (STA)[9] predicted that the acceptance of the pay offer of 5.5%, way below the pay demand of the Union, would pave the way for further attacks and in particular cuts in the education budget. An alternative perspective was visible through the initiative of the All London Parents Action Group, which called a meeting of over 4,000 in central London early in 1986 to discuss the fight against the Thatcher cuts. Many Labour Party Members of Parliament however did not want to get too involved fearing that their direct association with those conducting industrial action to defend the public services would have negative consequences for their own electoral fate. Although the STA campaigned vigorously to build links with the parents' initiative against the Tory strategy others failed to see the importance and the opportunities for building a teacher–parent alliance that could truly galvanize the campaign in education.

The left in the NUT had made progress over a number of years winning a significant base in the Inner London Teachers Association (ILTA), the largest branch of the Union, coterminus with the Inner London Education Authority (ILEA). The branch contained over 14,000 members working for the largest education authority in Europe with a reputation for progressive educational policies[10]. This combination, as events were to prove later, was one that Thatcher could not tolerate. Her supporters launched a series of attacks in the media against the ILTA and its officers the majority of whom were in the STA. Vicious personal attacks were initiated by Thatcher's supporters in papers such as the *Times Educational Supplement,* the *Daily Mail* and the *Daily Express.* At times these attacks were supplemented by those from aspirant Labour Members of Parliament anxious to disassociate themselves from trade union activity. The objective was to try to isolate Thatcher's most vociferous critics in education, in the most militant and arguably the best organized branch of the NUT.

Upon her re-election in 1987 Thatcher was determined to launch an offensive against comprehensive education[11] and the ILEA, which she saw as one of the most tenacious advocates for the system. The Education Reform Act 1988[12] was at the core of her strategy. It introduced legislation which simultaneously increased powers at the centre while introducing measures which would fragment the education system, breaking the links between schools and schools, and schools and local education authorities (LEAs).[13] Little wonder that that same piece of legislation specifically proposed and enacted the break-up of the ILEA, which ultimately lead to the break-up of the ILTA. In response ILTA had organized and lead strike action against the Bill as a whole and a mass campaign aimed specifically at London parents which won the backing of the overwhelming majority of parents for the continuation of the authority as a single unit despite the fact that they met with indifference at first from many in the union nationally and indeed hostility from leading Labour politicians who were happy to see the back of the ILEA and the union branch which they saw as a thorn in their side.[14]

By and large, the LEAs, like ILEA, had been responsible for the collective development of education within their local government area. Individual schools were given financial control of the running of their school through budgetary transferring of control to head teachers and governing bodies through a measure entitled "Local Management of Schools." Schools could go further being given the chance to "opt out" of local authority control to become grant maintained schools (GMS). Parents, notionally, were given a greater choice in the say as to which schools their child attended and to facilitate choice, schools were required to administer tests which were then used to construct league tables indicating each school's individual "performance."

The Tories believed that "opting out" would be the automatic choice for all parents but they were in many respects proved wrong. In order to opt out there had to be a ballot of all the parents to authorize it. The battle against GMS became a major campaign to defend the integrity of local education authorities as well as the comprehensive system. Conservative controlled Westminster City Council, a hotbed of Thatcherite neoliberalism, lead at one time by Dame Shirley Porter one of her closest allies in Local government, might have been thought an ideal place to demonstrate parents' enthusiasm for these new powers. Three proposals for opting out did occur in the city. In one, St Mary of the Angels, a Catholic primary school, the governors agreed that if the teachers were not in favor of the proposal to opt out then they would not go ahead with their suggestion. The teachers, backed by the local NUT branch, voted to stay in the authority and the whole idea was dropped. In a second example Westminster City School, a boys' secondary school, the head teacher persuaded his governing body that the school should opt out. The NUT locally, as elsewhere when these proposals arose, challenged the advocates of opting out to a public debate in front of the parents who were to vote. As a result of this debate and a vigorous campaign lead by NUT members in the school a parent/teacher alliance was struck, which resulted in an overwhelming vote by parents against the opt out proposal. Undoubtedly these results had a positive impact on the third school St Vincent de Paul's Catholic Primary School, which was attended by the daughter of John Patten, the Secretary of State for Education (1992 to 1994) in the Tory Cabinet. The vote against echoed the outcome at the other schools. Not a single school opted out of the education authority.

Battles of this kind took place up and down the country. It is notable that when the New Labour government introduced the idea of academies and then trust schools which we shall discuss later, they left out any suggestion that the decision to change the status of the school should be subject to any kind of democratic process which parents might be able to play a role in. Blair certainly learned from Thatcher. Democracy is a dangerous game.

Opting out however was not the only facet of the anti-comprehensive assault. Although it is true that there never has been a fully comprehensive system of education in schools in England and Wales, the majority of secondary age pupils, went to schools which were called, and operated on the general principle that they were "comprehensive." Children leaving their primary school at the age of 11, transferred to a local comprehensive secondary school without any form of selection and followed a curriculum common to all. Pupils in comprehensive schools follow the national curriculum which was introduced through the 1988 legislation referred to above. Although some children do go to private schools[15] and some to selective grammar schools, the overwhelming majority of children in England and Wales then attended comprehensive schools and did not go through any form of selection or testing to enter them. Pupil admissions have been for many years the result of a negotiated agreement between parents, schools and local education authorities.[16]

This process however was anathema to the neoliberals and the free-marketer Tories. They argued that the existing system did not allow individual parents to "choose" the school to which their own child went and furthermore that they needed some form of evidence on which to make their decisions. They accused schools and teachers of a lack of accountability, engaged in a process of collusion to deliberately hide the achievements or shortcomings of schools from public scrutiny. Despite the fact that David Blunkett, the incoming New Labour Education Secretary had made public declarations that he had no intentions of re-introducing selection at 11 he proceeded to attack the principles on which admissions to secondary schools had taken place by developing criteria that would allow increasing use of selective mechanisms. In what way was this to be done? Comprehensive schools were attacked for trying to provide a "one size fits all" education which failed to differentiate between children of differing abilities because, it was alleged, teachers worked on the basis that the lowest common denominator of ability defined the pace of work in an individual class and the ethos of the school.

FIGHTING THE TESTS

Although external selection of pupils at age 11 was largely impractical in many areas and downright impossible in some rural areas, the offensive against the comprehensive schools used the introduction of the nationally imposed Standardized Assessment Tasks (SATs), at 7, 11 and 14 to publicize league tables which parents could then use to chose between schools. Since for many choice was an illusion the objective consequence of the introduction of the SATs was to increase internal methods of selection through the promotion of streaming and setting. The whole process imposed an inflexible conformity to the national curriculum, increased the tendency to teach to the tests and produced a hierarchical league table that often said more about the social composition of the schools than about the teaching and learning within it.

The scores that schools achieved in the tests and in the public examinations at 16 and 18 became yardsticks to determine how "good" a school was deemed to be. The tests were criticized by many educationalists for imposing a curriculum that was narrow and inflexible and would lead to rote learning. Interestingly these criticisms echoed the arguments put forward in the 19th century by teachers opposed to the "payment by results" system which operated for a period of time. Then the teachers called it the "music tax" because the emphasis of the testing was on the "Three Rs"— reading, writing and arithmetic. Music, poetry and art in particular had been pushed to the margins as teachers strove to ensure that pupils were well prepared for the visit of inspectors upon whose judgement the school might pass or fail in its endeavour to win further funding.[17]

In 1993, as a result of the Education (Schools) Act 1992[18], the Office for Standards in Education (Ofsted) was established as a centralized mechanism to guarantee the implementation of the whole program by linking school performance results produced by the SATs with the inspection of each school, its teaching methodologies and the professional performance of individual teachers. Ofsted was viewed by many teachers as the ideologically driven inquisition policing the system, demanding a rigid adherence to the whole process.

When the SATs were first introduced into state schools there was at first little public reaction in England and Wales.[19] Even though they were piloted in 1990, modified and partially implemented in 1991, very few schools actually took part in them in 1992, and in 1993 a union backed boycott of the tests was held which revealed widespread opposition. By contrast in Scotland a substantial campaign was generated by parents who recognized their significance. They opposed the whole process whereby children were to be tested at 7, 11 and 14 and the school results ranked in league tables. They were critical of the suggestion that children at age 7 should be put through tests which might well lead to them being labelled and therefore prescribe the educational path they would take in the future. The campaign they built drew in the teacher unions and gathered momentum. South of the border in England the campaign was largely begun by a group of teachers belonging to the London Association for the Teaching of English (LATE) and activists from the STA working together. They developed a thorough critique of the impact of the SATs on the teaching and learning of English within schools taking this through to their national organization the National Association for the Teaching of English and more important into the NUTs to which the majority, though not all, belonged. A ballot of teachers of English in January and February 1993 revealed a 90% support for a campaign of action against the tests. It was through the development of this critique and seeking to engage with teachers of science and mathematics that the groundswell for the campaign developed.

Whilst the NUT annual conference in 1993 agreed to call for a boycott, on educational grounds, the smaller union involved in the action, the National Association of Schoolmasters Union of Women Teachers (NASUWT) took a more limited industrial approach to the question asserting that it was solely the additional workload burdens of supervising and marking the tests that they opposed. Whilst this route was taken in part to ensure that the boycott action conformed to the definition of an industrial dispute, under the terms of the Tory trade union legislation, the narrowness of the approach put constraints on the potential for building a campaign which could reach out to parents opposed to their children being put through the stresses of tests. The NASUWT withdrew from the boycott, thereby severely weakening the campaign, when the government promised external markers to undertake the additional work they had focussed on.

Although the NUT continued to fight alone the campaign was called off when a further review was promised.

Despite the fact that the SATs had become embedded, opposition to them continued leading once again in 2003 to calls for the implementation of a tests' boycott. Following a conference in June 2003 attended by teachers, parents, governors and others, the Anti-SATs Alliance was established to pursue the campaign. In addition to the alliance's work to produce masses of leaflets in English, others were produced in a variety of languages including Albanian, Arabic, Bengali, French, Serbo-Croat and Spanish to get the message over to all parents. The campaign won the support of leading children's authors including Alan Gibbons, Beverly Naidoo, Philip Pullman and many others. Postcards for MPs were prepared, speaker notes for parents, a "Frequently Asked Questions" leaflet and model letters to school governors calling on them to back their teachers in the boycott. A survey of teachers carried out for the NUT found that a massive 91% of those responding said the tests placed additional workload on teachers and 93.1% of primary and 85% of secondary teachers said they were stressful for pupils. Some 90% of teachers felt the tests diminished pupils' access to a broad and balanced curriculum. This view was strongest among primary teachers at 93.1% compared with secondary teachers at 84.3%. The condemnation of the tests was overwhelming.

In November 2003 the NUT launched a ballot for a boycott of SATs in Key Stage 1 and 2 and conducted a survey of its secondary members on their willingness to take action. Although 86.2% voted for the boycott, the NUT decided not to go ahead with the action because the turnout of 34.05% was less than that 50% required under the rules of the Union. At the time many questioned the wisdom of balloting the primary school members separately from their secondary colleagues and especially since they were isolated from the specialst subject teachers of English the majority of who remained strongly opposed to the tests.

The critique of the impact of SATs on the teaching and learning, which had much in common with the "Payment by Results" debate in the 19th century, was dismissed as "patronizing indulgent idealism. The neoliberals had powerful backers in the government and the army of Ofsted inspectors primed with the SATs evidence were prepared to go on the offensive against what they regarded as the romanticism of the "child centered" education which had been influential in the late 1960s, 1970s and part of the 1980s. The problem with the ideas of "child centered" education for the neoliberals was that it actually posited the notion that a child's socioeconomic, ethnic and cultural background, together with gender, were significant factors affecting a child's development. The idea that educationalists should take these factors into account to develop a pedagogical approach contradicted the need to assert the forces of the market and threatened to problematize the whole edifice of testing and ranking which had been constructed. The educational free-marketers believed that children should be exclusively judged by tests in schools, and the schools ranked on the basis of those test results.

The counter attack to this critique was ferocious and unremitting. David Blunkett, New Labour Secretary of State for Education speaking at an education conference in London in October 1997 criticized research by Peter Robinson a leading educationalist[20] at the London School of Economics (LSE) that highlighted the linkage between social disadvantage and academic achievement as "LSE silliness."[21] One of Blunkett's aides, Michael Barber, weighed in with a further attack in the pages of the authoritative *Times Educational Supplement*. James Tooley, a leading neoliberal educationalist was hired by Chris Woodhead, the chief inspector and head of Ofsted, appointed by Thatcher and retained by Blair, to investigate the value of educational research in liberal universities.[22] While Boris Johnson, later to become a Conservative Member of Parliament, said of the evolution of New Labour's educational policies that "this is nothing less than a triumph of Tory free-market ideology and, on the face of it a brutal snub to core Labour voters."[23]

POSTCOMPREHENSIVE MODERNISM

For Blair and others the education system they wished to develop was to be a "postcomprehensive" system which needed to "differentiate provision for individual aptitudes in schools."[24] Blair's principal spokesperson, Alastair Campbell, put it much more bluntly when he said that "the days of the bog standard comprehensive are over."[25] A "good school" was to be defined exclusively by its examination results and the grammar school and independent schools, of course without any reference to the non-school factors which might impact on children's learning, became the model to be emulated. No account was taken of the selective processes such schools employed or the real or relatively privileged socioeconomic backgrounds from which the vast majority of their children came.

The neoliberals attacked comprehensive education on the basis that there was little or no differentiation in the teaching and learning methods employed by comprehensive schools. At the core of this was an attack on the concept of mixed ability teaching (MAT) which, it was claimed, resulted in learning progressing at the pace of the least academically able child in a class, thereby "holding back" the more able. The critique of MAT was backed by a major propaganda offensive to deride its achievements, and to undermine its defence there was a related attack on educational research which in any way sought to defend it or even to question the assumptions and credibility of those who launched the offensive.[26]

Although the initial campaign against the SATs had strong backing from many teachers and notably from the NUTs there was a shortcoming in the campaign in that it failed to reach out to parents to explain the full impact of the testing regime. Although the parents of younger children were more hostile to the tests readily identifying the stresses that their children were put under, parents of older secondary age children were not won to the broader campaign against the tests. The situation in England and Wales was different from that in Scotland where parents had been at the forefront. That essential alliance, between teachers and parents, was evident from time to time but, apart from a few local important exceptions such as in Harrow, never flourished into a fully fledged united front across the whole of the country.

One other weakness of the campaign was that although the case against the tests was well made by teachers of English, the support amongst teachers of science and maths was less strong and less well established. The arguments were made but the critique did not have the same resonance since many teachers in these subject areas considered that the tests were value free, had a greater degree of objectivity and were less problematic than those in English. The major weakness lay in the failure to recognize the ideological role to which such tests were to be put and the key role they played in ranking and judging schools.

Ironically it had been Margaret Thatcher, as Minister for Education in the Government of another Conservative Prime Minister, Edward Heath who, in the early 1970s, had presided over the closure of large numbers of selective grammar schools which had flourished following the 1944 Education Act.[27] The '44 Act, introduced on a bipartisan basis by Conservative and Labour politicians, was seen as the product of a partnership agreement which incorporated the church schools and the selective grammar schools into the state system. The Act had left the privileged, private independent schools, often ironically referred to as "Public Schools," intact. In this it paralleled the legislation which introduced the National Health Service (NHS) leaving the privileges of medical consultants unchallenged, free to work in the private practice while undertaking work in state hospitals and indeed frequently using the publicly provided resources of the NHS to undertake their private operations.

In both instances the egalitarian, welfare aspirations that had stimulated the momentum for changes to education and health were tempered by compromises made with those whose privileges might otherwise have been challenged. Nevertheless the main changes, which were introduced in both spheres, were a product of pressure resulting from a profound sense of injustice among wide sections of society and especially sections of the working class born out of their personal experiences.

The changing face of the economy both in Britain and internationally to a certain degree revealed, some politicians argued, inadequacies and anachronisms in the educational system which had evolved in an economic era in which manufacturing had played a more key role.[28] Over 25% of Britain's manufacturing base disappeared, or some might argue was destroyed, in the first four years of the 1980s. Even where manufacturing remained it was progressively being confronted by technological changes which transformed processes and rendered some skills obsolete. Those politicians who proposed educational changes often put forward the case that they were necessary to ensure that British capital maintained economic competitiveness internationally but it also reflected employers' desires to introduce employee "flexibility" breaking whatever safeguards workers had won in some industries, such as print, against excessive exploitation. Although no substantial evidence could be produced to prove the link between education and economic progress some employers claimed, nevertheless the argument was readily appropriated by politicians and ideologues who utilized it to justify the changes they were pushing through.

From 1997, New Labour in government adapted very readily to this instrumentalist notion of education but their adoption of these views began before they were elected to office and their embrace of the concept of privatization was evident in the actions of key political figures in the years running up to the 1997 election.[29] The significant transformation which took place was that the newly elected government made a step change to expand the use of privatization measures and neoliberal concepts. Although the initial intervention was focused around questions of capital and revenue expenditure it was coupled with an ideological offensive on teaching and learning methodology.

A more cynical view of this orientation by the new government was that it was linked to the assessment made by Blair and others that to stay in government they needed to win the support of the "Thatcher generation" defined as the younger middle class who had benefited from Thatcher's economic policies and hence were driven by individualistic aspiration and absorbed by consumerist preoccupations.[30] This layer, New Labour politicians had assessed, was critical because, in the British political system, their votes would be key to winning marginal constituencies which would determine who would form the next Government. In the electoral system used in Britain the outcome of a general election could depend on some hundreds of votes in a limited number of key marginal constituencies.

EDUCATION ACTION ZONES

The neoliberalism introduced by Thatcher into the public sector was given a broader justification by the Blair government. This process was begun stealthily through the Schools Standards and Framework Act 1998[31] which, among a number of measures, introduced the "education action zone" (EAZ).[32] Each EAZ it was said "shall have as its main object the improvement of standards in the provision of education at each of the participating schools."[33] The central purposes of the initiative however was to break down the public/private interface thereby legitimizing the involvement of private enterprise in the public education system. This was well summed up by Graham Walker, education specialist of a company called Arthur

Andersen, the partner in the Newham EAZ and adviser to Department for Education and Employment, when he said in an interview

> If you look at the state education system. I think there's a general recognition that it's not providing what society wants, and that many people say that there is a crisis, and I think I would agree that there is a crisis, that we have to move to another level. And a lot of solutions that are relevant to the running of our schools and our education system generally are actually already in existence in the private sector, and the Education Action Zones are one way of really softening up and getting people ready in a more sophisticated manner than they can on their own as individual schools for this new way.[34]

The EAZs were to bring together a group of schools including primary and secondary schools, working with a private sponsor to develop educational programmes that were designed to address problems relating especially to the level of engagement by pupils from socially disadvantaged areas with the curriculum. The government was to put in an initial £500,000 and then a further £250,000 to be matched by another £250,000 by a sponsor from the private sector. Despite the fact that employers who were part of an EAZ were meant to make a financial commitment for the 3 years of the EAZ's lifespan, very few made any contribution whatsoever. Of the first 12 years established, the average contribution by the private employer in their first year of operation was £11,473, the rest being an "in kind" contribution ranging from cast off computers to provision of office space and meeting rooms for the management consortium that ran the EAZ.

The bids, submitted jointly by local education authorities and employers, to establish EAZs often referred to the advantages that would be gained by linking schools to the local employers. Business was not slow to appreciate the advantages that might come their way from such schemes. In Middlesbrough, a company called NTL entered a scheme with a very clear idea of their objectives. NTL's Business Director Bill Bates said,

> We wanted to make sure that children had the best opportunity we could give them to access . . . (new) . . . technologies. They will be the technologies of the future, they need to feel fairly comfortable in using them. And after all those children today will be our subscribers tomorrow.[35]

A great deal of the EAZ promotion emphasis by the government was centered on the ability of schools working within a zone to develop their own educational program and disapply the national curriculum. Although this seemed attractive to some it was criticized by others who drew attention to the tendency of the proposed schemes to adopt a narrow vocationalist curriculum.[36] This was quite explicit in some of the proposals put forward from areas like Lambeth. The campaign against EAZs launched by the

STA drew the comparison between the education practices of the zones and the "part-timers" system introduced in the early part of the 20th century, especially in working class areas of the north of England, where children would go to work, perhaps in a cotton mill, half the week and attend school the other half.[37] Some criticized this condemnation as over dramatic but there is no doubt that it hit home and many Government politicians were anxious to assert that there would be no "Gradgrind" curriculum in the EAZs. The critique of the EAZs was spelt out in a pamphlet called "Trojan Horses," which sold thousands of copies in NUT branches and helped consolidate opposition to the whole idea. A number of schools refused to join locally promoted EAZs, meetings were held in schools in Hackney, for example, and parents called on their governors not to become part of the zones. The debate was taken up in the pages of national newspapers like *The Guardian* carrying full page spreads, including an article by the author of this chapter.

Although it is not surprising that the curricula features of the EAZs were quietly dropped the initiative did in one important respect achieve its objective—the public/private interface was effectively established. In a sense the EAZ project was the forerunner of the city academies scheme that was first announced in September 2000. The academies were surrounded by the same rhetoric that had accompanied the EAZs. In the words of the Government Education Department,

> Academies are an integral part of the Government's strategy for raising standards in the most disadvantaged and challenging areas. They will raise standards by innovative approaches to management, governance, teaching and the curriculum. The involvement of sponsors from the voluntary and business sector or faith groups will allow them to bring their skills and expertise to each Academy.[38]

ACADEMIES

Once again private sponsors were invited to participate in the program. Anyone wishing to become a sponsor of an academy had only to make a contribution of £2 million and the government would provide the rest of the money necessary to fund building where new building was deemed necessary and to pay for all the running costs. The schools would then be handed over to the sponsors. "Each Academy is set up as a company limited by guarantee with charitable status and will have a board of governors responsible for the governance and strategic leadership of the school." As with the EAZ programme however little or no money has been forthcoming from the private sector. On 3rd May 2006 *The Guardian* reported that only 4 out of 27 academies had received the full £2 million pledged by sponsors and 4 schools opened in September 2005 had received no money whatsoever.[39]

Like many of the New Labour education policies they had their origin in the United States where the charter school had been introduced in much the same way. However in order to reinforce this policy the Government linked the whole academies program to the Building Schools for the Future proposals requiring local authorities to consider the establishment of academies before gaining access to any funds for the rebuilding or refurbishment of schools. Although the government is wielding the stick with one hand allegations have surfaced of honors being offered to induce potential sponsors to come forward. The matter has been investigated by the police although no prosecutions have followed.

Little wonder perhaps that the claims for the academy's program, designed to see 53 academies established by 2007 and 200 by 2010 with 30 in London by 2008 and 60 by 2010 were met with concern by educationalists. Learning from the problems confronted by the Tories resulting from parental ballots for opting out, the New Labour Government academies programme is being rolled forward without such democratic encumbrances. Notwithstanding that there have been numerous campaigns against the proposals to take schools off Local Authorities and hand them to private sponsors.[40]

The academies program frequently resulted in schools deemed to be underperforming, being renamed, perhaps rebuilt and then aggressively marketed. Understandably many parents and indeed teachers want to see children in new surroundings, however campaigners against the academies challenged the necessity for the involvement of private sponsors, many of whom had no connection with or experience of education. A vigorous campaign in Waltham Forest lead by the local NUT branch successfully opposed the proposal to replace McEntee Secondary School with an academy sponsored by the multimillionaire fashion designer Jasper Conran and dissuaded him from taking on the role. Conran's head of public relations put it somewhat diplomatically saying, "We have been conducting a feasibility study and have come to the conclusion that this is not right for us. There are several reasons why but we will not be discussing them."[41]

Elsewhere proposals for an academy in Doncaster were shelved, after protests against the sponsor by parents and teachers who were also uneasy about the creationist beliefs of the proposed sponsor. Public meetings took place in Newcastle bringing together local Members of Parliament, parents, teachers and trade unionists. An extremely effective local campaign, again built by teachers in the NUT was built around proposals for two academies in Islington. In one case the sponsors, a group of hedge fund speculators, were keen to set up a 5 to 18 years school and parents of children at some of the local primary schools joined forces with parents of children at the nearby secondary school. Public meetings, demonstrations outside the council buildings and outside the hedge fund company headquarters in central London all helped highlight the strong opposition to what was regarded as an outright attack on public education provision and comprehensive education.

In Brent an academy has been proposed and the local NUT occupied the land on which the building was to be erected. Within one week Andrew Rosenfeld, the sponsor withdrew from the scene. The local council set about looking for another sponsor and the struggle was continuing at the time of publishing.

Problems of a different nature cropped up in other cases. In London, Capital City Academy was dogged by complaints about the design of the building and ran into financial difficulties in April 2004, with the announcement of seven staff redundancies following the resignation of the head teacher after less than a year. After the sponsor of Westminster Academy, Chelsfield plc, was taken over by another company Multiplex, staff at the school remained in some doubts as to who was running things when Multiplex announced that they were no longer involved. Needless to say neither parents nor staff were informed about what was going on and the Westminster Local Authority washed its hands of the matter.

Campaigns against the academies have sprung up almost everywhere such a proposal has been mooted. In Birmingham, Bradford, Brent, Hackney, Islington, Lambeth, Lewisham, Merton, Milton Keynes, Norwich, Oldham, Southwark, Westminster and many other towns across England parents and teachers have established campaigning groups bringing together parents, teachers, school staff, students, governors, trade unions and campaign bodies like CASE (Campaign for State Education). In some instances these campaigns have developed to embrace activity concerning other educational issues such as schools reorganisations and the introduction of trust schools, as an alternative to the academy.[42]

The whole academies program has had to face a range of tribulations so much so that the government has been forced to introduce a variety of measures to positively encourage sponsors to become involved in the academies initiative. Sponsors have been made offers of "4 for the price of 3." One sponsor, the United Learning Trust was asked to contribute £1.5 million (instead of the customary £2 million) for 8 of the 11 schools it was proposing in September 2005.[43] A national scandal hit the academies supporters when Des Smith, a head teacher and council member of the Specialist Schools and Academies Trust (SSAT) resigned after allegations of a "cash-for-honors" offer resulting from comments he made.[44] Karen Buck MP, a former Labour Minister, threatened to take her child away from Paddington Academy, in Westminster, saying that she "didn't expect problems with deficits and building management before the end of the first term."

From an educational point of view many of the academy schools failed according to the Government's own criteria in terms of pupil achievement and the reports by the Ofsted Inspectors. In addition some academies were accused of massaging their examination results by expelling pupils who might bring down their league status in comparison to neighboring schools. One academy in Ealing in the academic year 2004/2005 expelled four times as many pupils as other local schools. Economically there have been problems in many of the schools. The National Audit Office, an authoritative public body, reported in 2007 that 17 out of the first 26 academies were running over costs. Westminster Academy declared redundancies in 2007 within months of being opened in September 2006. Private sponsors are coming forward who have a very specific evangelizing Christian agenda, promoting creationism and other bizarre ideas, without any concern for the views of the parents, pupils or staff.

It is these issues that have lead to a widespread questioning of the whole program. It is apparent that there are a disproportionate number of religious schools being created which raises further questions relating to admissions policies which allow for selective preferences to be used which have the possibility of creating mono-ethnic schools, because of their religious character. There is a real danger of predominantly white only Christian schools being created in some communities or schools with one religious ethos which is wholly inappropriate to the catchment area in which it might be situated. There is a real apprehension that the dynamic of this process will be to encourage the creation of religiously based selective secondary schools with a mono-cultural perspective.

In response to this scenario the Anti-Academies Alliance was established following a successful conference in London.[45] The Alliance brought together active local and national campaign bodies together with academics, trade unions including the NUT and political campaigners. The intention of the Alliance is to create a broad based united front of opposition to the neoliberal agenda embodied in the academies program and to turn back this offensive arguing for sustained investment and support for a "good local school for every child." Although the alliance is still in the first stages of construction, its political framework offers the most optimistic possibility that has been available to date. The campaign is trying to make a conscious effort to unify those local activists into a nationally focussed endeavour which is critical to halting the juggernaut of the academies program. National conferences are one way of doing this, for example that of 8 March 2008 (Anti Academies Alliance, 2008).

PRIVATE FINANCE INITIATIVE

Although the private finance initiative (PFI) had been introduced some years earlier under the Conservative Government it was not until the election of the New Labour Government in 1997 that it really took off.[46] The PFI, also called the public private partnership (PPP), was initially a scheme whereby private contractors could bid for capital building programs and then contract for the operation and maintenance of the buildings for a period up to 35 years in some cases. It later evolved and the capital building aspect of a contract was dispensed with.

The budget for education in Britain in 1997/98 was £39 billion. The estimated value of the replacement of the education "estate," which included approximately 24,000 schools, was put at around £58 billion. The financial size of any single school contract and the substantial financial benefits which might be made represented a massive opportunity to any successful bidder. Although PFI was introduced in 1992 it didn't really take off until the election of the New Labour Government five years later. The whole PPP/PFI scheme received a massive boost in 1997 when the New Labour Government Paymaster General, Geoffrey Robinson, invited Malcolm Bates, chairman of Pearl Assurance plc and Premier Farnell plc to review the operation of PFI.

Prior to the introduction of PFI a private contractor would be paid to build a new school to a local authority's specifications but any services or maintenance which might be needed to run the school thereafter would be provided by the authority itself. With the introduction of PFI/PPP one contractor might build the school and then themselves operate a range of services such as heating, maintenance and school meals through a long term contract. Later the nature of PFI/PPP contracts was to change away from the requirement that they had to involve a "design" and "build" component and the contracts themselves could vary in length from relatively short term—3 years—through to very long ones—60 years.

One of the earliest and most sharply contested campaigns against PFI took place around proposals to rebuild Pimlico School in Westminster, London. Pimlico, a secondary comprehensive, 11 to 18 school, was situated less than one mile from the Houses of Commons, in the City of Westminster with an education authority which was run by the Conservative Party. The school, which had been built in the 1960s and had won prizes for its design, stood on some of the most expensive real estate land in the whole of England, if not Europe.

The proposal to rebuild Pimlico School, first mooted in 1995 by the then Tory lead Department for Education and Science (forerunner of the DfES), was at the outset a classic PFI, a DBFO scheme—design, build, finance and operate. The intention was to pull down the school over a period of time and to replace it with a totally new one. The project had certain added attractions—selling off an acre of land and building about 200 dwellings which at 1996 at prices might well have sold in excess of £500,000 each.

It is interesting to look at how the Conservative dominated Westminster City Council dealt with this and just how the process worked out in favor of the private bidders and PFI. Normal requirements governing the use of land for building purposes were manipulated to suggest the cost to the public of building the school could be offset against the profits to be made.[47]

In the outline business case produced for the projected schools' PFI scheme in Haringey, another part of London, the PFI scheme costs were always being revised downwards while those for a public sector scheme were pushed up and up. In the case of schools in Haringey it was argued that the projected benefits of improved pupil performance in examinations guaranteed by a new school built under PFI would result in a greater degree of employability and therefore lessen the likelihood that young people would be a charge on public costs in the future. In this example as in most cases the judgements made were totally subjective and highly tendentious.

However things at Pimlico School didn't stop there—those who won the contract to build the new school would also win a contract to provide all the non-teaching services in the school.[48] They would be able to look at alternative uses for the school premises. All the existing employees, with the exception of the teachers and the office staff, would be transferred to the new company that would have the responsibility for the contract. The contract would be for a period of around 35 years. Although much was made of the fact that the existing staff would be transferred with their terms and conditions protected, past experience of PFI schemes often revealed this as ultimately a worthless guarantee.

An interesting feature of the Pimlico School PFI case was the role played by the then Shadow Home Secretary and New Labour leading figure and future Cabinet Member Jack Straw MP. He was absolutely committed to the PFI scheme and one of its most ardent advocates. Acting in his capacity as a member of the schools governing body he told everyone that "this is the only money being offered, and this is the only ship on the water. We have to go along this route." However just in case anyone was worried he also reassured them that this was nevertheless a "juggernaut that we could put the brakes on."[49]

His and the local council's determination to push the whole thing through was reflected in this account of events by Europe Singh, the Chair of Governors:

> Between 1998 and 2000, governors agreed eight separate resolutions hostile to progressing the PFI proposals. Unfortunately, it was never made clear that governors were able to terminate the project. Indeed, in 1997 we were misinformed that we had no such powers.
>
> For stakeholders, the sticking point turned on the feasibility of alternatives: . . . (for example one report said that) refurbishment was 30% cheaper, and did not require us to sacrifice a quarter of our playgrounds for housing.[50]

Although Westminster City Council wanted to enter into a deal which would have gotten them a £25 million subsidy to start a PFI project it was known at the time that a refurbishment program would cost a fraction of this. In the asset management plan which Westminster City Council Local Education Authority had to draw up to identify their priorities for rebuilding and refurbishment programs, the City Council projected, in 2001, that a mere £2.3 million should be spent on Pimlico School. This figure contrasts with the £2.5 million the Tory Government thought necessary to deal with problems in 1995. Pimlico was being punished for its resistance to PFI.

The principle way in which profits are garnered is through cuts that are made to the quality and cost of existing provision.[51] Although the PFI proposal in the case of Pimlico School excluded teaching and office staff from the transfer to the new private company[52] that would take over the school, the rest of the school staff would be transferred across and face pressure that would result in the worsening of their pay and conditions of employment. School staff, teachers and parents were well aware of the implications of what was being proposed.

This experience is the same as that in the United States. The Massachusetts Education Association teachers' union found that when companies took over a school and it became a Charter School, staff who had been long term employees of the school were sacked in a very short space of time.[53] Although in Britain the legal requirements of the Transfer of Undertakings Protection of Employment (TUPE) legislation[54] was meant to give protection to staff transferred from one employer to another, in practice it did not. In Tower Hamlets, London, Babcock and Brown, the bidding company, said TUPE would operate for 5 years but evidence from elsewhere suggested that even these promises are fairly meaningless assurances. New staff are generally recruited on new contracts, whereas existing staff transferred over are pressurized to change from their old contracts or face the rest of their careers standing still in the same post.

Those who wanted the PFI scheme to be pushed through at Pimlico School did not have their own way however. In order to push the project through, the government and the local City Council had to win the backing of the governing body of the school and it was right there that they began to run up against questioning which developed into opposition. The governing body, comprised of representatives of the local education authority, parents and teachers took their responsibilities to the school extremely seriously. They were concerned to know: What the cost of the proposal would be? What would happen to the children in the school while the new school was being built alongside the existing one? What would be the costs of a refurbishment as opposed to a complete replacement? They interrogated these issues in some detail, inviting the original school architect to make a report, inviting appropriate engineers to estimate the costs, requiring clear and specific answers as to what would happen to the existing building and the children in it while all the replacement work was going on.

PFI—THE HUMAN COSTS

Alongside the governors, staff at the school, though wishing to see improvements to their school buildings, recognized that the PFI proposal was about much more than its structure. They themselves would face a whole period of disruption while classrooms were pulled down and new ones went up right alongside. Given the likely levels of chaos staff might well start to look for posts elsewhere while new staff might be reluctant to apply for jobs in what many foresaw as a grand building site for several years. There was a concern at the proposed reductions in the play space available to the pupils in an inner London school with few outdoor amenities. The majority of the non-teaching staff in the main faced the prospect of being transferred to a new employer without any certain guarantees that their jobs, their pay or pensions would remain the same in the future. New non-teaching staff might be hired on quite different contracts, paid less, required to work longer hours and be exploited as a wedge to oust more longstanding staff who had some element of protection in their contracts.

One of the key factors which none of the outside agents appreciated was just what those who worked in the school thought about it. In fact the staff, both teaching and non-teaching, had a loyalty to the school and a commitment to the community they belonged to. They were not opposed to changes, indeed they had for many years complained about the need for a better level of maintenance to the building and sought support for capital investment in it but without the government or the local authority responding.

The anxieties of the parents were also evident and they were ready allies of the staff and those governors opposed to the plan. However the parents, staff and governors were not alone. The school sat in the middle of a rectangle of buildings in one of the most densely populated areas of London. It provided an open space for the residents with trees and a variation in the skyline from that of neighbouring buildings, allowing in more light than might otherwise have been there. At the weekends, during the holidays and outside of school hours, the space of the school provided relative quiet in comparison with the busy traffic of the nearby streets. The local residents took up the campaign worried that their neighborhood would become one grand building site.

Eventually the government and the local Westminster City Council conceded defeat but only after a prolonged period of campaigning which had fought them to a standstill. This was an outstanding victory for all concerned against a powerful array of opponents. This defeat of the PFI proposal was achieved in the end because the campaigners had been successful in bringing together a wide coalition consisting of parents, governors, staff, local residents, trade unions and students. The campaign was successful because of its imaginative use of a variety of tactics to challenge the proposal at every stage and because of the tenacity of those involved.[55] It revealed a potential which has inspired other campaigns that have faced the relentless march of privatization.

Inevitably because each and every PFI proposal was different the conditions that applied in the Pimlico School case were not replicated in subsequent PFI schemes. There were, and remain, many schools which are old and dilapidated and need to be replaced. The argument that PFI is the "only show in town" has become very powerful as central government quickly learned the lesson that it needed to impress schools' governing bodies that they had to go down that route. The government changed the ground rules of the PFI, no longer tying it to a building programme or to whole school projects. In the London Borough of Tower Hamlets the PFI contract covered the management of the schools premises and involved a cluster of schools.[56]

In this case each individual school governing body had to make a decision to be part of the process. Although in the end sufficient numbers did opt in to the process to make it commercially worthwhile, its viability was in some doubt at various stages because the company involved were concerned that the scale of the venture should, from their point of view, be profitable.

In this case the campaign against the PFI was able to take on a broader local character, linking schools together and bringing the collective energies and strength to the benefit of the individual institutions. The persistent dilemma in this and other similar examples which were to follow was that the opposition to the proposed privatization of the services had some difficulty in providing evidence of convincing alternatives to what was on offer. In her years in office Margaret Thatcher had coined the expression "TINA"—there is no alternative—and this was how the PFI schemes were presented to parents, pupils, governors, staff and often the local education authority itself. The long period of underinvestment in education throughout the Thatcher years had built up significant problems which needed to be addressed. The New Labour Government presented the PFI route as the only way that this could be carried out.

In the view of many of the Pimlico governors however the school paid a price for this absolutely time consuming process with hours and hours of meetings and incredible amounts of energy diverted to this whole process. The ideological obsessiveness of the government and the inflexibility of the city council took its toll on staff, students, parents and governors. The price of privatization is not simply the financial—it is a human cost too.

The neoliberal agenda of the Blair government was not confined of course to the essential infrastructure of education—it was never exclusively about the capital expenditure needed to replace the building stock, nor about its running, nor about the non-teaching staff, nor even about the "non-educational" aspects of the Education system. The essence of neoliberalism is a belief that the market should be the ultimate regulator of anything and everything—all aspects of life should be viewed as commodities and their worth determined by the choices that the consumers make. This would be as true for education and health as it might be for buying a washing powder or a car. All constraints which might interfere with the free and unfettered processes of "production," in its broadest sense, or with the consumers "choice" have to be removed. The distribution of the end product would be entirely determined by the ability of the consumer to pay the price in the market place.

PERFORMANCE RELATED PAY

The campaign against the SATs however was not over. It resurfaced as a matter of concern in the early 2000s with many of the same arguments prevailing. The Anti-SATs Alliance attempted to build the kind of links that would take the campaign out to a wider parental audience and address some of the weaknesses identified in the earlier campaign. However while the critiques were as sharp and articulate as before the SATs were now embedded in schools practice and were for younger teachers perhaps viewed in the same critical light. The changes that had taken place in education were now being transmitted to a new generation of teachers through the educational institutions of the universities and were becoming the norm.

This process was complimented by the introduction of new forms of pay arrangements backed by performance management mechanisms for teachers which gave greater power to individual schools and especially head teachers, to determine the salaries of individual teachers. Performance related pay was introduced which required the production of evidence which head teachers and governing bodies were encouraged to use to determine a teachers progress across the "threshold" and on up through the upper pay scales. The government has insisted on stronger forms of performance management designed to monitor the performance of each individual teacher in the most minute detail.

These changes are under challenge by some teacher organizations, not out of a fear of teacher accountability, but because the whole process robs teachers of the capacity to be innovative or to have any professional control over their practice as teachers.

Although the EAZ was tackled by campaigners at a local level, the academies program, though still fought by parents and teachers at the grass roots, has made tentative steps towards the development of a national campaigning strategy (See, for example Anti-Academies Alliance, 2008). In 2006 the Anti-Academy Alliance with its roots connected to activists in the NUT linked up with educational campaign bodies like CASE (Campaign for State Education) and others in an attempt to develop a broad based strategy in response to the government's program. In the 2008 local elections, four anti-academy councillors were elected to a District Council, Barrow Borough Council. (BBC, 2008)

NOTES

1. Most of the references in this chapter are to Education in England and Wales. Education in Scotland has always had a degree of independence and during the period discussed was not under the control of the Secretary of State for Education and some of the features referred to are not applicable. Education in Wales has also, especially since the establishment of the National Assembly for Wales (1998), developed a degree of autonomy.
2. The Ridley Plan *The Economist* 27th May 1978
3. The Ridley Plan was implemented by Thatcher—coal stocks were built up, power stations converted from coal to oil use and she appointed Ian McGregor as Chairman of the Coal Board to employ his US union-busting managerial techniques. She was determined to even the score for the defeat the Tories experienced in 1972 and 1974, described by one historian, A.J.P. Taylor as the miners' revenge for their "defeats of 1921 and 1926". McGregor provoked the NUM to strike in 1984 by announcing cuts at Cortonwood Colliery in Yorkshire, whilst Thatcher organized the Civil Contingencies Unit to coordinate the

state's response and through a variety of connections an alternative employer-friendly body called the Union of Democratic Miners was established based on the Nottingham coalfield to split the action of the NUM.

4. *Woman's Own* Interviewed by Douglas Keay, *"Aids, education and the year 2000!"* (pp 8–10) published 31 October 1987. Margaret Thatcher foundation: Retrieved 01/04/08 http://www.margaretthatcher.org/speeches/displaydocument.asp?docid=106689

5. Benn ,Tony (1994) *Diaries 1980–1990 "The End of an Era"* provides an insight into this period.

6. Tony Blair, Prime Minister speaking to British Venture Capital Conference 6/7/1999 said, "You try getting changes in the public sector and the public services. I bear the scars on my back after two years in government and heaven knows what it will be like after a bit longer."

7. The selective grammar school was the paradigm which was used as the referent for "better education" by both the Conservative and Labour Governments.

8. From 1979 to 1996 no less than 11 pieces of anti-trade union legislation were introduced by the Conservative Governments covering issues such as: industrial action, balloting, picketing, secondary action, removal of recognition rights, restriction on definition of industrial dispute, restrictions on area of dispute to 'own' employer, intervention in union internal democracy, attack on employee rights. Employment Act (1980), Employment Act (1982), Trade Union Act (1984), Public Order Act (1986),Employment Act (1988), Employment Act (1989), Employment Act (1990), Trade Union & Labour Relations (Consolidation) Act (1992), Trade Union Reform and Employment Rights Act (1993), Employment Rights Act (1996), Employment Tribunals Act (1996). Retrieved 01/04/08 http://www.opsi.gov.uk/legislation/

9. Socialist Teachers Alliance (STA) is an alliance of left activists which was formed in 1976 in response to the attacks on educational spending that had begun from the early 1970s onwards.

10. Maclure, Stuart (1990) *A History of Education in London 1870–1990*

11. Benn, Caroline and Clyde Chitty, (1997) *"Thirty Years On"* London Penguin Pp. 12

12. Education Reform Act 1988 Retrieved 01/04/08 http://www.opsi.gov.uk/acts/acts1988/ukpga_19880040_en_1

13. The most notable attack on Local Education Authority control was the break-up of the Inner London Education Authority (ILEA) which was at the time the largest education authority in Europe known for its championing of comprehensive education. The ILEA had, frequently with the encouragement of the Inner London Teachers Association (ILTA—the Inner London branch of the NUT representing over 14,000 teachers in the authority) developed polices on racism, sexism and conducted wide ranging reviews of primary, secondary, special education provision and the tertiary sector. The ILEA was eventually broken up in 1990.

14. Almost the whole of the ILTA Council were suspended by the Officers of the Union for organizing a one day strike against the Bill. The ILTA Officers received widespread backing from activists across the country. Although they were reinstated as a result of the decision by the lay Disciplinary Committee of the Union, the National Executive, upon appeal by the Officers of the national union, suspended some of the ILTA Officers for one year, banned them from office and expelled others. However the ILTA 8 were eventually exonerated by the fact that the National Executive itself subsequently called strike action and a judicial review reinstated them and criticized the actions of the National Officers.

15. Elite private schools in Britain are often confusingly called "public schools" having originally been founded to provide education for the "deserving

poor". In March 2007 the Independent schools estimated 7% of school age children went to the 2,500 private schools in the United Kingdom. In London the percentage rises to 13% of school age children.

16. Forms of selection are being reintroduced progressively—"postcode" selection (buying homes in a specific school's catchment area); faith based schools; specialist schools; academies.

17. Eagleton, Terry (2003) The struggle over English Studies (*Socialist Teacher* 49) gives an indication of the highly charged ideological backdrop of debates.

18. Education (Schools) Act of 1992 Office of Public Sector Information Retrieved 01/04/08 http://www.opsi.gov.uk/acts/acts1992/ukpga_19920038_en_1

19. SATs, and the National Curriculum to which they were tied, were never made compulsory for private schools.

20. Peter Robinson "Literacy, Numeracy and Economic Performance" (1997) *Reviews Support for Learning* 13 (1) , 47–48 doi:10.1111/1467–9604.00056.

21. Author's contemporaneous note.

22. *The Observer* Nick Cohen 5/4/98

23. Boris Johnson "The Monday Interview" *Daily Telegraph* 12/1/98

24. *The Times* 14/2/2001

25. *The Mirror* 13/02/2001

26. Socialist Teacher No. 65 1998 Jo Boaler (For a cogent defence of MAT:" Research studies in the UK . . . have shown that setted and streamed systems result in:

    a) disproportionate numbers of students who are working class, black or male being allocated to low sets and streams which do not reflect their ability. This seems to occur because it is difficult for teachers to make decisions about ability that are not influenced by such factors as behaviour, language, appearance, sex, ethnicity or social class

    b) the polarization of students into pro and anti school factions corresponding to their placement into high or low sets and the development of anti-school values amongst students in low sets

    c) the labelling of students in low sets which causes students to regard themselves as low attainers and perform at a level than is lower than their potential.

    [Sources: Abraham (1995); Ball (1981); Tomlinson (1987); Lacey (1970); Hargreaves (1967)] Retrieved 01/04/08 www.socialist-teacher.org/dossiers.asp?d=y&id=85

27. The Labour Government policy decision to promote comprehensive education in 1965 was implemented by Circular 10/65, an instruction to local education authorities to plan for conversion. Retrieved 01/04/08 http://www.oldmonovians.com/comprehensive/circular1065.htm

    In 1970 the Conservative party re-entered government. Margaret Thatcher became secretary of state for education and ended the compulsion on local authorities to convert. However, many local authorities were so far down the path that it would have been prohibitively expensive to attempt to reverse the process, and more comprehensive schools were established under Mrs Thatcher than any other education secretary.

28. See for example European Round Table of Industrialists (1994) *Education for Europeans "Towards the learning Society"*; Quiroz, Beatriz Madriaga, (2006) STEs—Intersindical *Spain: A Report to the Education Network of the European Social Forum*

29. See Ken Jones, 2003, *Education in Britain 1944 to Present* and the references to the speech by Labour Prime Minister James Callaghan at Ruskin

College , Oxford 18th October 1976. Retrieved 01/04/08 http://education.guardian.co.uk/thegreatdebate/story/0,9860,574645,00.html

30. NOP (National Opinion Poll) surveys identified the switch in votes by so-called C1 (non-managerial office workers) and C2 (skilled manual workers) as critical to the election victory in 1997. C1 voting Labour: 32% (1992) 47% (1997). C2 35% (1992) 54% (1997)
31. *Schools Standards and Framework Act of 1998* Retrieved 01/04/08 http://www.opsi.gov.uk/Acts/acts1998/ukpga_19980031_en_1
32. See Bernard Regan "Trojan Horses—Education Action Zones" *Socialist Teachers Alliance* pamphlet 1998. The pamphlet pointed out the origins of the policy lay in United States education initiative around "Charter Schools" and that it constituted the thin end of the wedge.
33. Schools Standards and Framework Act of 1998. Pp. 2
34. BBC *File on Four* (7/2/99)
35. *ibid.*
36. This debate sometimes intersected with debates around gender. See Carole Regan (1998) Boys Education (*Socialist Teacher* 65)
37. Regan, Bernard (1998) "*Trojan Horses—Education Action Zones*" Pp. 25
38. *The Standards Site*: Retrieved 01/04/08 www.standards.dfes.gov.uk/academies/faq/?version=1
39. *Yorkshire Post*, James Reed, Education Correspondent "Tony Blair's flagship academies are built with the help of sponsors who are supposed to provide around 10 per cent of the starting costs—usually £2m—and operate them once they open. But a letter seen by the Yorkshire Post shows that the Emmanuel Schools Foundation, which is supported by millionaire Sir Peter Vardy, was told last year it would only have to pay £2m towards its first three academies and £1.5m for each one after that." (4/10/2005)
40. See Beckett, Francis (2007) "*The Great City Academy Fraud*" London Continuum
41. *The Guardian* 3/12/2004
42 Although a Trust school does not require a private sponsor it still becomes a school independent of a Local Authority.
43. *The Guardian* 16/09/2005 A Department for Education and Science (DfES) spokesman confirmed the strategy: "Multiple sponsors have already demonstrated their commitment to the programme and have made a major financial contribution. Where a sponsor has already invested £6m across three academy projects, we allow them to commit £1.5m to the fourth and subsequent projects. £1.5m is a significant further investment, and given the commitment the sponsors have demonstrated to the programme, we consider this approach reasonable."
44. *The Guardian* 16/01/2006. In addition *The Sunday Times* reported that Mr Smith told a journalist posing as a potential donor's PR assistant that "the prime minister's office would recommend someone like [the donor] for an OBE, a CBE or a knighthood". Asked if this would be just for getting involved in the academies, he responded: "Yes . . . they call them services to education. I would say to Cyril's office that we've got to start writing to the prime minister's office." For a donation of £10m, "you could go to the House of Lords".
45. Anti-Academies Alliance. www.antiacademies.org.uk/
46. For a detailed account of privatization debate and developments see Regan, Bernard (2001) "*Not for Sale—The case against the privatization of Education*". (2002) *Privatization: a further threat to educational initiative and local government* Forum (2002) *Privatization—More to come*. Socialist Teacher Journal, Education and Social Justice. London (1998), Socialist Education Journal *Privatization* 17/03/2002, *A Challenge to London*

14/03/2004, We've just been robbed 03/04/2003. London, *He who pays the piper* Education Guardian (05/05/1998), Morning Star (19/03/2002), Regan, Bernard (2001) *FTSE, Dow Jones, NASDAQ, Nikkei—these are the new league tables* Socialist Teacher Journal, Campaign Group News, Tribune (2001), Labour Briefing (2003), Education Today and Tomorrow (1998)

47. *Public Finance* 4/11/1999. Many commentators in the field pointed out the hypocrisy of the systems used. As Jean Shaoul and Pam Edwards writing in *Public Finance* pointed out "While the Public Sector Comparator (for Pimlico School prepared by Westminster), assumes compliance with local authority guidelines for housing density and 25% social housing, the PFI consortium can ignore both. Hence it is able to put a higher value on the 'surplus' land, £10 million more, which swings the deal." Retrieved 01/04/08 http://www.publicfinance.co.uk/search_details.cfm?News_id=3238&keysearch=jean%20shaoul

48. Much of the information on Pimlico School is drawn from a number of committed campaigners, teachers and governors at the school who worked tirelessly over many years and from my own involvement as the local NUT Secretary in Westminster.

49. Source, Europe Singh, the Chair of Governors, from notes of meetings. Corroborated by governors present at the meeting.

50. Bernard Regan "Education Not for Sale" *Socialist Teachers Alliance* 2001. Also retrieved 21/04/08 from http://www.publicfinance.co.uk/features_details.cfm?News_id=8080

51. In studies undertaken for the public sector union UNISON the profits of the private companies are typically made by a reduction in the staffing costs—there would be fewer employees or the same staff paid at lower rates or indeed a combination of both. To quote one example from a study of a privatisation in the then publicly run prison service: "A security officer in a Securicor prison gets £14,000 per year for a 44 hour week whilst an HMP prison officer is paid £20,000 for a 39 hour week." Margie Jaffe UNISON Privatisation Report May 1999.

52. What was to be transferred was a constant matter of contention. See for example UNISON Publications London (2004) *The cost of PFI*. UNISON Newcastle City Branch.

53. For an interesting insight into the impact of privatization on teachers see Dexter Whitfield (2006) *The marketization of Teaching*.

54. *Transfer of Undertakings of Undertakings (Protection of Employment) Regulations 2006* Retrieved 21/04/08 http://www.opsi.gov.uk/si/si2006/20060246.htm

55. Pimlico school now (April 2007) faces the prospect of being turned into an Academy at the behest of Lord Adonis, one of Prime Minister Blair's education advisors. See Vicari, 2008.

56. Evidence concerning Tower Hamlets was gathered from the East London Teachers Association (NUT) and activists involved locally.

REFERENCES

Anti-Academies Alliance (2008) *Conference Against Academies: Conference leaflet.* Retrieved 23.06.08 from http://www.antiacademies.org.uk/index.php?option=com_remository&Itemid=41&func=fileinfo&id=73

British Broadcasting Corporation (BBC) (1999, February 7). *File on four.*

British Broadcasting Corporation (BBC) (2008) Anti academy fight ousts leader. *BBC News Online.* Retrieved 23.06.08 from http://news.bbc.co.uk/1/hi/education/7381927.stm

Beckett, F. (2007). *The great city academy fraud*. London: Continuum.

Benn, C., & Chitty, C. (1997). *Thirty years on*. London: Penguin.

Benn, T. (1994). *Diaries 1980–1990: The end of an era*. London: Arrow Books.

Boaler, J. (1998). Mixed ability teaching. *Socialist Teacher, 65*. Retrieved April 2, 2007, from http://www.socialist-teacher.org/dossiers.asp?d=y&id=85

Cohen, N. (1998, April 5). *The Observer*.

Eagleton, T. (2003). The struggle over English studies. *Socialist Teacher, 49*. Retrieved April 14, 2007, from http://www.socialist-teacher.org/dossiers.asp?d=y&id=161

European Round Table of Industrialists. (1994). *Education for Europeans: "Towards the learning society."* Retrieved April 20, 2008, from http://www.ert.be/working_group.aspx?wg=15.

Johnson, B. (1998). The Monday Interview. *Daily Telegraph*.

Jones, K. (2003). *Education in Britain 1944 to the present*. Cambridge: Polity.

Maclure, S. (1990). *A history of education in London 1870–1990*. London: Allen Lane.

The Mirror. (2001, February 13).

Public Finance. (1999, November 4).

Quiroz, B. M. (2006). *STEs—Intersindical Spain: A report to the education network of the European social forum, in advance of the Athens ESF May*. Retrieved April 14, 2008 from http://www.socialist-teacher.org/dossiers.asp?d=y&id=764

Reed, J. (2005, October 4). *Yorkshire Post*.

Regan, B. (1998a). *Education today and tomorrow*.

Regan, B. (1998b, May 5). *The Guardian*.

Regan, B. (1998c). Privatisation—More to come. *Socialist Teacher Journal, Education and Social Justice*.

Regan, B. (1998d). *Trojan horses—Education action zones*. London: Socialist Teachers Alliance.

Regan, B. (2001a). *FTSE, Dow Jones, NASDAQ, Nikkei*—These are the new league tables. *Socialist Teacher Journal, Campaign Group News, Tribune*.

Regan, B. (2001b). *Not for sale—The case against the privatisation of education*. London: Socialist Teachers Alliance.

Regan, B. (2002a, March 19). *Morning Star*.

Regan, B. (2002b) Privatisation: More to come. Socialist teacher.

Regan, B. (2002c) Privatisation: a further threat to educational initiative and local government. *Forum*, 44, (2) pp. 84-86.

Regan, B. (2003a) *Labour briefing*.

Regan, B. (2003b, April 3). *We've just been robbed*.

Regan, B. (2004, March 14). *A challenge to London*.

Regan, C. (1998). Boys education. *Socialist Teacher, 65*. Retrieved April 14 2007, from http://www.socialist-teacher.org/dossiers.asp?d=y&id=84

Shaoul, J. (1999). Lessons of Pimlico. *Public Finance*, 29 October 1999.

Thatcher, M. (1987). Aids, education and the year 2000! *Woman's Own*, October 31, pp. 8–10.

The Times (2001, February 14).

UNISON (2007) *Private Finance Initiative*. Retrieved 23.06.08 from http://www.unison.org.uk/pfi/index.asp

UNISON Publications. (2004). *The cost of PFI*. UNISON Newcastle City branch *How to exclude support services from BSF and PFI/PPP projects*. A best practice report for UNISON, GMB, NUT and NASUWT in Tyne and Wear centre for public services.

Vicari, A. (2008) letter to The Guardian, letters. June 18. *The Guardian*. Retrieved 23.06.08 from http://education.guardian.co.uk/policy/story/0,,2286107,00.html

Whitfield, D. (2006). The marketisation of teaching. The PFI Journal, 52, April 2006.

6 The Rouge Forum

Rich Gibson, Greg Queen, E. Wayne Ross and Kevin Vinson

> *Both for the production on a mass scale of this communist conscious-*
> *ness, and for the success of the cause itself, the alteration of men on*
> *a mass scale is, necessary, an alteration which can only take place*
> *in a practical movement, a revolution; this revolution is necessary,*
> *therefore, not only because the ruling class cannot be overthrown in*
> *any other way, but also because the class overthrowing it can only*
> *in a revolution succeed in ridding itself of all the muck of ages and*
> *become fitted to found society anew.*
>
> (Marx, The German Ideology)

INTRODUCTION

Ten years ago, the Rouge Forum initiated its work with this statement:

> The Rouge Forum is a group of educators, students, and parents seek-
> ing a democratic society. We are concerned about questions like these:
> How can we teach against racism, national chauvinism and sexism in
> an increasingly authoritarian and undemocratic society? How can we
> gain enough real power to keep our ideals and still teach—or learn?
> Whose interests shall school serve in a society that is ever more un-
> equal? We are both research and action oriented. We want to learn
> about equality, democracy and social justice as we simultaneously
> struggle to bring into practice our present understanding of what that
> is. We seek to build a caring inclusive community which understands
> that an injury to one is an injury to all. At the same time, our caring
> community is going to need to deal decisively with an opposition that
> is sometimes ruthless (Gibson and Peterson, 2006, p. 106).

This article briefly describes the theory and practice of the Rouge
Forum's last decade. In practice, the Rouge Forum's activists led mass boy-
cotts against high-stakes standardized exams in the United States, helped
lead sanctioned and wildcat teacher and student strikes and walk-outs

against the tests and military recruitment, and operated effectively inside professional groups as well as unions.

In theory, the Rouge Forum examined, often using a Marxist lens, questions such as: "What value do school workers or students create? Why have schools? How can educational workers and students keep their ideals and function inside their institutions? How do pedagogical methods influence substance?" In addition, Rouge Forum leaders published extensively in professional and popular journals, conducting serious research into both the social context of school, and daily life inside schools.

Rouge Forum has been challenged by many of the shipwreck questions of the left. Externally, Rouge Forum members faced the checks placed against any critical thinker/actor in an era when the encapsulation of thought is nearly complete. In addition, the Rouge Forum operated inside of a milieu of the left poisoned by a decade of opportunism and post-modernism, the whining of petit-bourgeoisie intellectuals who sought to disconnect the past, present, and future, in order to build self-serving atomized counter-movements.

Internally, the Rouge Forum sought to address parallel issues like the apparent contradiction between needing a serious organization prepared to fight a ruthless enemy with a centralized command, and the need to create an organization that offers people a rare chance to be truly creative and free. The Rouge Forum sought to fashion an integrated powerful movement, working against the stream of identity-based groupings operating without strategy, leaping from issue to issue, moment to moment.

How the Rouge Forum addressed these and other issues is the offering of this article.

WHAT IS THE ROUGE FORUM?

The Rouge River runs throughout the Detroit area. Once a beautiful river bounteous with fish and plant life, it supported wetlands throughout southeast Michigan. Before industrialization, it was one of three rivers running through what is now the metropolitan territory. Today the Rouge meanders through some of the most industrially polluted areas in the United States, past some of the poorest and most segregated areas of North America, with tributaries leading to one of the richest cities in the United States—Birmingham, Michigan. The Rouge cares nothing for boundaries. The other two Detroit rivers were paved early in the life of the city, and now serve as enclosed running sewers. Of the three, the Rouge is the survivor.

The Ford Rouge Plant built before and during World War I was the world's largest industrial complex where everything that went into a Ford car was manufactured. Seeking to extend his control to every aspect of production including the worker's life, mind and body, in the plant and out, Henry Ford instituted a code of silence, systematically divided workers along lines of national origin, sex, race, language groupings and set up segregated housing for the work force. He designed a, "sociology department," a group of social workers who demanded entry into workers' homes to ensure "appropriate" family relations and to see that they ate Ford-approved food (like soybeans), voted right, and went to church—the first social workers.

The Rouge Plant defined *Fordism*. Fordism centers on conveyor production, single-purpose machines, mass consumption, mass marketing, relentless surveillance, and seeks to heighten productivity via technique. The processes are designed to strip workers of potentially valuable faculties, like their expertise, to speed production, expand markets, and drive down wages. Fordism sees workers as replaceable machines, but machines capable of consumption. Henry Ford owned the Dearborn location of his plant, and its politicians.

Ford was and is an international car maker and a long-time practitioner of imperialism, the relentless battle for cheap labor, raw materials, markets, and social control that lies (against Lenin) within the origins of capital.

And, Henry Ford was a fascist. He contributed intellectually and materially to fascism and his anti-Semitic works compiled in his, "The International Jew," inspired Hitler. Ford accepted the German equivalent of the Medal of Honor from Hitler, and his factories continued to operate in Germany, untouched by allied bombs, throughout WWII.

At its height, more than 100,000 workers held jobs at the Rouge Plant. Nineteen trains ran on 85 miles of track, mostly in huge caverns under the plant. It was the nation's largest computer center, the third largest producer of glass. It was also its worst polluter. In 1970, the Environmental Protection agency charged the Rouge Plant with nearly 150 violations. When environmentalist volunteers tried to clean the Rouge River in June 1999, they were ordered out of the water. It was too polluted to clean. Today there are 9,000 workers at the Rouge Plant, most of them working in the now Japanese-owned iron foundry, though the great-grandson of Henry I promises to revitalize the plant, despite slipping behind Toyota as the number two automaker in 2007.

In 2006, Ford lost a record $12.7 billion and promised to cut 30,000 jobs, to close 30 plants in the next six years. In early 2007 Ford announced that process would accelerate, further devastating Michigan and especially Detroit, where the name "Ford," graces expressways, a football stadium, a major hospital complex, an auditorium, indicating the power of naming.

Henry Ford I ruthlessly battled workers organizing at the Rouge Plant. His Dearborn cops and goon squad—recruited from Michigan prisons and led by the infamous Harry Bennet who toured Detroit in a Ford convertible in the thirties, with lions in his back seat—killed hunger marchers during the depression, leading to massive street demonstrations. In the May, 1937, "Battle of Overpass," Ford unleashed his armed goons on United Auto Workers (UAW) union leaders, a maneuver which led to the battle for collective bargaining at Ford, and was the founding juncture to what was once the largest UAW local in the world, Local 600, led for years by radical and communist organizers.

Later, Ford granted collective bargaining rights and mandatory dues check-off, recognizing that he became the union's banker and, later still, his grandson readily agreed to organize all new Ford plants for the UAW, rightly seeing the union leadership as a useful disciplinarian for Ford's workers. By 2007, the UAW, despite a one billion dollar bank account, was dead in the water, having lost one million members from its high water mark of about 1.5 million, and having done nothing at all to mobilize job actions for 30 years, other than to organize to defeat them (Gibson, 2006).

On February 1, 1999, the boilers at the aging Rouge Plant blew up, killing six workers. The plant, according to workers, had repeatedly failed safety inspections. The UAW local president made a statement saying how sorry he was for the families of the deceased—and for William Clay Ford, "who is having one of the worst days of his life." The media presented the workers' deaths as a tough day for the young Ford, who inherited the presidency of the company. The steam went out of Local 600 long ago and the leaders now refer to themselves as "UAW-FORD"—proof that they have inherited the views of the company founder.

"The Rouge" represents the interaction of people, nature and work as humanity struggles in its great causes of production, reproduction, rational knowledge and the battle for freedom: the crux of political economy.

The Rouge never quit; it moves with the resiliency of nature itself. The river and the plant followed the path of industrial life throughout the world. The technological advances created at the Rouge, in some ways, led to better lives. In other ways, technology was used to forge the privilege of the few, at the expense of most—and the ecosystems which brought it to life. The Rouge simultaneously stripped people of humanity, yet united people in new ways, offering the possibility for a cooperative world. The Rouge seemed to be a good place to consider education and social action—to have Rouge Forums.

The Rouge Forum seeks to bring together educators, students, community activists and parents seeking an equitable and democratic society; the former governing the latter, depending on concrete circumstances. We ask questions like these: How can we teach against racism, national chauvinism and sexism in an increasingly authoritarian, inequitable and undemocratic society? How can we gain enough real power to keep our ideals and still teach—or learn? Whose interests shall school serve in a society that is ever more unequal? What role can schools play in the transformation of an unjust society? What is it that people need to know, and how do we need to come to know it, in order to take the risks necessary to transform the system of capital into a reasonably caring society where each can exhibit their own creativity?

We in the Rouge Forum are both research and action oriented. We want to learn about equality, democracy and social justice as we simultaneously struggle to bring into practice our present understanding of what that is. We seek to build a caring inclusive community that understands an injury to one is an injury to all. We know, however, our caring community will need to deal decisively with an opposition that is sometimes ruthless and has a central command.

We followed Marx's call to, "criticize everything," (Lenin, 1914) bringing into question the viability of our initial call for democracy, reviewing its inter-sections with equality, the need for organizational discipline and democracy's bourgeoisie foundations. At the same time, we have enough experience to recognize that we have all been wrong before and that friendship and mutual respect must arch above passionate criticism.

We hope to demonstrate that the power necessary to win greater equity/ democracy will likely rise out of an organization that unites people in innovative ways—across union boundaries, across community lines, across the fences of race and sex/gender. Good humor and friendships are a vital part of building this kind of organization, as important as theoretical clarity. Friendships allow us to understand that action always reveals errors—the key way we learn. We initially chose Brer Rabbit as a symbol to underline the good cheer that rightfully guides the struggle for justice. Every part of the world is our briar patch, though as the promise for perpetual war poisoned the atmosphere, Brer Rabbit is replaced by other symbols.

Although the first official meeting of the Rouge Forum was held at Wayne State University in Detroit, June 1998, the impetus for this meeting stretches back to 1994 and anti-racist and free speech activism within the National Council for the Social Studies (NCSS).

ORIGINS OF THE ROUGE FORUM: NATIONAL COUNCIL FOR THE SOCIAL STUDIES, PHOENIX 1994

At the 1994 meeting of NCSS in Phoenix, Arizona, two events galvanized a group of activists. First, Sam Deiner from the Central Committee of Conscientious Objectors (CCCO) was arrested for distributing leaflets at the conference; and second, the governing body of NCSS rejected a resolution condemning California Proposition 187 and calling for a boycott of California as a site for future meetings of the organization. These events fueled political activism the organization had rarely experienced and identified the need for organized action in support of free speech and anti-racist pedagogy. Moreover, these events highlighted the hostility of the largest professional organization for social studies educators in the United States to democracy within the organization and beyond.

THE ARREST AND TRIALS OF SAM DIENER[1]

Sam Diener was arrested for third-degree trespass on Saturday, November 19, 1994, at an NCSS sponsored concert of the U.S. Marine Corps

Band. Diener was a staff person for the CCCO and a registered exhibitor at the NCSS conference. Diener—whose work with the CCCO focused on countering the expansion of Jr. ROTC in schools—distributed small flyers, "Keep Guns Out of Our Schools!" The flyer criticized Jr. ROTC for its expense, discriminatory practices and militarization of the schools. Diener was arrested. When Diener protested, a security guard responded that he was acting on orders from the leadership of NCSS.

After his release, Diener began distributing a leaflet titled "Free Speech Censored at NCSS," lobbying NCSS leadership for an opportunity to present his case and have NCSS drop the charges. The president of NCSS, Bob Stahl, an Arizona State University professor, refused to allow Diener to address the organization's delegates.

A version of the events was given to delegates, Diener was portrayed as disrupting the concert. Members of the audience (social studies teachers with leadership positions) ridiculed Deiner's leafleting, many portrayed leafleting as a major crime. Some suggested Diener should be jailed, "the key thrown away."

Stephen Fleury, a member of the House of Delegates presented Diener's version of events based on the free speech leaflet Diener had been distributing. Fleury described the scene:

> As I began to read Diener's story, I felt momentary relief when the delegates began to laugh at what I perceived to be the absurdity and irony of Diener's arrest. Relief was quickly replaced with horror, however, when I realized the delegates' were amused that Diener (and others advocating for him) might believe that social activism was reasonable behavior at a social studies education conference . . . When the final vote was taken, however, the appeal to exonerate Diener was soundly defeated. (Fleury, 1998, pp. 4–5)

David Hursh and E. Wayne Ross later worked with Diener to distribute the free speech leaflet at the convention center. The executive director of NCSS, Martharose Laffey, threatened Diener with a lawsuit if the leafleting continued. On Monday November 21, Diener was allowed to present his case to the NCSS board of directors, but the board refused to assist Diener.

On November 22, Diener was arraigned and charged with trespassing. A series of trials ensued and in 1998 an appeals court reversed his conviction. After more than three years and four judicial hearings Diener prevailed.

Hursh (1998) says the Diener incident raises questions about whether the leading organization of civic educators in the United States tolerates diverse views. As Judge Alice Wright ruled at the pretrial hearing, Diener was ordered to leave the Civic Plaza "solely because of the content of the leaflets." Additionally, the actions of NCSS indicated that as an organization it supports the militarization of schools and society. Finally, Hursh (1998) argues that "the events surrounding Diener's arrest, the discussion in the NCSS House of Delegates, and the multiple appeals on the part of the prosecution, can only be interpreted as an effort to quash free speech."

CUFA, PROPOSITION 187, AND THE BOYCOTT OF CALIFORNIA

In November 1994—the same month the Denier imbroglio began—California voters passed the "Save Our State" initiative, Proposition 187. Provisions of the measure denied health care, social services and public education to immigrants without documentation. Under this law all city, county and state officials in California (teachers, counselors, and social workers) would be required to report any "suspicious" persons to the U.S. Immigration and Nationalization Service, nullifying sanctuary ordinances in many localities.

After Proposition 187 passed, the College and University Faculty Assembly of NCSS,[2] meeting in Phoenix, adopted a resolution condemning Proposition 187 and boycotting California as a future site for CUFA meetings.[3] A similar resolution presented to the NCSS House of Delegates in Phoenix was rejected by an overwhelming majority (Fleury, 1998). Ironically, the 1994 annual meeting of NCSS (and CUFA) was being held in Phoenix as a result of a NCSS boycott of Denver (the planned meeting site for 1994) in response to an amendment to the Colorado State Constitution that denied protection against discrimination based sexual orientation.

Following the Phoenix meeting, a small group of CUFA and NCSS members worked together as the Emergency Committee of Social Educators for Social Justice to publicize CUFA's decision to boycott California and encourage other organizations to do the same. Five hundred press releases announcing CUFA's actions were sent to media outlets. NCSS responded by attempting to suppress the emergency's committee's work; while the elected leadership of CUFA took no action to implement the resolution's provisions (Ross, 1997, 1998). The debate within CUFA regarding action (or non-action) on the boycott issue remained on low heat.

In the spring of 1997—three and a half years after the initiative was passed by California voters—the NCSS Board of Directors condemned California Proposition 187 (as well as the anti-affirmative action Proposition 209) and planned to provide a forum at the 1998 NCSS annual conference in Anaheim "to educate the social studies community and the public about the significant issues involved" in these measures. In addition, the NCSS Board decided to boycott California as a meeting site while Propositions 187 and 209 were in effect. The NCSS board of directors barely managed to pass this resolution (the vote was 9 to 8 with 3 abstentions), even though nearly every other leading education organization in the United States had taken similar stands.

In November 1997, at annual meetings of NCSS and CUFA in Cincinnati, Ohio, both groups retreated from previous decisions on the California boycott. The NCSS board of directors made a sudden behind-closed-doors about-face, rescinding their spring decision, apparently under pressure from leaders of the California Council for the Social Studies.

The executive director of NCSS—who had previously threatened the lawsuit against Diener—was invited by CUFA leaders to speak at their business meeting in Cincinnati. In her speech, Martharose Laffey advocated rescinding the original CUFA resolution, stating that the organization should not be "sidetracked by seductive but not so important issues" of racism and national chauvinism as represented in California Propositions 187 and 209. Following Laffey's comments and further debate, CUFA members voted by a 2 to 1 margin to reverse the 1994 boycott resolution and hold its 1998 meeting in Anaheim. (CUFA members, however, did vote to boycott California as a site for future meetings, as long as Proposition 187 was in effect.)

The CUFA reversal had a dramatic and immediate effect. Several leading members of the organization passionately condemned the move and resigned from the organization, including two African American board members—one of whom described the directions of CUFA and NCSS as in conflict with "deeply held convictions about social justice, equity, and democracy" (Ladson-Billings, 1998). In addition, the NCSS African American Educators of Social Studies special interest group decided it would not convene in Anaheim.

A small group of CUFA members (who became the founding members of the Rouge Forum) argued that it turned reality on its head to suggest that taking action against racism and national chauvinism was a diversion. They argued that the battle against irrationalism is exactly what should be taken up by the intellectuals of CUFA. Many CUFA members believed that the primary issue was the unity and solidarity of the two organizations (CUFA and NCSS). In a speech from the floor of the CUFA membership meeting in Cincinnati, Rich Gibson argued that unity and solidarity were indeed important, however the questions were: "Solidarity with whom? Around what purposes? Toward what end?"

Despite its reversal on the boycott, prior to the end of the Cincinnati meeting CUFA members voted that the 1998 Anaheim program should focus on analysis of the impact of racism and national chauvinism in educational institutions. Subsequently, a Diversity and Social Justice Committee was formed, with marginal impact.

The origins of the Rouge Forum trace right back to anti-racist, anti-imperialist, anti-chauvinist actions like those above. This set the tone.

Seven months later, an informal group was organized by Rich Gibson, Wayne Ross, Michael Peterson and others, and held its first meeting in Detroit. The meeting of perhaps 300 education activists was described by one participant as a, "72 hour conversation without end." People came and went, the agenda flowed with the ideas of attendees. Most found it a refreshing change from the routine of reading papers to each other. One important advantage was having access to a venue that was open 24 hours a day, offering a large room for plenaries and small breakout rooms—at no cost; testimony to the working class roots of Wayne State University.

Toward the close of the meeting, we chose the name, Rouge Forum, after the nearby Rouge plant, and all of its implications, and our dedication to open investigations of the world. We have never been troubled with the relationship to the French, "red," but that was not on the minds of the locals to whom Rouge means a river, and a huge factory in death throes, and the possibility to overcome. Since, we have been accused of being nothing but reds (hardly true, liberal democrats, libertarians, four U.S. troops in Iraq, socialists, anarchists, anarcho-syndicalists, and many others belong to the Rouge Forum). One vehement critic came up with the stretcher, "You people named yourself deliberately after the Khmer Rouge." We've stuck with the name for a decade and the reds inside the Rouge Forum seem comfortable with the action-oriented liberals and vice versa. Friendship, sacrifice for the common good (solidarity), all remain ethics of the Rouge Forum.

Continued activism within CUFA and NCSS remained a major topic of discussion at this meeting, issues included: continuing the dialogue on overt political action by both CUFA and NCSS, the social and political responsibilities of educators, the role of researchers and research findings in ameliorating social ills and the unique position of social studies curriculum and teaching as a force against racism and fascism. The ideas and actions of these social studies educators and their actions at the NCSS conferences during this period illustrate the activist roots of the Rouge Forum.

The following section explains a key operative principle for the actions of the Rouge Forum—the idea that schools hold a key position in North American society and educators play a critical role in the creation of a more democratic egalitarian society, or one that increases inequality and authoritarianism. At issue for the Rouge Forum, as Gibson and Ross succinctly put it in a 2007 article in *Counterpunch,* "school workers do not need to be missionaries for capitalism, and schools its missions." The metaphor is nearly perfect.

THE CENTRIPETAL POSITION OF SCHOOLS IN NORTH AMERICAN SOCIETY[4]

Schools hold centripetal and centrifugal positions in North American society. One in four people in the United States are directly connected to schools: school workers, students, parents. Many others are linked in indirect ways. Schools are the pivotal organizing point for most people's lives, in part, because of the de-industrialization and, in part, the absence of serious struggle emanating from the industrial working class (and its corrupt unions) despite its historical civilizing influence.

School is not merely school, but the point of origin for health care, food and daytime shelter and safety for many people. Schools are also huge markets (consider the bus purchases, architectural and building costs, salaries and potential for corruption), as well as bases for technological instruction and skill training. Schools warehouse children, serving as an important tax supported day care system for companies whose increasingly poorly paid workers come from dual income family who see their children an average of 20 hours less a week than they did in 1979. The beginning point in understanding the role teachers' play as major actors in a centripetally positioned organization is to understand the value teachers create within capitalist societies. This is what Marx [1867] (1985) had to say:

> The only worker who is productive is one who produces surplus value for the capitalist, or in other words contributes to the self-valorization of capital. If we may take an example from outside the sphere of material production, a schoolmaster is a productive worker when, in addition to belaboring the heads of his pupils, he works himself into the ground to enrich the owner of the school. That the latter has laid out his capital in a teaching factory, instead of a sausage factory, makes no difference to the relation. The concept of a productive worker therefore implies, not merely a relation between the activity of work and its useful effect, between the worker and the product of the work, but also a specific social relation of production, a relation with a means of valorization. To be a productive worker is therefore not a piece of luck, but a misfortune. (p. 644)

How do teachers create surplus value, adding to the self-valorization of capital? Teachers are both commodities and commodifiers. They train skills, promote ideologies, make possible institutional profiteering (remember milk or cola sales, architects, textbooks, bus makers, etc.) and above all teachers fashion hope, real or false. When schools fail in their role of fabricating hope, rebellion routinely follows, as France, 1968, demonstrated.

It follows that teachers create terrific value, not only in passing along what is known, but how it comes to be known; not just facts, or even dubious facts, but world views. Schools are battlegrounds in the combat for what is true—against the eradication of imagination. If the elites conceal the vital battle-fronts (like the very existence of exploitation), others (school workers) can reveal them, in work, knowledge, love and the struggle for freedom—and by holding the schools to their contradictory claims: schools for democratic citizenry or schools for capitalism. In schools the possible questions are: Can we understand the world? Can we change it?

While there is struggle on any job, in schools the struggle represents every aspect of social life, from the struggle over what is true, to the struggle for or against the military and war (of the 49 million youth in U.S. schools in 2005, half of them would be draft eligible in the following four years), to the struggle over wages, hours and working conditions, the struggle for hope itself—as before, when hope vanishes, uprisings often follow—and the fight for freedom, that being the foundation of learning anything important.

However, schools embedded within a capitalist nation, especially capital's most favored nation, are capitalist schools, their schools, not ours, until such time social upheavals or civil strife are at such a stage that schooling is either dramatically upended, or freedom schools operating outside capital's school supercede them.

There is a pervasive myth about the public nature of tax-funded schools. There is, after all, no single public U.S. school system, but perhaps six or seven different (inequitably collected) tax-paid systems, each teaching different substance, with educators using differing methods. For example, some schools in Detroit are preprison schools and pre-Walmart schools. As one heads into the Detroit suburbs, one encounters preteacher schools, and toward the upper end, predoctor or lawyer schools. The ruling classes rarely send their children to public schools. Rather, they choose private schools, like Michigan's Cranbrook, seated on acres of rolling green lawns in Bloomfield Hills. Or, they use private foundations to subsidize their segregated public schools, as in Lajolla, California where students have swimming pools and science labs while their black and brown counterparts to the south often do not have chairs.

A paradox of school is that the freedom to struggle for the methods to gain and test truth is often greatest in the richest and poorest schools where, in the former, parents and administrators seem to think that the lures of reading Marx will be overwhelmed by the Lexus waiting in the parking lot, and in the former, few people care what is taught, administrators focusing solely on test scores. However, too many youth learn that the construction of rational knowledge is a waste of time, undesirable; the crowing success of capitalist schooling. Even so, teaching against the destruction of reason is possible in U.S. public schools though the nooses of standardization and testing tighten each day.

The Rouge Forum took the lead in North America in re-establishing the role of Marxism and class struggle in education during a period when the "left," in education was reined in by postmodernist opportunists of all stripes, and the right sought to silence any form of dissent.

Given that the crisis of the present age is not merely a crisis of material scarcity, but also crisis of consciousness—that is, the abundance that is necessary for a democratic and egalitarian society is at hand, what is missing is the decision to gain it—the role of educators in creating critical, class, consciousness is even more vital. A base of solidarity, structured with an understanding of the collective value school workers of all kinds create, and the subsequent struggle to control value in the workplace and community makes defense possible.

The processes of school can, done well, go beyond demonstrating the well-springs of social change and justice, but those processes must leap beyond merely involving people in even critical construction of daily life. The counter-current to the democratic abolition of thought (quite possible in the emergence of fascism) is not solely to be found in the contradictory interests of production, but in the inexorable struggle for what is true. Ideas are key now.

Intellectual and practical works, the social praxis of school, are bases for the necessary envisioning of a better world and how to live in it. Clearly, it is not material conditions alone that challenge capital as the mother of inequality and injustice. Even crises do not overturn capital, rather they feed it. But, a profound understanding of how things are, how they change, and how we might live in better ways—in solidarity and creativity—that makes social change possible, and lasting.

In this context, in de-industrialized North America, where there is little reason to believe the industrial working class will be an initiator for democratic change for some time to come, school workers are positioned to assemble ideas which can take on an international import, and to assist in practices to challenge injustice. Social change can emanate out from schools, if it cannot be completed by school workers and students.

The Rouge Forum seeks answers to "what is up?" "what is to be done?" and "why do it?" and takes these questions of social justice as life and death issues—in schools and out. Being both research and action oriented, the Rouge Forum seeks to critique and engage in a reasoned struggle against standards-based education and high-stakes tests—lynchpins in the continued corporate hegemony of school. And the Rouge Forum identified and acted on a second choke point in schools, the military, especially military recruiters but also the Reserve Officer Training Corps.

In regard to the latter, Rouge Forum members have played supportive roles in city coalitions focused on driving recruiters and ROTC off K12 campuses, on the grounds that the lies of imperialist war have nothing to do with gaining and testing knowledge in a relatively free atmosphere: the project of schooling. However, there has been debate in the Rouge Forum about the wisdom of urging all youth out of the military (four Rouge Forum members are in the U.S. military in Iraq), when if social change is to be taken seriously, some youth will need to be urged in to the service, and in addition, for some youth the military service might be safer than home, just as school frequently is. Work against the military is connected to Rouge Forum action against what are called, "The Big Tests."

WHY STANDARDS-BASED EDUCATIONAL REFORMS AND HIGH-STAKES TESTING ARE KEY ROUGE FORUM ISSUES[5]

There is no place in the world that is growing more equitable and more democratic. To the contrary, commonly color-coded gaps of wealth and income expand across continents and within national populations. Carrot and stick, divide and conquer politics prevail behind a mask of globalism and prosperity. Total quality management, worker-to-worker campaigns, cooperative learning in schools, mystifies realities of exploitation and alienation. Talk of community is silenced by institutionalized pure self-ishness, the hubris of power and privilege: arrogant warfare for markets, cheap labor and raw materials. Freedom of choice becomes a pretense for a declining number of meaningful options, consumption.

Elites do not want citizens to understand how to unravel the roots of power. Moreover, elites do not want power, a corollary of fear, noticed. Instead, privilege wants to rule under flags of democracy, tradition, patrio-tism, respectability, reasonableness and perhaps above all, habit. This sums up to a numbing assault on human creativity and sensuality on one hand, and a razor-sharp hierarchical ordering, a grinding down made possible by largesse and a ferocious willingness to use terror and violence, on another.

The system of capital, grown by the war of all on all, requires profits, but is as deeply concerned with ideas, the consciousness necessary to make people instruments of their own oppression. No society reliant solely on technological might and the lures of covetousness—a society that cannot trust its citizens—can last. The injustice requisite within the birthrights of the capital system is permanent, however, standardized curriculum and high-stakes tests are not and reasoned struggle against them offers ways to come to better understand routes to challenge injustice.

REGULATING EDUCATION AND THE ECONOMY[6]

What has truly set the Rouge Forum apart from other schools-based groups in North America is the limited courage it took to link the system of capital to imperialism, to endless war, to racism, to the necessity of regimented curricula and high-stakes exams, a spiral of events that cannot be discon-nected. Only the Rouge Forum has made these connections. And only the Rouge Forum organized.

Without a crystal ball or the cursed prescience of Cassandra, Rouge Forum leaders began to warn middle school teachers, in 1998, "you are looking at the soldiers in the next oil war," and warned that the Big Tests were a pipeline to the military and meaningless, imperialist-based home-land jobs.

The Rouge Forum stood alone in developing a strategic and tactical analy-sis of existing conditions, well before 2001. This outlook was summed up by Rich Gibson in a keynote speech at the Rouge Forum conference in 2007:

> Our current context is this:
>   An international war of the rich on the poor, within that national wars based on inter-imperialist rivalry, within that appeals to nationalism, unit-ing people against false claims of united national interests when the very

real divide is social class, Within that, rising irrationalism, like religious mysticism, and rising racism, often born from religion, segregation to the point of incarcerating 2.1 million, Rising inequality as the rich grow much richer, the working classes get laid off and poorer, A media and cultural concentration on spectacles, like Anna Nicole, football, Judge Judy, while the question, "what war?" can be easily asked as war is on page five of USA Today, Constant surveillance into every aspect of life, The eradication of what were once limited liberties won by the industrial and earlier, even pre-industrial working classes, like the end of habeas corpus, Massive indebtedness within the US, and between the US and, especially, China, Nearly shocking imperial overstretch, with 739 permanent bases around the world and a secret military budget, A military fully exposed as weak, incompetent, and cowardly, but stretched so thin that a draft is surely on the horizon, Rising imperial rivals like Russia and China who also desperately need that oil, the cheap labor, and markets, of the world and especially the Caspian and Middle-East regions, A government fully exposed as an executive committee, and weapon of violence, of the rich.

And, as before, we are at a pivotal point in history, with financial and military crises at hand—handmaidens to the emergence of fascism.

Gibson went on to emphasize that resistance will take place as people are positioned in ways they must fight back; they have no choice, like the wildcat strikers who led Detroit teachers in two illegal job actions, the California Grocery strikers, and the massive immigrant-worker general strike in the United States on Mayday, 2006. At issue, however, is whether people can make sense of their circumstances, take charge of their collective lives, organize with ethical foundations, and fight for fundamental change in a manner that can sustain whatever is won, that is, to build a class conscious movement.

The Big Tests are designed to obliterate such a movement. The primary justification for the imposition of standardized curricula and/or the seizure of local schools by the state/corporate alliances has been poor test scores and high drop out rates, even though both of these measures are less a reflection of student ability or achievement than a measure of parental income. And, elites have argued that standardized curricula and high-stakes exams are a method of equalizing education, making the United States a greater meritocracy.

Since these same elites in the Carter, Reagan, Bush I, Clinton and Bush II regime are the people who demolished the social safety net in the United States, who now lobby hard to maintain a health care system that denies about one fourth of the children in the U.S. health care, and who do nothing about the massive homeless problem (setting aside their efforts outside the empire's homeland, like the hundreds of thousands of deaths of Iraqi children during the prewar sanction period), we dismiss that claim about equity out of hand. Instead, we choose to treat the question of the tests.

Research over two decades indicates test-based educational reforms do not lead to better educational policies and practices. Indeed, such testing often leads to educationally unjust consequences and unsound practices. These include increased drop-out rates, teacher and administrator de-professionalization, loss of curricular integrity, outright corruption, increased cultural insensitivity and disproportionate allocation of educational resources into testing programs, and not into hiring qualified teachers and providing enriching sound educational programs (Amrein & Berliner, 2002; Haney, 2000).

It is clear that scores on high-stakes standardized tests as well as drop-out rates are directly related to poverty, and none of the powers demanding school standardization is prepared to address inequality. The Rouge Forum has consistently maintained that the origins of the standards-based education reform are a direct result of increased inequality and authoritarianism—and war preparations. In fact, high-stakes tests are used to rationalize inequality and authoritarianism to promote the loyalty and obedience that are at the heart of nationalism and slavishness.

States have increasingly sought to punish low-scoring (less wealthy) schools and districts by cutting funding that might help raise test scores making them more "like" (via smaller classes, greater resources, increased staffing, modernized facilities) wealthier (read high-scoring) schools. Although the pro-standardization position has been hit with criticism—notably both from the Right, which sees standards-based reform as contradicting local school district autonomy, and from the Left, which sees it as racist, sexist and classist—one feature of the consensus view remains willingness to take such criticism seriously yet maintain it can satisfactorily be accommodated the prevailing framework. Thus while particular positions may differ marginally on the specifics (the devil is in the details), the demand for standards-based reform itself—the standardization imperative—goes unchallenged, at least among the alliance of conservative and liberal politicians, corporate elites, chief school officers and teacher union executives.

Inside this alliance is an insidious move on the part of elite stakeholders toward the corporate/state regulation of knowledge, a move that enables what Noam Chomsky (1998) calls "systems of unaccountable power" to make self-interested decisions ostensibly on behalf of the public when, in fact, most members of the public have no meaningful say in what or how decisions are made or in what can count as legitimate knowledge. This is purposeful. It involves the coordinated control of such pedagogical processes as goal-setting, curriculum development, testing and teacher education/evaluation, the management of which works to restrict not only what and who can claim the status of "real" knowledge, but also who ultimately has access to it (Mathison & Ross, 2002).

Consensus elites are among the same powerful few who make decisions about and promote such neoliberal (imperialist) policies and institutions as the General Agreement on Tariffs and Trade, the North American Free Trade Agreement and the World Trade Organization (GATT, NAFTA and the WTO) as good for the American public. This is a power-laden connection between the regulation of knowledge on the one hand and the regulation of the economy on the other, a joint effort by the politically, culturally and economically powerful (nominally on behalf of the public) designed to stifle community while simultaneously enhancing the profits of multinational corporations and the ultra rich. It is a reproductive and circular system, a power-knowledge-economics regime in which the financial gains of a few are reinforced by what can count as school (thus social) knowledge, and in which what can count as knowledge is determined so as to support the financial greed of corporations.

A conspicuous example is the social studies curriculum where, as John Marciano (1997) in *Civic Illiteracy and Education* argues, "students are ethically quarantined from the truth about what the U.S. has done in their name." This is particularly true with regard to U.S. perpetrated and sponsored aggression abroad, which is most often represented to students as unfortunate or accidental by-products of essentially humane policies that serve the "national interests," while what constitutes the latter remains unexamined. Those who administer the economy in their own self-interests are those who regulate the production and dissemination of knowledge and vice versa, all the while working superficially in the public interest but intentionally excluding any authentic public involvement. The leper's shroud of nationalism, "we are all in the same boat," overwhelms the reality of class struggle in official schooling.

In 2007, Gibson and Ross summarized the Rouge Forum position on liberal reformers like U.S. teacher union leaders who sought, not to abolish, but improve, the NCLB:

> We support the rising tide of education worker resistance to the high-stakes exams, as well as student and educator boycotts. We are sharply opposed to those false-flag reformers who seek to do anything but abolish the NCLB, its tests, and its developing national curriculum.

> Liberal reformers on this bent simply lend credence to a government that stands fully exposed as a weapon of violence for the rich, they disconnect the clear class and race domination in not-so public schooling from the empire's wars, and they mislead people into believing the dishonest motives of prime NCLB proponents. Above all, through their clear opposition to direct action versus the big tests . . . they simultaneously seek to destroy the leadership of a movement that could actually succeed, build support for laws and a state solely in service to capitalism, and they once again try to teach people that others, usually elites, will solve our problems, a vile diversion from the fact that no one is going to save us but the united action of us. (Gibson & Ross, 2007)

The first Rouge Forum in Detroit, was guided by the assumption that educators are centripetally positioned in our society; that they need, for their own good, to take clear and decisive stands on the side of the vast majority of citizens who are objectively hurt by racism and national chauvinism. From this initial assumption the Rouge Forum began its work within social studies professional organizations, but also built alliances with educators in the fields of special education and literacy as well as parents and students; and worked within the two major teacher unions.

REACHING OUT: BUILDING CONNECTIONS AND GRASSROOTS ORGANIZING[7]

These are times that test the core of every educator. In the context of an international war of the rich on the poor, intensified and thrown into hyper-speed by the terrorist attacks of September 11, 2001, economic collapse, harsh political repression and, in schools, the necessarily related rise of standardized high-stakes exams, school takeovers, vouchers, discrete phonics instruction, merit pay, militarization and the corporatization of schools under the guise of national unity—all combine to call into question what we are and what we stand for.

Collaboration of teachers' unions executives (whose high salaries—$450,000 for the National Education Associations' [NEA] Reg Weaver—are directly tied to the fruits of imperialism as demonstrated by the ties of the NEA, the American Federation of Teachers, and the CIA- sponsored National Endowment for Democracy) and many professional organizations in these international trends has raised many concerns. How can honest people organize?

The underlying complex processes of intensifying nationalism, racism, sexism, authoritarianism, irrationalism and forms of oppression, self-imposed or not, often seem overpowering, a series of small bullets coming in fast unison, so fast that it feels as if ducking one creates dozens of wounds from others. How shall we keep our ideals and still teach and learn?

In recent years, the impact of being a common target caused several members of distinct educational movements to come together for joint projects. Some groups are seriously considering the power of interdependence in seeking reason and social justice. As a result, advocates of the whole language approach to literacy education, inclusion, and critical pedagogy are engaging in more dialogue and have began to work together, to re-discover their natural unity—and seeing serious differences at the same time. The crux of those differences seems to revolve around the question: Can capitalism be reformed, tamed, made gentler, or not and, if not, then what? What comes of educational activism that does not address the system of capital?

A NATURAL UNITY? WHOLE LANGUAGE, INCLUSION AND CRITICAL PEDAGOGY

Rouge Forum members have sought to work closely with, and sometimes played leadership roles in, school reform movements like the Whole Schooling

Consortium initiated by Michael Peterson and Rich Gibson, the Whole Language movement (well established before the Rouge Forum) and the Inclusive Education movement. This has met limited success.

For a time, many people within the U.S. whole language movement saw their outlook as simply a teaching philosophy, a method, one that stood outside politics. The inclusive education movement likewise was viewed less politically. The idea of special education inclusion, however, has challenged ideologies and career paths. At the same time, the purportedly political critical pedagogy movement became so divorced from daily life, so steeped in the idealist befogged religious language of postmodernism, it lost sight of ways social change can be activated.

Perhaps born in the same well-springs, the three movements diverged so completely they lost sight of one another. A few individuals from each camp stay in touch, seeking to demonstrate the inseparability of political work, whole language, and critical teaching. Among this group at the university level, Patrick Shannon, Susan Ohanian, Carol Edelsky, Gerry Oglan, Steve Fleury, Michael Peterson, John Marciano and Richard Brosio, stand out.

The Rouge Forum argues that, the key question facing the world now—What is it that people need to know and how do they need to come to know it in order to arrange society in ways so they can be free, democratic, and creative?—is no longer just a question of industrial production, but rather it is a *pedagogical* one.

Critical pedagogy advocates have sometimes failed to acknowledge the elitist roots of their theory in Hegel's *Phenomenology of the Mind,* as in Paulo Freire's (2000) heavy borrowing from Hegel's chapter 8 in Freire's *Pedagogy of the Oppressed* (Gibson, 1994). Typically, critical pedagogy has served the interests of new elites (and self-promoting educators) rather than the interests of social democracy and economic equality, as in the ease with which banks and corporations took over Freire's claim to a critical method and used it in training programs. Critical pedagogy has, for the most part, served the selfish and ahistorical desires of postmodernism, not revolution. Freire, always protesting too much that he was becoming a marketed icon, was a revolutionary wherever he wasn't (Grenada) and a reformer where he was (Brazil). Trapped between subjective idealism (postmodernism), and mechanical materialism (old-time socialism), critical pedagogy danced too blithely around the vital tests of organization and ethics, key to the struggles ahead (Ross & Gibson, 2007).

Critical pedagogy, as represented by Freire (2000), failed the test of material equality and class consciousness. Too often, critical pedagogy located the source of oppression in the minds of people, rather than in a relationship of mind, matter, and motion: ideas linked to the understanding of alienated labor and class struggle, internalized oppression and authoritarian sexual relationships, and the fear of freedom and change (see Hill, McLaren, Cole & Ritkowski, 2002; McLaren, 2000). A truly exploratory, investigative pedagogy holds everything open to critique—but when it abandons reason, history and social practice as the test of knowledge, it becomes a system of oppression–an apostle for capitalism in new garb, speaking in obtuse tongues. But there is more to critical pedagogy than Freire.

The message of Whole Language is centered on the totality, the wholeness, inter-relatedness of knowledge. The focus of the inclusion movement has been the unity of people, all people. The heart of critical pedagogy is, or should be, that we can understand and transform the world—in the interest of masses of people–a clearer partisan view.

Whole Language, however, accepts uncritically the mental/manual division of labor that is academia, and a further division, form and substance. Most whole language leaders believe it is simply good that people read, ignoring what people read, toward what end? Slaves, and wage slaves, read. Germany and Japan in the 1930s were among the most literate societies in the world at the time; a problem in that the nations' peoples so quickly became fascists. Moreover, in ignoring the system of capital that surrounds all education activity, most whole language leaders seem to be partial to creating segmented people who at best want to simply reason their way beyond what is really still a master/slave relationship.

Absent an analysis of capital, they seek to rely on its government to solve problems; to replace bad phonics based programs with good whole language programs. Even so, the freedom (especially freedom of time to build close human ties) that has to stand as a beginning point for whole language, inclusive education, and critical pedagogy, means that there is at least a limited insurgent foundation for each movement and a point of unity.

JUSTICE DEMANDS ORGANIZATION: EXPANDING THE ROUGE FORUM ISSUES

The Rouge Forum moved to a leading role in school-based resistance. As the only group in North America that has connected imperialism, war, and the regulation of schooling, "The Rouge Forum No Blood for Oil" webpage became a focus of activity, both for researchers interested in a chronology of material related to the current and future oil wars, and for activists. Using a network developed over ten years of organizing in colleges of education and in K12 schools, the Rouge Forum, for example, initiated calls for school strikes, teach-ins, and freedom schools, which were adopted and carried out by school workers, students, and parents all over the United States at the outset of Iraq invasion in 2003. The calls for action swept well beyond the Rouge Forum's limited online base, cyberspace serving as a new outlet for organizing action.

Because Rouge Forum leadership shifted focus from opposing standardized tests to opposing a war *and* the tests, and because the organization sharpened its open criticism of capitalism, 374 people asked to leave the member-subscriber base by the end November 2001. They were replaced, though, by nearly 1,000. By 2007, the subscriber base was at 4,400, though it had remained so for three years, showing no quantitative growth.

There are serious limitations to the Rouge Forum work. Internally, the egalitarian and democratic outlook of its leaders has not been matched by a structure reflecting their mind set, or such was the case until the March 2007 Detroit Rouge Forum conference where the participants set up a steering committee with regional coordinators, easily identified chapters, so that anyone walking into the Rouge Forum could see where they might best exhibit their talents, yet remain as public or non-public as they choose, or, in Rich Gibson's words, "We want to be easy to see, but hard to catch."(Gibson, 2007c)

However, publication remains an issue. For example, leadership in editing the flagship of the Rouge Forum, its newspaper (http://www.rougeforum.org), shifted from founding professors to K12 teachers, Greg Queen and Amber Goslee, a significant step forward. But the two unpaid volunteers, working full-time jobs, without any external funding, were unable to carry the newspaper beyond a remarkable four-year stint. Members at the 2007 Detroit conference chose to continue the online publication of the Rouge Forum News, but to shift many articles to *Substance News,* published from Chicago by test-resister George Schmidt and his wife, Sharon.

The Rouge Forum influenced other labor groups like the California Grocery strikers in 2004 through research, publications and solidarity work. The organization has not, however, been able to successfully conduct the hoped-for kinds of freedom schooling that might help transcend resistance out of necessity, to revolutionary conscious action. Gibson noted that as a serious weakness in the Detroit 2007 conference (Emery, 2006).

Rouge Forum leaders conducted study groups, usually focused on the processes of dialectical materialism, the philosophical/practical foundation of Marxism, and led informal social film discussion groups, sometimes centered on more political films like, "Sir No Sir," on GI resistance during the Vietnam wars, on the history of teacher resistance with films like Charles Laughton's, "This Land is Mine," or the quasi-fictional "Blue Collar," but both the social and political groups have not been able to consistently sustain themselves over the years, some groups dissolving, others witnessing a passing parade of participants.

Over the course of six years, members of the Rouge Forum, Whole Schooling Consortium, and Whole Language Umbrella continued a friendly and productive association based on their clear commonalities. However, direct organizational ties are not firm. It is uncertain whether or not any of the organizations could withstand what could be political repression in the not too distant future.

Significantly, while the Rouge Forum fought racism and sexism perhaps harder than any other North American education-based group, it remains that the Rouge Forum has not fully bridged the race and sex/gender gaps that form the educator population the Rouge Forum draws from. Amber Goslee, the Rouge Forum webmaster, noted in the 2007 conference, that the organization would need to be transformed in practical ways, more inclusive, more dedicated to fighting internal forms of these Achilles' heel, if it would hope to have a lasting impact.

GRASSROOTS ORGANIZING

The Rouge Forum focused much of its work on grassroots organizing, rooted in establishing close personal ties, friendships with people. Working within as well as on the margins of various organizations we have had a number of successes. What follows is a brief description of many of the organizing strategies and tactics we have found useful.

Meetings, interactive conferences and teaching: Rouge Forum members made presentations at a variety of professional organizations including the American Educational Research Association, National Council for the Social Studies, The Association for Persons with Severe Handicaps (TASH), the International Social Studies Conference, Michigan Council for the Social Studies, and the Socialist Scholars Conference and have held a number of meetings and interactive conferences in Detroit, Albany (NY), Binghamton (NY), Rochester (NY), Orlando (FL), Calgary (Canada) and Louisville (KY). The united groups have also sponsored exhibitor booths at many of these conferences. Articles about the Whole Schooling Consortium and Rouge Forum have appeared in *Theory and Research in Social Education, Wisconsin School Board Journal, Substance, Counterpunch, the Nation* and *Z Magazine* among others.

England's Dave Hill, together with, in the USA and Canada, Susan Ohanian, Patrick Shannon, Ross, Vinson, Gibson, and many other Rouge Forum members have published extensively, pointing to the system of capital as the key problem in schools, and out. The sterling academic reputation won by, for example, E. Wayne Ross (former editor of the social studies journal, *Theory and Research in Social Education* and the editor of a series of books on public education) coupled with his activist stance have made it possible to inspire a new, younger generation of scholars and graduate students who appear poised to take leadership, not only in their own academic fields, but in the Rouge Forum. Like them, younger K12 teachers now move into leadership roles of the group, as older members seem willing to step aside.

Rouge Forum members joined, and assumed leadership in, community coalitions organized against the war, usually coalitions involving labor, leftists, grassroots collectives, and religious groups aimed at ending the war, but frequently involved in school organizing as well, such as the San Diego Coalition for Peace and Justice. As in other coalitions, Rouge Forum members assisted in developing strategies and tactics drawn from a careful analysis of the specific community linked to the workings of capital, identifying choke points similar to the Big Tests, as in the road to the airport in tourism-base San Diego (Gibson, 2007b).

In 2006 and 2007, four young Rouge Forum members traveled to Oaxaca, Mexico, the location of a mass community uprising, sometimes called the Oaxaca Commune, initiated by educators. There they joined in demonstrations against the regime which would cut off all of the Commune's hard-won communications systems, like the radio station, helped set up and defend barricades against troops, and engaged in the daily struggles about the goals and tactics of the movement. From their reports, Rouge Forum members published material in English in the United States, urging support from school workers in solidarity with the direct action efforts of the Oaxacans, and warning Oaxacans of the Trojan Horse union leaders who planned to arrive from the United States, a plan that was halted when Oaxacans became aware of the nature of the visits (Gibson, 2007a).

Rouge Forum members joined the editorial board of the journals, *Cultural Logic,* and the *Journal of Critical Education Policy Studies* (U.K.), creating new and respectable venues for newer radical scholars to find places for publication, voice and recognition. At the other end of the spectrum, some Rouge Forum members found it quite productive to participate in the many online educator discussion groups, like the California Resisters moderated by life-long education activist Susan Harman, where, over time, distant friendships were built which became close ties when job and community actions began.

In cooperation with the Whole Schooling Consortium and the Whole Language Umbrella, we co-sponsored the 2000 International Education Summit for a Democratic Society. It convened progressive educators, teachers, parents and community members locally and throughout the country. The Summit was an event designed to promote learning and skill development, dialogue, connecting urban, rural, and suburban schools and organizing to strengthen progressive education for an inclusive and democratic society. It linked art, music, drama, celebrations with ideas, organizing, relationship building. It was an interactive, action-oriented conference propelled by the belief that learning is both personal and social and that classrooms and other educational settings must be learning communities.

Our work in professional conferences brings the ire of reactionary scholars and bureaucrats. In 2004 at an NCSS conference, the audience shouted down a state bureaucrat, a test supporter, when he tried to aggressively wreck a workshop. And, in response, Rouge Forum members have targeted workshops by what are called *standardistos* with good humored guerilla theatre, like MEAP-SCHMEAP bingo, a bingo card distributed to the audience filled with common buzzwords, like "rigorous." The first to complete a card howls, "MEAP-SCHMEAP." MEAP is Michigan's state exam.

At conferences, we place flyers throughout the conference center, and we distribute flyers at social justice events, grocery stores, universities and schools. Flyers develop connections with potential allies and, importantly, provide an entre for face-to-face discussion. Our flyers serve as introductory notes and reminders when Rouge Forum members walk door to door in communities asking, for example, "what would a great school look like, what does your school look like, and what is between one and the other?"

In the planning of the many public activities like the demonstrations and teach-ins, we make contacts to local media and subsequently see our events reported through them, sometimes with a positive report, and sometimes not.

Many members also write op-ed articles or letters to the editor in local papers. We participate in radio and television interviews, usually focusing on the social context of educational reform, standards-based education and high-stakes testing, which often result from press coverage of our meetings or opinion pieces in newspapers and magazines.

The website, www.RougeForum.org not only informs folks of future Rouge Forum events but provides thousands of connections to information that facilitates a theoretical and practical understanding to achieve a more equal and democratic world. Beyond the baseline subscribers, nearly 200,000 people visited the Rouge Forum webpage in 2002, and, in early 2003, 4,000 people visited the webpage each week. By 2007, about 32,000 people a month visited the website, from all over the world, enough visitors to shut down the site toward the end of each month. The *Rouge Forum News* is archived on the Rouge Forum website as are video records of speeches at Rouge Forum conferences.

Demonstrations and other events: The Rouge Forum sponsored or co-sponsored numerous demonstrations in New York, Michigan, and California. In Michigan, we sponsored rallies to "GET RID OF THE MEAP." Our goals were to provide a place where people could comfortably take a public stand and to gain additional people with whom we could work. We had an "open mike" session and more than a dozen people spoke for 2 to 3 minutes each about their reasons for opposing high-stakes testing, specifically the MEAP. Following the march we met for refreshments and talk and made plans for continuing our work to educate others about high-stakes testing and what they can do about it.

We participate in community debates. In one such debate, in January 2005, the leader of the Michigan Chamber of Commerce and the executive director of merit awards (the department responsible for distributing the bribes that the State of Michigan pays out to primarily suburbanites for "passing" the state tests) presented opposing viewpoints, supporting standards-based education and high-stakes testing.

Early on we worked collaboratively with some Michigan state legislators to challenge other policy makers to take the tests that they expect students to take. Most of the legislators were no-shows. We encouraged parents, teachers and students to follow the example set by policy makers by boycotting the tests. Some Rouge Forum members feared that by bringing attention to the tests, it would legitimize them. We found two solutions to the problem. First, a participant was immediately handed a form to sign that would opt him/her out of the tests. Second, when policy makers were finished taking the tests, their scores were determined by the average income level of the district they represent. The best predictor of a school district's test scores is the average income of the parents. However, many Rouge Forum leaders felt strongly that electoral work is merely a direct route into deepened alienation, a process that looks for external saviors, when, "nobody is going to save us but us." That debate continues.

Members of the Rouge Forum brought two key resolutions to the National Council for the Social Studies conference in San Antonio (TX) on November 18, 2000. The two resolutions, reproduced addressed open access and free tuition to universities, and opposition to high-stakes tests. The motions were first presented to the members of the College and University Faculty Association (CUFA), composed of professors, the evening before the House of Delegates meeting of NCSS.

The motion on Open Access was defeated, about two-to-one, due at least in part to the opposition of multi-culturalist poverty hustlers and nationalists like counterfeit scholar Professor James Banks, who spoke fervently, worrying that free tuition might cut professors' salaries. The resolution opposing high-stakes tests, however, passed unanimously, a surprise for even the most optimistic of Rouge Forum members. The language of the CUFA resolution in opposition to high-stakes exams is the sharpest to come out of any of the professional organizations or the two education-worker unions. The NCSS House of Delegates voted down CUFA's high-stakes resolution, after very brief debate during which the members were warned that if the high-stakes were abolished, social studies teachers might lose their jobs. Meanwhile, related groups that oppose high-stakes exams began to circulate the resolution around the United States on email listservs, urging contact people to bring the proposal to union locals, PTA groups and administrator organizations. The resolutions influenced other professional groups that have developed statements on the deleterious effects of high-stakes testing (e.g., American Evaluation Association).

In 2004 and 2006, the Rouge Forum brought resolutions to NCSS that can be summed up by, "The US should get out of Iraq now." While CUFA passed these motions overwhelmingly, the members also virtually refused to discuss them and, in 2006, followed the CUFA chairperson's advice that, "we should pass this quickly and get on to the hors dwarves."

SUMMARY

The Rouge Forum exists because rank and file intellectuals and activists consistently made connections, not only between capitalism, imperialism, war and the regimentation of schooling, but between one another, persevering over years of practical resistance to authoritarian intrusions into their lives, and intellectual explorations into the struggle to not merely resist exploitation and alienation, but to transform it, now and in the future. The close personal ties, humility, dedication to equality, risk-taking, sacrifice for the common good, internationalism, anti-racism, anti-sexism, commitment to the celebration of aesthetics and creativity (fun), all forge an ethic that assisted Rouge Forum members to keep their ideals and stay afloat in a world that promotes a war of all on all. Those ethics helped bridge the gap between reformers and revolutionaries inside the Rouge Forum.

Today's educational practices are guided by educational policies, such as No Child Left Behind Act (US Department of Education, und.), that reflect the same obstacles to achieving education for democracy and social justice as identified by John Dewey (1966) early in 20th century—namely the powerful alliance of class privilege with philosophies of education that sharply divide mind and body, theory and practice, culture and utility: unacceptable disconnections. Our struggle is not new.

There is no "one best system" for organizing people to act for positive change, The Rouge Forum is one among many groups of committed activists who are contributing to the construction of a K–16 movement for progressive change in education and society, but the only one that takes on the system of capital, publicly and that stresses: Justice demands organization and sacrifice. It is our hope that by sharing our experiences in building a grassroots organization that our comrades in this struggle might learn something that advances the movement as a whole and that we might, in turn, learn from them.

NOTES

1. The basis of this section is David Hursh's (1998) detailed account of Sam Diener's arrest in, "The First Amendment and free speech at the National Council for the Social Studies: The arrest and trials of leafleteer Sam Diener," and Stephen C. Fleury's (1998), "A Sunday afternoon in the House of Delegates." Both papers were presented to the College and University Faculty Assembly of the National Council for the Social Studies as part of the symposium *The journey from Phoenix to Anaheim: Institutional identities and political engagements of CUFA and NCSS, 1994–1998,* Anaheim, California, November 19, 1998.
2. The College and University Faculty Assembly (CUFA) is an "associated group" of National Council for the Social Studies and operates as an autonomous organization within the larger structure of NCSS.
3. The CUFA Resolution on Proposition 187 was written and sponsored by Perry Marker, Stephen C. Fleury, and E. Wayne Ross. The text of the resolution can be found in Ross (1997).
4. This section draws on Rich Gibson's (2001). Outfoxing the destruction of reason and the introduction. *Theory and Research in Social Education* and *Cultural Logic, 4*(1). Available at http://www.eserver.org/clogic
5. This section draws from Rich Gibson's (2001) "Outfoxing the destruction of reason" (see note 4).
6. This section draws from Kevin Vinson and E. Wayne Ross (2001), "What We Can Know and When We Can Know It: Education Reform, Testing and the Standardization Craze," *Z Magazine.*

7. This section draws on E. W. Ross (Ed). Whole schooling: Implementing progressive school reform. In *The social studies curriculum* (Ed.), Albany: State University of New York Press.

REFERENCES

Amrein, A. L., & Berliner, D. C. (2002, March 28). High-stakes testing, uncertainty, and student learning. *Education Policy Analysis Archives, 10*(18). Retrieved April 29, 2003, from http://epaa.asu.edu/epaa/v10n18/

Chomsky, N. (1998). Domestic Constituencies. *Z Magazine*, May. Available at http://www.chomsky.info/articles/199805--.htm

Dewey, J. (1966). *Democracy and education.* New York: Macmillan.

Emery, K. (2006). *The freedom schooling curriculum.* Unpublished doctoral thesis. Available at http://www.educationanddemocracy.org/ED_FSC.html

Fleury, S. C. (1998, November). *A Sunday afternoon in the house of delegates.* Paper presented at the annual meeting of College and University Faculty Assembly of National Council for the Social Studies as part of the symposium, Anaheim, CA.

Freire, P. (2000). *Pedagogy of the oppressed.* New York: Continuum.

Gibson, R. (1994). *The Promethean literacy: Paulo Freire and pedagogy for social justice.* Unpublished dissertation. Available at http://www-rohan.sdsu.edu/~rgibson/freirall.htm

Gibson, R. (2006). *The torment and demise of the United Auto Workers Union.* Available at http://clogic.eserver.org/2006/2006.html

Gibson, R. (2007a). Oaxaca communards, beware the Trojan horse from the US. *Narco News.* Available at http://narcosphere.narconews.com/user/uid:306/notebook

Gibson, R. (2007b). Strategic planning and tactics in San Diego. *San Diego Peace and Justice.* Available at http://www-rohan.sdsu.edu/~rgibson/strategicplanningSD.htm

Gibson, R. (2007c). Speech to the 2007 Rouge Forum in Detroit. Unpublished.

Gibson, R. and Peterson, M. (2006). Whole Schooling: Implementing Progressive School Reforms (pp 103-126). Ross, E.W. (Ed.) *The Social Studies curriculum: Purposes, problems and possibilities.* New York: SUNY Press.

Gibson, R., & Ross, E. W. (2007, February). *Counterpunch, cutting the schools to war pipeline.* Available at http://www.counterpunch.org/gibson02022007.html

Haney, W. (2000). Myth of the Texas miracle. *Education Policy Analysis Archives, 8*(41). Retrieved April 29, 2003, from http://epaa.asu.edu/epaa/v8n41/

Hegel, G.W.F. [1807] *The Phenomenology of Mind.* Available at http://www.class.uidaho.edu/mickelsen/ToC/Hegel%20phen%20ToC.htm.

Hursh, D. W. (1998, November). *The First Amendment and free speech at the National Council for the Social Studies: The arrest and trials of leafleteer Sam Diener.* Paper presented at the annual meeting of the College and University Faculty Assembly of National Council for the Social Studies, Anaheim, CA.

Hill, D., McLaren, P., Cole, M., & Rikowski, G. (Eds.). (2002). *Marxism against postmodernism in educational theory.* Lanham, MD: Lexington Books.

Ladson-Billings, G. (1998). Letters. *Theory and Research in Social Education, 26*(1), 6–8.

Lenin, V. [1914]. *Karl Marx: A Brief Biographical Sketch.* Available at http://www.marxists.org/archive/lenin/works/1914/granat/ch01.htm#fwV21E029.

Marciano, J. (1997). *Civic illiteracy and education: The battle for the hearts and minds of American youth.* New York: Lang.

Marx, K and Engels, F. [1845]. *The German Ideology*. Available at http://www.marxists.org/archive/archive/marx/works/1845/german-ideology/chOld.htm.

Marx, K. (1985). *Capital* (Vol. 1). New York. International Publishers.

Mathison, S., & Ross, E. W. (2002). Hegemony of accountability in schools and universities. *Workplace: A Journal for Academic Labor, 5*(1). Available at http://www.cust.educ.ubc.ca/workplace/issue5p1/5p1.html

McLaren, P. (2000). *Che Guevara, Paulo Freire, and the pedagogy of revolution*. Lanham, MD: Rowman and Littlefield.

More on CUFA's resolution to boycott the NCSS California meeting. (1997, Spring). *CUFA News*, pp. 4–5.

Ross, E. W. (1997). A lesson in democracy? CUFA, Proposition 187, and the Boycott of California. *Theory and Research in Social Education, 25,* 256–258, 390–393.

Ross, E. W. (1998). Democracy and disagreements: Some things to do on our way to Anaheim. *Theory and Research in Social Education, 26,* 9–11.

Ross, E. W., & Gibson, R. (2007). *Neoliberalism and education reform*. New York: Hampton.

U.S. Department of Education (und.). *No Child Left Behind*. Available at http://www.ed.gov/nclb/landing.jhtml

Vinson, K. D., & Ross, E. W. (2001, March). What can we know and when can we know it? *Z Magazine, 14*(3), 34–38.

Vinson, K. D., & Ross, E. W. (2006). *Image and education: Teaching in the face of the new disciplinarity*. New York: Lang.

Young, I. M. (1992). Five faces of oppression, In T. E. Wartenburg (Ed.), *Rethinking power* (pp. 174–195). Albany: State University of New York Press.

7 Solidarity Building Dominican– Haitian Cross Cultural Education

John E. Lavin

INTRODUCTION

This chapter is a two-part invention in which I offer a series of historical and literary definitions for guerrilla pedagogy as an educational ethic that draws upon Paulo Freire as well as Chantal Mouffe and leaders of the transformative conflict resolution movement, David Moore and John McDonald. I, then, test my analysis by showing how guerrilla pedagogy reveals itself against V. S. Naipaul's novel, *Guerrillas* which rejects community-based education and E. R. Braithwaite's novel *To Sir, With Love*, which celebrates the Freirean paradigm of community-based learning. Finally, I take us to a Caribbean community whose educational program is driven by a discourse of radical listening for the purpose of collaborative advocacy that provides a voice to the voiceless.

LOST AT "THE CROSSROADS"

> I was driving the convent's station wagon near "The Crossroad" on one of the hottest days of the year when I saw a Haitian family carrying a child's coffin along the roadside with assistance from some friends and community members. They didn't really know me, but I stopped and asked if they would like to put the coffin in the car. That way, we could all ride to the gravesite. They said, "No, thank you, but we would like it if you would walk with us," and that's really what started the Crossroads project.
>
> —Sister Maureen, A North American Nun
> in the Dominican Republic[1]

Guerrilla pedagogy has its genesis in the historical concept that "guerrillas are by definition the weaker side" and that "their first duty is to survive" (Joes, 1996, p. 4). Their struggle, particularly in the postcolonial French, Spanish and Caribbean contexts, surmounted a revolution in 1803 led by

Toussaint L'Overture that resulted in the liberation of over 400,000 black Africans in Haiti from the threat of slavery. This "people's movement" was romanticized in early 19th century works such as William Wordsworth's (1807/1888) sonnet, "To Toussaint L'Overture" which elicited the image not of violence but of the "unconquerable mind" that L'Overture inspired in the poet. In this literary vein, the early 19th-century Spanish resistance to French colonizing forces was coined a *guerrilla* struggle. As a metaphor in Hispaniola, Spain and later in Cuba, the word, *guerrilla,* becomes an image of traumatic suffering endured by poor peasants and slaves whose human dignity is at the basis of their suffering. Francisco Goya's *Shootings of the Third of May* depicts what the Irish poet, Seamus Heaney (1973) describes as "thrown-up arms/And spasm of the rebel . . . His nightmares grafted to the palace wall" (p. 38). The emotions of grief and rage are at the core of the Spanish guerrillas' identity. It is upon this emotional, histori- cal and sociological terrain that this study defines guerrilla pedagogy as a Caribbean phenomenon that locates teaching and learning innovations among oppressed and disenfranchised people who become determined to transform their difficulties into theoretical conditions and political ethics that humanize, democratize and empower them. Their extenuating pov- erty and their encounter with military intimidation provide a daynamic background for educators to learn guerrilla community-building methods that have realized the voices and the stories that provoke recognition of human rights. The underlying need to tell and hear the tale of the voiceless emerges with an entire curriculum that advances the ability of educators to include new authors and works among the readings but, more importantly, to liberate the curriculum's potential for students and teachers to appreci- ate each other.

Thus, Guerrilla pedagogy is an ethic which is not rooted in violence but is based in a concern for humane treatment. Peter McLaren (2000), speaking of Che Guevara's guerrilla leadership, guides us to appreciate this concept of guerrilla pedagogy as a form of "love that became the seed- bed of each individual's revolutionary spirit" (p. 174). McLaren proceeds immediately to remind us that Paulo Freire's *Pedagogy of the Oppressed* traced Guevara's guerrilla spirit to its roots in a "dialogue with peasants" that was moved primarily by "[Che's] humility and capacity to love" (Freire as quoted by McLaren, 2000, p. 174).

On counterpoint, in this analysis, violence emerges as the assault against the human mind. For example, Eric Paul Roorda's (1998) *The Dictator Next Door,* recalls the disempowering curriculum that the United States Marine Corps used in the last century to establish the Dominican mili- tary police who would eventually impose marshal order on that Carib- bean nation to protect North American corporate interests. In this passage, Roorda quotes a *Marine Corps Gazette* article from December 1923 enti- tled "Training Native Troops in Santo Domingo" by Lieutenant Edward A. Fellowes:

> They [the U. S. Marines] continued to train Dominican officers and enlisted men at centers in Santo Domingo and Santiago, however, with courses on 'administration, topography, minor tactics, law, sanitation, signaling, military hygiene, military target practice and *lectures in obedience, loyalty, patriotism and espirit de corps.*' [italics added] (p. 20)

Guerrilla pedagogy is the alternative to the curriculum of "lectures in obedience [and] loyalty" that the United States made the premise of its colonial domination on the island in 1922 and 1923. However, Guerrilla pedagogy[2] is not a military challenge. It is a challenge to the ethical principles of subordination explicit in the curriculum noted by Eric Paul Roorda and enunciated in the words of Lieutenant Fellowes' "bullet points" of "obedience" and "loyalty."

In my work traveling to the Dominican Republic and El Salvador, I have observed and documented the indigenous knowledge and insight of poor, Caribbean communities that experience silence and oppression when order is imposed by outsiders, particularly by North Americans and Europeans whose interests originate in colonial times.[3] The alternative that I envision in guerrilla pedagogy is a dynamic counterpoint to the U.S. military's curricular plan for placing Caribbean people to live beneath the brunt of an obedient, loyal force.

In a wider social context, guerrilla pedagogy opposes the occupying of the Caribbean mind. On that precious cerebral ground, the guerrilla movement in pedagogy opposes both military force and violent counter insurgence. It is an educational initiative, not a military impulse, and emerges from a vigorous interest in the structures of thought and language enunciated by the Salvadoran poet, Roque Dalton (1999), who chose to dramatize the struggle of the Salvadoran poor not with guns and militia but within the literary framework of a theater and its stage and proscenium:

> The Republic of El Salvador, one of the smallest countries of the world in its territorial aspects, has been the scene, over the centuries, of a social drama of gigantic proportions. No doubt, that Salvadoran play has been, in large part, enacted in a theater which has been generally ignored. The economic powers that exploit and drain life from the Salvadoran people have extended a dense curtain over the real face of the country, to hide from the audience's view the humiliating scenes of reversal, conditions of hunger, landlessness and homelessness that prevail there; whereby, these unseen people are pushed to the margins and denied their most basic rights as human beings and forbidden from receiving the most basic advances of modern civilization and culture [my translation]. (p. 7)

Dalton (1999), here, represents a Latin American focus upon the dramatic stage and the discursive elements of how communities display and give voice to the challenges of their poverty and suffering. As a counterpoint to military intelligence, guerrilla pedagogy takes its line of reasoning from Caribbean thinkers such as Dalton who have posed the alternative of peaceful, collective, political awareness that draws back the curtain and allows the spectacle of humanity to engage the audience.

From Dalton's discourse between hidden stage and ignoring worldwide audience comes a curriculum determined not to obscure poverty with the oppressive "target practice" of "obedience" and "loyalty." Guerrilla pedagogy is a sociolinguistic movement to inspire exchange which recognizes poverty's impacts and seeks to learn from the condition of the poor. Dalton's focus upon literacy and the literary premises of this theater provides the dramatic framework for pedagogy to realize learning by way of humanizing exchange, and not more men with guns.

Guerrilla pedagogy, therefore, follows the precedent in Caribbean poets, dramatists, theologians and philosophers whose vision of humanity opposes violence by celebrating the sharing of imagination. The attention in Dalton focuses the poetic space of the stage as an ethical framework for understanding, recognizing the tension between performer and audience, and the building of public awareness. Dalton's definition of democracy is a literary stage exposing to public view the suffering of humanity. It is at once an aesthetic and sociological venue.

As a method for reading social justice, we witness a comparable humanity-based emphasis in Bishop Oscar Romero's (1999) poetry of language and thought in his distinctive style of "preaching." His sermons evoked not "obedience" from Salvadoran congregations but critical reflection. His theater, in this sense, was the church. In Romero's homily on workers' rights, he establishes the premises of collective meditation. Rather than ordering people to conform, he seeks sensitivity for the relationship between audience and theatrical actor. In a manner similar to Dalton's (1999) dynamic demand for the world to witness Salvadoran poverty, Bishop Romero asks his audience to consider the connections between the politics of poor people organizing labor unions and the awakening of public awareness. His homiletic plea connects him as priest with congregation in an appeal for the political awareness of his audience:

> I see a great value in calling attention today to the beloved workers, both men and women, both in the city and the countryside. I say this with keen awareness, right now, of the growing labor movement in our nation. The recent movement to form labor unions has much to tell us. From their mobilizing a deeply felt sense of solidarity among the unions and the workers in them, there has been an awakening. Something new has been born among us and a life that has been ignited must never be cut short and needs to be considered and nurtured, most certainly never suffocated [my translation] (Romero, 1999, p. 411).

When, as a Catholic cleric, Romero chooses to employ the pro-life rhetoric of "a life . . . that must never be cut short" in the advocating for the birth and protection of labor unions, his words become ironic. The Bishop is not compelling obedience in the Church's anti-abortion rule, but he is summoning the vision of the Church as people who need a voice for fair pay and social justice. His inversion of the pro-life metaphor asks the question: Without jobs, how can Salvadorans support more children? It is this social drama comparable to Roque Dalton's stage that provides Romero with an extended metaphor. He, first, advocates awareness for the right of poor people to participate in the drama of their abject poverty. He and they can, then, speak to their material needs. He refrains from crying out for wages, better living conditions, health care or food, however sorely all are needed. The Bishop's purpose is to identify as fundamental the pedagogical right to dialogue. It is a right to hear and be heard, to speak and to receive answers. He goes on:

> We should express to the workers among us a hearty congratulation on Labor Day, but our congratulations should acknowledge, as I said before, the concern, interest, struggle for solutions, as an invitation which complies with the upholding of workers' rights and their responsibilities. Workers urge the recognition of their rights in the realization that they, like their employers, are human beings, sons and daughters of God and that sincere dialogue, based on facts, must always be the first priority [my translation]. (Romero, 1999, p. 411)

The references throughout Romero's statement to communication across differences of class and gender is the underlying, subtle strength of a cause that puts "dialogue" forward as the discursive structure that will promote learning and teaching as well as the accomplishing of human dignity through the basic cause to promote human expression.

Guerrilla pedagogy works with the assumption that in the sociolinguistic frameworks are the essential elements of social transformation and community-building reform. As a theory of education, guerrilla pedagogy, issues from gestures deep in the organization of language and social movements crucially linked to advocacy and activism on a global level. Just as my travel from North to South has revealed to me political patterns; so, my reading across cultures has allowed me to understand analogies between the social injustices that writers seek to impact in both the Caribbean and North America. Writing in her double capacity as North American poet and human rights activist, Adrienne Rich (1993) conjectures the mind of a woman in a classroom that reveals this analogy:

> In the classroom
> eight-year-old faces are grey. The teacher knows which children
> have not broken fast that day,
> remembers the Black Panthers spooning cereal. (p. 143)

While the poet here alludes to the Black Panthers, a militant black party, founded in 1966 to endorse violent revolution, Rich's point is the impetus taken by the Black Panthers to sponsor programs for feeding the poor. On a deeper level, she draws upon the emotion, that same sense of the tragic affect[4] ("eight-year-old faces are grey") found also in Dalton and Romero, for the purpose of moving contemplation between author and audience, minister and congregation, teacher and student.

As such, guerrilla pedagogy follows the cause articulated by advocates of critical inquiry within Adrienne Rich's literary and political generation who are calling for deliberative democracy.[5] The proposition implicit in that cause to empower both women's bodies and minds is a cause to empower the sense of equity in the family, the community and the body politic. As such, guerrilla pedagogy addresses the needs of the poor that motivated Dalton and Romero to re-emerge by way of sociolinguistic structures that address the need to define education as a discourse in the cause of voicing the mental and physical abilities of poor people who continue to endure extensive suffering.

While this study sets in motion a dialogic dance of the perspectives from North and South regarding the goals of empowering healthy, literate and respectful communities in the classroom and beyond, it is also incumbent upon the project to address centers of harm that are revealed by the cynical definitions posed by V. S. Naipaul's (1975) novel entitled, *Guerrillas*. Naipaul's narratives reinforce colonial attitudes and oppose libratory practices that democratize pedagogy.

REPRESENTING RAGE IN THE FACES OF POSTCOLONIAL CARIBBEAN LITERATURE

Within a year of Paulo Freire's publication of *The Pedagogy of the Oppressed,* V. S. Naipaul completed the 1975 novel, *Guerrillas*. Naipaul more recently won the Nobel Prize in November 2001 for his writing on what the Swedish academy described as "the Islamic countries." While Naipaul's *Among the Believers* (1982) and, sixteen years later, his *Beyond Belief* (1998) brought his version of Islamic corruption, cultural loss and ineptness to the English speaking world, his first book to (mis)represent a Muslim comes in a Caribbean setting with the creation of Jimmy Ahmed, the protagonist of *Guerrillas*. According to a Western, patriarchal view of race and gender, V. S. Naipaul's *Guerrillas* produces a vision of desperation, fear and anger by inventing a collage of mouths in the mind of Ahmed who concludes the story with the brutal rape of an English tourist who is visiting the Caribbean island of which Ahmed is a native. Naipaul neatly arranges for Ahmed to append, "Haji" to his name and for another character to comment that Jimmy probably does not know what the word means. However, Naipaul introduces Jimmy as an obsessive pervert and places in his mind the following words to illustrate both his intellectual and emotional weakness, "Your mouth, Jane. As soon as I saw you, I knew you had a sweet mouth. We must christen it" (p. 234). The novel's network of images describes Jimmy's obsession with Jane's mouth by conflating many mouths in the novel's final act of murder. That scene is the moment of horror when Jimmy declares that his impression of Jane's mouth contains the reasons underlying his decision to murder her. Characters' mouths become Naipaul's theater of affect, a theater of attitudes and emotions that exhibit their rage and imprison them in Naipaul's novel where un-transformed, they remain like Dante's Ugolino (Canto XXXIII, Lines 21-25) eternally damned to repeatedly gnaw the back of the oppressor's head.

Jane's mouth makes Jimmy think of many mouths including the woman raped by Squire Lovelace in Samuel Richardson's 18th Century novel, *Clarissa,* as well as the mouth of Heathcliff's Catherine from the 19th Century novel, *Wuthering Heights* and the mouth of a woman raped at the beach by a group of local men on Jimmy Ahmed's Caribbean Island when he was just a boy. Jimmy's memories and fixations with mouths tell the story of his rage as carefully predicated by Naipaul upon colonial assumptions. The name of the victim, Jane, is reminiscent here of the whiteness of Tarzan's woman, Jane—moved by the novel out of context and vulnerable. It is important that Naipaul's Jimmy is a teacher whose pedagogy takes the form not of revolutionary community building but of rape and pedophilia. Naipaul's narrative sets a stage to (mis)represent Caribbean intellectual potential as paralyzed rage.

The school where Jimmy Ahmed teaches is an English morality play in which Naipaul (and the system that applauds his literary imagination) condemns rebellion against author(ity). In Naipaul's world, the "author" and the "teacher" must struggle for absolute cultural and political control. His story is English, not Trinidadian, although it is set in the Caribbean. Indeed, through ironies empowered by English books and attitudes, Naipaul's novel attacks the Freirean possibilities for the communal and constructivist sharing and learning that would revolutionize and transform self-damaging and other-damaging people into creative advocates of democracy. Naipaul poses an argument not only against the poor and marginalized of the Caribbean, but also against human potential on a global scale. Unfortunately, he has become the spokesperson for the Other.

GUERRILLA PEDAGOGY: A FORUM FOR LITERARY AND POLITICAL DISSENT

Educational theorists, led by Paulo Freire, have provided the basis of this pedagogy that informs our ability to appreciate stories from oral traditions as well as literary works, particularly innovative writings of the

Caribbean, whose primal scenes return continually to the words and images of poverty, violent conflict and social crisis.[6] The telling of stories in courts of law, theaters as well as schools gives shape to the scenes that create the occasion for individuals to share and to create their individual understanding through the interaction with others. In order for storytelling to have currency, the obstacles that arbitrarily divide speakers from listeners deserve critical re-consideration. Relationships and situations in which schools address conflict provide the curriculum with an opportunity to engage students in a storytelling process. Such crucial stories may fashion themselves against the negativity of a conflict wherein a spectrum of skills emerge, including communication, critical social analysis, criminal justice principles and legal process. If, however, schools implement patterns of pedagogy, discipline and labor relations that isolate workers and students and prevent them from fully telling their stories, the effect will be alienating. The storytelling theater that is the classroom and the hearing room will witness the limiting of literacy, intellectual sharing and critical action.

Homi Bhabha (1986) brings to crisis the critical concerns respectively with inter-textuality and with the pedagogy that motivates this study. Writing on "difference, discrimination, and the discourse of colonialism," Bhabha observes that, "Colonial power produces the colonized as a fixed reality which is at once an *other* and yet entirely knowable and visible" (p. 876). Epistemologically, Bhabha advances here a view of knowledge that reveals parallels between the classroom and the novel; (1) The classroom, like the literary work, becomes a colony when it insists that its students or (by comparison) its characters are completely knowable, predictable and/or without author(ity); and (2) The pedagogy of the classroom, as a socially constructed narrative, like the novel, becomes a discursive crisis with unknown elements when understood in terms the contention that "a struggle among adversaries is a struggle to establish a different hegemony, a transformation in the relations of power, rather than a substitution of one elite by another that leaves power relations substantially unchanged" (Mouffe as quoted by Worsham and Olsen 1998, p. 166). As Worsham and Olsen emphasize, via Mouffe's account, the emotions provide an occasion for deepening both understanding and for exchanging within the episteme that is the classroom, the courtroom or the colonial situation. According to Mouffe, the deepening of the narrative of the classroom or the novel to engage rage, grief or shame as humanizing affects becomes an opportunity for parties in a conflict to merge, exchange and transform emotions. In this transformative setting, rage can become mutual understanding, grief can turn into shared interest and shame can relieve tensions that formerly impeded the resolving of problems at impasse. Participants in the storytelling narrative, by seeking to collectively construct and simultaneously to learn from their story, can empower one another.

AFFECT OF RAGE INTO HOPE: CARIBBEAN
PEDAGOGY OF TRANSFORMATION

At the expense of Salvador Dali-like leaps and contortions, many Caribbean authors contemporary to V. S. Naipaul confront the same "affective demeanors" of disappointment and confinement with rage. Aime Cesaire (1971) of Martinique would compose a system of mouths parallel to Naipaul's. Cesaire writes,

> Our [Martinique's] hillsides explain why the suicide inflicted on himself the cutting of his hypoglossus and choked himself to death by inverting his tongue and swallowing it . . . and neither the teacher in the classroom nor the priest with his catechism can get a word our of this sleepy black boy, although they drum energetically on his shorn skull, for his voice is engulfed in swamps of hunger. (p. 38)

If Cesaire's poem here, *Cahier D'un Retour Au Pays Natal,* is like Naipaul's (1975) novel, in emphasizing the distorted facial expressions that humiliation and anger can inspire, Cesaire imagines and even romanticizes hope. The title of Cesaire's long narrative poem, *Notebook of a Return to My Homeland,* might easily have been the title of *Guerrillas* because the protagonist of both texts is a young Caribbean person returning home to the Caribbean from working and studying in Europe. Cesaire, however, frames the face in surreal series of changes that ultimately evoke an affirmative voice from his poem's main character, the young medical student whose story this desperate fantasy of tongue-swallowing suicide recounts. That transformation of the tongue becomes the basis of the student's vocation to speak for his people and simultaneously becomes an affect of liberation within the poem's patterns of facial images:

> I should come back to this land of mine and say to it, 'Embrace me without fear . . . If all I can do is speak, at least I shall speak for you.
>   And I should say further:
>   'My tongue shall serve those miseries which have no tongue, my voice the liberty of those who founder in dungeons of despair.' (p. 60)

Here the image of "My tongue shall serve those miseries" distills the author's ethical purpose to represent those afflicted by social injustice. The combination of Cesaire's experimental stream of images and rejection of Europe's literary traditions by writing in an obscure hybrid of poetry and prose offers a stark contrast with Naipaul's use of the conventional novel as a genre that exploits his subjects. Naipaul's unforgivingly precise portraits of pain and rage were an appropriate reminder of how people in colonial and postcolonial oppression become locked in states of rage.

Affect, the experience and expression of emotional states, is contagious. Its narrative elements can signify the infecting of a group with feelings signified by the facial features that participants recognize in one another as anger, sadness, guilt or grief. By analogy, there is an informative parallel between this body language and literary terms. The forum for communicating conflict can take shape either in a novel/poem's narrative pattern or in the way that the chairs in the classroom or courtroom are arranged. These arrangements of images can heighten or prevent interaction of victim and violator or author and reader. If interactive, democratic and attentive to the emotional and cerebral changes possible in groups and individuals, the text (whether a work of literature or the narrative of a community in crisis) will witness moment rich in collective problem-solving and, thus, transcendent. If authority remains isolated, the figures remain locked in the scheme of rage. Thus, the responses of Caribbean writers to the educational and judiciary limits imposed on their lands by colonial history inform us about a deeply human universal need for negotiation in the voicing of grievances.

When Naipaul's character, Bryant (who is a student in *Guerrillas'* Back to the Land commune where Jimmy Ahmed is the head teacher) gazes in the dark of the cinema at the face of Sidney Poitier, Naipaul tells the story of Bryant's isolation and his inner person. Bryant, like his teacher, Jimmy, is a gangster and a killer. Inherent in this student–teacher relationship is Naipaul's critique that community-based, popular education is premised in hate and ignorance. It is a dangerous and hurtful scene. The Caribbean student and teacher's rage is a causistry for acts that deny hope and/or learning. Bryant's gaze and the pedagogical connection with Poitier's face is a poignant, primal scene in the telling of the Caribbean story. For Naipaul and his readers, it is the anatomy of failure:

> The second film was for the Love of Ivy. It was Bryant's favorite; it made him cry but it also made him laugh a lot, and it was his favorite. Soon he had surrendered to it, seeing in the [Sidney] Poitier of that film a version of himself that no one—really no one, and that was the terrible part—would ever get to know: the man who had died within the body Bryant carried, shown in that film in all his truth, the man Bryant knew to be himself, without the edginess and the anger and the pretend ugliness, the laughing man, the tender joker. Watching the film, he began to grieve for what was denied him: that future in which he became what he truly was, not a man with a gun, a big profession, or big talk, but himself, and as himself was loved and readmitted to the house and to the people in the house. He began to sob. (Naipaul, 1975, p. 31)

Naipaul's image of Bryant crying silently in the cinema, offers a vision of suppressed feelings. In silence, Bryant gives up the potential that he believes he possesses as an individual capable of opening himself to laugh, to joke, and even, at the critical moments, to share love with others. V. S. Naipaul displays a hellish educational environment, which imposes colonial versions of authority, history and literacy upon readers and the people that he characterizes. Dialogue between Poitier's face and Bryant's private tears is an intimate space that has the potential to be dialectic between the colonial rage and the postcolonial forgiveness, between the unilateral oppression and the shared authority, between a fear of uncertainty and a love of learning. Large epistemological issues loom in the demeanor of Sidney Poitier. However, Bryant remains confined in grief and inarticulate fury. In counterpoint, the metaphor of the classroom as the colony is enlivened by the Caribbean fictions in which Poitier's loving manner challenges the audience to take emotional and intellectual risks.

TO SIR, WITH LOVE: DISCARDING BOOKS FOR HUMAN EXCHANGE

When Sidney Poitier in the 1966 film, *To Sir, With Love,* throws his students' British standard O-Level examination texts into the rubbish, a moment in Caribbean literature-cum-pedagogy has reached a critical pitch. Sidney Poitier is playing the character of Mark Braithwaite in that scene. In this persona, Poitier proclaims to the students, "We're going to talk, you and I, but we'll be reasonable with one another . . . If at any time I say anything that you do not understand or with which you do not agree, I would be pleased if you would let me know." E. R. Braithwaite's (1959) novel, also titled *To Sir, With Love,* provided the text for the film's screenplay. Thus, the cinematic pedagogy of hearing and telling students' stories began in a complex, written narrative. The role of the actor, Sidney Poitier, in portraying the teacher who throws out the books and addresses his students from a poor, working class London neighborhood, dramatizes the quintessential educator as cultural worker. The witness to both the novel and the film observes students and teachers constructing knowledge by sharing stories of the classroom. The role of the dictator (and the taking of dictation) disappears in this novel's analogy between justice and educational systems. If in Naipaul's *Guerrillas* the classroom is a structure of powerlessness like the colonial economy in which information and power are banked and held by an elite authority figure (the teacher), the Caribbean classroom in Braithewaite's *To Sir, With Love* becomes a revolutionary space defined by relevance, shared interest and collective benefit. The Poitier classroom reveals a Guyanese teacher in London teaching students conflict resolution skills, sensitivity and interest in decision-making, health, fashion and sexuality. One can imagine Bryant thriving in such an environment.

The author of the novel upon which the film *To Sir, With Love* was based came to Britain from Guyana in the early 1950s. Like Barbadian novelist, George Lamming and Trinidadian V. S. Naipaul, Braithwaite migrated to Britain with memories of the English-speaking Caribbean under colonial rule. In Braithwaite's *To Sir, With Love,* the protagonist played by Poitier displays deeply felt fears, uncertainties and defenses.

Sidney Poitier's persona as Braithwaites' protagonist reveals a Caribbean pedagogy at work in the film to invert patriarchy and to assert a collective, dialogic spirit. One of the film's visually compelling moments occurs when a student named "Seale," the only student of African heritage, suffers the misfortune of his mother dying during the last weeks of the school year. His classmates decide to buy flowers for Seale's family. They explain, however, to their teacher (played by Poitier) that no one can "afford" in their neighborhood's socioeconomic scheme to be seen visiting the home of a "colored" person. At this cinematic instant, Sidney Poitier plays the affect of trying to minimize the hurt he feels at witnessing the coldness of racism from the students for whom he has planned and hoped and cooked and healed so many wounds. Poitier's cinematic interpretation of the novel, nonetheless, transcends woundedness. The black teacher's consolation, which becomes consummate in Poitier's facial expressions and body language, embodies a turning-point paradox. Poitier's face plays, in a single moment, the realization that the teaching opportunity is to learn and to share a lesson on hate. Poitier's character has taught students to feel and to reflect. He pauses eloquently to encourage them to think and feel together. In that pedagogical negotiation, one student, Gillian, feeling deeply her teacher's hurt volunteers to go to the mourning Seale's house with the flowers. Not only has she learned to compose her story as a work in progress, but she has also fallen in love with her teacher and has crossed the race line by breaking the tension in Poitier's affect of painful understanding when she volunteers to take the flowers to Seale's home.

The character, who Poitier plays, decides, at the conclusion of the film that teaching will become his vocation and that, within the struggle of London's poor, he can sustain a transformative revolution both within himself and his students.

NAIPAUL'S PEDAGOGY AS PEDOPHILIA

Jimmy Ahmed, the protagonist of *Guerrillas,* writes out, in his novel within that novel, an impassioned account of the primal scene that will provoke Jimmy to torture, rape and kill a woman named "Jane" who is visiting his native Caribbean island from England. As author of purple prose, Jimmy imitates the voices in Bronte's *Wuthering Heights* and Richardson's *Clarissa* to feed his ego by describing himself from the perspectives of adoring English women, past and present. Jimmy is, also, Naipaul's argument against popular education and his rebuttal of Paulo Freire as well as the character played by Sidney Poitier in *To Sir, With Love.* Like a coil within a coil, Jimmy's writing articulates only rage within the novel that Naipaul has arranged for him to display his scenes of isolation and decapitation.

When Jimmy finally murders Jane, Bryant, the young man whom Jimmy has also sexually and personally dominated, awaits, armed with a cutlass. Naipaul details the stabbing with precision. Jimmy, self-absorbed, thinks of a woman murdered at the beach many years previous who has now become his analogue for the murder in progress. Jimmy has written about Jane and, now, as he violates her, he shows himself unable to recreate a cogent Caribbean narrative of his experience or to draw together the English stories upon which the novel has predicated his murder motives. Jimmy associates Jane's body with the ground where she will be killed and buried, but, as she dies, the Caribbean will become again an unsolvable puzzle in a mire of disjunct pieces for Jimmy to negotiate. The earth, Jane's face, and the faces of women from other tales by Bronte and Richardson are interchangeable in the killing scene:

> He was squatting on the ground, beside the dry pit of the septic tank and the heap of dug out earth, looking at the earth and not the face, and not seeing the earth. He saw a day of sun at the beach, sea and sky bright beyond the coconut grove, the girl bleeding on the fender of the car, accepting water from his cupped hands, and love coming to her frightened eyes. But the eyes below him were closed. (Naipaul, 1975, p. 238)

Jane has become the literal and the philosophical ground upon which Jimmy has been allowed by the author of *Guerrillas* to exist. Jane, the tourist, dies, consuming Jimmy, but the reader/tourist is guided by V. S. Naipaul through a system of images in which the land visited might as well disappear as the story/journey closes, simultaneously dissolving the natives who exist for the sake of the visitor. Our guide has translated the events into a dialect of standard English for novel readers. Leaving the beach, we are prepared to close the book and throw it at Jimmy as well as the culture that he has been deployed to represent.

Inherent in the scene of Jane's murder is the literary convention of *Guerrillas*. As all writing happens in a repetition of thoughts, images, and words between the writer's lips and the page, between the reader who repeats the writer's inscription and the author, and among the fictional characters who may (in the novel within the novel) be either readers or writers, *Guerrillas* motivates the repetition of ideas and words and images in a series of disparate pairs that echo, reflect, and imitate one another. It is colonialism in letters. The colonizer seeks the repetitions of the metropole's flag and language and books on the familiar terrain of the colony where the unfamiliar is to be assimilated and exploited rather than explored. In the colonial's failure to imitate the imposed standards is a necessary disparity which designs inferiority for the "other" who will benefit rather than perplex the colonizer. So, a series of uneven reflections are set up around Jane's murder.

The actual work of Jane's murder is carried out by Bryant, whom Naipaul describes as "very ugly, damaged from birth,"—a flawed mirror image. Jimmy holds Jane, but Bryant is confirmed an inferior duplicate as he stabs her. Indeed, Naipaul confirms Bryant's dependence upon his teacher by having him cry, "Help me, Jimmy," when he is committing the stabbing. The plan that Bryant executes is implanted and master-minded by Jimmy. And it is Bryant who falls dupe to the scheme of avoidance that Jimmy and Jane have played in their sexual encounters. The reader knows that Bryant owes Jane a dollar that Jimmy wishes to pay back with knives. In the course of the novel, Bryant has also served Jimmy and Jane sexually. After the "disappointment" of Jane's body, Bryant has been made to satisfy Jimmy's sexual debts with "warm firm flesh and his relieving mouth and tongue" (Naipaul, 1975, p. 76) in the pairing of Jimmy's narcissistic impulses to avoid intimacy with the womanly unknown of Jane and to know only his own image in his flawed double. Bryant is used up in a pairing that becomes a perverse tripling.

Bryant's education has been a process of his losing his genitals as well as the rest of his body. Jimmy turns to him to feel his "stomach muscles, tensed and dipped" (p. 61) and then a series of sentence fragments disclose "lower past the navel, to the hard curve, the springy hair, a man after all, the concealed complete beauty." In this passage, Bryant's penis is eliminated by the pneumonic device of "concealed complete beauty" and never named or described. His body is re-cast to accommodate Jimmy's fantasies. The structure of Bryant's colonial education unfolds according a process of pairing or imitation in which Bryant's identity is conceded. He exists to conform to Jimmy's singular wishes to know nothing outside himself. Bryant's anatomy of "warm firm flesh" is erased to the status of "hard curve," neither male nor female, a space to be occupied. Jimmy removes himself from the intimacy of stabbing Jane by managing and producing Bryant's scene of slaughter in which this other self gets the murder committed just as *Guerrillas* gets V. S. Naipaul's masterpiece accomplished by scheduling Jimmy's elaborate failure to write an English novel.

The continuum of damage or discourse of rape and murder, within a story of rape and murder that V. S. Naipaul has "arranged," like a box within a box within a box, for Jimmy Ahmed is an erasure of the Caribbean.

In contrast to *Guerrillas,* E. R. Braithewaite's (1959) *To Sir, With Love*'s main character, Mark, encourages his student, Gillian, to dance with him at the graduation party, and, in the novel's metered, periodic sentences, the scene assumes an eloquence in which teacher and student respectfully express deep feeling for one another,

> She waited until the first few bars of the beautiful evergreen "In the Still of the Night" floated over the room then turned and walked towards me, invitation large in her clear eyes and secretly smiling lips. I moved to meet her and she walked into my arms, easily, confidently as if she belonged there. There was no hesitation, no pause to synchronize

our steps; the music and the magic of the moment took us and wove us together in smooth movement. I was aware of her, of her soft breathing, her firm roundness and the rhythmic moving of her thighs. She was a woman, there was no doubt about it, and she invaded my mind and my body. The music ended, all too soon. We were locked together for a moment, then released.

Thank you, Gillian.

"After I leave school, may I come and see you sometimes?"

"Of course, I'd be pleased to see you any time."

"Thank you. Bye Sir."

"Bye Gillian." (p. 186)

While the first-person narrator feels expressively and openly for the young woman, he sustains the Freirean dialogue, allowing her to ask the questions and to depart according to her will. He has allowed her the space to make decisions that take the form of action. Delivering the flowers to Seale and dancing with the teacher of color are boundaries to be crossed in the context of Braithwaite's Britain. The novel and the film celebrate the collaborative construction of knowledge between teacher and student.

This is the ethic, the culture and the sense of political action and community that pervades both E. R. Braithewaite's novel by the ironic title *To Sir, With Love* as well as the film by the same name made popular in the visage of Sidney Poitier. The Poitier role as teacher is a rich icon revealing the transforming of emotions and the crucial meaning of crossing boundaries of class, race and gender.

RADICAL LISTENING: AN ACT OF GUERRILLA PEDAGOGY

I was going house-by-house to visit every family in the barrio, when I came to a shack that was all locked up. But, I could hear someone breathing inside, and I knew that there was a person in there. I left. But then, I was really bothered by this, and I went back, undid the lock and went in only to find a little abandoned infant, covered in filth and starving to death. I took her home. And, even though, all of the neighbors told me, "that little baby's dying, Altagracia, you are crazy to try to save her like this. You're going to suffer so bad when she dies." I just kept trying. And, thank god, she lived and stayed with us and became one of our children. So, today, Porfirio says that we didn't save Michelle, when she appeared in our path but that she saved when she found us in her path and that we have been allowed to stay with her and that she has showed us how to confront the suffering that we all must share in our community. There's no doubt in my mind that Michelle breathed life into us.

—Altagracia, The Crossroads, Dominican Republic[7]

Altagracia did not "discover" this child and/or save her life. The Haitian infant, discovered and "saved" Altagracia and, from appearance, Porfirio too. What question should I ask now? I have an idea. "Porfirio, why are you crying?"

Porfirio

Don't you see? We all ended up here from somewhere else and most people are headed out of here as soon as possible. You noticed what a wasteland this is. Right? So, poor people on this island are treated like trash. A dam is built in the mountains near our homes and the government just dumps us somewhere else. People in Haiti who can't find jobs come here in search of work and food. And they don't get much of either work or food. And they don't get much of either come here heading somewhere else. They go to Santo Domingo or to Puerto Rico or to New York, if possible. People get moved around this country like trash, used up and dumped.

Well, here's my point. People are not trash! [Porfirio isn't crying anymore. He's on his feet and he's pointing his finger at me, with passion.] Little Michelle used to wonder why her parents abandoned her. And, I always have emphasized to her that they loved her very, very much. We all knew her mother. No one knows if she was arrested and detained and deported. No one knows if she was forced to go somewhere else in search of a job and just wasn't able to return. One thing I've always emphasized to Michelle is that her family loved each other very much, cared for each other very much, and that, if they're alive, they probably hope to return to her, but that we love her as a daughter. You see, when you don't assume that people are trash, you become a better person, yourself. A lot of people speak ill about Haitians in this country, but they are just like us. And we are all struggling.

Porfirio calms down, and I reassure myself that he's not upset at me the finger pointing was just to emphasize a deeply held conviction. The women and men in support of the United Women of The Crossroads Project are all activists regarding the rights of Haitian children. It is impossible in practice for a child born of Haitian parents to become registered as a Dominican citizen and gain access to the rights, such as attendance at schools and treatment in public health facilities.[8] According to Altagracia and Porfirio, most Haitians live in constant fear of being arrested. Porfirio points out that, "The adults are arrested and detained by the police. Many times, they are not allowed to bring their children. The children become abandoned in the community. They are separated from their parents by the military police. It is a horrible scene to watch. And, I'll tell you. You wouldn't dare interfere."

One of the priorities of the community meetings, I learn from Altagracia, was registering Haitian children in the school, either by trying to force doctors to issue birth certificates that could be used in seeking documents or by adopting Haitian children.

Altagracia takes the initiative to redirect the discussion and to explain that the Women's Group would meet once a week, in the evenings, for no more than three hours. They formed committees and would have smaller committee meetings to, for example, compare notes on their visits in the community. The process of going door-to-door in the community was an important method because it enlisted more participation and also helped the group to fine tune their understanding of the issues.

FRIDAY IN THE POSTCOLONIAL CLASSROOM

On March 12, 2003, while I was guiding a group of North American students through the poorest barrios of Santo Domingo, Dominican Republic, I arranged for them to meet Rev. Jorge Cela, S.J., Director of a community education Center located in the neighborhood known as *La Cienaga (the swamp)*. The war in Iraq had not yet been declared, and it was to Fanon that Cela referred us, stating:

> Fanon tells the story of the seemingly good grandmother that will return from the market having left a bomb there that killed more than forty people. Fanon's purpose was to examine the symptoms of the rage within her. Right now, Americans need to search for understanding in the wounds described by Fanon. The conflict has its origins in poverty that accompanied the colonialism to which Fanon's life in the Caribbean testified. Your nation is on the brink of war, and, rather than advocate negotiation, exchange, as well as sensitivity that comes with humanizing education, violence is imminent.[9]

The movement to elucidate emotional responses by reading literature of the Caribbean is a conscious decision to practice deliberative democracy.

Frantz Fanon (1963) in *The Wretched of The Earth* begins his analysis of Fredrich Engels by quoting Engels' claim that "[J]ust as Crusoe could procure a sword for himself, we are equally entitled to assume that one fine morning Friday might appear with a loaded revolver in his hand, and then the whole 'force' relationship is inverted. Friday commands and it is Crusoe who has to drudge" (p. 25). Fanon emphasizes here the word, "force" and adds his own interpretation of Crusoe by concluding that "guerrilla warfare, that instrument of violence of the colonized, would amount to nothing if it did not count as a new factor in the global competition between cartels and monopolies" (p. 25). However expressly committed to violence Fanon may seem, his accomplishment is to expose the untransformed anger inspired by the Crusoe/Friday analogue. Fanon poignantly asks throughout this analysis in which he quotes Engels' version of the Crusoe/Friday tale,

"Who am I in Reality?" (p. 182), or "How does torture make you feel?" (p. 198). Fanon is, thus, posing these questions about identity and emotion, as a French-speaking Caribbean man whose European training positioned him in Algiers of the 1940s and 1950s to empathize with African people caught in a struggle with colonial inequities and injustices. Like the peoples of so many islands who have lost their indigenous language and political standing as European rule was imposed, Friday is an icon. The South African novelist, J. M. Coetzee (1986), has the protagonist of his novel, *Foe,* conjecture that "The story of Friday's tongue is a story unable to be told . . . That is to say, many stories can be told by Friday's tongue, but the story is buried within Friday, who is mute. The true story will not be heard till by art we have found a means of giving voice to Friday" (p. 118). As educators, our dilemma is acknowledging the stories that lie untold within students. To illustrate this theoretical claim, I am throughout this investigation testing how the classroom takes the shape of a colony *in micro* and how my project as an educator has become a postcolonial liberation from traditional western hierarchies that are colonial dictatorships. Implicit in this work is the proposition that the poorest women, men and children on our planet possess an experience from which we can learn by proportions of a high magnitude about human potential. This critical project is given unity by literary figures who have addressed Friday's silence, subservience and loss of identity.

In the dialectical continuum of exchange moved by the telling and re-telling of stories, there is an interplay of thought and feeling which integrates and inspires cultural, social appreciation of differences. Friday's identity in my classroom has become an opportunity for individuals to reject the terms of slavery and to locate and to affirm positive images of race and gender in the cause of composing healthy, imaginative interpretations of themselves.

GUERRILLA PEDAGOGY: A SEARCH FOR AUTHOR(ITY)

A crisis of authority is at the origin and foundation of this study. Fictional characters such as the peasants depicted by Goya in the *Shootings of the Third of May* are unfrozen as we enter their scene to examine their plea for life as guerrillas. Robinson Crusoe and Emile leave the bounds of the respective novels in which the western tradition has sentenced them. The slave, Friday, is imagined to speak his mind quite beyond the expectations of the role stated for him by Daniel Defoe (1972). Indeed, the women and men, whose interview statements appear here, provide a wide range of historical, cultural and political references in this study. The central motivation has been to describe a democratic discourse that tolerates the constructing of a story concurrently from radically diverging viewpoints for the purpose of learning about a shared humanity rather than conceding to the impulses to conflict that motivate unilateral power, war, confusion, harm and literal mindedness.

NOTES

1. The full name and identity of Sister Maureen as well as other historical, non-fiction figures whom I interviewed between January 2003 and January 2005, will remain undisclosed at their request.
2. Jody Norton (1994) uses the term guerilla pedagogy in critically assessing teaching strategies in American literature that reflect both the exhaustion of canonicity and an awareness of the multiple problematics of race, ethnicity, gender and sexual orientation.
3. I traveled to the Dominican Republic between January 2001 and January 2004 as the Director of Saint Joseph's University's Comey Institute of Labor Relations, and educational program for adults to improve their literacy and knowledge of labor rights. I traveled to El Salvador between January 2000 and July 2001 in the same capacity.
4. Moore & McDonald (2000) describe *affect* as expressions of face and mouth and have connected the reading of the human face and other body language to the reading of emotions that resut in the transformation of conflict. They explain the process with special attention to the face. "As an *affective* program is triggered, the face displays the basic expression that English language calls interest, fear, surprise, distress, anger and enjoyment" (p. 138).
5. Chantal Mouffe (2000) conjectures that a crucial step occurs when "collective passions will be given ways to express themselves over issues which, while allowing enough possibility for identification, will not construct the opponent as an enemy but as an adversary" (p. 102). Mouffe's proposition supports the occasion for the telling of the individual's story through literature or in cultural settings whose oral traditions allow emotions to be expressed. The practice of telling our own and hearing others' stories provides the primal scene for Mouffe's "agonistic pluralism" because, as Mouffe opines, "the prime task of democratic politics is not to eliminate passions from the sphere of the public, in order to render a rational consensus possible, but to mobilize those passions towards democratic designs" (p. 103).
6. Paulo Freire (1979) elevated his vision for educating the poor of Latin America to a high, romantic ideal when he described learning as "communion." Freire identified Cuba as the defining scene for the empowerment of oppressed people by way of the ethic that he constructed within his pedagogical theory. Freire used the term, *communion,* to mean a "fusion . . . [which] can exist only if revolutionary action is truly human, empathetic, loving, communicative, and humble, in order to be liberating" (p. 171). Freire proposed education as a means of empowering Cuban farmworkers or *campesinos.* The sequence of abstract values inherent in this definition is a conceptual framework for his pedagogy. His conditions of "human, empathetic" and "loving" emphasize the primacy of emotion in this process; while "communicative" and "humble" acknowledge discursive and ethical values that he believed to be necessary for liberation.
7. On May 18, 2003, I interviewed Altagracia and Porfirio (names changed to assure anonymity) about their experience in organizing a committee in order to improve living standards in their community near Bani, Dominican Republic, which originally lacked running water, electricity, access to medical care facilities as well as schools and education. I interviewed them in Spanish and have subsequently translated my notes into the text quoted above. I was visiting the Dominican Republic as a North American teacher accompanying students and colleagues for the purpose of observing and learning from communities of poor Haitian refugees and Dominicans. Working with a group

of North American nuns living in a nearby town and with the guidance of a Cuban Jesuit, Rev. Jorge Cela, S.J. stationed in Santo Domingo, the women created a cohesive network. They first learned how to form consensus by sharing perspectives on issues impacting their lives, by reflecting collectively and by working in collaboration with one another. Their earliest accomplishments were to make decisions and to, then, plan the action necessary for bringing practical improvements to their lives. Once they had accomplished a method for their meetings in which they both communed and communicated effectively, they decided to advocate for the founding of a school. Their experience reveals the Caribbean heritage which these women brought to life in working within cultural circles. In addition, the ways in which the women described changing in the course of their experience displays a transformative process from rage and grief into creative emotional states that inform our way of thinking about educational and legal forums.

8. Two studies describing poverty and discriminatory abuses experienced by Haitian workers and their families in the Dominican Republic are: *De Este Lado de la Frontera/From this side of the Border* (Badillo, 1998) and *El Otro Del Nosotros /The Other Within Us (*Centro de Estudios Sociales Padre Juan Montalvo, S.J. y One Respe, 1994). Badillo explains that, although laws exist that permit Haitians to naturalize in the Dominican Republic, "the majority of those who flee Haiti in poverty do not have money to afford food, let alone to pay for documents and legal procedures (p. 9).

9. Fr. Cela's concern, expressed in his article, "Constructing Democracy Together," appearing in *Estudios Sociales,* is to provoke reflection among students for the purposes of (1) deciphering information in groups that may allude us as isolated individuals and (2) slowing down the process of our comprehension in an age when information has been "so jet-streamed, so beamed, and so faxed, emailed and broadcast in such volumes that we cannot possibly digest or synthesize it in a comprehensible way" (Cela, 2002, p. 83, my translation).

REFERENCES

Aligheiri, D. (1996). *The Inferno.* Translated and edited by Robert Pinsky. New York: Farrar, Strauss and Giroux.

Badillo, A. (1998). *De este lado de la frontera [From this side of the border].* Santo Domingo, Dominican Republic: Centro de Estudios Sociales Padre Juan Montalvo, S.J. y Servicio Jesuita a Refugiados/as.

Bhabha, H. (1986). The other question: Difference, discrimination and the discourse of colonialism. In F. Barker, P. Hulme, M. Iversen & D. Loxley (Eds.), *Literature, politics and theory* (pp. 148-172). London: Metheun.

Braithwaite, E. R. (1959). *To sir, with love.* London: Bodley Head.

Bronte, E. (1998). *Wuthering Heights.* London: Oxford Univserity Press. (Original work published 1847).

Cela, J. (2002, March). Construir la democracia juntos [Building Democracy Together]. *Estudios Sociales, 35*(127), 79–89.

Centro de Estudios Sociales Padre Juan Martalvo, S.J.y One Respe (Father Juan Montalvo Centre for Social Studies and One Respe - centre for co-existence, solidarity and shared projects) (1994). *El Otro del Nosotros (One of us).* Santo Domingo, Dominican Republic: Author.

Cesaire, A. (1971). *Return to my native land.* Paris: Presence Africaine.

Coetzee, J. M. (1986). *Foe.* New York: Penguin.

Clavell, J. (Producer & Director). (1966). *To sir, with love* [Motion Picture]. United Kingdom: Columbia (British) Productions.

Dalton, R. (1999). *El Salvador* (10th ed.). San Salvador, El Salvador: University of Central America Press.

Defoe, D. (1972). *Robinson Crusoe*. London: Oxford.

Fanon, F. (1963). *The wretched of the earth*. New York: Grove.

Freire, P. (1979). *Pedagogy of the oppressed*. (Trans. Myra Bergman Ramos). New York: Continuum.

Heaney, S. (1973). *North*. London: Faber.

Joes, A. (1996). *Guerrilla warfare: A historical, biographical, and bibliographical sourcebook*. Westport, CT: Greenwood.

McLaren, P. (2000). *Che Guevara, Paulo Freire, and the pedagogy of revolution*. New York: Rowman & Littlefield.

Moore, D., & McDonald, J. (2000). *Transforming conflict*. Sydney: Transformative Justice Australia.

Mouffe, C. (2000). *The democratic paradox*. London: Verso.

Naipaul, V. S. (1975). *Guerrillas*. London: Deutsch.

Naipaul, V. S. (1982). *Among the believers*. London: Vintage.

Naipaul, V. S. (1998). *Beyond belief*. New York: Random House.

Norton, J. (1994). Guerrilla pedagogy: Conflicting authority and interpretation in the classroom. *College Literature*. *21*, 136–157.

Rich, A. (1993). *Selected poetry of Adrienne Rich*. New York: Norton.

Richardson, S. (1971). *Pamela or Virtue Rewarded*. Boston: Houghton Mifflin.

Romero, O. A. (1999). *La voz de los sin voz* [*The Voice of Those Without a Voice*]. (Edited by J. Sobrino, 5th ed.) San Salvador, El Salvador: University of Central America Press.

Roorda, R. (1998). *The dictator next door*. New York: Viking.

Wordsworth, W. (1888). *William Wordsworth: The complete poetical works*. London: Macmillan.

Worsham, L., & Olson, G. (1998, December). Rethinking political community: Chantal Mouffe's liberal socialism. In L. Worsham & G. Olson (Eds.), *Race, rhetoric and the postcolonial* (pp. 165–201). New York: State University of New York Press.

8   Learning From the South
The Creation of Real Alternatives to Neoliberal Policies in Education in Porto Alegre, Brazil

Luís Armando Gandin

INTRODUCTION

This chapter describes and analyzes the experience of the Citizen School in Porto Alegre, Brazil, a progressive city-wide educational reform created as a viable alternative to the market-based reforms being implemented worldwide. The article examines how the city administration—the "Popular Administration" led by the Workers' Party—implemented radical changes in the way schools build their curriculum (a process that starts with a research in the community and is controlled locally at the school), organize their governance (with empowered School Councils and elected principals and curriculum coordinators), and relate to the local state (with democratically elected assemblies that determine the goals of the whole school system). The chapter also discusses some of the successes and potential problems of the proposal and its implementation. The overall conclusion is that there is something to be learned from the new relationship established between the state and the poor communities where the schools are situated and from the new forms of social accountability created by the Citizen School project.

THE CITIZEN SCHOOL PROJECT IN PORTO ALEGRE, BRAZIL

Neoliberal policies are as powerful for the new realities they create as for what they exclude from our social imaginary. These days, subaltern and dissident discourses and practices are not propagated and are portrayed as "old-fashioned." Nevertheless, organized subaltern groups have been voicing a clear message for a long time: There are other ways to organize education and there are concrete ways to implement them. But when these voices come from periphery countries,[1] it is even more improbable that they will be heard. This chapter deals with one of these subaltern voices that have gained the space of local state policy: the Citizen School project, being implemented in Porto Alegre, Brazil.

The policy—and its implementation described in this chapter—is important because it provides discursive and institutional weapons to the struggle against market-based one-size-fits-all models in education. The lesson that the Citizen School project teaches us all is exactly this one: There is no model that can be replicated everywhere. No progressive reform in education can be implemented if the context is ignored. If this project is to be tried elsewhere, what should be done is not a replication but rather a translation, which is always a recreation of the original, one that makes sense in the new site.

The Citizen School project is far from complete and has flaws and contradictions, but it represents a new way of conceiving education and this alone deserves a close examination. It is a proposal that searches for responses for the educational problems in places other than the market-based policies that center their solutions in testing and economic accountability. In this chapter, I will present the conception and the basic mechanisms created to implement this conception and evaluate its strengths and some of its contradictions. But first let me describe and analyze the context in which the Citizen School project is situated.

THE CONTEXT—LOCAL AND GLOBAL

Porto Alegre is a city of almost 1.5 million people, situated in the southern region of Brazil. It is the capital of the state of Rio Grande do Sul, and the largest city of the region. From 1989 to 2004, it was governed by a coalition of leftist parties (the Popular Administration), under the general leadership of the Workers' Party (Partido dos Trabalhadores or PT, formed in 1979 by a coalition of unions, social movements and other leftist organizations). The Popular Administration was reelected three consecutive times, thus giving it and its policies even greater legitimacy. Despite the recent electoral loss that replaced PT in 2005 after 16 years in the municipal administration, the basic structures of the project are still in place. The fact that the winning coalition of parties (a centrist alliance) had to promise not to change the major set of policies put in place by the PT government in order to be elected, is a clear indicator of how organic these policies became to the daily life of Porto Alegre's citizens.

The goal of the educational policy of the Popular Administration was to promote real involvement of the communities in the education of their children and to learn from the experiences of community organization. There is clearly a radical difference between this proposal and the neoliberal ones. It is important, therefore, to understand the global context where the Citizen School project is situated before we examine the practical elements of the proposal.

The rhetoric of neoliberalism insists on the importance of education in solving the problems of capitalism. Several reports show how education has failed to efficiently provide workers with the appropriate skills.[3] What is the proposed solution? Neoliberal proponents say that there is only one way to solve this crisis: to apply the logic of the market to the educational system. They say that, just like in other spheres of society, the intervention of the state and the control of the unions over the workplace are disastrous for school efficiency. Competition is the only force that will end the historical inefficiency in schools that are currently controlled by the corporatist power of the teacher's unions and the bureaucratic structure of school districts or local Departments of Education.

It is important to emphasize that the process of turning neoliberalism into a hegemonic project is not one that can be done once and for all; it is always a process (rather than a state) where articulations have to be constructed, reconstructed and struggled over in relation to the historical circumstances of each specific social formation.

The concept of articulation provides us with a tool to understand the complex and historical "work" involved in constructing and maintaining hegemony. It also helps us to understand that the apparent homogeneity and solidness of a given discourse is actually a historical construction, one that has to be constantly renovated. A connection that is established between groups and specific ideologies is not "necessary" or given; it cannot be easily deduced from a central dominant ideology. It is better understood as an articulation, a non-necessary and more or less contingent connection made possible in a specific context and in a specific historical moment. "Conservative modernization," a movement lead by an alliance of neoliberal and neoconservative groups aiming at building a new market-based, socially conservative common sense in society, is a good example of a successful articulation.

GLOBALIZATION: A SPACE OF CONTRADICTIONS

It is important to recognize here that, although there is a clear global movement towards conservative modernization that has to be acknowledged in order to understand the constraints that alternative reforms face, specific realities in each society will pose different challenges to this hegemonic movement. When dealing with the conservative modernization movement, one gets tempted to use the current discourse of globalization to assume that what happens in the Brazilian context is a mere transfer of the policies of the core countries to the ones in the periphery. However, what I encountered in my research of educational policy implementation in Brazil was not a monolithic implementation of conservative policies originally conceived in the core countries,[2] transferred to that country, but re-articulations and hybridisms formed in the struggles between global and local hegemonic forces and between hegemonic and counter-hegemonic forces.

Although globalization is a process that has been able to reach even remote locales, it has been generating very different consequences, depending on the local realities. When a globally hegemonic discourse reaches a national context, it produces a hybrid product, a complex set of consequences. As Ball (1998) says, referring to education, "the new orthodoxies of education policy are grafted onto and realised within very different national and cultural contexts and are affected, inflected and deflected by them" (p. 133). So, when this adaptation of a global hegemonic discourse occurs at a local level, not only does it have to be reconfigured and rearticulated to "make sense" in the particular context—this is exactly the nature of a hegemonic discourse, one that "makes sense" and is local and not foreign—but it also has to account for the opposition and resistance of local groups.

THE CREATION OF THE PRECONDITIONS TO THE CITIZEN SCHOOL PROJECT

How does this discussion apply to the case of the Citizen School project? Because neoliberal policies cannot merely be imposed but must also win the consent of the agents involved in education, spaces are created where it is possible to construct alternative practices. The Citizen School rearticulates these spaces and turns them into opportunities for its project. One of the problems with the idea of operating in the gaps is that the hegemonic forces set the agenda, and the progressive movements must operate within the field constructed by these forces. The difference with the Citizen School project is that it only uses the spaces and gaps created by neoliberal policies and creeds to launch an alternative project, one that has a radical new logic. So rather than operating in the gaps, the Citizen School proposes a field with different priorities and assumptions and starts to foster a real alternative educational proposal. Rather than being merely tactical, this project builds a new strategy.[3]

When the discourse of conservative modernization reaches Brazil and, more specifically the city of Porto Alegre, some interesting rearticulations are forged. One of the ideas stressed by this discourse is the definition of education as the solution for the capitalist crises. If "we" prepare the students for the increasingly competitive new capitalism, "we" will be better prepared to excel in the globalized market, says the dominant educational rhetoric. Education is stressed as a targeted sphere for transformation in this hegemonic discourse.

In the hegemonic discourse the emphasis on education is related to the will to colonize this space and produce an educational environment more in tune with the economic needs of the market. But when this global process and its mediation through federal policies reach Porto Alegre, contradictions are created and a process of rearticulation is forged. If it is true that the hegemonic discourse tries to colonize the educational sphere, it is also true that it creates unintended spaces for alternative experiences, because the common sense idea that education will solve the problems of the country allows real investment in education. The Popular Administration uses this space to prioritize education in a country where education for the poor has been neglected. Once the space is occupied by the rhetoric calling for more investment in education, the Citizen School can deploy its alternative project, with its realignment of priorities, and invest in a transformative project of education for the excluded. The Popular Administration can also start to recuperate and, at the same time, reinvent concepts such as "autonomy," "decentralization," and "collaboration," currently rearticulated by neoliberals. These concepts had a completely different meaning in the popular movements in Brazil and now have to be disarticulated from neoliberal discourse and rearticulated to the Citizen School project.

Taking advantage of the hegemonic decentralization discourse expressed in Brazilian educational policy in the early 1990s, the Popular Administration was able to construct a system that does not have to follow any federal curricular directives and can be structured in cycles of formation, an option anticipated in the educational law. While the governments of other state capitals were only complaining about the neoliberal effects of decentralization that were giving them more responsibility without more resources, the Workers' Party in Porto Alegre, while strongly protesting at the lack of resources, explored every aspect of the decentralization proposals and used them to construct a real alternative. Rather than performing only the minimum that the federal legislation demanded from municipal systems, Porto Alegre created a democratic Municipal Council for Education, able autonomously to regulate education in Porto Alegre and to explore every possibility that the law allowed to construct an alternative school structure and an alternative curriculum.

This does not mean that the battle has been won by the Popular Administration. New articulations are forged by the hegemonic groups and education remains a site of struggle. But the important point is that no hegemonic action can block all spaces simultaneously, and even its own discourse can be rearticulated to favor counter-hegemonic purposes. And that is what the Citizen School project has done.

Nonetheless, no progressive policy can be a real alternative without changing the structures that discourage and impede the implementation of the new project. It is necessary to evaluate whether the Citizen School is able to construct a different structure, one that acts both as a stimulant for the intended change and as a real example of the alternative in action, a reality that can work as an anchor for new experiences. This is what I will do in the next section.

THE CITIZEN SCHOOL PROJECT

Historically, as a rule, schools in Brazil have had little autonomy. In the majority of states and cities, there are no elections for the city or state council of education (traditionally a bureaucratic structure, with members appointed by the executive), let alone for principals/head teachers in schools. The curriculum is usually defined by the secretariats of education of the cities and states. The resources are administered in the centralized state agencies; schools usually have very little or no financial autonomy.

Although Brazil has recently achieved a very high level of initial access to schools, the indexes of failures and dropouts are frightening. This reality is where the central purpose of the Citizen School, and the entire educational project of the Popular Administration, begins. It represents a sharp contrast with the policies that produced such indexes. The field of education has become central to the Popular Administration's project of constructing new relations between state, schools and communities. The Citizen School is organically linked to and considered a major part of the larger process of transforming the whole city.

The municipal schools of Porto Alegre are all situated in the most impoverished neighborhoods of the city—in *favelas*. This is because the expansion of the system occurred recently (since the Popular Administration took office in 1989), and the schools were built in the zones where there was a clear deficit of educational opportunities.

The Citizen School project was constructed explicitly as an alternative to the marketization ideology around education, and it is clear that the notion of citizenship is used overtly as a way of opposing the process that views knowledge as a commodity. The Citizen School wants to create citizens and not mere consumers. According to the Municipal Secretariat of Education (SMED), citizens are the ones that have the material goods necessary for survival, symbolic goods necessary for their subjectivity, and political goods necessary for their social existence (Azevedo, 1999, p. 16).

In order to construct the principles that would guide the actions of the Citizen School, a democratic, deliberative and participatory forum was created in the form of a Constituent Assembly. This project was constituted through a long process of mobilization of the school communities (using the invaluable lessons learned in the mobilization for the Participatory Budgeting), and it had the goal of generating the principles that would guide the policy for the municipal schools in Porto Alegre.

The process of organization of the Constituent Assembly took a good deal of time. The whole process started in March of 1994, lasted 18 months, and involved thematic meetings in the schools, regional meetings, the Assembly itself, and the elaboration of the schools' internal regulation. The themes that guided the discussion were school governance, curriculum, principles for living together and evaluation.

The Constituent Assembly decided on the radical democratization of the education in the municipal schools as the main normative goal of the Citizen School project. This radical democratization would have to occur in three dimensions: democratization of access to school, democratization of knowledge and democratization of governance. These three principles would be the ones guiding every action in the municipal system of Porto Alegre. These three principles changed the structure of the schools and the relationship between schools and the SMED. I now examine these changes.

DEMOCRATIZATION OF ACCESS TO SCHOOLS

If the schools were to have an impact on the lives of the children living on the most impoverished neighborhoods of Porto Alegre—where the municipal schools are situated—the initial access to schools had to be a priority. For the Popular Administration, guaranteeing this access was, therefore, the first step to promote social justice to communities historically excluded from social goods.

Granting access to all children in school age is not as easy as it might sound. Historically, Brazil has had an enormous number of children who did not attend school. National statistics show that this has been changing rapidly, but in 1991, when the Popular Administration was just starting, and even in 1994, when the Citizen School project had only been in existence for one year, the situation was grave in terms of initial access to schooling. Almost 17% of the Brazilian children in school age were not being formally educated in 1991 and in 1994 this number dropped to almost 13%.

This was a central preoccupation for the Popular Administration and the SMED, and the definition of democratization of access to schooling as one of the central priorities is a proof of it. The SMED invested in building more schools and increasing the number of teachers prepared to work on these schools.

When the Workers' Party was elected in 1988, the city of Porto Alegre had only 19 K8 schools ("fundamental education," as it is called in Brazil, that is to say, schooling for those between ages 6 and 14), with 14,838 students and 1,698 teachers, curriculum coordinators, and educational supervisors. Under the Popular Administration the number of students grew at a remarkable rate. Between 1988 and 2000, the number of students in fundamental education increased by 232%. This number shows how profound the impact of the actions of the SMED has been in Porto Alegre and, although the comparison is not between equal circumstances, it is worth pointing out that between 1991 and 1998 the number of school-age children in Brazil increased by only 22.3% (INEP, 2000, p. 53).

The number of fundamental education schools increased by 126% under the Popular Administration government (and if we consider all the schools under the municipal government—including the schools geared towards early childhood, adolescents and young adults, and special education—the increase rate is actually 210%). It is important to point out that these schools were all constructed in very impoverished areas of the city and that the majority of new schools were actually built inside or around *favelas*. This means that the schools are not only bringing back students who drop out of state schools, but they are also creating a space for many children who never attended school and possibly never would have were it not for the new municipal schools.

But guaranteeing initial access to school does not guarantee that these children will benefit from school. In order to really democratize the access to schools, in 1995 the SMED started to propose a new organization for the municipal schools. Instead of keeping the traditional structure of grades with the duration of one year (first to eighth in the fundamental education), the idea was to adopt a new structure called Cycles of Formation. It is important to note that the idea of reorganizing the curriculum and the space time of the schools in cycles instead of grades does not originate from Porto Alegre. What the Citizen School was implementing was not new per se, but a new configuration that, according to the SMED, would offer a substantially better opportunity for dealing with the need for democratization of access and knowledge.

The administrators at the Secretariat were convinced that the issue of access to schools could be dealt with in a much better way using cycles. According to the SMED, "the cycle structure offers a better way of dealing seriously with student failure, because its educational perspective respects, understands, and investigates the socio-cognitive processes that the students go through" (SMED, 1999a, p. 11). The idea is that by using a different conception of the equation learning/time, the Citizen School would not punish students for allegedly being "slow" in their process of learning. In this new configuration, the traditional deadline—the end of each academic year—when the students had to "prove" that they had "learned," was eliminated in favor of a different time organization. The establishment of the cycles is a conscious attempt to eliminate the mechanisms in schools that perpetuate exclusion, failure and dropouts, as well as the blaming of the victim that accompanies these.

The schools now have three cycles of three years each, something that adds one year to the elementary and middle education (one year of early childhood education inside the schools, expanding elementary and middle education to nine years). This makes the municipal schools responsible for the education of kids from 6 to 14 years old. The three cycles are organized based on the cycles of life: each one corresponds to one phase of development, that is, childhood, pre-adolescence and adolescence. The idea is to group together students of the same age in each of the years of the three cycles. This aims at changing the reality in the majority of public schools that cater to popular classes in Brazil and the one the SMED was faced with when the Popular Administration started to govern the city: Students with multiple failures inside classrooms intended for much younger children. By having students of the same age in the same year of the cycle, the SMED claims to remotivate the kids who have failed multiple times.

In the schools using these cycles, students progress from one year to another within one cycle; the notion of "failure" is eliminated. Despite this victory, the SMED understood that the elimination of mechanisms of exclusion was not enough to achieve the goal of democratization of knowledge. Because of this, the Citizen School created several mechanisms that aim at guaranteeing the inclusion of students. It established Progression Groups for the students that have discrepancies between their age and what they have learned. The idea is to provide these students who have experienced multiple failures in the past with a stimulating and challenging environment where they can learn at their own pace and fill the gaps in their academic formation that exist because of the multiple failures they experienced. Furthermore, the Progression Groups are also a space for the students who come from other school systems (from other city or state schools, for example) and have experienced multiple failures to be given more close attention so that they are ultimately integrated into the cycles, according to their age. The idea here is that the school has to change its structure to adapt to the students, and not the reverse, which has been historically the case (Souza et al., 1999, pp. 24–25).

This idea of constructing a new structure to better respond to students needs led to the creation of another entity: the Learning Laboratory. This is a space where students with more serious learning problems get individual attention, but also a place where teachers conduct research in order to improve the quality of the regular classes. For the students with special needs, there are the Integration and Resources Rooms, which "are specially designed spaces to investigate and assist students who have special needs and require complementary and specific pedagogic work for their integration and for overcoming their learning difficulties" (SMED, 1999a, p. 50)

With all these mechanisms, the Citizen School project not only grants initial access, but also guarantees that the educational space occupied by the subaltern children is a space that treats them with the dignity, respect, and quality necessary to keep them in the school and educate them to be real citizens.

DEMOCRATIZATION OF KNOWLEDGE

Curriculum transformation is a crucial part of Porto Alegre's project to build active citizenship. It is important to say that this dimension is not limited to access to traditional knowledge. What is being constructed is a new epistemological understanding about what counts as knowledge as well. It is not based on a mere incorporation of new knowledge within the margins of an intact "core of humankind's wisdom," but a radical transformation. The Citizen School project goes beyond the mere episodic mentioning of cultural manifestations or class, racial, sexual and gender-based oppression. It includes these themes as an essential part of the process of construction of knowledge.

In the Citizen School project, the notion of "core" and "periphery" in knowledge is made problematic. The starting point for the construction of curricular knowledge is the culture(s) of the communities themselves, not only in terms of content, but in terms of perspective as well. The whole educational process is aimed at inverting previous priorities and instead serving the historically oppressed and excluded groups. The starting point for this new process of knowledge construction is the idea of Thematic Complexes. This organization of the curriculum is a way of having the whole school working on a central generative theme, from which the disciplines and areas of knowledge, in an interdisciplinary effort, will structure the focus of their content.

The schools are encouraged to follow steps for the construction of the thematic complex and for the translation of the macro discussions into curriculum. These steps involve acknowledging and studying the context where the school is situated, through participatory research conducted by the school collective in the community, selecting statements gathered in the research that are significant and representative of the aspirations, interests, conceptions, and cultures of the community, and elaborating principles that can guide the curriculum building process in the school.

The thematic complex provides the whole school with a central focus that guides the curriculum of that school for a period of time that can be one semester or an entire academic year. After having determined the principles, the larger contribution of each knowledge area for the discussion of the thematic complex, and the conceptual matrix—a web of concepts from the knowledge area, rather than isolated facts or information that the teachers understand are essential to use when dealing with the thematic complex—the teachers have meetings organized by their knowledge areas and by each year in the cycles, to elaborate and plan the curriculum. Teachers have to "study" their own knowledge areas and elect the concepts that would help to problematize the thematic complex. They also have to work collectively with teachers of other areas in order to assemble a curriculum that is integrated and dense enough to simultaneously address the issues listed in the thematic complex.

According to one of the "creators" of this conceptualization, in the context of the Citizen School project, "the thematic complex brings about the perception and comprehension of the reality and makes explicit the worldview that all the ones involved in the process have" (Rocha as cited in SMED, 1999a, p. 21). Because the thematic complex is closely related to social problems, the process makes teachers search for the relation of their discipline to social reality as a whole. Finally, because the starting point for the thematic complex is popular knowledge or common sense, teachers are also forced to think about the relation between official knowledge and this common sense. Therefore, this approach deals simultaneously with three problems of traditional education: the fragmentation of knowledge, the "apparent" neutrality of school content and the absolute supremacy that traditional schools grant to scientific/erudite knowledge over local knowledge of the communities, especially very impoverished ones—as is the case in Porto Alegre.

The Citizen School project conceives the organization of the curriculum around a thematic complex not only as a form of generating alternative knowledge inside the curriculum, but also as a form of political intervention.

> To teach using thematic complexes not only generates the possibility of selecting knowledge that is significant to students but also presents us with the perspective of having a tool for analysis that can help students to organize the world they live in, so that they can understand it and act upon it through a critical, conscious, and collective social practice. (Goroditch & Souza, 1999, p. 78)

The traditional rigid disciplinary structure is broken and general interdisciplinary areas are created. These areas of study are given the names of social expression, biological, chemical and physical sciences, socio-historic and logic-mathematical.

To give a concrete example of how this works, I now describe how the socio-historic knowledge area proceeded, in one school of Porto Alegre, to organize its curriculum. After the phase of carrying out research in the community, the school elected "the quality of life in the *favela*" as its thematic complex. The socio-historic knowledge area had to construct the principle of that area, that is, the contribution of this area to deal with the elected thematic complex. This area expressed its possible contribution as "the individual and collective transformation of the citizen, in his/her time and space, recuperating his/her origins, aiming at improving the quality of life, taking into account the ideas of the community where this individual is situated." (SMED, 1996b)

From the major thematic complex—the quality of life—three sub-themes were listed by the teachers in the socio-historic area: rural exodus, social organization and property. In the rural exodus sub-theme, the issues reflected the origin of the community—living now in a *favela,* but originally from the rural areas. This is a common story in the *favelas* where people who had nothing in the rural areas came to the cities only to find more exclusion. In this sub-theme, the issues discussed were migration movements, overpopulation of the cities, "disqualification" of the working force, and marginalization. In the sub-theme social organization, the issues were distributed in terms of temporal, political, spatial and socio-cultural relations. The issues, again, represent important questions in the organization of the community: the excessive and uncritical pragmatism of some in the neighborhood associations, and cultural issues such as religiosity, body expression, African origins, dance groups and samba schools. In the third sub-theme—property—the issues were directly linked to the situation of the families in the favela, living in illegal lots with no title, having to cope with the lack of running water, basic sanitation and other infrastructure problems, the history of this situation and of the struggles for lots legalization, and their rights (of having basic public goods in the neighborhood) and duties (of understanding the importance and the social function of taxation) as citizens.

This example shows the real transformation that is occurring in the curriculum of the schools in Porto Alegre. The students are not studying history or social and cultural studies through books that never address the real problems and interests they have. Through the organization in thematic complexes, the students learn history by beginning with the historical experience of their families. They study important social and cultural content by focusing on and valorizing their own cultural manifestations. It is important to note that these students will ultimately still learn the history of Brazil and the world, including "high" culture, but these will be seen through different lenses. Their culture will not be forgotten in order for them to learn "high status" culture. Rather, by understanding their situation and their culture and valuing it, these students will be able to simultaneously learn and will have the chance to transform their situation of exclusion. By studying the problems (rural exodus, living in illegal lots, etc.) and not stopping there, but studying the strengths of self-organization (in neighborhood associations and in cultural activities and groups), the Citizen School helps to construct alternatives for the communities living in terrible conditions.

This shift of what is considered the core or the center of knowledge affects not only the pedagogical conception that guides the daily life in the classrooms; it also transforms how the school itself functions as a whole. This conception of knowledge now is spreading throughout the entire school system. The project not only serves the "excluded" by generating a different formal education for students, but also serves them by creating an innovative structure that makes it possible for the community of those who have historically been excluded to regain their dignity (both material and symbolic).

DEMOCRATIZATION OF GOVERNANCE

The first mechanism that guarantees the democratization of governance is the Constituent Assembly and the Congresses of Education. They not only provide a space to decide on the administration of the project, but also allow for real participation in the definition of the goals of the Citizen School.

Among the mechanisms created to democratize the governance of the educational system in Porto Alegre, the School Council is a central element. Its role is to promote the democratization of the decision-making process and governance in education in Porto Alegre. A product of the political will of the Popular Administration and the demands of social movements involved in education in the city, the school councils, established by a municipal law in December of 1992 and implemented in 1993, are the most important institutions in the schools. They are formed by elected teachers, school staff, parents, students, and by one member of the administration, and they have consultative, deliberative and monitoring functions.

The task of the school council is to deliberate about the global projects for the school, the basic principles of administration, to allocate economic resources, and to monitor the implementation of the decisions. The principal and her/his team are responsible for the implementation of these policies defined by the school council.

In terms of resources, it is important to say that, before the Popular Administration took office, there was a practice (common in Brazil) of a centralized budget. Every expense (even the daily ones) had to be sent to the central administration before it was approved, and then, the money was sent to the school, or a central agency would purchase the product or the service necessary. In such a system, the school council would have "their hands tied," with no autonomy at all. The SMED changed this structure and established a new policy to make the amount of money available to each school every three months. According to the SMED, this was the measure that instituted the financial autonomy of the schools, which allowed the schools to manage their expenditures according to the goals and priorities established by the school council. At the same time that it creates autonomy, this measure gives parents, students, teachers, and staff who are present in the council a notion of social responsibility in administering public money, and it teaches them to hierarchize the investments with solidarity in mind (SMED, 1999b).

The school council also has the power to monitor the implementation, through the principal and her/his team, of its decisions (SMED, 1993, p. 3). In fact, the school council is an empowered structure in the schools. It is the main governance mechanism inside the schools, and its limitations are only the legislation and the policy for education collectively constructed in democratic fora. Decisions about the curriculum can be part of the deliberation, and the inclusion of parents, students and staff (or even teachers, if we consider the traditional school) in this process is a great innovation of the model.

Along with the school council, another structure guarantees democratic spaces in the Citizen School: In the municipal schools of Porto Alegre, the whole school community elects the principal by direct vote. The one responsible for the implementation of the decisions of the school council, that is, the principal, is her/himself elected defending a particular project of administration for the school. There is a legitimacy that comes from this fact. The principal is not someone that necessarily represents the interests of the central administration inside the school councils, but someone with a majority of supporters inside that particular educational community. Principals have a great degree of embeddedness and, because of this the SMED feels that it is possible to avoid the potential problem of having someone responsible for the concretization of the deliberations occurring in the school councils who is not connected with the project. But the responsibility of the community does not stop there: through the school council, the school community has a way of monitoring the activities of the principal and holding her/him responsible for implementing its democratic decisions.

The direct election of the one responsible to implement the directives created by the school council, also elected directly by the school community, represents a mechanism that aims at generating the principle of democratic management at the local level of the school.

ASSESSING THE SUCCESS OF THE NEW EDUCATIONAL STRUCTURES

The democratization of access is certainly an important aspect of the Citizen School project and the SMED was able to advance substantially on this area. The SMED knew that it would have to attack the problem of dropouts if it really wanted to democratize access to schools. The SMED recognized that the dropout problem is not an accident, but something structural in the society, as pointed out by Apple (1996, p. 90). By drastically reducing the number of students who abandon school and therefore dramatically increasing their chances of having better opportunities, the Citizen School project attacks a central problem. The students who stay in school are able to experience the alternative educational program designed by the Citizen School and will be able to learn about and, it is hoped, fight against the circumstances that led so many of them to drop out of school in the first place. The data speaks for itself: The dropout rate fell from more than 9% in 1989 to around 1% in 2003 (SMED, 2003).

Together with the cycles, another practice that has served to radically reduce dropouts is the close monitoring of student attendance. By employing an aggressive policy of visiting the homes of the parents of students who fail to show up at school after a number of days and explaining to them how harmful it is to their children not to attend school, the Citizen School was able to reduce the dropout rate significantly. Involving the whole community and the neighborhood associations in this monitoring has been another successful strategy. In fact, the drastic reduction of dropouts appears also to be related to the involvement of the communities with the school.

The "care" that the communities dedicate to the schools is readily apparent as well. While state schools are constantly damaged, robbed, and vandalized, the municipal schools are usually not targeted in this manner. The schools do not have any significant problems, and even the older ones are in very good shape. This is not something to be taken for granted. All over the country, and even in the state schools in Porto Alegre, there are complaints from teachers, students and parents about the material conditions.

By valuing teachers, changing the whole environment of the schools, involving the community with the school as a public institution, and insisting that every student counts, the Citizen School project clearly attained its goal of democratizing access to school. In doing so, the Citizen School made possible a level of access to public benefits that are not usually available to students of public schools in Brazil. The numbers show this clearly: The numbers of students tripled from 1989 to 2000.

In order to evaluate the degree by which the project has succeeded in democratizing knowledge, several elements must be examined. One of these elements is the organization of the school in cycles of formation rather than traditional grades. As I showed before, there is a political conception of knowledge and learning behind the choice of radically changing the organization of the schools. The SMED has been investing heavily in teacher education and teacher salaries in order to make sure the priority of education in its schools is the learning process of the students. The elimination of repetition is only one of many measures, integrated in a whole new conception of schooling that involves a deep discussion of what is valued as knowledge and what is *real* democratization. Therefore, the lack of repetition does not mean the lack of evaluation and monitoring of the learning process of the students.

There is, nevertheless, another mechanism created by the SMED that is directly connected with the democratization of knowledge: the thematic complex. The thematic complex is a methodological technique constructed in order to deal with a serious challenge. The problem that the Citizen School project creators were faced with was how simultaneously to value and work with the knowledge and culture of the community and to make the accumulated body of human knowledge available and accessible to the students. The question did not exactly end there, because the Citizen School project also wanted to help students (and teachers) to construct new knowledge in the process of dialog between and problematization of local and official knowledge. For the Citizen School project, only knowledge that is emancipatory—that is, that helps the students to establish relations between phenomena, between their own lives and the larger social context—is knowledge worth pursuing in schools.

Nevertheless, the Citizen School project does not claim that the schools should abandon traditional school knowledge. The creators of the Citizen School project know that this knowledge is absolutely necessary for the advancement of the students in the school system. They also insist that the students who attend the municipal schools should not be denied the "accumulated knowledge of humankind." There are several educational programs for poor students that end up offering them a "poor" education, claiming that they will not need better education because they will end up in jobs that only require basic skills. This is something that the Citizen School strongly fights against in its programs with teachers. It is necessary to break with the dominant cultural models that say that students who live in *favelas* have deficits because they are poor (Paes da Silva & Vasconcelos, 1997).

While insisting that students from the *favelas* should have access to the same quality of education that wealthier students have in Brazil (and, as I described above, the material conditions that the schools offer for these students are in fact similar to the ones that some lower middle-class students have in some of the private schools), the Citizen School also wants to problematize the notion that the knowledge offered to these students should not be scrutinized and criticized. Any kind of knowledge should always be submitted to criticism. This can be better understood by Santos' notion of "double epistemological rupture." Santos (1989) claims that

> the double epistemological rupture represents a work of transforming both common sense and science. While the first rupture is essential to the constitution of science—something that does not change common sense as it was before science—the second rupture transforms common sense based on science. With this double rupture the goal is to achieve an enlightened common sense and a prudent science . . . , a configuration of knowledge that being practical is still enlightened and being wise is still democratically distributed. (p. 54)

This is a notion that can help the municipal schools in Porto Alegre to use traditional school knowledge with the students but not simply teach it as if it were neutral. Santos and Freire contribute to the understanding of the need to be critical of such knowledge and not act as if there were some "stock of knowledge out there, not problematic at all, about which there is a general accord" (Silva & McLaren, 1993, p. 43).

The epistemological rupture that plays such a major role in the Citizen School is a sign that the project is being successful in the construction of a real progressive alternative in education. The challenge to what counts as knowledge, to what counts as core and periphery, represents the essence of the democratization of knowledge. Instead of creating isolated multicultural programs or content that has little efficacy in the context of a largely dominant whole structure, the Citizen School project has been creating a structure, with popular participation, in which the question of diversity of cultures has space to flourish. The Citizen School has created spaces where multicultural practices are organically integrated, not merely added superficially to a bureaucratically determined structure that is averse to "difference." To construct a powerful and democratic set of multicultural experiences, the whole institutional structure was changed.

In this sense, the Citizen School advances in relation to the "mainstream" notion of multiculturalism. In fact, "multiculturalism is too easily depoliticized" (Pagenhart, 1994, p.178). It is exactly this depoliticization that the Popular Administration wants to avoid. The project seems perfectly to fit what Giroux (1995) calls an "insurgent multiculturalism," one where "all participants play a formative role in crucial decisions about what is taught, who is hired, and how the school can become a laboratory for learning that nurtures critical citizenship and civic courage" (pp. 340–341).

In terms of the democratization of governance, the constituent assembly is a core element. The major policy directives formulated by the SMED derive from this assembly. This marks a significant departure from the traditional model, in which decisions are handed down from above while implementation is left to the schools. Through their elected delegates, schools and their communities are actively involved in the construction of the major educational policies in Porto Alegre. This is a unique aspect of the Citizen School project. Fung (1999), who studied the Local Schools Council in Chicago and classified them as highly positive, nevertheless suggests that "centralized interventions, themselves formulated through deliberation, would then further enhance the deliberative, participatory, and empowered character of otherwise isolated local actions" (p. 26). This combination, suggested by Fung as ideal, is exactly what has been achieved in Porto Alegre.

Another important element to emphasize is that the experience in Porto Alegre has been serving as a viable alternative to the neoliberal market-based solutions for management and monitoring of the quality of public schools in Brazil. Involvement of the parents and of the students in important decisions and active monitoring in the school (not merely peripheral decisions) gives them a real sense of what "public" means in public school. At the same time, because the SMED has been able to involve teachers actively in the transformations—as well as to help improve their qualifications and their salaries—instead of merely blaming them and their unions for the problems in education (common practice in the neoliberal driven reforms), the Popular Administration has been able to include every segment of the schools in the collective project of constructing a quality education in the impoverished neighborhoods where the municipal schools are situated. Thus, instead of opting for a doctrine that merely treats the parents as consumers of education (treated itself as a commodity), the Citizen School became an alternative that challenges this idea. Parents, students, teachers, staff and administrators are responsible for working collectively, each contributing their knowledge and expertise, to create better education. In this way, the Citizen School has defined itself as a concrete and effective alternative to the market logic that offers only competition and "exit" as solutions.

In the Citizen School project the active involvement of the community in the schools represents a mechanism to guarantee a better performance of the school and to hold teachers and administrators accountable to the parents. The school council, with its powers to deliberate, regulate and monitor together with the Congresses of Education, where the rules are constructed, represents a mechanism that can generate schools that offer a better quality of education.

As I have shown above, the Citizen School truly has been a project for the excluded. Not only students, however, have been benefiting from the quality education they receive. Parents, students and school staff, usually mere spectators of the processes in the traditional school, are now part of the structure of governance inside the school council and bring their knowledge "to the table." In fact, the whole process challenges the cultural model that says that poor and "uneducated" people should not participate because they do not know how to do so.

SOME CONTRADICTIONS AND POTENTIAL PROBLEMS

Thus far my evaluation of the experiment in Porto Alegre has been very positive. The project, in fact, has been making real progress in its goals of democratizing the schools and the educational system as a whole. Nevertheless, any project that tries to accomplish such a large range of innovations as the Citizen School does will inevitably face challenges and certainly will have contradictions. As Hargreaves (1997) says, "restructuring is not an end to our problems but a beginning" (p. 352). This section of the chapter will deal with some of these challenges and contradictions.

A contradiction of the implementation of the project is the role of common sense. I quoted above Santos' (1989) points about the need for a double epistemological rupture, one that deals with the transformation of both common sense and science in the construction of new emancipatory knowledge. This very sophisticated vision does not seem to prevail, nevertheless, among all the senior members and advisers of the SMED.

Analyzing documents and the texts of interviews, I was able to identify a discourse that stresses the need of replacing common sense with more politicized or critical thought. The words used by many SMED people in the interviews were "overcome," "question" and "challenge" when talking about common sense. These statements suggest a discourse that is not informed by the insights of Santos. They presuppose the encounter of a discourse that already "overcame" common sense (that of the teachers) with a discourse that still operates within the boundaries of common sense (among members of the community). But teachers, according to these members of the SMED, might also be operating from the standpoint of common sense. As one senior member of the SMED, still talking about the construction of the thematic complex, said: "the problem is that many times rather than questioning and challenging the common sense of the community, teachers actually agree with it." (personal communication) The rationale here is something like this: "How can teachers agree with the statements of the community? How can they participate in this distorted vision?"

Such words, used by members of the SMED, emphasize the negative connotation of common sense and suggest that it needs to be replaced by a more enlightened and critical view. The use of these terms actually indicates that the speakers are operating within a discourse based on the Marxist tradition of defining ideology as "false consciousness." This is *one* tradition within Marxism, one that does not represent the whole body of Marxist thought.

The contributions of Gramsci (1997), Hall (1996) and Apple (1996) have stressed the need to see common sense as practical knowledge and to understand the good sense in it. Nevertheless, the statements of the members of the SMED seem to put them at odds with these contributions.

There is a flagrant contradiction between using the notion of false consciousness to characterize common sense and, at the same time, insisting that one must start from it, connect with it, in order to construct knowledge in the school. If common sense is always filled with false consciousness, why bother starting with it? One could suppose that this would be a valuable exercise for the students to learn how they should *not* think. The problem with this line of reasoning is that it directly contradicts the entire Citizen School project emphasis on the need to use the culture of the students in the learning process. It would make no sense to use the culture of the students only to denounce it as problematic. This would have deleterious consequences rather than being beneficial.

Another potential problem of the Citizen School project is the issue of sustainability. The question to ask is: Is it possible to maintain this mechanism and to generate beneficial results (in the case in question, participatory decision-making) over time?

The problem of sustainability in the case of the Citizen School refers not only to the capacity of continuing to bring people to participate in the mechanisms that were created, but also refers to the quality of participation. If the mechanisms continue to have members of all segments (parents, students, staff and teachers) making decisions while a rigid hierarchy remains among these segments, then the mechanism will not function properly. Because the goal of the Citizen School project is not only to make parents and students participate in the decision-making process, but to do it actively, in a democratic way, the nature of the participation is a fundamental question in the evaluation of the goals of the project. Hence, discussing sustainability in the context of the Citizen School project also involves discussing how to preserve active and engaged participation among all the segments.

In the case of the school councils, there is a serious risk that teachers, who have the technical knowledge of the institution, will dominate the decisions. Some teachers may even feel that this is only natural, because they are the ones who understand educational issues, but this contradicts the goals of the school councils. These sites should be a place where teachers, students, parents and staff learn together how to better manage a school, not only financially but also pedagogically. Apparently this is not yet happening to a full extent in the schools of Porto Alegre and this should certainly be addressed by the administration.

There is certainly a need for attention to the challenges that the schools are faced with. As I stated above, the difficulties and contradictions can jeopardize the whole project if not taken seriously. There is, however, a sign that should be viewed with optimism. In all of the schools there are very active groups of teachers who are critical and who look for better ways to deal with the problems of the proposal and for how to reinvent it in daily life.

The kind of environment that the Citizen School fosters, where critical thought and action are valued as assets, where teachers have spaces to talk and to look for better ways of constructing projects that continue the radical democratization proposed in the first congress of education and the collective of the schools, is something that is now deep-rooted in the schools. The active criticism that the schools have against the SMED and the understanding that conflict should not be suppressed because it is the source of new ideas, are signs that the schools are headed in the right direction; that is, they are producing critical subjects, the critical citizens of which the proposal talks. Because schools are spaces where the proposal is implemented, it will be there, in the interactions of teachers, students, parents and directive teams that these contradictions and problems will have to be faced.

FINAL REMARKS

With schools that dramatically improve access and decrease dropout rates, with a curriculum that challenges what knowledge should be taught, and with democratic governance structures that stimulate participation and community involvement, the Citizen School project can provide a concrete example of alternative to reforms based on the introduction of markets as the ultimate arbiters.

In the municipal schools of Porto Alegre, I encountered teachers with a renewed hope in the possibility of constructing a radically different school from the one they attended. I witnessed teachers actively creating a curriculum for their school through interacting with the communities and meeting regularly at times especially allocated and institutionally guaranteed for dialogue about their methodology and their goals with the specific network of concepts they are developing with their students. Rather than being pressured for a kind of accountability that only looks at test results, these teachers are socially, politically and culturally responsible for providing quality education for their students. Quality in this context is not reduced to accumulation of information, or even ability to establish connections among concepts; it is also linked to the schools' capacity to generate a culturally-embedded curriculum that engages students in creative thinking and, to a certain extent, in actions that could lead to social transformation in the future.

While the world-wide emphasis is on testing, economic accountability and blaming the victims, Porto Alegre is showing that it is possible to create an alternative space, where articulations can be forged and where new common sense around education can be created. It is possible to create a space where children and the community feel connected to the schools, where their voices are not only heard but are crucial to the solutions and therefore feel that the school serves them.

The greatest differential of the Citizen School is the real change in the source of solutions for the problems in education, such as lack of responsiveness of the schools to students and parents or absence of real and meaningful learning. Rather than looking to the market as the model site for positive influence and change, or to expert knowledge as the only foundation for promoting education, the Citizen School project sees community involvement and valorization of local knowledge as the starting points to a transformative learning experience. The solution will not reside on an expert telling the dwellers of the favelas what to do, but on a real dialogue between the so-called popular knowledge and scientific knowledge.

Finally, I end with the words of a teacher in one of the schools:

> The kind of transformation we are doing is not one that can easily be measured by statistical data. We can show the increase in enrolled kids, the sharp reduction in dropouts from the schools, but we cannot easily show data about the radical change in the way teachers, parents, and teachers perceive the role of education and the nature of knowledge. These are not easy quantifiable, especially in reports and in the media that expects numbers.

Perhaps the Citizen School project has to come up with a creative way of constructing new common sense around how we understand and assess successful schools. Rather than using economic accountability as the model, we should be thinking about cultural and social accountability, with inputs from the communities involved in the educational process. If the Citizen School, together with other progressive experiences around the world, could reinvent the way we evaluate quality education, perhaps we could overcome the age of standardized tests and outcome-based evaluation (for an initiative towards this goal, see Pedroni & Gandin, 2006). This would be a crucial contribution for rethinking a rigorous academic education towards social justice.

ACKNOWLEDGMENT

A slightly longer and modified version of this text appeared as Gandin, L. A. (2006). Creating real alternatives to neo-liberal policies in education: The Citizen School Project. In M. W. Apple, & K. Buras (Eds.), *The subaltern speak: Curriculum, power, and educational struggles*. New York: Routledge.

NOTES

1. The terms "core" and "periphery" were coined in the 1960s in the context of the critique of the, then dominant, modernization school of thought. In the "developmentalist" approach, states were seen as independent entities located at various stages along a universal development path. States were thus classified according to a series of descriptive characteristics (Wallerstein 1985). Against this universalizing view of the development process, dependency theorists introduced the concepts of "core" and "periphery"

to highlight the relational nature of countries' position within the world-economy. . . . The development of the core and underdevelopment of the periphery are indeed analyzed as the two sides of a single process of capital accumulation (Souza 1990: 104). The core/periphery hierarchy is seen as "a reproduced feature of the capitalist world-economy rather than simply a lag between developed and less developed countries" (Chase-Dunn 1990: 19). In this view, the world is a system in which core countries' advantage is based on the exploitation of the periphery and any country's gain represents a loss for others. (Peschard, 2005: 2) See also Leher, 2008.
2. More information about this can be found in Molnar (1996, 2006a, 2006b); Gee, Hull, and Lankshear (1996).
3. For more on this discussion on tactics and strategy see Certeau (1984).

REFERENCES

Apple, M. W. (1996). *Cultural politics and education*. New York: Teacher College Press.
Azevedo, J. C. (1999). Escola, Democracia e Cidadania [School, Democracy, and Citizenship]. In C. Simon, D. D. Busetti, E. Viero, & L. W. Ferreira (Eds.). *Escola Cidadã: Trajetórias [Citizen School: Trajectories]*. Porto Alegre, Brazil: Prefeitura Municipal de Porto Alegre - Secretaria Municipal de Educação.
Ball, S. J. (1998). Cidadania Global, consumo e política educacional. [Global Citizenship, consumption, and educational policy] In L. H. Silva (Ed.), *A Escola Cidadã no Contexto da Globalização [The Citizen School in the context of globalization]* (pp. 121–137). Petrópolis, Brazil: Vozes.
Certeau, M. (1984). *The practice of everyday life*. Berkeley: University of California Press.
Fung, A. (1999). *Deliberative democracy, Chicago style*. Unpublished manuscript.
Gee, J. P., Hull, G., & Lankshear, C. (1996). *The new work order: Behind the language of the new capitalism*. Boulder, CO: Westview.
Giroux, H. (1995). Insurgent multiculturalism and the promise of pedagogy. In D. T. Goldberg (Ed.), *Multiculturalism: A critical reader* (pp.325–343). Cambridge, MA: Blackwell.
Goroditch, C., & Souza, M. C. (1999). Complexo Temático. [Thematic Complex] In L. H. Silva (Ed.), *Escola Cidadã: Teoria e prática [Citizen School: theory and practice]*. Petrópolis, Brazil: Vozes.
Gramsci, A. (1997). *Selections from the prison notebooks* [Ed. Hoare, Q. & Smith, G. N.] (Reprint, 1st ed. 1971). New York: International Publishers.
Hall, S. (1996). The problem of ideology: Marxism without guarantees. In Morley, D., & Chen, K. (Eds.), *Stuart Hall — Critical dialogues in cultural studies* (pp. 25–46). London: Routledge.
Hargreaves, A. (1997). Restructuring Restructuring: Postmodernity and the prospects for educational change. In A. H. Halsey, H. Lauder, P. Brown, & A. S. Wells (Eds.), *Education: culture, economy, society* (pp.338–353). Oxford: Oxford University Press.
INEP. (2000). *Education for all: Evaluation of the year 2000*. Brasilia, Brazil: Author.
Leher, R. (2009) Brazilian Education: Dependent Capitalism and the World Bank. In D. Hill and R. Kumar (Eds.) *Global neoliberalism and education and its consequences*. New York: Routledge.
Molnar, A. (1996). *Giving kids the business: The commercialization of America's schools*. Boulder, CO: Westview.

Molnar, A. (2006a) The Commercial Transformation of Public Education. *Journal of Education Policy*, 21, pp. 621–640.

Molnar, A. (2006b) *School Commercialism: from Democratic Ideal to Market Commodity.* New York: Routledge.

Paes da Silva, I. & Vasconcelos, M. (1997). Questões raciais e educação: Um estudo bibliográfico preliminar. [Racial Issues and Education: a preliminary bibliographical study] In S. Kramer (Ed.), *Educação infantil em curso [Early childhood education in motion]* (pp. 38–66). Rio de Janeiro, Brazil: Escola de Professores.

Pagenhart, P. (1994). Queerly defined multiculturalism. In L. Garber (Ed.), *Tilting the tower* (pp.177-185). New York: Routledge.

Pedroni, T. C., & Gandin, L. A. (2006). *Building cosmopolitan solidarity across borders: Educational movements for the dispossessed in Brazil and the United States.* Paper presented at the College and University Faculty Assembly (CUFA) Conference, Washington, DC. November 2006.

Peschard, K. (2005). *Rethinking the semi-periphery: Some conceptual issues.* Retrieved January 15, 2007, from http://www.ualberta.ca/GLOBALISM/pdf/semi-periphery.lnk.pdf

Santos, B. S. (1989). *Introdução a uma ciência pós-moderna [Introduction to a postmodern science].* Porto, Portugal: Afrontamento.

Silva, T. T., & McLaren, P. (1993). Knowledge under siege: The Brazilian debate. In P. McLaren & P. Leonard (Eds.), Paulo Freire: A critical encounter (pp.36-46). New York: Routledge.

SMED (1993). *Projeto Gestão Democrática — Lei Complementar no. 292 [Democratic Governance Project — Bill 292].* Unpublished text.

SMED (1999a). Ciclos de formação – Proposta político-pedagógica da Escola Cidadã [Cycles of Formation — Citizen School's Political-Pedagogical Project]. *Cadernos Pedagogicos*, 9 (1), pp. 1–111.

SMED (1999b). Official homepage of the SMED. Retrieved December 15, 1999, from http://www.portoalegre.rs.gov.br/smed

SMED (2003). Boletim Informativo – Informações Educacionais. [Information Newsletter – Educational Information] Year 6, No. 11. Newsletter

Souza, D. H., Mogetti, E. A., Villani, M., Panichi, M. T. C., Rossetto, R. P., & Huerga, S. M. R. (1999). Turma de progressão e seu significado na escola. [Progression Groups and their meaning in the school]. In S. Rocha, & B. D. Nery (Eds.), *Turma de progressão: a inversão da lógica da exclusão [Progression Groups: avoiding the exclusion logic]* (pp. 22–29). Porto Alegre, Brazil: SMED.

9   Resistance to the GATS

Antoni Verger and Xavier Bonal

INTRODUCTION

Since the World Trade Organization (WTO) was constituted in the year 1995, there have been a constantly increasing number of critics and protests in reaction to the organization and its free trade agreements. One of the main free trade agreements of the WTO is the General Agreement on Trade in Services (GATS). GATS has been strongly condemned by a broad variety of actors (social movements, trade unions, development non-government organizations [NGOs], local governments, public universities, etc.) because of the inclusion of education in its scope. The main criticism of this agreement is that it stipulates the application of regulations for free trade in the education sector—and all other services sectors (Fredriksson, 2004; Hill, 2006; Scherrer, 2007).[1] The GATS also aims to promote the commercialization of educational services through successive rounds of negotiations (Verger, 2008). These negotiations take place on an international scale (basically, in spaces such as the WTO headquarters in Geneva or the WTO Ministerial Conferences). It means that, as we shall see, many of the struggles and other kind of reactions against WTO and GATS are of a similarly global nature. However, key decisions over the GATS are being taken at the state level (Vlk et al, 2008) and consequently, initiatives for resistance are also being also developed in local and national spaces.

In this chapter, we shall be looking into the causes and motives for these reactions against the GATS (specifically, we will focus on the critical interpretations of GATS and its main effects on the education field), the main organizations that have risen up against the GATS and the commercialization of public assets that it involves, and the initiatives for resistance that have taken place (what social movements analysts call action repertories). Finally, we will analyze the impact of these initiatives on the process of negotiating the agreement and the functioning of the WTO itself. To make it, we will distinguish three impact dimensions: substantive, procedural and symbolic.[2]

THE REASONS FOR THE STRUGGLE: FOCUS
ON THE MEANING REPERTORIES

Any response initiative is based on challenging the dominant ideologies and influencing public opinion, the media and certain elite groups (McAdam, 1998). In many cases, these actions are constructed collectively in platforms for debate. In terms of the struggle against the inclusion of public services in the GATS the process of defining meanings takes place in such stable arenas as social forums and local authority forums.[3] It should be said that this process involves the contributions of a highly extensive epistemic community, with the participation, among others, of committed academics and militants/activists dedicated to research. The involvement of these experts contributes to the interpretation of the legal language, so often complex and ambiguous, that predominates in the text of the agreement, as well as in the analysis of its impacts.[4] Their work contributes to placing certain issues in the public eye, as well as enabling activist nucleuses to know better the opponent, and to guide, legitimize and develop the struggle.

We shall now explore the main repertories and frames of meaning[5] that have been constructed in opposition to the inclusion of education in the GATS. The analysis of frames of meaning enables us to touch upon the subject of the articulation of the discourse of the protest and the meanings shared by its participants, and also those on which there are divergences (Hunt, Benford, and Snow, 1994). These divergences normally relate to the extent to which the reality is interpreted.[6]

For purposes of the analysis, we distinguish between two dimensions of the meaning frames, the *explicative* and the *predictive*. Explicative frames are focused on the identification of a problem and an understanding of it. Sometimes, those explanations aim to convince the public that the adversities are not arbitrary, and injustices are not natural phenomena, but rather that they are the result of the actions of specific agents or a certain system of rules. So, the aim is to identify the causes and factors responsible for a problem, to attribute intention to its actions, and to demonstrate that its particular interests contradict common good. Meanwhile, the predictive dimension involves those repertories aimed at possible or desirable social change and which, therefore, reflect upon the effect and raison d'être of social mobilization.

Explicative Frames

The aim of GATS, like other WTO agreements, is to promote greater quotas of freedom for trade on a worldwide scale and therefore facilitate the economic activity (foreign investment and export operations) of business groups. Protest initiatives against the GATS consider that the agreement is there to serve the interests of large multinational firms, many of which, through their pressure groups, have a large capacity to influencing on WTO negotiations (Wesselius, 2002). Different organizations consider that the synergies between the private business sector and the WTO break the rules of democratic fair play (Rikowski, 2003; Sinclair, 2000).

As for the problem of including the education sector in the GATS, these are some of the most common interpretative repertories on the tongues of social movements and other agents:[7]

1. *Violation of educational sovereignty:* As a result of any commitments a government makes within the framework of GATS, public administration loses its capacity to control and plan its educational systems. GATS involves major changes in the domestic regulation of the education sector in such a way that those governments that submit their education sectors to the agreement lose their sovereignty over the establishment of education policies.
2. *Extension of the education market:* GATS promotes the liberalization of the education sector, the protection of educational activity of business and the introduction of greater amounts of competition. In this sense, it favors the notion that the market, rather than the state, should respond to the increasing demand for education.
3. *Commercialization of a social right and educational inequality:* The concept of education as a social right is incompatible with the concept of it as a commodity. GATS aims to subject the supply of education to free trade rules. It therefore contributes to students' access to education being conditioned by their purchasing capacity, which has a negative effect on educational equality and equal educational opportunities.
4. *Educational quality:* GATS does not deal with issues related to the standards of educational quality, meaning it facilitates the presence of low-quality education suppliers, whose activities are based more on profit than on the educational *ethos*. Moreover, according to the GATS regulations, certain standards of educational quality could be considered barriers to free trade and should be eliminated.
5. *Employment rights:* Any liberalization process (in the education sector too) risks a reduction in the power of trade unions, as well as the introduction of greater quotas of labor deregulation and flexibilization.
6. *Cultural homogenization:* The less educational service companies modify their curricular packages, and the less they adapt it to the different realities of international students, the greater their profit rates will be. Moreover, in the international education market, English will become an even more hegemonic language as a result of the national origin of the main suppliers of education, but also because the use of one single language will reduce the costs of producing transnational education.
7. *Disadvantages for southern countries:* The effects of GATS could be more serious in poorer countries. In these countries, due to their lack

of competitiveness, the flows of investment and commerce of education are clearly unfavorable. Education centers in southern countries (both private and public) will not only have fewer possibilities for accessing the markets of the north, but may even be displaced by international competition in their own countries.

8. *Brain drain:* GATS makes it easier for qualified professionals to work abroad. Therefore, the agreement promotes the "brain drain" phenomenon by which the countries of the south lose cultural capital and high-level human resources.

In many cases, the diagnosis regarding the inclusion of education in GATS is carried out from profound frames of meaning. In this sense, the diagnosis overlaps with a *master frame of meaning* that suggests that the current economic globalization is the central problem. Consequently, GATS is considered one instrument more for the expansion of capitalism on a global scale and for the institutionalization of neoliberalism. Moreover, different frames of meaning often appear aggregated. Consequently, GATS is related to such global problems as the commodification of social rights and other spheres of life, labor exploitation, privatization and its social costs, free trade and the north–south economic fracture, and so forth.

Predictive Frames

On the prediction level, two dominant repertories are distinguished, one of *partial attribution* and another of a more disruptive nature, or *absolute attribution*.[8] The discourse of partial attribution does not aim to alter the grounds of the agreement. Proposals that follow this logic are focused on the demand for a moratorium in negotiations until independent and reliable evaluations are made, on the revision and modification of specific articles of the agreement, on the introduction of better guarantees in the domestic regulation disciplines, on advances in the safeguard mechanisms, on more democracy in the negotiation process (more consultation with civil society, publication of the demand and offer schedules of member countries, publication of the meetings minutes) and so forth.

However, the repertory for absolute attribution demands that education and other public services be excluded from GATS negotiations. It is proposed that the internationalization of these services be tackled from a different perspective to the commercial one (with a more cultural and cooperative nature). Consequently, there are other platforms that are more adequate than the WTO for dealing with the matter, such as UNESCO itself. Moreover, this latter repertory can be associated to a more profound area that considers the problems of the system of free trade in general (and not just the free trade of educational services) and which suggests alternatives to liberal trade theory based more than anything else, on the people's needs and more solidarity in relationships between nations.

It should be said that one actor could adopt both types of repertory at the same time.[9] That is because they are not incompatible; it is rather than the absolute attribution repertory is more ambitious (in terms of the results proposed) than the partial attribution one.

MAIN ACTORS ON THE BATTLEFIELD

The most opposed positions to the WTO and GATS can be found in the organized civil society sphere. Social movements that criticize the WTO have come together in different campaigns and networks and have channeled their message through a wide range of struggle repertories: local and global, confrontational and negotiable, applying political pressure or influencing public opinion, in the street or lobbying. However, social movements do not hegemonize the field of resistance against GATS. Other actors, such as local governments, public universities and such international organizations as UNESCO have also expressed their rejection and promoted initiatives aimed at neutralizing the effects of GATS on education and public services.

Social Movements

Civil society's protests against WTO and GATS cannot be understood as the sum of discontinued and unconnected campaigns and neither can they be related to the configuration of a new thematic movement like the ecologist or pacifist ones. In many cases, the mobilizations are generated by a new political subject that involves different features with respect to preceding movements. We are referring here to the *movement of movements*. It is a phenomenon of collective action that can be typified as being multidimensional, in the sense that it is the result of the confluence of different agents that had mainly been acting in a disarticulated way; an internal and horizontal way of working typified by operating as a network; being territorially international; generating generally unconventional actions; and offering a radical and global interpretation of the problems being dealt with. The fact that the WTO should be the target of the criticism of so many different sectors has opened up a platform from which many struggles that until then had operated in a fragmented way could be recomposed. These involve the participation of activists from northern and southern countries, and such movements as ecologists, squatters, feminists, unemployed workers, agricultural workers, trade unions, international solidarity organizations, indigenous movements and so forth.

In order to understand the dimension of movements against WTO and GATS they can be located in the *cycle of protest*[10] that began in the mid-1990s and during which the movement of movements was configured. Moreover, the struggle of anti-WTO/GATS movements was intensified as a result of precipitating factors (those which create a feeling of urgency and accelerate mobilizations in favor of the action in such a way that they develop into massive, plural events) such as the Ministerial Conferences (MC) of the WTO.[11] In the countersummits that were held on occasion of the MCs, it can clearly be seen how multidimensional and plural the characteristic collective action of the current cycle of protest is. This recomposition of struggles is also typically of a territorially international nature. So, campaigns against WTO and GATS perceive the scenario for the fight as being the whole planet, because in order to influence an agent that operates globally, the response also needs to take place on a similarly global scale.[12]

The first of the social movements' main acts of protest against the WTO goes back to May 1998 in Geneva, where the organization was holding its second MC. However, the movement against the WTO did not attract much media attention until the Seattle MC, held in November 1999. Between 50,000 and 80,000 people took part in protests those days against the WTO, known as "The Battle of Seattle," which contributed to the non-establishment of an ambitious round of WTO negotiations that were to be called the "millennium round." In the Cancun countersummit, on occasion of the fifth MC, 980 organizations came together (242 more than in Seattle) from 83 different countries. The Cancun MC made it clear just how global the fight against the WTO was when the acts of protest were reproduced in more than 100 countries around the world.[13]

Meanwhile, reactions of social movements to the GATS go back to the Uruguay Round[14] when certain voices opposed the commercialization of services that this round was advocating. However, it was not until the year 2000 (when the first round of negotiations of GATS was implemented, called *GATS2000*) that the first initiatives for opposition and mobilization against the agreement emerged with major continuity or resonance. From then on, different campaigns would emerge, some of which were based around the different sectors affected by GATS. Of these, education has been one those to play a more central role. As a result of that, the threats that GATS implies for education have made their way into the discourse and agendas of propublic education movements, as shown by the final declarations of recent editions of the World Education Forum and other social forums.[15]

Specifically, the organizations that most actively take part in campaigns against the inclusion of education in GATS are teachers unions,[16] student movements and NGOs with a critical view of north–south relations.

Other Actors in the Struggle

The research about social struggles tends to be focused on the activist field. However, it has to be considered that the struggles (although to a different extent) can also be developed by more formalized institutions. The inclusion of education in GATS has generated reactions from other actors, which include the following:

a. *Public universities:* Many universities, rather than opposing the internationalization of education (which they consider a constituent practice of the university system) oppose the commercial approach to the internationalization of education promoted by GATS. For this and other reasons, they have publicly displayed their rejection of GATS on several occasions. For example, in 2001, different associations of public universities, along with other organizations, signed an agreement that said,

> Higher education exists to serve the public interest and is not a "commodity." . . . Our member institutions are committed to reducing obstacles to internationalisation of higher education using conventions and agreements outside of a trade policy regime. This commitment includes, but is not limited to, improving communications, expanding the exchange of information, and developing agreements concerning higher education institutions, programs, degrees or qualifications and quality reviewing practices . . . authority to regulate higher education must remain in the hands of competent bodies as designated by any given country. . . . Nothing in international trade agreements should restrict or limit this authority in any way. (AUCC, ACE, EUA, & CHEA, 2001, p. 1)

The reactions in the university sector have been especially intense in the Latin American region. At the third *Cumbre Iberoamericana de Rectores de Universidades Públicas* (Iberamerican Summit of Public University Rectors, Porto Alegre, April 2002) the *Porto Alegre Letter* was signed in which the rectors expressed their "profound concern about the policies promoted by the WTO, which seem to favour the international commercialisation of education services, as if they were common commodities."(CIRUP, 2002, p.1). This same repudiation of GATS was expressed in the 33rd chancellors meeting of the *Asociación de Universidades del Grupo de Montevideo,* which involves the participation of universities in the countries of the southern cone of Latin America. Meanwhile, such universities as Lima and El Salvador have also issued similar declarations to their governments (UdL, 2002; UdES, 2003).

However, it should be said that another set of universities, both public and private, see more opportunities than threats in GATS. That is the case with the universities grouped in the Universitats 21 consortium. This consortium's objective is to "provide its members with a significant role in the global commercialisation of HE" as "in an international business environment in which an increasingly lucrative global educational market is being developed, a strong, high profile international network of universities has better commercial possibilities."

b. *Local governments:* Several regional and municipal governments, above all from northern countries, have also expressed their rejection to GATS. In this case, the response has been triggered by the fact that GATS stands for an international legal framework to which all local government service policies must be subordinated. In Article I of GATS it is emphasized that the agreement is applied to the measures adopted by member countries that affect the commercialization of services "including those measures adopted by the local governments of member countries" (WTO, 1994, n.p.). The local governments' disagreement is increased by not being able to formally participate in the negotiation of the agreement. This question is yet another indicator that the decentralization of the management of certain services has not been accompanied, on the scale, by cession of political sovereignty.

Left wing local governments consider that another of the main risks of GATS is that it obstructs the implementation of policies for promoting citizen welfare. With respect to this question, in the declaration of the Assembly of European Regions (AER) of November 2004 it is stated that negotiation of GATS should consider

the established values and standards of the European Union, such as human rights, in particular workers' and children's rights, and social and environmental standards, as the Assembly of European Regions does not share the principle of total submission to the global logic of unregulated competition and free trade."(Sussex 2005, pp. 2-3).

c. *United Nations (UN):* Different UN bodies have publicly expressed their concern with respect to GATS. Such is the case with the High Commissioner for Human Rights (HCHR) who warns that the agreement could be incompatible with the application of policies that promote Human Rights (HCHR, 2003). In the field of education, criticisms of GATS have been channeled through UNESCO. Members of their staff have repeatedly expressed their concern about the commercialization of education promoted by GATS. These include the role played by Marco Antonio Rodrigues Dias, the former director of the Higher Education Division of UNESCO, who has become one of the main analysts to denounce the negative effects of GATS on education systems. In fact, he organized the UNESCO World Conference on Higher Education (October 9, 1998, Paris) and its final declaration that had a big impact, states that Higher Education is a public good, as well as warns about the current market-driven reforms on higher education.[18] This declaration has been interpreted as a direct criticism of the GATS rules on the educational field (Rodrigues Dias, 2002, 2002b).

It is important to state that, since it was created, UNESCO has played a gradually decreasing role in the global governance of education. This organization, which works on a very limited budget, finds itself under the shadow of the World Bank (which uses its credits to hegemonize educational cooperation in southern countries) and the OECD (which is the main educational forum in developed countries). The recent insertion of education into the WTO's system of regulations through GATS has worsened this tendency as it makes it difficult for UNESCO to adopt a major role in the internationalization of the education arena. However, UNESCO has reacted to a certain extent, and is promoting (as we shall see in the next point) certain initiatives to make a stand against the rules that the WTO aims to impose upon the fields of education and culture.

ACTION REPERTORIES

The political activity of GATS critics has been manifested in a number of initiatives. Opting for one type of action or another can be a response to ideological or strategic criteria. Also, the type of institution promoting the initiative can widen or limit the scope for action.

  a. *Direct action:* Direct action is a public action, normally collective and planned, which aims to achieve an immediate objective. Direct action, as it takes place in the public arena, is especially efficient for visualizing a problem and transmitting a series of concerns and demands to political elites and to public opinion. This type of action tends to be performed by social movements and can be developed on different levels of conventionality. In other words, it can be more conventional (protest marches, concentrations, etc.) or less (occupying spaces, interrupting the flow of traffic, etc.). More conventional actions need to get a lot of participants together in order to make enough impact. Meanwhile, the less conventional actions, as they are more novel expressions and often more forceful, need less participation in order to achieve certain results.

Both types of action have appeared in the struggles against the WTO. However, a large sector of movements has opted for more destructive and less conventional ones. This question is clearly illustrated by reviewing the actions that took place during the Cancun and the Hong Kong Conferences. In those mobilizations thousands of people tried to interrupt the summit by blocking the ways into the Convention Centers; they also pulled down the metal barriers that protected the negotiators; large multinational department stores were ransacked; groups of farmers blocked the routes of trucks transporting the merchandise of major companies in the food sector; others stripped off naked on Cancun beach and used their bodies to write the words "NO WTO"; Korean farmers and fishers tried to reach the Convention Center by swimming or sailing through Hong Kong's bay. Also, in Cancun and Hong Kong the division was broken between what are usually considered the *inside* and *outside* struggles as a sector of NGOs accredited to the conference promoted direct action within the Convention Center, such as the common exhibition of banners during meetings and press conferences.[19]

As far as we can see, direct actions against WTO are characterized by disruptions and confrontations with authority. However, specific campaigns against GATS rather than direct actions used to be expressed through other repertories such as political pressure and monitoring.

> b. *Political and legal pressure:* The WTO (2004) itself recognizes that the leaders of civil society can be quite efficient when it comes to exerting influence on governments to change their position. In fact, many of the campaigns against GATS aims to influence the outcomes of negotiations by exerting political pressure, providing technical knowledge to delegations (above all to southern countries) or advising them on the most appropriate decisions to make.[20] To do this, experts from civil society organizations meet members of different delegations from the south, publish reports on the impact of the liberalization of trade, organize public meetings and so forth. However, it should be mentioned that it is not only trade unions and human rights organizations that exert pressure on delegations. "Civil society" of business origin also organize their pressure groups, and with many more resources than the former. It is illustrative that in the Cancun MC one hundred lobbyists from humanitarian organizations had to counter the work of 700 lobbyists from the transnational companies that attended the conference.

Political pressure is not only exerted by experts. It can also be popularized through such initiatives as the signing of statements or mass mailing and emailing for transmitting certain demands. So, in reference to GATS different statements have circulated that express the main concerns and proposals with respect to the agreement.[21] These statements are aimed both at WTO delegations and the governments of member countries (ministry of trade, ministry of education, etc.).

Public universities have also been highly active to exert political pressure. Several universities and university associations have demanded their governments to not liberalize the education sector in the framework of GATS negotiations. For example, in the "Carta de Porto Alegre", Iberoamerican chancellors insist that their governments "do not subscribe any commitment on educational matters to the framework of the GATS or the WTO."

Country	GATS Free Zones (and Similar)	Civil Society Implied
France	600 local governments have demanded more transparency in the negotiations and a moratorium in the GATS; some have declared *GATS free zones*, among these the city of Paris.	ATTAC-France
Belgium	171 Flemish communities have signed motions against the GATS and water supply services.	11.11.11
Switzer-land	Geneva and Lausanne are GATS free zones; governments of 15 cantons and 25 communities have presented different motions regarding GATS.	Attac-Switzerland
United Kingdom	26 local governments have signed motions in which they express their concern about the effects of the agreement.	Union and NGO campaigns such as World Development Movement
Austria	280 declarations regarding GATS made by municipalities, including Vienna; these declarations reject greater liberalization of quotas for public services and insist on an immediate moratorium in the negotiations.	Stop GATS Campaign
Italy	The provinces of Genoa and Ferrara as well as such communities as Turin have passed motions against the GATS.	NGO platform and Italian trade unions
Canada	Declaration by the Federation of Canadian Municipalities (represents some 1,000 cities) which is strictly opposed to municipal services being included in the agreement.	Council of Canadians Attac-Quebec
Australia	Declaration by the Australian Local Government Association (represents 700 local governments) that demands that certain service be excluded from the GATS.	Australian Services Union (ASU)
New Zealand	Declaration by the Local Government New Zealand federation that represents the 86 local authorities in the country.	Arena
India	200 Panchayat (local governments) demand of the government a moratorium in negotiations until they have evaluated the impact of the agreement.	Equations, Manthan and Global South
Spain	Declaration against GATS by the Andalusian parliament; city councils in Andalusia, Extremadura and the Basque country have declared themselves GATS free zones.	Attac

Source: (Sussex, 2005)

The same thing occurs with many local governments through the constitution of what are known as GATS free zones. This initiative consists of local governments declaring, in a symbolical way, GATS free zones by passing municipal motions. These motions are presented by social movements from the area or directly by parliamentary groups that form the local council. In different countries, this initiative has managed to generate public debate into the GATS, but most of all it is a measure for pressurizing those governmental authorities that take a direct part in the negotiations of the agreement. For the moment, this proposal and other similar ones have proliferated in several northern countries.

   c. *Public information and monitoring:* Different civil society and local government organizations (such as the AER) focus their work on monitoring GATS negotiations. These organizations monitor the process of negotiating and publishing related information through press releases, internet distribution lists, web sites, news bulletins and so forth. Some of the subjects that receive the greatest attention are progress of agreements in different sectors, corporations that exert pressure in different WTO decision making arenas, bullying to the delegations of southern countries,[22] changes that are introduced to different matters of the GATS text that are already opened (methodology of negotiation, domestic regulation disciplines, etc.)[23]; the public declarations of the delegations of member countries or of the WTO staff, and so forth. One of the last successful campaigns in the framework of this repertoire was organized before the Hong Kong MC. It started when European Union (EU) pushed for changing GATS negotiation rules with the aim of forcing Member Countries to open their services more quickly. But Civil Society uncovered this plan and publicly supported those countries that did not support the proposed change.[24]

With respect to the education sector, it is of particular importance the monitoring undertaken by *Education International,* which is spread through the "GATS Update" and "TradEducation News" bulletins.

   d. *Creation of global legal frameworks:* The struggle against free trade agreements can also involve the legal environment. In this sense, some organizations claim that the Universal Declaration of Human Rights, Civil and Political Rights pacts, Economic, Social and Cultural pacts and other international human rights and environmental agreements are imperative regulations that cannot be violated by free trade agreements like GATS (Teitelbaum, 2004).[25] But many governments constantly violate the cited declarations and mechanisms to ensure compliance with their content are non-existent or inefficient. However, most free trade agreements and the WTO itself contain mechanisms to ensure that members comply with the acquired commitments. If they do not respect them they face major economic and commercial sanctions.

In the field of education, UNESCO (concretely, the Quality Guarantee section of the Higher Education Division) along with the OECD, trade union organizations and university centers, have promoted an initiative that, if consolidated, may stop some of the negative effects of the commercialization of education promoted by the WTO. We are referring to the "Guidelines for the evaluation of quality in the internationalization of educational services" (UNESCO, 2005). This initiative aims to make it difficult to commercialize low quality educational services, which tends to have a greater affect on the populations of southern countries, where the mechanisms for the evaluation of quality do not tend to be so developed (Malo, 2003; Guni, 2006). Although this is not an especially radical initiative, the project is being sabotaged by the countries that have adopted a more commercial focus in the internationalization of their educational services as they consider that the guidelines might affect the profit rates of their education industries.

Another recent UNESCO initiative, the "Convention on the protection and promotion of cultural expressions" could also clash with the economic interests of the major powers and with GATS logic. This convention stipulates, in an implicit way, that trade agreements should be subordinated to the protection of cultural diversity, while WTO regulations stipulate that the free market should regulate this issue, like so many others. Countries like the United States and Israel voted against the Convention because they consider that the protection of certain cultural expressions could lead to protectionism and unfair competition. (Chan-Tibergian, 2006)

THE IMPACT OF MOBILIZATION

In analyzing the performance of the campaigns against GATS and WTO we can differentiate between the impact on public policies and the symbolical impact. Impact on policies can be *substantive* (when it affects the result of the political decision making process) or *procedural* (when the impact refers to the facilitation of new administrative processes or the creation of new and stable arenas and mechanisms for participation). Meanwhile, *symbolical* impact refers to changes to social or individual systems of values, attitudes, opinions and behaviors, along with the formation of new collective identities (Gomà, Ibarra, et al., 2002). In this sense, social movements (as well as other actors) are characterized as being agents for influence and persuasion that aim to challenge the dominant interpretations of various aspects of reality (Sabucedo, et al., 1998).

a. *Substantive impact:* On a substantive level, campaigns against the WTO have contributed to the way this organization's agenda has taken more consideration of the needs of developed countries (although this impact often appears more in the rhetorical field than in the *real politik*). Campaigning has also contributed to make it more difficult for the negotiations to progress and to the failure of the MCs such as Seattle and Cancun. However, it also has to be said that the blocking of negotiations and the continued failure of the conferences responds largely to internal discrepancies between WTO members. The center-periphery perspective seems very useful for understanding these discrepancies, as (to put it very briefly) northern countries aim for southern countries to liberalize their services and adopt agreements to guarantee the investments of their countries, while the countries of the south aim for the north to open their agricultural markets. Moreover, some of them (such as India), aim to establish agreements on trade of "natural persons." But neither of the two blocks is making moves in these areas of negotiation.

Despite the undisputable weight of factors that are extrinsic to the struggles, the activity of movements has to be contemplated in the analysis of WTO negotiations. For example, in the Seattle MC, the social mobilization was unexpected, disruptive and forceful. A huge amount of uncertainty among the delegations attending the conference was generated in the street, which damaged the secretive and anonymous nature that characterized WTO negotiations. Joseph Stiglitz and other authors consider that the Battle of Seattle "was a shock" and provoked an intense soul-searching among the WTO staff and delegations (Stiglitz, 2002; Wilkinson, 2002). At the same time, the political pressure or technical advisement exerted by many humanitarian organizations is a resource that is highly valued by some delegations from southern countries. Some of them, due to a lack of resources, are not able to actively participate, even to assist, in the negotiation meetings.[26]

Meanwhile, campaigns against the inclusion of education and other "sensitive" sectors in the GATS framework have also performed very well. For example, faced by the pressures of civil society, the European community issued a report that guarantees that commitments would not be established for education, health and cultural services in the present GATS round of negotiations. (ICSTD 2003) A similar effect was achieved by the main teaching unions of Brazil and Argentina when, in October 2004, the education ministers of those countries signed a declaration in which they agreed not to liberalize the education sector and, even more relevantly, to "actively prevent education from being negotiated as part of the GATS framework." (IE-AL 2004:1) One year later, all the education ministers of Mercosur member countries and the educational sections of the main unions signed a very similar declaration. In this case, the signatories express special concerns about the limitations in the educational policy space, as a consequence of GATS commitments.[27]

b. *Procedural impact.* In its beginnings, the WTO aimed to stay fairly anonymous to avoid providing resources to public information and, therefore, to be more effective (Jiménez, 2004). But as the protest has intensified, this organization has had to respond to criticism of its lack of transparency and to adopt new dispositions regarding relationships with civil society (Scholte, 2000). Some of these dispositions include: delegations being able to meet "in a constructive way" with NGOs; NGOs being able to attend MCs and to publish position papers on the WTO website; access to documents that are not restricted and to information by means of an electronic bulletin; the possibility to take part in different forums—virtual forums, lunchtime dialogues, workshops, public symposiums, etc. (WTO, 1996). However, the WTO considers that, despite the demands for it to become even more transparent, it can do no more because that would affect the confidentiality and effectiveness of negotiations. Other WTO sources also state that only "responsible" NGOs that aim to make a "productive contribution" can access the channels for participation, in such a way that it will make no concessions to "groups whose specific objective is to undermine or destroy the WTO in its current form" (WTO, 2004, p. 44).

On a procedural level, as we said before, many civil society organizations have recently concentrated their efforts on a reactive campaign that involves avoiding modifications to the methodology for negotiating GATS as proposed by the EU (Sinclair, 2006). The EU, along with other developed countries, proposed—just before Hong Kong MC—that the GATS methodology should be less flexible. One of their main proposals was that countries had to liberalize, by imperative, a minimum number of sub-sectors of services at each round (EC, 2005, 2005b). As well as civil society, many delegations from southern countries expressed their rejection to this proposal because most of them, due to strategic or ideological reasons, do not wish to liberalize their services—either voluntarily or forced. Finally, the most radical European proposals were not accepted in Hong Kong, although some methodological changes to advance the liberalization process were introduced (Sinclair, 2006).

3. *The symbolical impact:* Symbolical incidence is a recurring objective of campaigns against WTO and GATS.[28] This objective can be achieved through direct action. For such a purpose, the "Battle of Seattle" was especially effective. After the first day of mobilizations, one media company stated that "the population went to bed one night not knowing that there was a thing called WTO and woke up the next full of curiosity to find out about the subject" (Barlow & Clark, 2000, pp. 4–5). So, as a result of the mobilizations in Seattle, the WTO suddenly shot into public awareness. The collective actions of social movements put a devastating finish to the anonymity of the organization.

In reference to the struggles against the GATS, GATS free zones, as a result of the political debate they generate, have become an especially adequate initiative for drawing public attention to a generally little known matter.

Some organizations, in turn, have designed educational and leisure materials to explain what GATS is and what it implies in an amenable manner.[29]

Finally, we should mention the fact that WTO actively participates in the duel of ideas in which certain sectors have come to challenge. WTO's anti-poverty and anti-development rhetoric can be understood in the context of this duel—and its legitimacy crisis.[30] Meanwhile, the WTO (through the Division of Information and Relation with the Media) uses a large amount of resources for persuading public opinion of "the advantages of free trade" (WTO, 2000; WTO 2004). The WTO staff also aim to respond to GATS critics in a document titled *GATS: Facts and Fiction*. The aim of this document consists of "debunking the myths and falsehoods surrounding GATS" (WTO, 2001).

CONCLUSION

The WTO is one of the multilateral organizations most criticized by the global civil society, as well as other agents. One of the main criticisms of this organization is its aim to apply free trade regulations and norms, through GATS, to education and other (public) services. A broad range of actors (social movements, local governments, UNESCO, etc.) perceives multiple risks in the liberalization and commercialization of education services. Consequently, a wide range of repertoires of action has been promoted to resist and to promote alternatives to the liberal policies promoted by the WTO in the field of education. Although a thorough analysis of the impact of these struggles is extremely complex, we could consider that if these struggles had not occurred, the liberalization of education and other public services would have made far more progress than it has.

NOTES

1. It needs to be noted that GATS does not single out education: It is merely one of the services captured in its wide mandate.
2. When tackling this subject it should be considered that general campaigns against the WTO, of their many demands, contemplate the problems of commercializing education and other public services. However, campaigns against the inclusion of education in the GATS make up just one small part of the full spectrum of the struggle.
3. Some events that have recently taken place on the subject are the "GATS and Education" seminar organized by Education International at the UNESCO headquarters (Paris, April 2005) and the European Convention of Local Governments, "Against the GATS, for the Promotion of Public Services" (Liege, October 2005; Geneva, October 2006).
4. Some of the research groups that work on the activist line of research in relation to the GATS are GATSWATCH, the Polaris Institute, Education International, and some members of the GENIE network.
5. The frames of meaning are filters through which we interpret reality, perceive opportunities and represent behaviors.

6. The deep frames of meaning are those that represent a global analysis of social structure and are therefore characterized by the extent of the reality to which they are referring.

7. These critical repertories can be found in such works as (Frase and O'Sullivan, 1999; Nunn, 1999; Worth, 2000; Barblan, 2002; Kelk & Worth, 2002; Knight, 2002; Robertson, Bonal, & Dale 2002; Rodrigues Dias, 2002a; Aboites, 2004; Caplan, 2001; Ginsburg, Espinoza, Popa, & Terano, 2003; IE, 2003; Kelsey, 2003; Rikowski, 2003; Robertson & Dale, 2003; Schugurensky & Davidson-Harden, 2003; García-Guadilla, 2003; Altbach, 2004; Feldfeber & Saforcada 2005; COL/UNESCO, 2006; Rosskam, 2006; Hill, 2006; Rikowski, 2007; Devidal, 2008; Naghorne, 2008).

8. This section is based on such statements and public declarations as "Stop the GATS attack" (www.gatswatch.org/StopGATS.html), "Take GATS out of education" (*www.gatswatch.org/educationoutofgats*), "Stop the GATS power game" (www.tradeobservatory.org/library.cfm?refID=73165), "Call to participate in the General States of local governments against the GATS" (http://www.eg-contre-agcs.org/article.php3?id_article=33), *Stop the GATS power play against citizens of the world!* (www.ourworldisnotforsale.org).

9. As reflected in some of the statements analyzed.

10. Tarrow (1994) defines the cycle of protest as a phase of intensifying conflicts and confrontation in the social system. Any cycle of protest is characterized by the rapid diffusion of collective action from more mobilized sectors to less mobilized ones. (Tarrow, 1994).

11. The Ministerial Conference is the main decision making body of the WTO. They are held at least every two years.

12. This idea is reflected, for example, in the document "Call for mobilization toward the WTO meeting in Cancun 2003" (www.movsoc.org).

13. Observatorio Social de América Latina (http://osal.clacso.org).

14. Round of negotiations held between 1988 and 1994 that resolved the constitution of the WTO.

15. According to the final charter of the second edition of the World Forum on Education (Porto Alegre, July 2004) one of the priorities of the agenda of propublic education movements should consist of "rejecting any national or international agreement that promotes the commercialisation of education, knowledge, science and technology, especially in relation to the WTO's framework."

16. Including Education International, an international confederation of trade unions involving 248 unions operating in 166 countries (www.ei-ie.org).

17. Universitas 21 (2003) as quoted in Schugurensky and Davidson-Harden (2003, p. 343).

18. See "World Declaration on Higher Education for the Twenty-First Century: Vision and Action." Available at www.unesco.org/education/educprog/wche/declaration_eng.htm

19. For instance, one of the press conferences of P. Mandelson (trade commissioner of EU) in the Hong Kong Ministerial was interrupted by a group of activists that, dressed as Santa Claus and singing Christmas songs, expressed that the "development package" that rich countries were offering to southern countries as a negotiation strategy was really "empty."

20. With respect to the education sector, *Education International* used to organize lobby meetings in key moments of the negotiation. See, for instance *Trade Education News,* issue number 7 (Hong Kong MC) and issue number 10 (June '06 cluster services in Geneva). In: www.ei-ie.org.

21. See footnote 8.

22. On this subject see also (Jawara and Kwa 2004).

23. Remember that GATS is an incomplete text (Nielson, 2003).

24. See for instance "Open Letter to WTO Director General—Pascal Lamy: Redefining what consensus means in the WTO?" (ww.focusweb.org) or "Call to Action to Protest the WTO Negotiations in Hong Kong" (www.nadir.org).
25. For example, in Article 103 of the Charter of the UN it states that "In the event of a conflict between the obligations of the Members of the United Nations under the present Charter and their obligations under any other international agreement, their obligations under the present Charter shall prevail" (Teitelbaum, 2004:15).
26. For example, at the Doha MC, Haiti could not send one delegate while the United States had more than 300. Many southern delegations do not have permanent offices in Geneva and do not have the capacity to promote procedures in the Organ for Solution of Differences (IATP, 2003; Kapoor, 2004).
27. See also, www.me.gov.ar/dnci/**mercosur**/docs/declaracion **conjunta** 2005.rtf (last accessed June 10, 2007).
28. For example, in the "Strategy Meeting for Social Movements against the WTO" (Mexico City, November 2002) one of the main axes of action was defined as "winning the support of public opinion against the WTO through mass information campaigns and education."
29. Some of these resources (dynamics, puzzles, card games) can be found on the Polaris Institute website (www.polarisinstitute.org) and on the Public Services International website (www.psiru.org/educindexnew.asp). WTO-Poly was also created to raise awareness of the WTO; it emulates sarcastically the popular Monopoly board game (www.wtopoly.de).
30. An example of this is the name of the present round of negotiations, the "development round," which was promoted after the "millennium round" was frustrated in Seattle. See also some of the general secretary's speeches: "Lamy says that commerce is the missing piece in the jigsaw puzzle of development," "Lamy: Commerce is a 'fundamental instrument' in the fight against poverty" (www.wto.org).

REFERENCES

Aboites, H. (2004). Derecho a la educación o mercancía: La experiencia de diez años de libre comercio en la educación mexicana [Right to education or commodity. The ten years experience of free trade in Mexican education]. *Memoria. Revista Mensual de Política y Cultura* 187. Retrieved in September 5, 2005, from http://memoria.com.mx/node/425.

Altbach, P. G. (2004). Higher Education Crosses Borders. *Change*, 36 (2), 18–24.

AUCC, ACE, EUA, & CHEA (2001). Joint Declaration about HE and the GATS. Retrieved August 31, 2007, from http://socrates.aucc.ca/_pdf/english/statements/2001/gats_10_25_e.pdf

Barblan, A. (2002). The international provision of higher education: do universities need GATS? Paper presented at the *Global University Network for Innovation First General Assembly*, Hangzhou, September 2002.

Barlow, M., & Clark, T. (2000). *The Battle after Seattle*. A working paper for strategic planning & action on the WTO. Retrieved September 15, 2004, from www.polarisinstitute.org/pubs/pubs_after_seattle.html

Caplan, R. (2001). GATS: in whose service? *Nexus Magazine*, 8 (3). Retrieved September 2004, from http://www.nexusmagazine.com/backissues/0803.conts.html

Chan-Tibergien, J. (2006). Cultural Diversity as Resistance to Neoliberal Globalization: the Emergence of a Global Movement and Convention. *Review of Education* 52: 89–105.

CIRUP (2002), *Carta de Porto Alegre* [Porto Alegre letter], Porto Alegre: Cumbre Iberoamericana de Rectores de Universidades Públicas. Retrieved October 22,

2004, from http://www.grupomontevideo.edu.uy/Documentos_y_publicaciones/ Documentos/Carta_Porto_Alegre.htm

COL/UNESCO (2006). *Higher Education: Crossing Borders: A Guide to the Implications of the General Agreement on Trade in Services (GATS) for Cross-Border Education.* Paris, Commonwealth of Learning / UNESCO

Devidal, P. (2008). Trading Away Human Rights? The GATS and the Right to Education: A Legal Perspective. In D. Hill and R. Kumar (Eds.) (2009) *Global Neoliberalism and Education and its Consequences,* pp.71–99. New York: Routledge.

EC (2005). Common Baseline for the Services Negotiations. Non-Paper, *Draft,* June 2005.

EC (2005b). Non Paper on Complementary Methods for the Services Negotiations. Possible Elements. Communication from the European Commission—WTO Council of Trade in Services. TN/S/W/55, October 2005.

Feldfeber, M., & Saforcada, F. (2005). *OMC, ALCA y educación. Una discussion sobre ciudadanía, derechos y mercado en el cambio de siglo [WTO, FTAA and education. A discussion on citizenship, rights and market in the new century],* Buenos Aires: Centro Cultural de la Cooperación.

Frase, P., & O'Sullivan, B. (1999). *The future of education under the WTO.* Retrieved February 8, 2004 from www.corporations.org/democracy/wtoed.html

Fredriksson, U. (2004). Studying the Supre-National in Education: GATS, education and teacher union policies. *European Educational Research Journal* 3(2): 415–441

García-Guadilla, C. (2003). Educación superior y AGCS. Interrogantes para el caso de América Latina [Higher education and GATS. Questions for the Latin American case]. In García-Guadilla, C. (Ed.) *El difícil equilibrio. La educación superior como bien público y comercio de servicios [The difficult equilibrium. Higher education as a public good and trade in services].* Caracas: Editorial Latina, 109–209.

Ginsburg, M., Espinoza, O., Popa, S., & Terano, M. (2003). Privatisation, Domestic Marketisation and Internacional Commercialisation of Higher Education: vulnerabilities and opprtunities for Chile and Romania within the framework of WTO/GATS. *Globalisation, Societies and Education* 1 (3), pp. 413–445.

Gomà, R., Ibarra, P., & Martí, S. (2002). *Creadores de democracia radical. Movimientos sociales y redes de políticas públicas [Radical democracy creators. Social movements and public policies networks].* Barcelona: Icaria.

HCHR (2003). *Human Rights and Trade. Paper prepared for the 5th WTO Ministerial Conference.* New York: Commission on Human Rights, Economic and Social Council- UN.

GUNI (2006). *Higher Education in the World 2007. Accreditation For Quality Assurance: What Is At Stake?* Global University Network for Innovation Conference Report. Barcelona: Mundi-Prensa.

Hill, D. (2006). Education Services Liberalization. In E. Rosskam (Ed.) *Winners or Losers? Liberalizing public service,* pp. 3–54. Geneva: ILO.

Hunt, S., Benford, R. and Snow, D. (1994). Marcos de acción colectiva y campos de identidad en la construcción social de los movimientos [Collective action frames and fields of identity in the social movements construction]. In Laraña, E., & Gusfield, J. (Eds.), *Los nuevos movimientos sociales. De la ideología ala identidad [The new social movements. From ideology to identity].* Madrid: CIS, 221–252.

IATP (2003). *WTO Decision Making: A Broken Process.* Retrieved March 18, 2004, from www.tradeobservatory.org

ICSTD (2003). European Commission presents services liberalisation offer. *Bridges Weekly Trade News,* 7 (4), February 6, 2003.

IE-AL (2004). *Declaración de Brasilia [Brazilian Declaration].* San Pedro, Belize: Internacional de la Educación—Oficina Regional para América Latina.

IE (2003). *Globalization, GATS and Higher Education.* Retrieved September 10, 2004, from www.ei-ie.org/hiednet

Jawara, F., & Kwa, A. (2004). *Behind the scenes at the WTO: the real world of international trade negotiations. Lessons of Cancun.* London-New York: Zed Books.

Jiménez, C. (2004). De la Ronda d'Uruguai a Cancún [From the Uruguay Round to Cancun]. *Revista dCIDOB,* 89, pp. 8–13.

Kapoor, I. (2004). Deliberative Democracy and the WTO. *Review of International Political Economy,* 11 (3), pp. 522–541.

Kelk, S., & Worth, J. (2002). *Trading it away: how GATS threatens UK Higher Education.* Retrieved March 4, 2004, from www.peopleandplanet.org/tradejustice/executivesummary.pdf.

Kelsey, J. (2003). Legal Fetishism and the Contradictions of the GATS. *Globalisation, Societies and Education,* 1(3), pp. 321–357.

Knight, J. (2002). Trade *in Higher Education Services: The Implications of GATS.* Retrieved August 31, 2007, from www.obhe.ac.uk/products/reports/publicaccess-pdf/March2002.pdf.

Malo, S. (2003). La comercialización de la educación superior [Trade in higher education]. In García-Guadilla, C. (Ed.), *El difícil equilibrio. La educación superior como bien público y comercio de servicios [The difficult equilibrium. Higher education as a public good and trade in services]* (pp. 101–107). Caracas: Editorial Latina.

McAdam, D. (1998). Orígenes conceptuales, problemas actuales, direcciones futuras [Conceptual origins, current problems and future directions]. In Ibarra, P., & Tejerina, B. (Eds.), *Los movimientos sociales: transformaciones políticas y cambio cultural [Social movements: political transformations and cultural change]* (pp. 89–110). Madrid: Trotta.

Nielson, J. (2003). A Quick Guide to the State of Play in the GATS Negotiations. Paper presented at the *OECD Forum on Trade in Educational Services.* Trondheim, November 2003.

Nunn, A. (1999). *The GATS: an impact assessment for Higher Education in the UK.* Retrieved May 5, 2004, from http://www.esib.org/commodifi cation/documents/AUTImpact.pdf.

Rikowski, G. (2003). Schools and the GATS Enigma. *Journal for Critical Education Policy Studies.* 1 (1). Retrieved October 25, 2004, from http://www.jceps.com/index.php?pageID=article&articleID=8.

Rikowski, G. (2007). Schools and the GATS Enigma, in E. Wayne Ross & R. Gibson (Eds.) *Neoliberalism and Education Reform,* Cresskill, NJ: Hampton Press.

Robertson, S., Bonal, X., & Dale, R. (2002). GATS and the education services industry: the politics of scale and global reterritorialization. *Comparative Education Review,* 46 (4), pp. 472–496.

Robertson, S., & Dale, R. (2003). This is what the fuss is about! The implications of GATS for education systems in the North and the South. Paper presented at the *UK Forum for International Education and Training.* Commonwealth Secretariat. May 2003.

Rodrigues Dias, M. A. (2002). Utopía y comercialización en la educación superior del s. XXI [Utopia and trade in the higher education of the XXI Century]. In M. A. Rodrigues (Ed.), *Lecciones de la Conferencia Mundial sobre Educación uperior: Perspectivas de la Educación Superior en el s. XXI [Lessons from the World Conference on Higher Education: Higher Education prospects in the XXI Century].* Madrid: CRUE, 11–44.

Rodrigues Dias, M. A. (2002b). Educación Superior: ¿bien público o servicio commercial reglamentado por la OMC? [Higher Education: public good or tradable service regulated by the WTO?] Paper presented at the *III Cumbre Iberoamericana de Rectores de Universidades Públicas,* Porto Alegre, April 2002.

Rosskam, E. (Ed.) (2006). *Winners or losers? Liberalizing public services.* Geneva: ILO.

Sabucedo, J. M., Grossi, J. & Fernández, C. (1998). Los movimientos sociales y la creación de un sentido común alternativo [Social movements and the creation o fan alternative common sense]. In Ibarra, P., & Tejerina, B. (Eds.), *Los movimientos sociales: transformaciones políticas y cambio cultural [Social movements: political transformations and cultural change]* (pp.165–180). Madrid: Trotta. Hill-2 2nd.

Scherrer, C. (2007). GATS: commodifying education via trade treaties. In K. Martens, A. Rusconi and K. Leuze (Eds.) New Arenas of Education Governance: The Impact of International Organizations and Markets on Educational Policy Making. London, Palgrave.

Scholte, J. A. (2000). Cautionary Reflections on Seattle. *Millenium. Journal of International Studies, 29*, pp. 115–121.

Schugurensky, D., & Davidson-Harden, A. (2003). From Córdoba to Washington: WTO/GATS and Latin American education. *Globalisation, Societies and Education,1* (3), pp. 321–357.

Sinclair, S. (2000). *GATS: How the WTO's new services negotiations threaten democracy.* Retrieved February 12, 2004, from www.policyalternatives.ca.

Sinclair, S. (2006). *Crunch Time in Geneva. Benchmarks, plurilaterals, domestic regulation and other pressure tactics in the GATS negotiations.* Retrieved February 8, 2007, from www.policyalternatives.ca.

Stiglitz, J. E. (2002). *Globalization and its Discontents.* London: Penguin.

Sussex, E. (2005). *Local and Regional Reaction to GATS and Similar Trade Rules.* Retrieved October 15, 2005, from http://www.ourworldisnotforsale.org/printfriendly.asp?search=386.

Tarrow, S. (1994). *Power in movement: social movements, collective action and politics.* Cambridge: Cambridge University Press.

Teitelbaum, A. (2004). El ALCA está entre nosotros: Los tratados bilaterales de libre comercio [The FTAA is between us. The free trade agreements]. *Presentation at the III International Conference on Rights and Guarantees, Buenos Aires, September 2004.*

UNESCO (2005). *Guidelines for Quality Provision in Cross-border Higher Education.* Paris: UNESCO.

Verger, A. (2008). Measuring Educational Liberalisation. A Global Analysis of GATS. *Globalisation, Societies and Education* 6(1): 13–31.

Vlk, A., Westerheijden, D. & Wende, M. (2008). GATS and the steering capacity of a nation state in higher education: case studies of the Czech Republic and the Netherlands. *Globalisation, Societies and Education* 6(1): 33–54.

Waghorne, M. (2009) The Public Services International. In D. Hill (Ed.) *Contesting Neoliberal Education: Public Resistance and Collective Advance.* New York: Routledge.

Wesselius, E. (2002). Behind GATS 2000: Corporate power at work. *TNI—The WTO Series, 4.* Retrieved March 15, 2004, from http://www.tni.org/reports/wto/wto4.pdf.

Wilkinson, R. (2002). The World Trade Organisation. *New Political Economy* 7, pp. 129–141.

Worth, J. (2000). The threat to higher education. A briefing on current WTO negotiations. Retrieved November 24, 2003, from www.peopleandplanet.org/tradejustice.

WTO (1996). Guidelines for arrangements on relations with Non-Governmental Organizations [WT/L/162]. Geneva: World Trade Organisation.

WTO (2000). *10 benefits of the WTO trading system.* Geneva: World Trade Organisation.

WTO (2001). *GATS—fact and fiction.* Geneva: World Trade Organisation.

WTO (2004). *The Future of the WTO.* Geneva: World Trade Organisation.

10 Teacher Conflicts and Resistance in Latin America

Dalila Andrade Oliveira

INTRODUCTION

Since the 1990s many Latin American countries have undertaken reforms in education, motivated by the need for improved access to schooling. Many of the reforms have been controversial, since broader accessibility has come at the cost of quality in education. Studies have shown that attempts to reduce costs and incorporate previously excluded social classes into mainstream education have led to serious repercussions in the development of the education system and have directly affected teachers' working conditions and income (Birgin, 2000; Tiramonti, 2001; Oliveira & Melo, 2004; Hill, 2009; Oliveira, 2006b; Rosskam, 2006). The reforms have been part of a broader restructuring process toward a more capitalist system, which in Latin America has led to state reforms that have deeply impacted relationships between state and society (Salama & Valier, 1997).

Many Latin American countries had not yet made education universally available by 1990. This could be attributed to an array of political and economical crises and authoritarian governments, which have exacerbated social inequality and poverty. The general reforms implemented in Latin American countries during the 1990s followed the goals of globalization and the politics of the neoliberal paradigm. They consisted chiefly of reductions in government spending.

The reforms attempted to adapt the education system in order to produce a labor force for the legal market and to fight poverty through targeted social policies. They established new regulations mainly focused on school administration—the school as a center for planning and management; per capita financing; broadening and standardizing national examinations; institutional evaluation; and participation of the community in school administration (Medina & Kelly, 2001; Birgin, 2000; Fanfani, 2005; Feldfeber & Oliveira, 2006).

They also changed the structure of educational systems in both physical and organizational terms, in the hope of improving productivity, expressing a management model that despite focusing on public and state institutions, was strongly rooted in the market (Barroso, 2003; Lessard, 2004). Changes in working relationships in schools have taken place since the beginning of these reforms, due to policies related to career and salaries, and have interfered with the professional identities of these workers increasing professional conflict and tension have demanded investigation into the conditions of teaching professionals in light of these trends.

The goal of this chapter is to discuss the nature and cause of teacher conflicts, which in the context of these reforms have manifested themselves as resistance to the educational guidelines established by national governments. It is understood however, that these conflicts are part of a much broader modern crisis of change in the traditional organization of work and society.

The conclusions drawn in this article are based on research carried out in Latin American countries using data on teacher conflicts from 1998 and 2003, gathered from the national and official press (Oliveira & Melo, 2004; Gentili & Suarez, 2004). Teacher conflicts have been categorized as organized/unorganized and conscious/unconscious instances of collective resistance. When linked to the results of other research developed by our research group[1] on the work of teachers in Latin America (Oliveira, 2006b) and in conjunction with contemporary theory, hypotheses have developed concerning the condition of teaching professionals specifically, as distinct from other classes of workers.

THE LATIN AMERICAN CONTEXT

Language and political orientation have dually represented major obstacles to progress and development in the Latin American world. Although Spanish is the most commonly spoken language through out Central and South America, the richest and most populous South American country, Brazil, is officially Portuguese speaking. This reality has compromised the potential for cultural uniformity among Latin American countries. And Latin American integration has been historically troubled by nationalist agendas. According to Ianni (1988), revolutions and movements for independence are rooted deeply in the same cultural mindsets upon which many South American countries were founded.

Recent elections of new Latin American governments—for example of indigenous leader Evo Morales in Bolivia, Lula from Brazil, who rose from an working-class industrial background—demonstrate common contemporary cultural demands, those associated with the recognition of the condition of poor workers. In both the cases of Brazil and Bolivia can trace a bourgeoning desire for genuine equality. The fight against exploitation is seen as a national concern in which the nation is understood in cultural and even racial terms, and in which territoriality becomes a secondary aspect. These movements therefore express the struggle for the recognition of the nation, which becomes an increasingly more autochthonous entity, against elitist and authoritarian governments, groups which have served international rather than national interests for many decades.

According to Ianni (1988) the conflicts between society and the state constitute practical and theoretical challenges that have always been present in Latin American countries, both on the continent and on the islands:

> It is a commonly held belief that a civil society is feeble and unorganized, characterized by inherent political instability. Many feel that structural dualities are historically precedented and cannot be avoided: archaic vs. modern; patrimonial vs. rational. . . . They are forces juxtaposed to push society forward and drag it backwards at the same time, making progress labyrinthine and evasive. (p. 2)

Ianni (1988) identifies a vicious cycle, fuelled by historically present poverty, violence and authoritarian governance. For him, Latin American history is rife with precarious, provisory, unresolved, racially-complicated, misplaced and folkloric aspects.

> Nations without a people or citizens: only individuals and population. . . . That is why they say that the state is strong, democracy episodic and dictatorship recurring. The dominating elites—military, civil, oligarchic, corporate, technocratic—have the knowledge and the power. (p. 2)

In Ianni's (1988) opinion, conflicts between civil society and the state stem from a series of crises, coup d'états, dictatorship and interruptions of democratic process. According to him, these are ultimately responsible for the separation between the agendas of civil society and of the state, since the elite revolutions that have occurred in Latin American countries have not solved the basic question of national identity. The formation of a people as a group of citizens did not occur in most of the countries. Workers, farmers, employees, as well as many other classes of indigenous, black or white individuals have not had full access to citizens' rights.

This question is at the center of the debate on education in Latin America. Social, racial, regional and cultural diversity and inequality observed in political and economical terms show that a nation's physiognomy is very different from its people—a fact often contradicted by current South American governments. School systems, as microcosms within their nations, have not escaped the complications of this paradox: Since they are organized according to models that are often not of Latin American origin, they manifest themselves in systems that reflect the inequitable and ambivalent structure of society, resulting in conflicts on several levels. According to Tiramonti (2001), inequalities have developed in different ways in each country. In countries and whose educational systems were rapidly expanded and modernized, the increase in availability of public education generated a segmentation process within the public systems. In others countries (for example, Colombia and Brazil) the incorporation of emergent sectors into public education led to a withdrawal of the elites from public education, a trend which fundamentally undermined the quality of public space, and jeopardized the process of socialization and integration of the newly incorporated demographic groups.

The prevailing movement in the field of education is for inclusion and equality for all according to the tenets of citizenship, and this is merely a microcosm of a broader social agenda. Indigenous peoples, blacks, women, farmers and above all the poor, identify themselves with each other as equals and demand a social inclusion, in which education plays an important role. Yet these movements are part of a complex social dynamic, in which the demand for affirmative action policies are not balanced with a guarantee of basic universal rights.

LATIN AMERICA

Through the analysis of these conflicts, our aim is to understand the response of teachers to the reforms in question, responses which have brought new pressures and responsibilities without adapting working conditions. Circumstances vary within and among different national contexts, depending on the infrastructure type, teaching materials and work relations. They have put greater demands on teachers, who increasingly have become responsible for the schools' and students' performance, and for their own education.

Novel teaching and evaluation processes, and curricular adaptations have resulted in prolonged working hours and an overload of professional responsibility. Schools have been pressured to measure success according to economic criterion, propelled by new external evaluation systems. These demands have made schools seek alternative financing by means of help from the community and partnerships with the private sector, whose contributions have fundamentally undermined the integrity of "public" space.

The public administration paradigm adopted is based on technical criteria imported from the private sector. Its use has led to changes in the composition of the institutions and their relationship with the community, and to a breakdown in working relationships, a fact that has threatened the stability of public sector employment. This destructurizing is reflected in the deregulation of work relations, and a process of strategically curtailing workers' resistance. Limitations imposed on public sector unions and the non-recognition of their right to strike, to say nothing of punitive measures against those who participate in protests and strikes, are evidence of this trend.

Latin American state reforms have taken place at a critical historic juncture in which capitalism is remobilizing toward a clash with nationalistic agenda, the latter having been the prevailing ideology in Latin America.

Many economists consider the 1980s as a lost decade, characterized by years of crisis culminating in the so-called "debt crisis" (Calcagno, 2001). Several countries in Latin America reached the 1990s with threatened or exhausted welfare capacities and escalating levels of poverty and unemployment. International organizations, such as those associated with the United Nations (UN), played an important role in this process. They encouraged, mobilized and controlled the processes by which South American governments adapted themselves to the resurgence of capitalism and to new approaches to the regulation of public policies in general, including education.

Consequently, during the 1990s attempts were made to universalize education and eradicate illiteracy according to the agreements signed by Brazil and Mexico during the World Conference, *Education for All* in Jomtien. An attempt was further made to combine various technical measures to administer public funds invested in this sector. The combination of these factors resulted in greater availability of educational services, but at the expense of the resources, and an undermining of quality.

During the period of protectionist national development in Latin America, (roughly 1940 to 1960) modernization of society was centered on economic progress, and the school systems were oriented toward this end. Social policies were universally oriented, characterized by a concession of social rights by the state, though concessions won were typically precipitated by mass demonstrations of workers. Although Latin America was still far from a "welfare state," this period brought considerable economical prosperity, urbanism, access to school, social security policies and public health. Even though these services were precarious in most countries, they were responsible for bringing society into a new phase of development. Across the world, these years represented the apex of a social regulation model, in which the unions played an important role as interlocutors (Castel, 1999).

From his analysis of the period, Tiramonti (2001) concluded that teaching professionals and their unions were the major contributors to forging of a more inclusive society in Latin America. Their dominant role in this movement—at its peak in Latin America—can be traced to the rapid expansion in the middle classes, a group which had traditionally demanded greater public emphasis on educational services. Consequently, the unions were incorporated into the control structure and encouraged to participate in the standardization processes and regulation of members and their activities.

According to Tiramonti (2001), in the context of both the "social state" established in Latin America in the 1940s, and because of the predominance of Human Capital Theory which developed along with Latin America's economical growth in the 1960s and encouraged the development of national education systems, there was an increase in student enrollment, and an incorporation of previously excluded social demographics. In many of these countries, the unions played an active role in standardizing and regulating the sector. In some instances, as educational systems developed, they even helped to define teachers' statutes. Although unions played an official role in regulation during this period, their exact role varied from country to country according to type of local institutional governance, the attitudes of the governing elites and the dynamics of local political.

UNIONS AND THE ORGANIZATION OF EDUCATION WORKERS

Unions have been losing their power continuously throughout the last two decades and have been considered incapable of reacting to the demands of recent work changes. In Latin American countries, specifically those in the Mercosul group,[2] the freedom of unions has been restricted, their supranational incarnations fragmented, and it has become more difficult for the workers in different regions to collaborate on a common cause. This loss of power has been attributed to decreasing union membership and waning participation by workers.

Factors contributing to this process include: The decreasing number of legal, regulated occupations, especially in the most important industrial centers, technological progress, deregulation of work relationships and increasing non-regulated work. In this context, right-wing criticism of the role of unions has contributed to their loss of power. Neoliberal sectors, which demand autonomy, freedom from unions and oppose labor laws on the grounds that such laws amount to protective legislation, claim that these institutions embody high levels of corporatism, and subscribe to nationalist, conservative and backward-looking ideology. These criticisms were designed to reduce union power at the source, and to question the legitimacy of their right to act as representatives of the workers' interests.

An interesting point is that conservative critics of the unions champion the same rhetoric of autonomy and freedom of workers' movements as the neoliberals, but with different goals. In their case, the separation of the unions from the state is part of a broader agenda to consolidate an ongoing process of deregulating worker's rights, to eliminate protective and discriminatory laws, and to curtail the government's role in the process. The goal is to establish new laws that reflect the same contract logic that controls civil and commercial work relations.

The crises faced by unions the world over have corresponded to the crises of modern institutions in general (Dubet, 2002). The unions have played a highly ambiguous role throughout the 20th century. They have legitimized capitalist development based upon exploitation of the labor force, while paradoxically providing a much needed platform for democratic struggle and resistance to many forms of exploitation. The general crisis of the unions however, takes on particular significance in the case of teachers.

According to Tiramonti (2001), the emergence of teachers' unions in various countries was linked to the development of education systems, the accumulation models adopted and the need for the state to expand its social foundation. Thus, countries in which modernization occurred the fastest and most democratically, and which had already witnessed considerable improvement in their education systems since the beginning of the century, also recorded early teachers' movements.

These movements became unions in the second part of the century, as part of the restructuring of the social order, as a result of Latin America's response to the crisis of capitalism in the 1930s through the implementation of the postwar Keynesian proposals. Such was the case in Argentina, Chile and Mexico. In Brazil's case, the union structure implemented in the 1940s had a corporative and authoritarian character. It was based on Mussolini's *Carta del Lavoro* (work charter), which connected the unions to the state through the concession of the rights of grant, unity and tax, and saw state involvement in the financial establishment and support of unions, which remains in effect even today, despite changes introduced by the Federal Constitution of 1988.

Prior to this period, public sector workers, including most teaching professionals had been prohibited from organizing unions. During the political thaw in Brazil in the late 1970s and early 1980, public workers in the education sector in several Brazilian states participated actively in strikes, including hunger strikes, demanding the right to establish a free and autonomous workers' union. It was the struggle for professional recognition for an array of workers in the public education sector, including teachers, support staff and other employees in the school system.

As part of the resistance to authoritarian governance, movements were organized to promote the struggle for accessible public education. Many of these were of a socialist and libertarian bent. The fight for a new society included the demand for a new educational mandate. These movements, eminently humanist, combined a defense of universal access to education with a priority to improve the working conditions of teachers. And they were based on the recognition of the need for a class-based organization of society, a society concerned with the defense of workers' rights in general.

From these movements came the desire to regard all education professionals, teachers, support staff and administrative workers, as equals. The debate surrounding professional identity led to conflicts, however, both in terms of the recognition of individual workers and from the perspective of the workers' unions. Now, some 30 years later, it has become clear that tensions stemming from divisions of work and power within the schools remain, and this is evidence that this unity was not soundly built (Oliveira, 2006b).

In Brazil during this period, teachers' unions organized themselves to uphold the following principles: to protect the rights and interests of the class and of each individual education professional, including retired workers; to develop solidarity among the entire group of education professionals; to combat all forms of exploitation and oppression. The desire to promote these ideals led to a new educational policy geared to meet the interests of the workers. The unions became representatives of this group, and solidified their independence and autonomy from employers, religious organizations, political parties and the state.

Since the 1990s, wage-freeze policies have undermined Latin American education professionals' purchasing power and impoverished the class. Further deterioration has stemmed from measures to curtail labor legislation, permit greater contract freedom, and eliminate salary-protection laws. The increase in the number of teachers hired on a temporary basis and under unacceptable conditions in the public sector is a significant example of this trend. Yet in some cases, as in Brazil, salary policies in the public sector are heterogeneous: salaries vary according to career, type of work contract—temporary or long term—working schedules, level and class type, years of service, amount of responsibility, contractual bonuses and levels of education achieved.

In Latin America today, teachers' challenges have been profoundly altered within the context of the new regulations. Latin America must now respond to new forms of resistance from education workers, professionals who are feeling unprecedented pressure from deteriorating working conditions, caused by the new low-quality homogenization of education brought on by recent reforms. Latin America has suffered a congruent fate to that of the unions' as a result of restructuring, a decrease in legal, regulated work, salary decreases and loss of power in negotiations with governments. The unions' greatest challenge has been to defend themselves as institutions, and the workers as a category, and this task has been complicated by their role as intermediators between civil society and the state in favor of education. This struggle is most apparent at the institutional level where the interests of the unions are different from those of the workers.

A characteristic of teachers' unions is that conflict has developed mainly on the issues of salary and working conditions. It is a turbulent dynamic (Nuñez, 1990), but one which nevertheless allowed the establishment of a give-and-take relationship between the state and the unions that has made cooperation possible. The conflict becomes a mechanism for testing participants' mettle, while making negotiation possible and constantly updating the reluctant alliance between the parties. Each negotiation allows the union to renew its credentials as mediator and negotiator of basic demands, and furnishes governments with issues on which to garner political consensus. The system works through the continuous renewal of hope for future improvement, a process which (conveniently) constantly reaffirms its usefulness. The demand for better salaries and working conditions has been and still is the primary mandate of education unions in Latin America.

This raises the question of whether is it possible to discuss education and teacher conflicts from a continental perspective as though Latin America were a single entity. How can we engage in a discussion of an entire continent without ignoring its internal diversity? To what extent has social criticism reproduced already established discourse, specifically that used by international organizations to refer to undifferentiated policies applied throughout this group of distinct nations? How can we recognize diversity without forgetting the notion of totality and, at the same time, the reference to universality?

TEACHERS' CONFLICTS AND THE NEW EDUCATIONAL REGULATIONS IN LATIN AMERICA

The new wave of popular democratic governments in Latin America could be the sign of a new era, in which there will be a rupture with the discontinuous process pointed out by Ianni (1988). We have experienced a wave of progressive governments in the sub-continent, having started in the past decade with the governments of countries such as Venezuela, Brazil, Argentina, Uruguay, Bolivia, Ecuador and most recently, Nicaragua (2006). Despite support received from the working classes, bartered for with election promises, these governments have continued the educational reforms started by their predecessors. For this reason, it is not possible to obtain an illuminating picture of the reforms carried out in the last decade in Latin America without including those that occurred in the so-called democratic popular governments. Even in countries that have experienced radical changes in forms of government, there has been a strong appeal for compensatory temporary policies, focused on the most socially vulnerable groups, rather than structurally stable ones based on universal and sound principles. The *Bolsa-Escola* (school grant) in Brazil, Mexico and Argentina, and the quota policies in public universities in Brazil are some examples. In addition, there is the maintenance of previous governments' external evaluation systems (Chile, Brazil and Argentina) and the creation of per capita financing, based on a market logic (Chile, Brazil, Argentina and others), derived from the monetarization of the social relations, all introduced into the educational context via the neoliberal reforms.

These governments were elected by a social base different from the one which supported previous authoritarian governments. Therefore they do not fulfill the expectations of popular sectors, which expect new policies from new governments, including new educational programs. South American social movements have tabled new educational proposals that can be appropriated and implemented in other parts of the continent, such as those which were formulated during MST's (Brazil's Landless Worker's Movement) struggle for land property, the *Barrios de Pie* in Argentina[3] among others. However, despite similarities in their political objectives, these movements have not yet come together to develop a new educational proposal for Latin America. The institutional power of the governments and international organizations in Latin America has defined the limits on ways in which education can be organized in the region.

CATEGORIZATION AND ANALYSIS OF THE CONFLICTS

The teacher conflicts identified in the survey occurred in five different countries in Latin America (Argentina, Brazil, Peru, Mexico and Ecuador), and they can be traced to nine distinct motivations: salary, profession, social security, assistance, work relations, working conditions, union relations, school administration and educational policy (Oliveira & Melo, 2004). There are without doubt numerous factors that should be considered in the analysis of the reasons for these conflicts. Special attention should be paid to aspects related to the current context, such as the reforms taking place in the last years and their consequences for the worker's lives.

These conflicts acquire new significance with the process of educational regulation implemented in each region, such as the reforms that have occurred in the most recent decades. We shall define as salary-related, demands for a long-term career plan, salary bonuses, on-time payments, fully paid vacations and other benefits, salary adjustment for inflation and compensation for losses. Those classified as concerning the teaching profession itself are: salary campaigns, recognition and inclusion of new forms of workers into the career plan, the concession of two- and five-year salary increases, in addition to a "wage floor" as defined by law. Social security issues are demands for social security and for non-termination of pensions on account of accident or death. We considered as assistance-related, demands for improvements in health assistance and expansion of the network of medical and dental assistance services. Under work relations we grouped demands related to work contracts, in particular to the condition of directly hired professionals (without the legal application process), outsourced labor, and those who had passed the qualification exams but were not granted the position. Conflicts related to working conditions are demands for improvements of the physical conditions under which teaching takes place, as well as policies for improving teaching conditions, such as: decreasing the number of students per classroom; decreasing the number of lessons taught and hours worked and granting bonus vacation.

Union-related conflicts were defined as issues concerning the union representation of workers and their relations with public administration. Under the category of school administration are demands related to the technical division of labor, power and hierarchy and personal control relations, such as demands for reviewing dismissal processes; formal hiring practices via public examinations, direct elections for head teachers; and career progression independent of evaluation by immediate superiors. Finally, we considered as educational policy issues those referring to demands and proposals concerning the administration of the system, financing or legislative changes. Among the conflicts identified in the period studied, clearly the most significant were salary and professional matters.

It would be premature to state that the present survey confirms the thesis that characterizes union movements as corporatist, defending immediate rights for the workers' group, such as salaries and other bonuses. It is in fact impossible to know whether work and payment conditions are the immediate cause of disputes over salaries, or if the reduced union action has been caused by other political elements, such as bureaucratic union directives, or auto-incompetence and loss of touch with the grassroots. And the unions themselves express their difficulties to mobilize the class they represent.

However, it is important to mention that during the time the survey was carried out (Oliveira & Melo, 2004), the main source of information about the conflicts were the unions themselves by means of their files, archives, press releases and personal statements. Accordingly, even data about workers' participation in protests and demonstrations can vary considerably, depending on the person interviewed. Data obtained from the unions on protest participation was generally more optimistic than that furnished by the government. The methodology used in another study (Oliveira, 2006a) made it possible to use the workers themselves as informants, by means of observation and discussion of the working process itself. A comparison of these two studies has given us perspective on the ideological gulf that exists between unions and school employees today.

By observing their development, it is clear that teacher conflicts have neither a beginning nor an end, but instead are constantly evolving. Solutions and negotiations have only ever led to partial results and teachers have often found themselves back at work without the impasse having been resolved. And more often than not, the leading role played by teachers as protagonists in these conflicts is made very clear to the other education workers.

PARTICULARITIES OF EDUCATIONAL WORK AND ITS RELATED CONFLICTS

Many studies about the nature of work organization at schools can be found in the educational literature of the 1980s and 1990s. The focus of the debate was the emergence of teaching as a profession rather than its historical relationship with the clergy, and at the same time, the threat of proletarianization and the defense of the distinctiveness of teaching work in comparison to factory work. The emergence of the teacher as a professional and the necessity for teachers to defend themselves against broad standardization in the education systems is reflected in the debate surrounding the organization of educational work. This movement has also brought greater consciousness of and attention to the traditional mechanisms of control and exploitation. These became known as the theses of proletarianization and professionalization (Apple, 1995; Hargreaves, 1998).

Analysis of the changes that occurred within the Latin American context suggests that teacher conflicts reflect inherent more deeply rooted elements of inequality in Latin American society. However, as far as the teaching profession is concerned, there is no consensus in the specific literature about surplus value exploitation of employees in public schools. According to some authors (Enguita, 1991) the theory of value does not apply to the public sector. We believe that the capital work conflict does exist in the public sector, in which work relations evolve in a capitalist way. This is particularly exacerbated in situations involving imposed reforms and restructuring, such as those found within the context studied. The conflicts emerging under such circumstances lead to discord among the workers, both individually and collectively. These can be demonstrated by the technical and hierarchical divisions within schools. According to Castoriadis (1985), the positive attitude of the working classes lies in the fact that they simply do not allow themselves to be defeated by such contradictions. On the contrary, they keep trying to overcome them on several levels. The essence of this fight consists in the autonomous organization of workers and ultimately, the reorganization of society. The same author also identifies two kinds of proletarian struggles, which he characterizes as explicit and implicit. The first has to do with their organization and explicit action in unions, parties and strikes. Implicit struggles are those understood as a specific instance of a continuing action and ongoing organizational process in everyday life at the workplace. The struggle is composed of action, organization and both formal and informal objectives. According to Bernardo (1991) resistance is necessarily present in the capitalist production process and is even responsible for its development, since workers resort to several complex ways of resistance and revolt, which have in common an immediate consequence: the reduction of the working time in the production process.

According to Bernardo (1991), resistance forms may be classified as active or passive, and as individual or collective. Among passive individual forms are those aimed at reducing working time, with no open conflict and not the result of a kind of organized worker protest, such as deliberately poor-quality work, absenteeism, alcoholism and the use of drugs. The alarming amount of sick leave due to health issues among teachers nowadays should call our attention to this phenomenon. Active individual forms are related to open conflict, albeit sometimes performed in a stealthy way by single workers, with no collective deliberation, such as sabotage, theft and aggression against managers. The high levels of violence in schools reflect students' poor behavior but also the lack of enthusiasm of teachers caused by their deplorable working conditions. These individual ways of resistance violate specific production standards and reproduce the principle of the disciplinary bases of capitalism: individualization. Individualism is encouraged in this regulatory mode, in which the subjectivity of each worker is mobilized towards a view according to which each one should individually look for means of ensuring their personal and professional success, since there is no guarantee for all. The means of evaluation are growing ever more individualized, making it possible to evaluate personal results as well as the time needed to achieve them.

When gathered into a single system, collective forms of resistance have as a reference point the totality of the individuals that act together. They are passive when directed by the union management or other leaders that assume the initiative, guidelines and control of the struggle, generally without effectively consulting the workers. They reproduce workers' isolation and the fragmentation between collectives, while union leadership serves as an indispensable mediator between the struggle and the collective units of members and becomes an agent of social discipline. However, as mentioned previously, such protest works. During active collective struggles workers organize themselves at their own initiative, leading to the active participation of all who collaborate, expressing interest for the control of the process. It is an extreme and not very common type of manifestation of the conflict and therefore antagonistic to capitalist discipline. Diffuse resistance or that based on collective or group actions by means of ambiguous or fragmented practices, but with a particular logic, can evolve into acts performed within the spaces free from dominant imposition, which requires support, adherence and cooperation in a balance of refusal, acceptance and conformism. The opposite would be rebelliousness, appropriation and reinvention. Conflicts are omnipresent in social life and can assume numerous shapes. They may be distinguished through their nature and goals.

Teacher conflicts present certain particularities and cannot be analyzed within the wide spectrum of capital and work relations if we do not take into account the relative autonomy of teaching as a profession, the specificity of pedagogical work and the final goals of education. Only by taking such aspects into account is it possible to understand why, in many cases, the forms of resistance of these workers are not only those of demanding better working conditions and salaries, but also of expressing broader social interests, such as a high quality universal education in a more just and democratic society.

FINAL CONSIDERATIONS

The analysis of the manifestation of conflict and resistance in the Latin American context indicates a turbulent reform process involving the state and the educational system, which has brought losses to its workers and limited the potential for change. This is because these reforms were based on reduction of public costs and on structural adjustments affecting social policies, assigning a double task to education: to form the labor force necessary for economic development and at the same time to contribute to the reduction of poverty (Oliveira, 2000). The presence of these two distinct mandates, in the context of a new social regulation in which universalism is stripped of its significance as a measurement of social justice; one can perceive a tendency to blur the distinction between diversity and inequality.

The analyses contained in this chapter are related to various forms of conflicts and resistance, which were observed and documented within different boundaries of time and space. Therefore, they do not show the complexity of the workers' struggle or the numerous ways of expressing their interests. These records indicate that issues related to salary, profession and the defense of workers' rights are still most frequently at the core of their struggle and protests. This can be attributed to the deplorable working and salary conditions experienced by these professionals, which have been exacerbated in the past few decades.

The way in which these struggles develop and their results indicate that union rhetoric and proposals have become distant from schools and education workers. The unions have lost touch with the current reality of workers' conditions. Because of reforms undertaken in recent years, we are now faced with a new organization for workers in the educational sphere. This indicates that school is not the same as it was when the unions were created. Unions seem to ignore the existence of new educational regulations, and the teachers' new, highly vague and subjectively defined roles. Many now feel responsible for their working performance, professional advancement and even for students' success or failure.

Tiramonti (2001) observes that to defend and justify their actions, unions resort to several rhetorical models, including classicist interpellations, refutation of the development model, demands for the recovery of the educational role of the state, claims related to the situation of excluded citizens, the demand for professional recognition and also the recovery of proposals to institute the market logic in order to organize the educational system. Between these extremes are hybrid discourses deriving from a continuous negotiation with the real situations faced by the unions. Unions are trying to remobilize members with issues, for example, that are not exclusively connected with salary demands, but instead with professional esteem and recognition of the intellectual value of work.

In the Latin American context, where new governments with new educational programs are emerging, the gulf between the movements organized by unions, political parties and the various forms of autonomous and ordinary manifestations may endanger the admittedly unprecedented possibility of Latin American integration as a genuine expression of its people. Educational policies developed with the struggles and experiences of the workers as a reference point are abandoned in favor of those developed by specialists from international organizations, powerful outside groups which lobby against Latin American and African poverty. The preference for external counsel betrays an agenda which favors technique over policy, disguised under the euphemism of participation. The political-economical dependence of these governments on such organizations and the fact that education occupies a secondary position in this context overshadows the importance of this struggle. As observed by Ianni (1988):

> There are critical circumstances under which the state and civil society move away from each other. The people resist and subsist with organized and concentrated violence in the militarized state, which serves the great capital. However, they seem to be roaming, lost in the solitude of the pampas, plateaus, coasts, mountains, valleys, woods, fields and building

sites. Many are forced to be confined inside themselves. They look like sleepwalkers, zombies coming from a non-existing country. (p. 2)

The complicated issues of universal rights and recognition of diversity is at the root of Latin American social conflict, and in particular those from the educational sector. Unrealistic governmental policies often flounder shortly after their inception. The unions take too long to notice their failure and exacerbate the problem by playing the role of the political parties and governments supported by them. This has been a constant contributor to ruptures and institutional struggles. The daily resistance movements do not acquire their own logic, and cannot be a reliable barometer of current change. The integration of Latin American movements emerging in this context seems to be the only possible way of fighting the isolation described by Ianni (1988), so that Latin American peoples are finally able to illuminate the solitude of the pampas, valleys and mountains, and free themselves from marginalization.

ACKNOWLEDGMENTS

I would like to thank Tristan McCowan and Roland Graham for their help in the final revision of the translation of my text.

NOTES

1. A research group comprised of the combined efforts of (1) GESTRADO–UFMG, a research group from the Federal University of Minas Gerais on the politics of education and the work of teachers; and (2) RedEstrado, a network of researchers under CLACSO, (Latin American Council of Social Sciences) on the work of teachers.
2. The signatories to the Mercosul group are Argentina, Brazil, Paraguay and Uruguay.
3. Born in December 2001, the Barrios de Pie movement resulted from the need of a national organization for workers and unemployed who had been struggling for workers rights and education. See www.barriosdepie.org.ar.

REFERENCES

Apple, M. W. (1995). *Trabalho docente e textos: economia política das relações de classe e de gênero em Educação. [Teachers and Texts: a political economy of class and gender relations in education]*. Porto Alegre, Brazil: Artes Médicas.

Barroso, J. (2003). *A escola pública: regulação, desregulação e privatização. [The Public School: regulation, deregulation and privatization]*. Porto, Portugal: Asa Editores.

Bernardo, J. (1991). *Economia dos conflitos sociais*. São Paulo, Brazil: Cortez.

Birgin, A. (2000). La docencia como trabajo: la construcción de nuevas pautas de inclusion y exclusión. [The job of teaching: the construction of new patterns of inclusion and exclusion]. In P. Gentili & G. Frigotto (Eds.), *La ciudadanía negada: políticas de exclusión en la educación y el trabajo. [Citizenship Negated: policies of exclusion in education and work].* (pp. 221–239) Buenos Aires, Argentina: CLACSO.

Calcagno, A. (2001). Ajuste estructural, costo social y modalidades de desarrollo en América Latina. [Structural Adjustment, Social Cost and modalities of development in Latin America]. In E. Sader (Ed.), *El ajuste estructural en América Latina costos sociales y alternativas. [Structural Adjustment in Latin America: Social Costs and Alternatives]* (pp. 75–98). Buenos Aires, Argentina: CLACSO.

Castel, R. (1999). *As metamorfoses da questão social: uma crônica da questão social. [The Metamorphoses of the social question: a chronic social issue].* Petrópolis, Brazil: Vozes.

Castoriadis, C. (1985). *A experiência do movimento operário. [The experience of the workers' movement].* São Paulo, Brazil: Brasiliense.

Dubet F. (2002). *Le déclin de l'institution. [The decline of the institution].* Paris: Seuil.

Enguita, M. F. (1991). *A ambigüidade da docência: entre o profissionalismo e a proletarização. [The ambiguity of teaching: between professionalism and proletarianisation].* Revista Teoria & Educação. Porto Alegre, N. 4.

Fanfani, E. T. (2005). La condición docente. [The condition of teachers]. Buenos Aires, Argentina: Siglo Veintiuno Editores.

Feldfeber, M., & Oliveira, D. (2006) *A Políticas educativas y trabajo docente: nuevas regulaciones, nuevos sujetos? [Education Politics and Teachers' Work: new regulations, new subjects?].* (Comp.). Buenos Aires, Argentina: Centro de Publicaciones Educativas y Material Didactico.

Gentili, P., & Suarez, D. (Eds.). (2004). *Reforma educacional e luta democrática— um debate sobre a ação sindical docente na América Latina. [Educational Reform and democratic struggle—a debate on teachers' union action in Latin America.]* São Paulo, Brazil: Cortez.

Hargreaves, A. (1998). *Os Professores em Tempos de Mudança: O Trabalho e a Cultura na Idade Pós-Moderna. Alfragide. [Changing Teachers, Changing Times: teachers' work and culture in the Postmodern Age].* Portugal: Editora McGraw-Hill de Portugal.

Hill, D. (2006) Education Services Liberalization. In E. Rosskam (ed.) *Winners or Losers? Liberalizing public service*, pp. 3–54. Geneva: ILO.

Ianni, O. (1988, January/March). A questão nacional na América Latina. [The national question in Latin America]. *Estudos Avançados*, 2 (1).

Lessard, C. (2004). L'obligation de resultats en éducation: de quoi s'agit-il? Le contexte québécois d'une demande sociale, une rhétorique du changement et une extension de la recherche. [Requiring Results in Education: What is this? The Quebec context of social demand, a rhetoric of change, and an extension of research]. In C. Lessard, and P. Meirieu (Eds.), *L'obligation de resultats en education. [Requiring Results in Education]* (pp.23–48).Montréal, Quebec, Canadá: La Presses de L'Université Laval.

Medina, S. A., & Kelly, E. P. (2001). Professionnalisme et procés de formation: l'expérience latino-américaine. [Professionalism and teacher training: the Latin American Experience]. *Revue Éducation et Sociétés (N. 6/2000/2).* Paris: Département De Boeck Université.

Nuñez, I. (1990). Sindicatos de maestros, Estado y Políticas Educacionales en América Latina. [Teacher Unions, the State, and Education Politics in Latin America]. In *Final do século: desafi os da educação na América Latina, [Challenges of Education in Latin America at the end of the Century].* M. L. P. B., 1990 NUÑEZ, I. M. L. P. B. Franco e D. M. L. Zibas, Cortez Editora.

Oliveira, D. A. (2000). *Educação básica: gestão do trabalho e da pobreza. [Basic education: the management of employment and poverty]*. Petrópolis, Brazil: Vozes.

Oliveira, D. A., & Melo, S. D. (2004). *Estudio de los confl itos en los sistemas educativos de la región: agendas, actores, evolucion, manejo e desenlaces. [Study of conflict in the regions education systems: agendas, actors, evolution, management and outcomes]*. Santiago, Chile: LPP/UERJ/OREALC/UNESCO. (Relatório de estudo de caso do Brasil).

Rosskam, E. (Ed.) (2006) *Winners or Losers? Liberalizing public services*. Geneva: ILO.

Salama, P., & Valier, J. (1997). *Pobrezas e desigualdades no terceiro mundo. [The Poor and the Unequal in the third world]*. São Paulo, Brazil: Nobel.

Tiramonti, G. (2001). *Sindicalismo docente e reforma educativa na América Latina na década de 1990. [Teacher trade unionism and educational reform in Latin America]*. PREAL,19.

11 The State Apparatuses and the Working Class

Experiences From the United Kingdom: Educational Lessons From Venezuela[*]

Mike Cole

ABSTRACT

In the Introduction to this chapter, following French Marxist Louis Althusser, I briefly examine the roles of the Repressive State Apparatuses (RSAs), and the Ideological State Apparatuses (ISAs) in forging consensus to capitalist norms and values. The chapter is divided into three parts. In the first part, I discuss the role of what I have described as the governmental/political RSA/ISA in the United Kingdom in promoting neoliberal global capitalism and imperialism and forestalling social revolutionary change. In the first part I also make a few observations on the special role of the UK monarchy. Next I consider to what extent the educational ISA is the dominant *ISA*. In the second part of the chapter, as a contrast to the political and economic "consensus" which has been engineered in the United Kingdom, I look at current developments in Venezuela—at social democracy in action, and socialism in embryo. I also pose the question: Is there a need to amend Althusser's RSA/ISA thesis in the light of these developments. In the third part of the chapter, I make some suggestions as to how three important strands in the UK national curriculum might be used to break "the last taboo" how they might facilitate the creation of spaces for discussions in schools of the alternative to global neoliberal capitalism—world socialism.

INTRODUCTION

At the turn of the century, socialist scholar and revolutionary, and university and college union (UCU) activist Tom Hickey (2000, p. 177) declared

---

This chapter is adapted from Cole, M. (2008). The working class and the State Apparatuses in the UK and Venezuela: implications for education. *Educational Futures*. April 2008.

that young workers in Britain "will carry, as did their forebears, a political potential of historic importance." Hickey was referring to the role of the working class as agents of the revolutionary transition to socialism. He concluded that "[i]t is a potential, however, of which they might spend their lives in ignorance" (p. 177).

My initial response was one of shock and surprise that the suggestion was being made by a fellow Marxist that the British working class might be lost for socialism for up to a generation. I must now say that I think Hickey was right. The prospect of socialist revolutionary change in Britain is *possibly* off the cards for the foreseeable future.

To understand how and why this has happened, it is useful to look at the role in forging consensus to capitalist norms and values of what Louis Althusser (1971)[1] has described as *the state apparatuses*. For Marxists, *the state* is considered to be far more than "government." Althusser (1971, pp. 143–144) makes a distinction between what he calls the *repressive state apparatuses* (RSAs; government, administration, army, police, courts, prisons) and the *ideological state apparatuses* (ISAs; religion, education, family, law, politics, trade unions, communication, culture).

The RSAs operate primarily by force and control. This can be by making illegal the forces and organizations (and their tactics) that threaten the capitalist status quo and the rate of profit. Thus, for example, restrictions are placed on strike action and trade union activities. More extreme versions of RSA action include heavy intimidation policing and other forms of state-sanctioned political repression and violence by the police and armed forces (Hill, 2001a, p. 106; see also Hill, 2001b, 2004, 2005).

The ISAs, on the other hand, operate primarily through ideology—promoting the values and attitudes required by capitalism. However, it needs to be pointed out that the two state apparatuses function both by violence and by ideology. It is worth quoting Althusser (1971) at length:

> What distinguishes the ISAs from the (Repressive) State Apparatus is the following basic difference: the Repressive State Apparatus functions "by violence," whereas the Ideological State Apparatuses' *function "by ideology."* I can clarify matters by correcting this distinction. I shall say rather that every State Apparatus, whether Repressive or Ideological, "functions" both by violence and by ideology, but with one very important distinction which makes it imperative not to confuse the Ideological State Apparatuses with the (Repressive) State Apparatus. This is the fact that the (Repressive) State Apparatus functions massively and predominantly *by repression* (including physical repression), while functioning secondarily by ideology. (There is no such thing as a purely repressive apparatus.) For example, the Army and the Police also function by ideology both to ensure their own cohesion and reproduction, and in the "values" they propound externally. In the same way, but inversely, it is essential to say that for their part the Ideological

State Apparatuses function massively and predominantly *by ideology,* but they also function secondarily by repression, even if ultimately, but only ultimately, this is very attenuated and concealed, even symbolic. (There is no such thing as a purely ideological apparatus.) Thus Schools and Churches use suitable methods of punishment, expulsion, selection, etc., to "discipline" not only their shepherds, but also their flocks. The same is true of the Family. . . . The same is true of the cultural IS Apparatus (censorship, among other things), etc. (pp. 144–145)

The ruling class, and governments in whose interests they act, tend to prefer, in normal circumstances, to operate via ISAs. For example, introducing trade union legislation to limit the right to strike presents less problems for the state than physically attacking strikers; changing the school curriculum to make it more in line with the requirements of capital, and thereby foreclosing pupil/student dissent, is less messy than sending in the riot police or the troops to deal with demonstrations that are "threatening peace and order." The ISAs also tend to be deemed more legitimate by the populace (Hill, 2001a, p. 106).

PART ONE: THE STATE APPARATUSES IN THE UNITED KINGDOM

The Government/Political RSA/ISA

As we have seen, Althusser (1971) identifies a number of state apparatuses, all of which are important. For my purposes here, however, I will concentrate in this part of the paper on what I have termed the government/political RSA/ISA. The government is for Althusser part of the RSA (Althusser, 1971, pp. 143–144), and the political ("the political system, including the different Parties," p. 144) is decidedly an ISA. As we saw in the long quotation immediately above, however, both RSAs and ISAs operate by force and ideology. It is for this reason that, while Althusser distinguishes between RSAs and ISAs, I have adopted the formulation, "the government/political RSA/ISA."

This RSA/ISA has made seem inevitable not only *capitalism per se,* but has also successfully hailed *neoliberalism* as healthy, *globalization* as part of the natural order and *U.S.-led imperialism* as unstoppable. In order for all this to work, there is also a need for the socialism to be believed to be no longer viable. I will deal with each of these capitalist triumphs in turn.

Capitalism as Inevitable

The political ISA has been spectacularly successful in securing ruling class hegemony in the United Kingdom. Not only is capitalism presented as "inevitable," it is also hailed as natural. Capitalism presents itself as "determining the future as surely as the laws of nature make tides rise to lift boats" (McMurtry, 2000, p. 2). Capitalism is made to seem unalterable and the market mechanism "has been hypostatized into a natural force unresponsive to human wishes" (Callinicos, 2000, p. 125). Ironically, the capitalist class and their representatives who used to deride what they saw as the metaphysic of "Marxist economic determinism" (economic processes determine all else, including the future direction of society) are the ones who now champion the "world-wide market revolution" and the accompanying inevitability of "economic restructuring" (McMurtry, 2000). Capitalism is praised,

> as if it has now replaced the natural environment. It announces itself through its business leaders and politicians as coterminous with freedom, and indispensable to democracy such that any attack on capitalism as exploitative or hypocritical becomes an attack on world freedom and democracy itself. (McLaren, 2000, p. 32)

Neoliberalism as Healthy

Martinez and García (2000) have identified five defining features of the global phenomenon of neoliberalism:

1. *The rule of the market:*
   - The liberation of "free" or private enterprise from any bonds imposed by the state no matter how much social damage this causes;
   - greater openness to international trade and investment;
   - the reduction of wages by de-unionizing workers and eliminating workers' rights;
   - an end to price controls;
   - total freedom of movement for capital, goods and services.

2. *Cutting public expenditure:*
   - Less spending on social services such as education and health care;
   - reducing the safety-net for the poor;
   - reducing expenditure on maintenance, for example, of roads, bridges and water supply.

3. *Deregulation: Reducing government regulation of everything that could diminish profits:*
   - Less protection of the environment;
   - less concerns with job safety.

4. *Privatization: Selling state-owned enterprises, goods and services to private investors, for example:*
   - Banks;
   - key industries;
   - railroads;

- toll highways;
- electricity;
- schools;
- hospitals;
- fresh water.

5. *Eliminating the concept of "the public good" or "community":*
   - Replacing it with "individual responsibility";
   - pressuring the poorest people in a society to find their own solutions to their lack of health care, education and social security.[2]

Neoliberalism is presented *ideologically*—as healthy competition, as freedom from the constraints of meddling and interfering governments. It is conflated with "modernization" and "reform"—a wholesome alternative to "the nanny state" and a dependency culture. On a world scale, it works also to varying degrees by repression, some of which is brute force and violence.

Globalization as Part of the Natural Order

Globalization became one of the discursive orthodoxies of the 1990s and continues to hold sway into the 21st century. It is proclaimed in the speeches of virtually all mainstream politicians, in the financial pages of newspapers and in company reports; it is common currency in corporation newsletters and shop stewards meetings (Harman, 1996, p. 3). Its premises are that in the face of global competition, capitals are increasingly constrained to compete on the world market. Its argument is that, in this new epoch, these capitals can only do this in so far as they become multinational corporations and operate on a world scale, outside the confines of nation states. The argument continues: This diminishes the role of the nation–state, the implication being that there is little, if anything, that can be done about it. Capitalists and their allies insist that, since globalization is a fact of life, it is incumbent on workers, given this globalized market, to be flexible in their approach to what they do and for how long they do it, to accept lower wages, and to concur with the restructuring and diminution of welfare states.

Globalization is, in fact, as old as capitalism itself, but it is a phenomenon that alters its character through history (e.g., Cole, 1998, 2005, 2008). This is because one of the central features of capitalism is that, once rooted, parasitic-like, it grows and spreads. This double movement is thoroughly explored by Marx (1887/1965) in *Capital* and elsewhere (for a summary, see Sweezy, 1997). The adoption of neoliberal policies has given a major boost to globalization, both de facto and ideologically. Marxists are particularly interested in the way in which the concept of globalization is used ideologically to further the interests of capitalists and their political supporters (for an analysis, see Cole 1998, 2005), of the way in which it is used to mystify the populace as a whole, to suppress class consciousness, and to stifle action by the Left in particular (e.g., Meiksins Wood, 1998; Cole, 2008).

For Tony Blair, for example, globalization was part of the natural order: "I hear people say we have to stop and debate globalisation. You might as well debate whether autumn should follow summer" (Speech to the Labour Party Conference, 2005). Blair's rhetoric provides a prime example of the ideological justification for globalized neoliberal capitalism. Like neoliberalism, globalization *in practice* takes on a brutal repressive mode, with capitalists touring the globe in the search of the cheapest labor it can find, or ruthlessly exploited both legal and "illegal" migrant workers in the home country.

Imperialism as Unstoppable

As far as imperialism is concerned, that the United States is involved in major new imperial adventures, for example, in Iraq and central Asia, is being recognized by a wide spectrum of political opinion, with wide support from neoconservatives, and condemnation from some political liberals and others, and of course Marxists (Cole, 2008; for information on the political affiliation of these various writers, see Cole, 2004). That the Blair Government was involved by way of fawning ideological acquiescence and support, along with substantial material support in the way of troops must surely be widely accepted. I have discussed at length elsewhere (Cole, 2008) the vicissitudes of U.S. imperialism—save it to note here that, despite massive opposition, principally by way of street demonstrations, the U.S. and British ruling classes get away with imperialist adventures, simply because most people think they cannot do anything to stop it. Necessary as they are, demonstrations are just that—a protest about what is happening. Demonstrators do not expect world imperialist leaders to say, "ok, you're right—we'll pull out of Iraq and Afghanistan." Indeed we are told that the "war on terror" goes on until there are no more terrorists. In reality, of course, the so called "war on terror" begets more terrorism, which in turn is used to legitimate the continuation of the "war on terror" and so on and so on.

The material effects of imperialism, of course, entail states in their most repressive, most brutal, most uncompromising modes, with respect to both the imperial subjects, and with respect to the (young) occupying troops— the modern equivalent of cannon fodder.[3]

Symptomatic of the success of the Government/political RSA/ISA is the fact that pro-imperialist Gordon Brown (in his first face-to-face meeting with Bush in April 2007, Brown stressed there would be no change of policy in Iraq or Afghanistan) has, despite personal differences between himself and Blair seamlessly replaced Blair as British Prime Minister.

Socialism as No Longer Viable

While neoliberal global capitalism is portrayed as healthy, normal and inevitable, and imperialism is perceived as unstoppable despite massive opposition, socialism is portrayed as something that is aberrant, as something that happened in the past and *failed,* and will not happen again. Thatcherism bears much responsibility for this. The collapse of the Soviet Union was used to back up the claim that socialism is no longer viable. Socialism was portrayed as synonymous with Stalinism. Congruent with her success in championing the free market as the only viable way to run economies was the apparent success with which Margaret Thatcher seemed to wipe social-ism off the agenda of political change in Britain—essential if Britain were to move in the direction of labor market compliance and labor flexibility. Fol-lowing the late 1980s revolutions in Eastern Europe and the Soviet Union, Marxism, Thatcher argued, was now extinct and outmoded. Therefore the Labour Party was now also extinct and outmoded. It is precisely the suc-cess of this formulation which projected Tony Blair, a neoliberal, to center stage—a savior of the Labour Party—but only if the Labour Party became reformulated as "New Labour."

"New Labour" was coined as part of an orchestrated campaign to dis-tance the party from its socialist and (radical) social democratic roots, to "modernize" it—in other words, to establish an unequivocal pro-capitalist base for itself. For Blair, the "founding principle of New Labour" was "the partnership we have tried to build with [business] . . . and it will not change" (*Guardian,* 2001b). This underlines why Blair, described and reported in Britain's most popular tabloid by Margaret Thatcher as "probably the most formidable Labour leader since Hugh Gaitskell" (*Sun,* 1995), in 1995 abandoned the anti-capitalist Clause IV from the party constitution—for Blair a crucially important step forward, and signalling the future direc-tion that New Labour would take.[4] In the same year, in Hayman Island, Australia, Tony Blair declared to Rupert Murdoch and the world that "the era of the grand ideologies, all encompassing, all pervasive, total in their solutions—and often dangerous—is over" (Blair, 1995, p. 12).[5]

The Special Role of the Monarchy

In addition to the political/government RSA/ISA, the monarchy in the United Kingdom continues to make a major contribution to the ideological role of the state, in that it "normalizes" a massively hierarchical society. As Althusser (1971) has argued, above the ensemble of state apparatuses is "the head of State, the government and the administration" (p, 138). Althusser has also pointed out that "the English bourgeoisie was able to 'compromise' with the aristocracy and 'share' State power and the use of the State apparatus with it for a long time" (p. 154). This "arrangement" continues, albeit in modified form, up to the present day. In the United Kingdom, the head of state is, of course, the Queen. The monarchy, though not as popular as it used to be—"Princess Di as the fairy princess"—is still thriving. The royal family continue to receive mass attention in the media, much of it favorable. Their outrageous activities are normalized and con-doned. For example, the vast wealth they have, their private planes and boats, the large number of servants they employ are all generally portrayed as "necessary" for such important people, who are seen as an "asset" to the nation. If one of the princes spends thousands of pounds on a night out—when Prince William split up with Kate Middleton in April 2007, he racked up a £11,000 bar bill in one night—this is reported neutrally by the tabloids, as "understandable." The aristocracy and the monarchy are not under any imminent threat of extinction. The Queen receives £7.9 million per year from taxpayers via the Civil List, while the income due to the heir to the throne, The Prince of Wales's Office from the Duchy of Cornwall (created in 1337 by Edward III) amounts to £14.067 million (The Duchy of Cornwall, 2006).

THE EDUCATIONAL ISA—THE DOMINANT ONE?

I have attempted to demonstrate the importance in the forging of capitalist hegemony of the government/political RSA/ISA, and to a lesser extent, the significance of the Queen as head of state, and the rest of the monarchy and the aristocracy in legitimizing hierarchies. For Althusser, however, it was the educational state apparatus that was paramount. As he put it, whereas the religious ISA (system of different churches) used historically to be the major ISA, the ISA "which has been installed in the *dominant* position in mature capitalist social formations . . . is the *educational ideological apparatus*" (Althusser, 1971, p. 153).[6] Althusser (1971) argued that schools are particularly important for inculcating the dominant ideology, since no other ISA requires compulsory attendance of all children eight hours a day for five days a week. Althusser suggested that what children learn at school is "know-how"—wrapped in the ruling ideology of the ruling class. Gordon Brown's (2002, *The Guardian*) declaration, in a speech embracing "inevitable globalisation," that teaching the "entrepreneurial culture" should start in schools, serves to uphold Althusser's contention. Indeed, from September 2005, new funding of £60 million a year was made available from the Department for Education and Science (DfES) to support a new scheme to promote enterprise education in all English secondary schools. Ken McCarthy, a school governor at Swanlea School—a hub school in the Schools' Enterprise Education Network (SEEN)—noted that the scheme provided "skills and attitudes required for the modern workplace" (DVD viewable at DfES, 2007). SEEN aims to support "all schools to embed an enterprise culture" (DfES, 2007). In addition, in the light of the inquiry by Lord Leitch in 2006, which warned that Britain's competitiveness and economic growth would suffer by 2020 unless the workforce was better trained (Lepkowksa, 2007, p. 1), a new secondary curriculum is scheduled for introduction in September 2008, which according to Lepkowska is "part of a major overhaul of teaching . . . to make sure that every pupil is motivated and engaged in class and ultimately prepared for the workplace" (p. 1).

In portraying capitalism as the norm, and keeping discussions of socialism out of the school curriculum, and the teacher education curriculum (Hill, 2007) education is indeed a prime ISA. In the United Kingdom, for example, "education, education, education" was New Labour's main mantra. From a Marxist perspective, it is possible to identify both a *Capitalist Agenda for Education* and a *Capitalist Agenda in Education*. The former relates to the role of education in producing the kind of workforce that is currently required by global capitalist enterprises, and is thus about making profits *indirectly,* while the latter is about making profits directly (for analyses, see Hill, 2004a, b, c; Cole, 2007; Rikowski, 2005; Hatcher, 2006). The *Capitalist Agenda for Education* is clearly part of the ISAs, whereas the *Capitalist Agenda in Education* is part of the accumulation process at the base.[7]

The businessification of schools is about to intensify. In a speech to the City of London in June 2007, Gordon Brown stated that if Britain was to meet the challenges of globalization, improving education and skills had to be the priority: "[i]n future every single secondary school and primary school should have a business partner—and I invite you all to participate" (Gordon Brown as cited in BBC, 2007b).

This is not, of course, to say that there is no resistance from educational workers. Althusser (1971) was well aware of this. As he put it:

> I ask the pardon of those teachers who, in dreadful conditions, attempt to turn the few weapons they can find in the history and learning they "teach" against the ideology, the system and the practices in which they are trapped. They are a kind of hero. But they are rare. (p. 158)

Ways to initiate discussions in schools on the democratic world socialist alternative to global capitalism are discussed in the last section of this chapter.

PART TWO: THE STATE APPARATUSES IN VENEZUELA

Social Democracy in Practice/Socialism in Embryo

If I am right that the formation and development of class consciousness in Britain has been forestalled for the foreseeable future, where in the current era might Marxists look to for inspiration and guidance? In the rest of this chapter I discuss the initiatives of the socialist government of the Bolivarian Republic of Venezuela.[8] In Venezuela, neoliberal capitalism is not seen as "inevitable," nor indeed is capitalism itself. President Hugo Rafael Chávez Frías[9] is against neoliberalism and imperialism. As he remarked in 2003:

> In Venezuela, we are developing a model of struggle against neoliberalism and imperialism. For this reason, we find we have millions of

friends in this world, although we also have many enemies (as cited in Contreras Baspineiro, 2003).

Chávez talks about globalizing socialism, rather than global capitalism:

> Faced with the outrageous excesses of the powerful, our only alternative is to unite ... That's why I call upon all of you to globalize the revolution, to globalize the struggle for ... freedom and equality. (as cited in Contreras Baspineiro, 2003)

In January 2007, the utilities sector and the country's largest telecoms company were nationalized, and in May 2007, Chávez took control of four major oil projects worth $30 billion (PDVSA, the state oil company has held majority control since 2005). Also in May 2007, Venezuela pulled out of the International Monetary Fund (IMF) and the World Bank.

The Missiones

Central to the Bolivarian Revolution are the "Missiones"—a series of social justice, social welfare, anti-poverty, and educational programs implemented under the administration of the Chávez government. The Missiones use volunteers to teach reading, writing and basic mathematics to those Venezuelans who have not completed their elementary-level education. In addition, they provide ongoing basic education courses to those who have not completed such education, and remedial high school-level classes to millions of Venezuelans who were forced to drop out from high school.

The Bolivarian University of Venezuela (UBV) is particularly significant in the struggle for social justice. Previously the luxurious offices of oil oligarchs, UBV has opened its doors to thousands of students. This program's goal is to boost institutional synergy and community participation in order to guarantee and provide access to higher education to all high school students.[10] UBV, which recently had its first 1,078 graduates (70% of which are women) has to be seen in the context of the established university system in Venezuela. Like many others in Latin America, it has traditionally primarily served a limited, better-off section of the population. Access for the poor majority has been extremely restricted, partly because of the financial costs of university study, but also because of a deeply entrenched system of corruption and patronage governing entry procedures and so forth. Since 1998, the government has raised the number of university students in the country from 366,000 to 1,200,000. This is a *genuine* widening participation initiative.

Chávez has announced that he aims to create 38 new universities in the current phase of the "Bolivarian Revolution." The state universities go out to the people in the *barrios,* as well as the people coming to them, with the government aiming for more than 190 satellite classrooms throughout Venezuela by 2009.

The Missiones are not confined to education. Other Missiones are concerned with health, providing a free service to the poor by giving access to health care assistance to 60% of the excluded population through the construction of 8,000 popular medical centers: providing a doctor for every 250 families (1,200 people), increasing the life expectancy of the population, and contributing to a good standard of life for all.

Yet other Missiones aim at assisting the sport skills of students, senior citizens, pregnant women, people with disabilities, and anyone wishing to improve their standard of life and health, and include high performance sport, and vocational training for work. There is also a mission which sells food and other essential products like medicines at affordable prices, along with a massive program of soup kitchens (British Venezuela Solidarity Campaign, 2006).

Crucially, there are Missiones to restore human rights to numerous indigenous communities, and to hand over land titles to farmers in order to guarantee food for the poor and to foster a socialized economy and endogenous development (British Venezuela Solidarity Campaign, 2006).

Finally, Negra Hipólita Mission, one of the newest created by the national government, was launched on January 14, 2006, in order to fight poverty, misery and social exclusion; a new stage in the struggle against inequality. The Bolivarian Republic of Venezuela is committed to set Venezuela free from misery (British Venezuela Solidarity Campaign, 2006).

Social Democracy and Socialism: Is There a Need to Amend the RSA/ISA Thesis?

The Missiones are, of course, classic examples of social democracy, somewhat akin to the policies and practice of the postwar labor governments in Britain. What distinguishes the Bolivarian Revolution, however, is that these reforms are seen both by the Chávez government and by large sections of the Venezuelan working class as a step on the road to true socialist revolution, since for Chávez "[t]he hurricane of revolution has begun, and it will never again be calmed" (as cited in Contreras Baspineiro, 2003). Elsewhere, Chávez asserted: "I am convinced, and I think that this conviction will be for the rest of my life, that the path to a new, better and possible world, is not capitalism, the path is socialism, that is the path: socialism, socialism" (Lee, 2005).[11]

At this point it is useful to return to Althusser and the Marxist theory of the State. In classical Marxist theory, the capitalist state must be overthrown rather than reformed. As Althusser (1971) put it:

> the proletariat must seize State power in order to destroy the existing bourgeois State apparatus and, in a first phase, replace it with a quite

different proletarian, State apparatus, then in a later phases set in motion
. . . the end of State power, the end of every State apparatus. (p. 142)

However, Althusser's analysis did not extend to the possible existence of
states which advocate their own destruction. As Chávez proclaimed at the
World Social Forum in 2005:

> We must reclaim socialism as a thesis, a project and a path, but a new
> type of socialism, a humanist one which puts humans, and not ma-
> chines *or the state* ahead of everything. That's the debate we must pro-
> mote around the world (emphasis added; as cited in Hearne, 2005)

More recently (January 8, 2007), Chávez has created "communal councils"
and has referred to "the revolutionary explosion of communal power, of
communal councils" ("Chavez: I am also a Trotskyist," 2007). This is a
project for rebuilding or replacing the bourgeois administrative machin-
ery of local and state governments with a network of communal councils,
where the local populations meet to decide on local priorities and how to
realize them.

With the communal councils [Chávez said, in perhaps his most clearly
articulated intention to destroy the existing state] we have to go beyond the
local. We have to begin creating . . . a kind of confederation, local, regional
and national, of communal councils. We have to head towards the creation
of a communal state. And the old bourgeois state, which is still alive and
kicking—this we have to progressively dismantle, at the same time as we
build up the communal state, the socialist state, the Bolivarian state, a
state that is capable of carrying through a revolution. ("Chavez: I am also
a Trotskyist," 2007)

"Almost all states," Chávez continued, "have been born to prevent revolutions. So we have quite a task: to convert a counter-revolutionary state
into a revolutionary state" (as cited in Piper, 2007a, p. 8). The communal
councils are intended to bring together 200 to 400 families to discuss and
decide on local spending and development plans. Thirty thousand communal councils are intended, and provide, in the words of Roland Dennis, an
historic opportunity to do away with the capitalist state (as cited in Piper,
2007a. p. 8)

If it is the case that genuinely supports socialist revolution from below,
which will eventually overthrow the existing capitalist state of Venezuela,
then, for Marxists, he must be seen as an ally. Whether he is or not, however, is less important than the fact that he is openly advocating *and* helping to create genuine socialist consciousness among the working class.

For example, swearing in the new ministers, in the wake of his land-
slide presidential election victory, late in 2006, Chávez declared that they
will be in charge of pushing forward his government's project of implementing "21st century socialism" in Venezuela (Wilpert, 2007), which

Chávez defines as "fundamentally human, it is love, it is solidarity, and our Socialism is original, indigenous, Christian and Bolivarian" (as cited in Hampton, 2006).[12] More recently, Chávez advised all Venezuelans to read and study the writings of Leon Trotsky, and commented favorably on *The Transitional Programme,* which was written by Trotsky for the founding congress of the Fourth International in 1938 (Martin, 2007). Trotsky's pamphlet begins with a discussion of the objective prerequisites for a socialist revolution.

Trotsky's concept of "the permanent revolution," Chávez went on, is an extremely important thesis.[13] Chávez underlined Trotsky's idea about the necessity for conditions for socialism to be ripe and expressed his view that this is certainly the case in Venezuela (Martin, 2007).

Chávez continued,

> Trotsky points out something which is extremely important, and he says that [the conditions for proletarian revolution] are starting to rot, not because of the workers, but because of the leadership which did not see, which did not know, which was cowardly, which subordinated itself to the mandates of capitalism, of the great bourgeois democracies, the trade unions. (as cited in Martin, 2007)

For me, this statement is indicative of Chávez' belief in the importance of grass roots working class consciousness and action.

Martin (2007) agrees,

> [s]ince Chávez started talking about socialism in January 2005, this has become a major subject of debate in all corners of Venezuela. Chávez's statement that under capitalism there was no solution for the problems of the masses and that the road forward was socialism represented a major step forward in his political development. He had started trying to reform the system and to give the masses of the Venezuelan poor decent health and education services and land, and he had realised through his own experience and reading that this was not possible under capitalism. (p. XX)

In the last few months Chávez has become increasingly impatient at the delaying tactics of the bureaucracy and the counter-revolution in Venezuela. He has made clear that when he talks of building socialism, he is talking about doing it now, not in the long distant future (Martin, 2007). In his comments about Trotsky he stressed the point:

> Well, here the conditions are given, I think that this thought or reflection of Trotsky is useful for the moment we are living through, here the conditions are given, in Venezuela and Latin America, I am not going to comment on Europe now, nor on Asia, there the reality is another,

another rhythm, another dynamic, but in Latin America conditions are given, and in Venezuela this is a matter of course, to carry out a genuine revolution (as cited in Martin, 2007).

Leading figures in some of the Bolivarian parties have refused to join in Chávez' new United Socialist Party, the United Socialist Party of Venezuela (PSUV) formed two weeks after his election success on December 3, 2006, fearing the development of revolutionary consciousness among the workers. To one opponent's statement that he was in favor of "democratic socialism," Chávez replied that the problem was that "I am a socialist and he is a social-democrat," and he added, "I am in favour of revolutionary socialism" (as cited in Martin, 2007).

In talking about the need for a revolutionary leadership Chávez also quoted from Lenin on the need for a revolutionary party in order "to articulate millions of wills into one single will," which "is indispensable to carry out a revolution, otherwise it is lost, like the rivers that overflow, like the Yaracuy that when it reaches the Caribbean loses its riverbed and becomes a swamp" (as cited in Martin, 2007). Chávez argued that PSUV must be the most democratic party Venezuela has ever seen, built from the bottom up, inviting all the currents of the Venezuelan left to join.

He also insisted that it must not be dominated by electoral concerns, nor by the existing leaders of the existing coalition parties. He criticized the way the Bolshevik Party in Russia came to suffocate rather than stimulate a battle of ideas for socialism, noting how the marvelous slogan of "all power to the soviets" degenerated into a sad reality of "all power to the party." For Chávez, this points towards precisely the kind of mass, democratic, revolutionary, political organization that is needed (Piper, 2007b)

Capitalists and their political supporters are intent on spreading disinformation about the Chávez Government. In particular, there are numerous attempts to label the government nondemocratic or "dictatorial."[14] In actual fact, according to a survey released by the Chilean NGO Latinbarometro (Wilpert, 2006) apart from Uruguay, Venezuelans view their democracy more favorably than the citizens of all other Latin American countries view their own democracies. Moreover, Venezuela is in first place in several measures of political participation, compared to all other Latin American countries. The percentage of citizens surveyed who indicated satisfaction increased more since 1998, the year Chávez was elected, than any other country. The percentage expressing satisfaction increased from 32% to 57% in those eight years. In terms of political participation, Venezuelans indicate that they are more politically active than the citizens of any other surveyed country.

As Martin (2007) concludes,

[t]he political thinking of Chavez is in tune and reflects the conclusions drawn by tens of thousands of revolutionary activists in Venezuela,

in the factories, in the neighbourhoods, in the countryside. They are growing increasingly impatient and want the revolution to be victorious once and for all[15]

PART THREE: IMPLICATIONS FOR EDUCATION IN THE UNITED KINGDOM: THE LAST TABOO

Chávez devoted a May 15, 2005 call-in television program to education. Attending the inauguration of a new high school, he presented a "new educational model for a new citizen." In direct contrast to Gordon Brown's view (2002) that teaching the "entrepreneurial culture" should start in schools, for Chávez, competition and individualism in schools must give way to unity, brotherhood[16] and solidarity. "We are all a team, going along eliminating little by little the values or the anti-values that capitalism has planted in us from childhood" (Chávez, as cited in Whitney, 2005 para. 2).

Great strides, with respect to legislation (Nixon, 2008), have been made over the last decade in promoting equality of opportunity and equality of gender, race, disability and sexuality. This has been the case in schools, and in further and higher education. Some improvements have also been made to the curriculum itself. However, capitalism is not directly discussed, nor are the values that it promotes addressed in a critical analytical context. Moreover, social class, however, except in the narrow though nonetheless important sense of working class underachievement, has been left out. It is high time to redress this and for children and young people to learn about capitalism and social class, and their accompanying massive inequalities, in a wide-ranging and meaningful way. From an early age, children have the right to know what it is really going on in the world. Judy Dunn (as cited in Epstein, 1993) has shown that children are aware of the feelings of others as early as their second year of life and *can* therefore "decenter" and are thus amenable to understanding issues of equality.

There are some positive developments in schools related to globalization, to world poverty and to ecology, but no space is provided for a discussion of *alternatives* to neoliberal global capitalism, such as world democratic socialism. Discussing world democratic socialism in schools may be seen as *the last taboo*. It is time to move forward and bring such discussions into the classroom in schools, colleges and universities. Paulo Freire (1972) urged teachers to detach themselves and their pupils from the idea that they are agents of capital, where *banking education* (the teacher deposits information into an empty account) is the norm and to reinvent schools as democratic public spheres where meaningful *dialogue* can take place. Given the fact that global capitalism is out of control (e.g., Cole, 2008), the very survival of our planet is dependent on such dialogue. Neoliberal capitalism, in being primarily about expanding opportunities for large multinational companies, has undermined the power of nation states and, as we saw above, exacerbated the negative effects of globalization on such services as healthcare, education, water and transport.

World capitalism's effects on both the "developed" and "developing world" should be discussed openly and freely in the classroom. Capitalism and the destruction of the environment are inextricably linked to the extent that it is becoming increasingly apparent that saving the environment is dependent on the destruction of capitalism. Classroom debate should therefore include a consideration of the connections between global capitalism and environmental destruction. McLaren and Houston (2005) have argued that "escalating environmental problems at all geographical scales from local to global have become a pressing reality that critical educators can no longer afford to ignore" (p. 167). They go on to cite "the complicity between global profiteering, resource colonization, and the wholesale ecological devastation that has become a matter of everyday life for most species on the planet" (p. 167). Following Kahn (2003), they state the need for "a critical dialogue between social and eco-justice" (McLaren & Houston, 2005, p. 168). They call for a dialectics of ecological and environmental justice to reveal the malign interaction between capitalism, imperialism and ecology that has created widespread environmental degradation which has dramatically accelerated with the onset of neoliberalism. Environmental issues and their interrelationship with global neoliberal capitalism and the new (U.S.) imperialism are discussed at length in Cole (2007a; see also, Feldman & Lotz, 2004).

CONCLUSION

In the first part of this chapter I began by suggesting that Louis Althusser's (1971) concepts of RSAs/ISAs are a good way of explaining and understanding why the working class in the United Kingdom has been interpellated to acquiesce in global neoliberal capitalism. With respect to U.S.-led imperialism, I argued that, while this is opposed by a large number of people, a sense that we cannot stop it has been successfully imposed. At the same time, socialism has been triumphantly distorted and discredited by the ruling class. The monarchy and the aristocracy, I suggested, helps engender a natural sense of hierarchy. I concluded the first part of the chapter by a consideration of the educational ISA as the dominant ISA.

In the second part of the chapter, I turned to the Bolivarian republic of Venezuela, which I commend to be a good model of social democracy in action, and socialism in embryo.

In the third part of the chapter, I suggested that, if we are to address *all* equality issues, including social class, if we are to offer a truly democratic dialogic education, if we are to consider all possible ways of saving the planet, it is imperative to break through *the last taboo*. A meaningful evaluation of global neoliberal capitalism is a necessity, as is a serious consideration of the world socialist alternative.

I began this chapter by quoting Tom Hickey. Hickey is right that young workers in Britain carry a political potential of historic importance. There is much work to do if that potential is to be realized. In this endeavor, I believe that the Left in education have an important role to play. This chapter has concentrated on a small part of the work of Louis Althusser, who, as noted, has sometimes been criticized for his structural determinism. Let me finish with a quote from that other great European Marxist, Antonio Gramsci, who is celebrated for his belief in human agency. Gramsci famously called for continued determination, even in the direst of circumstances, in the belief that resilience will result in meaningful change even in the face of adversity. As Gramsci (1921/1978) put it:

Our pessimism has increased, but our motto is still alive and to the point: "pessimism of the intellect, optimism of the will."

ACKNOWLEDGMENTS

I thank Dave Hill, Alpesh Maisuria, Carol Smith, Paul Warmington, Ian Woodfield and Richard Woolley for their very helpful comments on this chapter. As always any inadequacies remain mine.

NOTES

1. It is not the intention of this chapter to evaluate the work of Althusser as a whole. A structuralist Marxist, Althusser is widely perceived to be deterministic, in denying the power of "human agency"—the ability of people to successfully struggle to change things (but see his reference to "teacher heroes" below). It is also not my intention to address what has been described as the internally contradictory nature of both his ISA essay and his wider corpus of work (for a discussion, see for example, Callinicos, 1976). However, the particular Althusserian concepts referred to in this chapter are illuminating, I argue, in understanding political and other events in the United Kingdom over the last 30 years or so, and in trying to understand current developments in Venezuela.
2. Neoliberalism *in the economic sense* as is described here has its origins in 19th century liberalism, which was based on the ideas of Adam Smith. Smith and others advocated no government intervention in economic matters. Economic liberalism prevailed throughout the 19th and early 20th centuries. It was proceeded by welfare economics based on the ideas John Maynard Keynes. Keynes believed in mass government spending to create full employment and to create jobs in times of depression. Keynesian economics had a great influence on President Roosevelt's "New Deal" in the United States, and on the mixed economy (part state/part private ownership), a major feature in Britain from the end of the World War II until the 1970s. Liberalism's "neo" or new incarnation arose as a result of shrinking profit rates which encouraged capitalists, with the connivance of sympathetic governments, to launch a world offensive—to seek unfettered profit making around the globe to compensate for these shrinking profits. With respect to economics, the

current dominant ruling faction in the United States (George W. Bush and his followers) epitomizes neoliberal thinking. With respect to other spheres of life—culture, morality and so forth—the faction has been described as— neoconservative" (or "neocon") and, taking cognizance of its strong right-wing Christian leanings, as "theo-conservative" or "theo-con." "Liberal" *in the political sense,* on the other hand, is used in Britain to describe "middle-of-the-road" politics. In the United States, it refers to those whose politics is considered to be "on the Left." (for an analysis of various political perspectives, see Hill, 2001c).

3. Travelling regularly between Lincoln and Brighton by train, I sometimes come across British troops on their way to the airport, some apparently not knowing whether they are then off to Iraq or Afghanistan. These are *young working class* men (I have not yet encountered any young women yet)—in Britain it is possible to enlist at seventeen years of age. It is easy to forget the reality of the everyday existence of these young people when the media is saturated with the glorification of neoimperialist "adventures." At the time of writing (May 2007), fourteen teenagers, as members of the British armed forces, one of them a young woman, have died during the present conflict in Iraq (McVeigh, 2007, p. 9)

4. In 1959, Hugh Gaitskell had attempted without success to abolish Clause IV, the clause of the Labour Party constitution at that time that committed the Labour Party:

> to secure for the workers by hand or by brain the full fruits of their industry and the most equitable distribution thereof that may be possible upon the basis of the common ownership of the means of production, distribution, and exchange, and the best obtainable system of popular administration and control of each industry or service.

This Clause IV was printed on Labour Party membership cards. It had been adopted in 1918. It was removed by Tony Blair at the Labour Party conference of 1995, a defining moment in the transition from Labour to New Labour.

5. What Blair meant was that the grand ideology of socialism is over, and that the grand ideology of capitalism is now the only option. He repeated this belief in his aforementioned speech to the (British) Labour Party Conference, on October 2, 2001, when he declared that "ideology . . . in the sense of rigid forms of economic and social theory . . . is dead" (*Guardian*, 2001a, p. 5). Again, the subtext is *socialist* theory, not capitalist or neoliberal theory, is dead.

6. To what extent, Althusser might have modified his views on education as being the dominant ISA, given the current hegemony of organized religion (neoconservative distortions of Christianity and distortion of Islam by certain groups; Althusser, 1971, was concerned with the Christian—Roman Catholic—religion only) is open to debate. In addition, the proliferation of the mass media in its numerous guises might have encouraged Althusser to attribute a more central role to the communication ISA. In fact, Althusser (1971, p. 155) has noted the significance of this ISA which crams "every 'citizen' with daily doses of nationalism, chauvinism, liberalism, moralism, etc, by means of the press, the radio and television." It is a measure of the success of the communications ISA that in the United Kingdom, the decidedly *right-wing* tabloid newspapers are read by approximately 90% of mass tabloid newspaper readers (Bilton, 2007, p. 7). Althusser (1971) has also highlighted the cultural ISA as having a similar cramming role. With respect to this latter ISA, Althusser specifies "the role of sport in chauvinism [as being] of the first importance" (p. 155). In the case of the United Kingdom, sport is of paramount importance. The (mainly male) working class is preoccupied with sport—particularly football. If there

were the same enthusiasm for socialist change, with equal numbers of women involved, we would indeed be in a revolutionary situation.

7. Marxists differentiate between the economic base or infrastructure—the capitalist economy—and the superstructure, of which the ISAs form part.

8. The adjective "Bolivarian" is derived from Bolivar. Simon Bolivar, an anti-colonialist revolutionary of Basque origin, was born in Caracas in 1783. In 1819, he created the Angostura Congress which founded Gran Colombia (a federation of present-day Venezuela, Colombia, Panama, and Ecuador).

9. Chávez was elected President in 1998, and assumed office in February, 1999. He was re-elected in 2000 and in 2006. There was a failed right-wing coup against him in 2002 (for an analysis, see the video by Bartley & O'Briain, 2003).

10. I had the privilege to teach a course at UBV for a week in 2006. The course was entitled *Introduction to World Systems: Global Imperial Capitalism or International Socialist Equality: Issues, and Implications for Education*. Standards are very high—with seminar discussions and debate comparing more than favorably with universities I have taught in the United Kingdom and around the world. However, at UBV, advanced theory is very much linked to practice—that is, to improving the lives of people in the communities from where the students come. Students are almost 100% working class at UBV. While teaching there, I met a police officer who was studying for his second degree. He told me how the Chávez Government was humanizing the police force. He reckoned that Chávez has the support of about 75% of the Caracas police.

11. One thing that symbolizes the revolution for me was the way in which, at the start of my last seminar at UBV, one of the caretakers arrived to unlock the lecture theater, and then sat down, listened to and actively contributed to my seminar. His question was what percentage of the British working class did I think were revolutionary socialists. When I told him that the percentage was very very small indeed, he seemed somewhat bemused.

12. I have dealt elsewhere (Cole, 2008) with my own views on what should be the nature of 21st century socialism. Suffice it to say here that it must be democratic, feminist, anti-racist, anti-homophobic and anti-ageist. As the Venezuelan revolution progresses, it is important that there is a just sexual division of labor inside and outside the home (Blanco, 2007).

13. Ex-Prime Minister Tony Blair is calling for a different sort of "permanent revolution"—a permanent neoliberal revolution—in "public service reform" to meet the public's "high expectations." Blair spoke of frustration at "forces of conservatism" in public sector unions who end up competing "over who can flag up the most resistance to change" (BBC, 2007a).

14. In May 2007, Chávez was criticized by the Communications ISAs of the West for "closing down" the Venezuelan TV channel, RCTV (one among an estimated 95% of anti-Chávez media outlets). In actual fact, the Venezuelan Government has chosen not to renew its license, which expired on May 27, 2007, to broadcast via Channel 2. RCTV can continue to operate freely on cable or satellite, despite it's violation of numerous laws, including "incitement to political violence" (most notably its active support for the military coup against Chávez in April 2002), its non-cooperation with tax laws, and its failure to pay fines issued by the telecommunications commission. RCTV's activities would have violated most countries' broadcasting legislation, including Britain and the United States. Channel 2 is to be given over to public service broadcasting, open to all political parties (Venezuela Information Centre, 2007)

15. Support for Chávez, with varying degrees of reservation, seems to be unanimous among the left British revolutionary parties. An exception is *Workers*

Liberty, which has at least three objections to Chávez. First, Chávez is "a Bonaparte figure" (Hampton, 2006), who is heading "towards state capitalism, headed by a Bonapartist bureaucracy" (Hampton, n.d.), and the United Socialist Party of Venezuela (PSUV) "will be a top down affair" (Hampton, 2007). Second, "Chávez's combination of military personality-politics and limited social reforms from above fits a pattern"—Peron in Argentina and Vargas in Brazil, who despite taking some "left-wing" measures, were in many ways "very right-wing" (Thomas, 2006). Elsewhere Paul Hampton (n.d.) argues that "Chávez is a career soldier, with over 20 years in the military. That conditions his politics." Third, *Workers Liberty* has expressed is concerned about Chávez's "friends," including Mahmoud Ahmadinejad, the President of Iran (Hampton, n.d.), and Alexandr Lukashenko, president of Belarus (Broder, 2007). I will respond briefly to each of these three objections. With respect to the first objection, I have dealt with this at length and have argued that Chávez is not heading towards state capitalism, but towards socialist revolution. As far as the relationship between Chávez's military background and the RSAs is concerned, this needs further analysis, and a possible further amendment of Althusserian Marxism—the possibility of a benign military state apparatus. Indeed, there is a precedent for this in the 1974 Carnation Revolution in April 1974 in Portugal, when the post-Salazar dictatorship was overthrown by left middle ranking officers and other sections of the army, many of whom were Marxist. With respect to *Workers Liberty*'s last point, I have to say that I share their concerns about *some* of Chávez's friends. While I understand why, in his foreign dealings, Chávez is attempting to make alliances with anti-U.S. imperialist forces, such alliances are, for me, also problematic.

16. Not having the original Spanish version makes it impossible to know whether Chávez actually used this non-inclusive terminology. To put this in context, however, it should be pointed out that the 1999 constitution makes the use of non-sexist language obligatory (Blanco, 2007, p. 9).

REFERENCES

Althusser, L. (1971). Ideology and ideological state apparatuses. In *Lenin and philosophy and other essays (pp.127–187)*. London: New Left Books. Available at http://www.marx2mao.com/Other/LPOE70ii.html#s5 (accessed May 6, 2007).
Bartley, K., & O'Briain, D. (2003). *The revolution will not be televised* [Video]. Available at http://video.google.com/videoplay?docid=5832390545689805144
BBC. (2007a). *Blair seeking "permanent" reform.* Available at http://news.bbc.co.uk/1/hi/uk_politics/6763665.stm (accessed July 19, 2007).
BBC. (2007b). *Brown plans "world class" schools.* Available at http://news.bbc.co.uk/1/hi/uk_politics/6224364.stm (accessed June 22, 2007).
Bilton, J. (2007, May 14). Freesheet fiasco compromises the press's image. *The Guardian,* p. 7.
Blair, T. (1995, July 7). *Speech at NewsCorp leadership conference.* Hayman Island, Australia.
Blanco, J. (2007). Venezuela: Is our socialism "feminist"? *Socialist Outlook, 12.* Available at http://www.isg-fi.org.ukspip.php?article497.
British Venezuela Solidarity Campaign. (2006). *Bolivarian achievements: Socialmissiones.* Available at http://www.venezuelasolidarity.org.uk/ven/web/2006/missiones/social_missiones.html (accessed March 31, 2007).
Broder, D. (2007). *Chavez makes another friend.* Available at http://www.workersliberty.org/node/6674 (accessed June 21, 2007)

Brown, G. (2002). *The Guardian*. March 29.

Callinicos, A. (1976). *Althusser's Marxism*. London: Pluto.

Callinicos, A. (2000). *Equality*. Oxford: Polity.

Chavez: "I am also a Trotskyist." (2007). *Socialist Outlook Editorial. Spring.* Available at http://www.isg-fi.org.uk:80/spip.php?article430.

Cole, M. (1998). Globalisation, modernisation and competitiveness: A critique of the New Labour project in education. *International Studies in Sociology of Education, 8*, 315–332.

Cole, M. (2004). US imperialism, transmodernism and education: A Marxist critique. *Policy Futures in Education, 2,* 633–643. Available at http://www.wwwords.co.uk/pfi e/content/pdfs/2/issue2_3.asp#15 (accessed May 6, 2007).

Cole, M. (2005). New Labour, globalization and social justice: The role of education. In G. Fischman, P. McLaren, H. Sunker, & C. Lankshear (Eds.), *Critical theories, radical pedagogies and global conflicts (pp.3–22).* Lanham, MD: Rowman and Littlefield.

Cole, M. (2007). Neo-liberalism and education: A Marxist critique of New Labour's five year strategy for education. In A. Green, G. Rikowski, & H. Raduntz (Eds.), *Renewing dialogues in Marxism and education: Openings.* (pp.103–116). Basingstoke, England: Palgrave Macmillan.

Cole, M. (2008). Marxism and educational theory: Origins and issues. London: Routledge.

Contreras Baspineiro, A. (2003). Globalizing the Bolivarian revolution Hugo. Chávez's proposal for our América. Available at http://www.narconews.com/Issue29/article746.html (accessed May 4, 2007).

DfES. (2007). *Enterprise education in schools conferences 2007*. Retrieved May 19, 2007, from http://livegroup.co.uk/enterpriseeducation/.

The Duchy of Cornwall. (2006). Available at http://www.duchyofcornwall.org/managementandfi nances_fi nances_analysis.htm (accessed May 9, 2007).

Epstein, D. (1993). *Changing classroom cultures: Anti-racism, politics and schools.* Stoke-on-Trent, England: Trentham Books Feldman, P., & Lotz, C. (2004). *A world to win: A rough guide to a future without global capitalism.* London: Lupus Books.

Freire, P. (1972). *Pedagogy of the oppressed*. Harmondsworth, England: Penguin.

Gramsci, A. (1978). Unsigned, L'Ordine Nuovo. In Q. Hoare (Ed. & Trans.), *Selections from political writings (1921–1926).* London: Lawrence and Wishart. (Original work published 1921) Available at http://www.marxists.org/archive/gramsci/1921/03/offi cialdom.htm (accessed May 10, 2008).

The Guardian. (2001a, October 3). p. 5.

The Guardian. (2001b, November 6). p. 2.

Hampton, P. (2006). *Chávez wins election, but what about the workers. Available at* from http://www.workersliberty.org/node/7388 (accessed June 21, 2007).

Hampton, P. (2007). *Chávez presents timetable for new party*. Available at http://www.workersliberty.org/node/7925 (accessed June 21, 2007).

Hampton, P. (n.d.) *Support Venezuela's workers, not Chávez*. Available at http://www.workersliberty.org/fi lestore2/download/7636/venez010207.pdf (accessed June 21, 2007).

Harman, C. (1996). Globalization: A critique of a new orthodoxy. *International Socialism, 73,* 3–33.

Hatcher, R. (2006). Privatisation and sponsorship: The re-agenting of the school system in England. *Journal of Education Policy, 21,* 599–619.

Hearne, R. (2005). *World social forum 2005—The movements fight on*. Available at http://www.swp.ie/socialistworker/2005/sw236/socialistworker-236-3.htm (accessed May 4, 2007).

Hickey, T. (2000). Class and class analysis for the twenty-first century. In M. Cole (Ed.), *Education, equality and human rights (pp.162–181)*. London: Routledge/Falmer.

Hill, D. (2001a). Equality, ideology and education policy (pp.7–34). In D. Hill & M. Cole (Eds.), *Schooling and equality: Fact, concept and policy*. London: Routledge.

Hill, D. (2001b). The national curriculum, the hidden curriculum and equality. In D. Hill & M. Cole (Eds.), *Schooling and equality: Fact, concept and policy* (pp. 95–116). London: Routledge.

Hill, D. (2001c). State theory and the neo-liberal reconstruction of schooling and teacher education: A structuralist neo-Marxist critique of postmodernist, quasi-postmodernist, and culturalist neo-Marxist theory. *The British Journal of Sociology of Education, 22, 137–157*.

Hill, D. (2004a). Educational perversion and global neo-liberalism: a Marxist critique. *Cultural Logic: an electronic journal of Marxist Theory and Practice*. Available at http://eserver.org/clogic/200402004.html (accessed May 12, 2008).

Hill, D. (2004b). Books, Banks and Bulletts: Controlling our minds- the global project of Imperialistic and militaristic neo-liberalism and its effect on education policy. *Policy Futures in Education*, 2, 3–4, pp.504–522 (Theme: Marxist Futures in Education). Available at http://www.wwwords.co.uk/pfie/contents/pdfs/2/issue2_3/asp (accessed May 12, 2008).

Hill, D. (2004c). Enforcing capitalist education: Force-feeding capital through/in the repressive and ideological educational apparatuses of the state. In D. Gabbard & E. W. Ross (Eds.), *Defending Public School Education under the Security State (pp.175–189)*. New York: Praeger.

Hill, D. (2005). State theory and the neoliberal reconstruction of schooling and teacher education. In G. Fischman, P. McLaren, H. Sünker, & C. Lankshear, (Eds.), *Critical theories, radical pedagogies and global conflicts (pp.23–51)*. Boulder, CO: Rowman and Littlefield.

Hill, D. (2007). Critical teacher education, New Labour in Britain, and the global project of neoliberal capital. *Policy Futures in Education, 5* (2). Available at http://www.wwwords.co.uk/pfie/content/pdfs/5/issue5_2.asp (accessed June 20, 2007).

Kahn, R. (2003). *Paulo Freire and eco-justice: Updating pedagogy of the oppressed for the age of ecological calamity*. Available at http://getvegan.com/ecofreire.htm (accessed September 4, 2007).

Keynes, J.M. (2007). *The General Theory of Employment, Interest and Money*. London: Palgrave Macmillan. (Original work published 1936).

Lee, F. J. T. (2005). *Venezuela's President Hugo Chavez Frias: "The Path is Socialism."* Available at http://www.handsoffvenezuela.org/chavez_path_socialism_4.htm (accessed May 4, 2007).

Lepkowska, D. (2007April 3). Teachers promised freedom. *Education Guardian*. Retrieved June 20, 2007, from http://education.guardian.co.uk/curriculumreform/story/0,,2048219,00.html.

Martin, J. (2007, April 26). Chávez recommends the study of Trotsky, praises *The Transitional Programme. In Defence of Marxism*. Available at http://www.marxist.com/chavez-transitional-programme.htm.

Martinez, E., & García, A. (2000). What is "neo-liberalism:" A brief definition. *Economy 101*. Available at http://www.globalexchange.org/campaigns/econ101/neoliberalDefined.html (accessed May 6, 2007).

Marx, K. (1965). *Capital, vol. 1*. Moscow: Progress. (Original work published 1887).

McLaren, P. (2000). *Che Guevara, Paulo Freire and the pedagogy of revolution*. Oxford: Rowman and Littlefield.

McLaren, P., & Houston, D. (2005). Revolutionary ecologies: Ecosocialism and critical pedagogy. In P. McLaren (Ed.), *Capitalists and conquerors: A critical pedagogy against empire (pp.166–185)*. Lanham, MD: Rowman and Littlefield.

McMurtry, J. (2000). Education, struggle and the left today. *International Journal of Educational Reform, 10,* 145–162.

McVeigh, K. (2007, May 8). Pride and tears over rising toll of teenagers sent to war. *The Guardian,* p. 9.

Meiksins Wood, E. (1998). Modernity, postmodernity or capitalism? In R. W. McChesney, E. M. Wood, & J. B. Foster (Eds.), *Capitalism and the information age.* New York: Monthly Review.

Nixon, J. (2008). Statutory frameworks relating to teachers' responsibilities. In M. Cole (Ed.), *Professional attributes and practice for student teachers and teachers: Meeting the QTS standards (pp. 64–89).* London: Routledge.

Piper, S. (2007a). After the elections: A new party for the Venezuelan revolution. *International Viewpoint.* Available at http://www.internationalviewpoint.org/spip.php?article1188&var_recherche=chavez (accessed May 17, 2007).

Piper, S. (2007b). Venezuela: The challenge of socialism in the 21st century. *Socialist Outlook, 12.* Available at http://www.isg-fi.org.uk/spip.php?article496.

Rikowski, G. (2005). *Silence on the wolves: What is absent in New Labour's five year strategy for education* (Occasional Paper). Brighton, England: University of Brighton, Education Research Centre. (Available from ERC, University of Brighton, Mayfield House, Falmer, Brighton, BN1 9PH; email: Education. Research@brighton.ac.uk).

Smith, A. (1998) *The Wealth of Nations.* Oxford: Oxford University Press. (Original work published 1776).

Sun. (1995, July 21).

Sweezy, P. (1997). More (or less) on globalisation. *Monthly Review, 49*(4), 1–4.

Thomas, M. (2006). *"Left" backs Hugo Chávez—We say solidarity with the workers!* Available at http://www.workersliberty.org/node/7293 (accessed June 21, 2007).

Venezuela Information Centre. (2007). *The truth about RCTV.* Available at http://www.vicuk.org/index.php?option=com_content&task=view&id=186&Itemid=29 (accessed May 27, 2007).

Whitney, W. T., Jr. (2005). Education gets huge boost in Venezuela. *People's Weekly World.* Available at http://www.pww.org/article/view/7279/1/275/ (accessed May 13, 2007).

Wilpert, G. (2006, December 20). Poll: Venezuelans have highest regard for their democracy. *ZNET Daily Commentaries.* Available at http://www.zmag.org:80/sustainers/content/2006–12/20wilpert.cfm (accessed May 17, 2007).

Wilpert, G. (2007). *Chavez swears-in new cabinet for "Venezuelan path to socialism."* Available at http://www.venezuelasolidarity.org/?q=node/32 (accessed May 4, 2007).

12 Socialist Pedagogy

Peter McLaren and Juha Suoranta

INTRODUCTION

Socialist pedagogy (as well as Marxism) has had several conceptual and historical uses both in social theory and in various political practices. It has become fashionable even among leftist intellectuals to abandon the socialist movement as a rite of passage of becoming political "mature." In addition to the largely mythological uses that are functional for the reproduction of the transnational capitalist class, socialism and its pedagogical principles have been treated as a worthy political philosophy containing highly pertinent ideas, insights and arguments for social scientific analysis as well as for developing diverse social and educational practices that offer a much needed counterpoint to a society imprisoned by capital's law of value. In this sense the aim for truly critical social and educational theory has always arguments for the ongoing development socialist theory and pedagogy by recognizing their potential but also by their limitations. Our attempt to develop a radical humanistic socialism and socialist pedagogy—in part by de-writing socialism as a thing of the past—assumes the position that socialism and pedagogical socialist principles are not dead letters, but open pages in the book of social and economic justice yet to be written or rewritten by people struggling to build a truly egalitarian social order outside of capitalism's law of value.

SOCIALISM AND SOCIALIST PEDAGOGY

Studious observers of history's mighty tapestry of revolutionary struggle have born witness to numerous forms and practices of socialism and socialist pedagogies, often tightly and intricately woven in the public debate such that different patterns and designs become less distinct from one another, especially at a time of rampant historical amnesia such as ours. As much as we look forward to that fateful day that socialism will make its impress in all aspects of political life and that capitalism will be solemnly declared by historians to be part of the prehistory of socialist society, we readily acknowledge that the progenitors of socialism made their longest and most striking strides across the stage of world history during the Enlightenment (see Wilson, 2003).[1]

Most modern forms of socialism consist of comprehensive yet also conflicting visions and worldviews with distinct views of society, human beings, education and other earthly matters. But if there has been one gloriously protean idea—on recurrent leitmotif in the vast archive of socialism's variegated display of different social formations and political formulations and their corresponding pedagogies, it has to do with the centrality of the collective character of the social as well as the unequal nature of liberal capitalist society and its corresponding social arrangements.

Socialism throughout the 20th century largely has been seen as a casualty of Cold War politics. The vaunted political historians guarding the legacies of Western democracies—governments dedicated to buttressing social equilibrium while reproducing the privileging hierarchies and asymmetrical relations of power associated with capitalist states—have in the thrall of impulses towards Eurocentrism and revisionism, often ignored or denigrated socialism as a desirable or even distinctive ideology, revolutionary praxis or radical philosophy. Particularly in North America, socialism and its educational principles, polemics and practices have often been viewed by mainstream historians as ultimate threats to capitalist democracies, whose desideratum is the boundless freedom to accumulate capital's surplus value for private gain (and whose own history is replete with fascism, genocide, war and hunger). Socialism as an ideology continues to be viewed with intensifying urgency by the Bush administration, as reflected (to cite only one example) in the tendentious misrepresentation of the push towards socialism for the 21st century by the government of Venezuelan President Hugo Chávez. Consequently, the calumniating commentaries coming out of the Western corporate media have frequently demonized socialism as an atavistic remnant from the swampland of prehistory—as a half-living, half-dead monstrosity still stalking humankind and the new world order, despite the progressive rationalization of social life under capitalism. Part of this has to do with the failure of the political left in the United States, who not only have failed to deliver capitalist society from its gangrene of racism, sexism, fascism and homophobia, but also have been unable to rid themselves of the establishment propaganda and political untruths that have tended to become "part of the left's own intellectual apparatus" (Herman, 1997, para. 19). But it is also because socialism has often been conflated unproblematically in the hoary rhetoric of anti-communism with despotic regimes and totalitarian police states—Stalin's Soviet Union, Pol Pot's Cambodia, Peru's Sendero Luminoso, and the regime of North Korea's Kim Jong-II being four frequently cited examples. (Of course no mention is made of the role of millions of deaths of innocent civilians in the malignant attempt by the United States to maintain authoritarian control over the capital system as a whole and to secure its position as the supreme power of global hegemonic imperialism, except to suggest that such regrettable slaughter is more the result of collateral damage [more in character with a pardonable solecism than a war crime] in the global war on evil and terror than a concerted attempt at obliterating any and all opposition to free market capitalism.)

Socialism and socialist pedagogy (as well as Marxism) has had several conceptual and historical uses both in social theory and in various political practices (see, Burawoy & Wright, 2000). Sometimes—as in the above-mentioned cases—it has been propagated as a comprehensive worldview often in rigid forms of dogmatic enunciations—in other words, as modes of "non-knowledge"—and as "bad faith" formulaic panaceas for social ills. Additionally, socialism and socialist education have been dismissed as a senseless and antiquated utopianism, with little relevance to contemporary incarnations of critical social theory, cultural contestation or oppositional praxis. It has even become fashionable among intellectuals in some quarters to abandon the socialist movement as a rite of passage of becoming politically "mature" and to display the new found disavowal of one's radical past and abandonment of one's socialist convictions in the most trite anti-communist rhetoric (i.e., by equating Bolshevism with Stalinism), as if in the expurgation of their past sins they had finally rolled back the iron curtain of historical deceit and exposed to the sunlight of their newly won enlightenment the mummified corpse of Lenin, turning it to dust under its dignified (albeit old-fashioned) black suit. Unleashing their incinerating assault of reason had finally put the stake in the heart of the Great Beast.

In addition to such largely mythological uses that are functional for the reproduction of the transnational capitalist class, socialism has been treated—mainly by those less convinced of capital's universal beneficence—as a worthy political philosophy containing highly pertinent ideas, insights and arguments for social scientific analysis as well as for developing diverse social practices that offer a much needed counterpoint to a society imprisoned by capital's law of value. In many of these contexts, socialism has been defined not as a doctrine, a body of readymade truths, or an ideology, but as an unfinished endeavor, and an open and subjunctive "what if" category in need of revalorization and resolute reconstruction. In this sense the aim for truly critical social and educational theory has always arguments for the ongoing development socialist theory and pedagogy by recognizing their potential but also by their limitations. Our own attempts to develop a radical humanistic socialism—in part by de-writing socialism as a thing of the past—assumes the position that socialism and pedagogical socialist principles are not dead letters, but open pages in the book of social and economic justice yet to be written or rewritten by people struggling to build a truly egalitarian social order outside of capitalism's law of value.

SOCIALIST EDUCATION'S GLOBAL REACH

Historically speaking, the most dramatic attempt at adapting and developing socialist pedagogy occurred in the Soviet Union, a Communist republic founded by Lenin's Bolsheviks during the October Revolution in 1917, and fatally brought to a conclusion by President Mikhail Gorbachev 74 years later. Socialist educational principles were designed to create a *homo sovieticus,* a term coined by Aleksandr Zinovjev, a severe critic of the Soviet system who maintained that the Soviet political system contributed to making its citizens lazy, jealous, crooked, indifferent, unreliable and opportunistic.

After the Russian Revolution in 1917, the Communist Party's Central Committee reformed the Russian educational system according to socialist principles. Soviet educator Anton Makarenko (1888–1939) quickly ushered Soviet educational thinking into the international arena. Socialist pedagogy attracted number of visitors around the world, especially from developing countries but also from the western world; among the early visitors was John Dewey who arrived in the Soviet Union in the summer 1928. In the book, *Impressions of Soviet Russia,* Dewey reported his experiences, having been particularly impressed by some aspects of the Soviet "collectivistic mentality," and the collusion of school and state. This concept fitted with Dewey's overall idea of schooling as a means of developing an "associated life," a term describing those educational processes which connected people to each other, provoking human interdependence by means of collective learning. Dewey might have had a romanticized picture of the Soviet regime—one that was not unusual in parts of the United States during the first decades of the 20th century. Many communist-minded working-class youth at the time were drawn to the romantic images of the Soviet Union "as a place where the country belonged to 'the people,' where everyone had work and free health care, women had equal opportunities with men, and a hundred different ethnic groups were treated with respect" (Zinn, 2005, p. 147). Of course, considering the long sweep of the history of communist police states whose real conditions of existence tended to controvert the import of its propaganda machine, we should be disappointed but not surprised. In the Soviet period, education was centralized like it is at present in many European countries, especially in Scandinavian Social Democracies; of course, schools and teachers have relatively large substantial and pedagogical autonomy inside the national curricula in the Nordic countries unlike the Soviet Union where the teaching of Marxist–Leninist doctrine was an important element of the Soviet school curricula. The underlying philosophy was built around socialist ethics that stressed the primacy of the collective over the interests of the individual. At first Soviet pedagogy promised moral preparation of life and was designed to guarantee the victory of the revolution; it "was expected to have intensive effects by transforming the behavior, ideas, and very identity of pupils during and after their time in the schools" (Ewing, 2005, p. 42). But in addition to the teaching of very positive socialist values, Soviet-style socialist education, especially in the years of Stalin, emphasized the ultimate in instrumental, bloodless and technocratic rationality, where the bureaucratic state in its rigid didacticism functioned as an uber-pedagogue bent upon turning out a citizenry that would unquestioningly accept its revolutionary goals and its retrograde practices of realizing them:

> The revolutionary dream of the Bolsheviks and the Stalinists was to transform the whole country into one huge workhouse or factory, which would be directed in a completely scientific-technological manner. In this utopia, politics were replaced with "scientific management" and practical reason (*phronesis*) was seen as a branch of modern technology, also as merely an application of general scientific laws. Such utopias were not Bolshevist in origin, but they were very common in utopia literature—both in socialist and non-socialist literature (such as Comte or Bellamy). Many men of practice like Benjamin Franklin, Henry Ford, and Fredrick W. Taylor were also interested in the idea of rationalising life in its entirety, not just the work or labour aspects of life. (Mäki-Kulmala, 2003, p. 307)[2]

Regis Debray (2007) laments the "Bolshevization" of socialist culture by the Communists and its "standardization" by the Socialists, claiming that socialist culture was, early on, "paradoxically attached" to an elitist and bourgeois (and even aristocratic) curriculum. He writes,

> Socialism was marked during the first half of the 20th century by an educational universe that despised technical knowledge, commerce, industry, and even maths, but taught Latin and Greek as living languages. . . . The didacticism, ponderousness and rigidity of Soviet discourse, its moralistic gloom, are what ensue when a school turns upon thinking and subdues it with an iron fist. The handbook becomes the curriculum, and the result is crude simplification, stereotypes and cant. (pp. 15–16)

While Debray's (2007) comments perhaps say more about his own bourgeois and elitist predilections than he would care to admit, it remains clear, never the less, that there was too little emphasis on human development in the Soviet educational system.

Other forms of socialist education influenced by but also independent of the former Soviet Union have been employed in various countries in different continents. Perhaps the best-known example in Africa is Tanzania under Julius Nyerere's (1922–1999) presidency. Nyerere was known in his country as *Mwalimu,* a teacher with a socialist vision of education. In the Arusha Declaration of 1967 he stated as follows:

The objective of socialism in the United Republic of Tanzania is to build a society in which all members have equal rights and equal opportunities; in which all can live in peace with their neighbours without suffering or imposing injustice, being exploited, or exploiting; and in which all have a gradually increasing basic level of material welfare before any individual lives in luxury. (Nyerere, 1968, p. 340)

Regis Debray (2007) has recently discussed the "scholastic implications' of political history as it concerns the history of the school in the struggle for socialism. He writes that

The "battle for education" always featured high on the left's agenda; socialism, as the pedagogy of a world-view, knew that its own survival was at stake here. Any militant enrolling in a school of socialist thought must first have absorbed the habits of the schoolroom. The socialist's code of honour was modeled on that of the good schoolboy: he who can put up with the boredom of the classroom will triumph over the class enemy. (p. 14)

While trade unionism and workers' movements clearly existed before the arrival of mass schooling, socialism as an educational project was a strong step forward along the path of socialist struggle cluttered by leaflets and cobblestones stained in blood. According to Debray (2007):

It was the educational project of socialism that lifted its vision beyond that of unions and guilds. Its parties were created on the strength of the conviction that class is an instinct, but socialism is a raising of consciousness. The job of the school was thus not incubation but production. This accounts for the intensive focus on educational questions. "For every school that opens, a prison is closed." The mystique of the emancipated and emancipatory school was a tribute rendered by the working-class parties to the bourgeois state. (p. 14)

Teachers were among the earliest socialist activists in Europe. Debray (2007) notes that

Numerous teachers . . . once hurried back and forth between blackboard and rostrum. The First International (1864) and the Workers' Educational League (1867) pooled their staff, premises and periodicals. One of the first acts of the Paris Commune was to appoint a Commission of Education, headed by Edouard Vaillant. Louise Michel, deported to New Caledonia with the Commune's suppression, immediately opened a school there for the Kanaks. . . . From its inception in 1920, the French Community Party recruited its star cadres from the ranks of schoolteachers and professors. The best-established branch of the International between the wars was the education workers' section headed by Georges Cogniot, a practicing Latinist. Mill workers had provided a focus for the communist imaginary during the first industrial revolution; miners and steel workers took over that role during the second. But it is the primary schoolteacher, with his Spartan or sententious modesty, who reveals the extent to which organized socialism's roots lie in the pre-industrial culture of the Enlightenment. (pp. 14–15)

Latin American countries have witnessed a number of significant experiments in socialist pedagogy over the past century. The quintessentially pukka socialist, Fidel Castro, whose early ateliers for socialism were the guerrilla encampments in the thickets of the Sierra Maestra, hastily installed by *los barbudos,* established universal public services after the victory of the socialist revolution in Cuba. In 1960, only a year after the revolution, Fidel decided to manumit a people enslaved by Batista's brutal capitalist regime; accordingly, he abolished illiteracy by recruiting 120,000 volunteers to teach illiterate peasant of all ages to read in the remote rural areas. Most of the teachers were high school students equipped only with books and gas lanterns. Public education, with over 98% literacy rate, is among the most impressive successes of the socialist revolution, especially given the 40-year-long U.S. embargo against Cuba.

Before the Cuban revolution, in the 1930s Mexico, the Partido Nacional Revolucionario (PNR), the precursor of the current Partido Revolucionario Institucional, promoted attempts to develop public education that was socialist in character. Mexican progressives and revolutionaries were inspired by the ideas of Soviet educational theorists. Mexican socialist pedagogy stressed collective learning and organization for adults and children, and the acquisition of productive habits through collective gardens and cooperatives. During the period of socialist education, a new curriculum for national history was implemented in order to emphasize the primary role of workers and peasants in the revolution. Schoolteachers and other educators were involved in socialist pedagogy, and became key movers in people's political mobilization (Vaughan, 1997).

In 1994, in one of the poorest states of Mexico, a few hundred members of the The Zapatista Army of National Liberation (*Ejército Zapatista de Liberación Nacional,* EZLN) invaded the regional trade centers of San Cristobal and Ocosingo in the state of Chiapas in order to put an end to their oppression. Taking their name from one of the great leaders of the Mexican Revolution (1910–1920), Emiliano Zapata, the Zapatistas view have placed themselves at the forefront of a 500 year-old struggle to resist imperialism and colonial power. The opening salvo of their struggle—a struggle that is aimed at controlling their own resources, including their land, and at winning the right to govern themselves according to their indigenous traditions—coincided with the signing of NAFTA and the removal of Article 27, Section VII, in the Mexican Constitution (see Hilbert, 1997) which had guaranteed land reparations to indigenous groups throughout Mexico.

Viewing the contemporary political system of Mexico as one that is overwhelmingly oppressive due to what they claim is its purely representative nature and glaring disconnection from the people and their needs, the Zapatistas founded a popular autonomous movement by creating their own government (which they claim exercises power from the "bottom up" rather than the "top down" and autonomous educational program independent of the neoliberal impositions of the national and international power elite. The true and authentic value of the Zapatistas' autonomous pedagogy, according to Roberto Flores (2006), is highlighted in the global context of capitalist attack on progressive educational reforms. The Zapatistas struggle for autonomous education, firmly rooted in applied socialist principles, is particularly appealing for it offers a concrete example to transition into a proactive mode of struggle opposing "the impositions of state power," (para. 13) and the stranglehold of neoliberal capitalism. Thus, as Flores states, "A new global system of oppression backed by overwhelming military force begs of all social movements an appropriate, proactive and non-violent model for resistance, justice and change that transcends national borders and promotes global change through a corresponding transnational strategy." (para. 13) In a new stage of capitalist decrease, a new analysis and look is needed for socialism, and its educational principles. The Zapatistas' autonomous method, as Flores puts it,

> does not focus on reforming nor on overthrowing a corrupt system but instead concentrates on building a new one. Zapatistas' main goal is the creation of autonomous community spaces within which participatory democracy dominates and a process of conscientizacion allow for the development of its own pedagogical paradigm. The Autonomous model aims to build protected spaces that are incubated from the destructive ideology of those in power to allow for direct democracy to create an autonomous pedagogy. A basic premise of the autonomous model is that autonomous education cannot exist outside of the context of the autonomous community. There is a dialectical relationship between the two in that autonomous education is part of building the autonomous community and the autonomous community helps to develop autonomous education. A corollary to this premise is that the autonomous community is interdependent with the autonomous municipality and the municipality interdependents on the autonomous region, etc. In this global context, where dependence is absolutely necessary, transnationalism is natural enemy to autonomy. It is no coincident that the Zapatistas rely so heavily on international (global) support and protection to their peaceful approach. (para. 18)

It is remarkable that when a certain Marxist–Leninist city boy and poet, Rafael Guillén, eventually known as Subcomandante Marcos, first moved to Chiapas as part of a plan to educate the indigenous people, he himself became educated by them (Gotlieb, 2006, p. 7). In this respect, the Zapatista pedagogy is not another top-down educational model lead by state, but exemplifies new dialogical and democratic principles of socialist education, especially those emphasizing localization of education and government by calling for "a move beyond solidarity to a consideration of the possibilities for linking multiple, heterogeneous struggles as well as for transformations between and within sectors and locales" (Bahl & Callahan 1998, p. 24).

In Nicaragua, the Sandinistas applied socialist pedagogy in their efforts to establish their society after the decades of U.S.-funded terror. In 1979, the Nicaraguan people, led by the Sandinistas, overthrew the brutal Somoza dictatorship (supported by the United States). The Sandinistas established a stable, pluralistic society in which the death penalty was abolished, hundreds of thousands of poor families were given titles to the land and schools were built. As noted by Nobel Peace Prize Laureate and playwright, Harold Pinter (2005):

> A quite remarkable literacy campaign reduced illiteracy in the country to less than one seventh. Free education was established and a free health service. Infant mortality was reduced by a third. Polio was eradicated. The United States denounced these achievements as Marxist/Leninist subversion. In the view of the US government, a dangerous example was being set. (para. 39)

Paulo Freire's prominent influence both in Latin America, Africa and elsewhere should also be mentioned. In his letters, Freire (1978) noted how most African countries were simply adapting, at independence, the old colonial governmental and educational systems and mind sets (which were still in place). During the 1970s he visited several African countries like Guinea-Bissau, and Sao Tomé and Principe where he worked "as a militant educator who tried not to separate his task from the liberation cause of the oppressed" (Gadotti, 1994, p. 47). He exchanged his pedagogical ideas also with President Julius Nyerere, and in his teaching remembered to refer to the Tanzanian experience, and the courage of the Tanzanian people in refusing to accept prefabricated educational solutions, and fighting against educational imperialism (see also McCullum, 2005). In Latin America, especially, Freire's inheritance has been—if possible—even more important than in other parts of the world.

Among the latest chapters of radical socialist initiatives in education on a national scale can be found in Venezuela's Bolívarian revolution. Venezuela's educational policy is based on the writings of Simon Rodriguez, the teacher of Simon Bolívar, and other radical educators such as Freire and others. The path to socioeconomic change in Venezuela has been in various ways different than almost any other revolutionary road in the past. As Marta Harnecker (2005) points out, "what is happening in Venezuela is a *sui generis* process that explodes preconceived schemes of revolutionary processes."(p.9). Among the unprecedented characteristics of the revolutionary process is its start with Hugo Chávez's overwhelming electoral

victory and popular support; this support has continued as important governmental reforms in areas of the constitution and the law have proceeded
apace, along with changes in economic, social, and educational policies.
A political vanguard party does not lead the revolutionary process, but
instead a former member of the military, who in the early 1990s organized
a military coup against the previous regime. The revolutionary process
integrates several political ideologies and is not guided by any one ideology,
that is Marxism, alone (Harnecker, 2005, pp. 9–10). If there is one explicit
ideology in Venezuelan politics it is Bolívarianism. It does not use the language of class struggle, or create class antagonisms but speaks for the new
integration of Latin America. Istvan Meszaros (2007) writes:

> Bolivar called equality "the law of laws," adding that "without equality
> all freedoms, all rights perish. For it we must make sacrifices." All this he
> professed in a truly uncompromising sense. And to prove with deeds the
> validity of his own deeply held principles and beliefs, he did not hesitate
> for a moment to free all of the slaves of his own estates, in his resolve to
> give as broad a social base as possible to the struggle for a complete and
> irreversible emancipation from deeply entrenched colonial rule. (p. 56)

There is no universally accepted definition for Bolívarianism, but in the Venezuelan case it means the following governmental principles: economic and
political sovereignty (anti-imperialism), grassroots political participation of
the people via popular votes and referenda (participatory democracy), economic self-sufficiency (in food, consumer goods, etc.), instilling in people a
national ethic of patriotic service and equitable distribution of Venezuela's
vast oil profits. Clearly these principles reflect the spirit of Bolivar's lifelong
strong views. Meszaros (2007) is worth quoting at length on this issue:

> Bolivar's "law of laws," legal equality, was considered by him absolutely
> indispensable for the constitution of a society that would be politically
> sustainable against the powers that internally tended to disrupt its poten-
> tial development, and tried to violate and even to nullify its sovereignty in
> its international relations. Moreover, he insisted that "physical inequal-
> ity" must be counteracted unfailingly under all circumstances, because
> it is an "injustice of nature." And he was realistic enough to admit that
> legal equality could not do the job of correcting physical equality beyond
> a certain extent and in a limited way. Not even when the legal measures
> introduced the legislators were of a fundamental social significance, as
> indeed his liberation of the slaves happened to be. What was required in
> order to make the given social order truly viable was the transformation
> of the whole fabric of society (pp. 57–58)

In recent years President Chávez has tried to eliminate corruption in
its various forms, and negotiate with the elite to get its participation to

the new democracy. He has stated strongly that the United States is a real danger for Latin America as well as to other parts of the world as it tries to impose its dominance and imperialist hegemony in the area by spreading the vicious capitalist plague in the name of freedom and democracy (Harnecker, 2005, p. 10).

The Bolívarian Circles, with over 2 million members, are the most basic form of participation, forming the backbone of the democratic revolution of Venezuela. Usually they consist of seven to fifteen people committed to the defense of the revolution and the mandate of the 1999 Bolivarian constitution, and unlike neighborhood associations, the Bolívarian Circles are involved in countrywide and international issues (Chavez, Rodrigo, & Burke, 2003). President Chávez describes Bolívarian Circles as drops of water which form a stream, and eventually, a river when unifying with other drops: "there should be a Circle on every corner, in every neighborhood, in every town, in the petroleum fields, in the factories, in the schools, in the technical schools, in the Bolívarian schools, in the bodegas, in indigenous communities" (Chávez, 2005, p. 162).

Chávez's educational reform is based on the themes of "coexisting, knowing, and doing." He has called upon fellow Venezuelans to reject the "imperialistic anti-values" of previous governments, and to "rescue the authentic Christian values, lost by the capitalist model." Chávez has also asserted that education is a "vital aspect" of the Bolivarian political program and his government is committed to improving the quality of the educational system and transforming its traditional project through the construction of 'Simoncitos' (preschools) as well as other Bolivarian educational institutions—from schools and high schools to universities and technical schools. In his weekly public speeches Chávez has blamed the capitalist media campaigns for filling the people with poisonous lies by teaching them to overvalue money and leading them to believe that the poor are a useless social waste. Chávez has stressed such values as unity, brotherhood and solidarity above competition and individualism (Wagner, 2005).

Greatly impressive are the Bolivarian Missions with their emphasis on human development and the creative capacity of all individuals to create democratic social formations able to address local needs in the context of a larger project of human emancipation by means of political transformation. These missions consist of anti-poverty and social welfare programs. We were fortunate to be able to visit some of them. In one year, the Chavez government was able to graduate 1,430,000 Venezuelans from Mission Robinson, a program launched in June 2003. Volunteers who work for Mission Robinson teach reading writing and arithmetic to illiterate adults using the "Yo Si Puedo" ("Yes I can") method developed in Cuba. This method uses a combination of video classes and texts which, in only seven weeks, bring students to a basic literacy level. Indigenous peoples are taught to read and write in Spanish and in their own languages, in line with the indigenous rights outlined in the 1999 Bolivarian Constitution, Articles 199, 120 and 121. (Mission Robinson

International has just been launched in Bolivia). Mission Robinson II provides basic education up to sixth grade, and Mission Robinson III teaches functional literacy and links these efforts to the creation of production units. Mission Ribas, a two-year remedial secondary school program (that teaches Spanish, mathematics, world geography, Venezuelan economics, world history, Venezuelan history, English, physics, chemistry, biology and computer science), targets 5 million Venezuelan dropouts. This program has a community and social-labor component, where groups use their personal experience and their learning to develop practical proposals to solve community problems. Unemployed graduates of Mission Ribas (known as "lanceros") are encouraged to enroll in Mission Vuelvan Caras (Turn Your Faces or About Face), where they receive training in endogenous development and are eventually incorporated into the formal economy. Mission Sucre provides a scholarship program in higher education to the most impoverished sectors of Venezuela, graduating university professionals in thee years as opposed to the traditional five years.

In sum, socialist pedagogy has a long and diversified history especially in accordance with revolutionary times in various parts of the world (see Ewing, 2005). True socialist pedagogies and revolutionary movements have always meant persistent struggle for social justice and radical humanization of society. In furthering radical humanization it still needs examples of vibrant movements like those mentioned above, and others, which join forces with revolutionary parties in reciprocal learning for political, economical, ecological, social, and cultural change. In this perspective, as Youngman (1986) put it, "learning is conceived as the product of purposeful activity within the environment, an activity through which people change themselves and their surroundings. . . . Socialist pedagogy is therefore founded on the learners' study of and participation in the struggle to control production and society" (p. 211).

AIMS OF SOCIALIST EDUCATION

While there is much talk about labor today, and the decline of the labor movement, what is important for educators to keep in mind *is the social form that labor takes*. In capitalist societies, that social form is human capital (Rikowski, 2005). Schools are charged with educating a certain form of human capital, with socially producing labor power, and in doing so enhancing specific attributes of labor power that serve the interests of capital. In other words, schools educate the labor-power needs of capital—for capital in general, for the national capital, for fractions of capital (manufacturing, finance, services, etc.), for sectors of capital (particular industries, etc.), or for individual capital (specific companies and enterprises, etc.), and they also educate for functions of capital that cut across these categories of capitals (Rikowski, 2005). General education, for instance, is intentionally divorced from labor-power attributes required to work within individual capitals and is aimed at educating for capital-in-general. Practical education tries to shape labor-power attributes in the direction of skills needed within specific fractions or sectors of capital. Training, on the other hand, involves educating for labor-power attributes that will best serve specific or individual capitals (Rikowski, 2005).

In so far as one of the central goals of socialist pedagogy is to challenge the canonical unfolding of a capitalized ideological hegemony, and its progressive integration into the historical flow of our everyday lives, it is important to note that capital needs to be described not only as the subsumption of concrete, living labor by abstract alienated labor but also as a mode of being, as a unified social force that flows through our subjectivities, our bodies, our meaning-making capacities. Schools educate labor-power by serving as a medium for its constitution or its social production in the service of capital. But schools are more than this, they do more than nourish labor-power because all of capitalist society accomplishes that; in addition to producing capital-in-general, schools additionally *condition* labor power in the varying interests of the marketplace. But because labor power is a living commodity, and a highly contradictory one at that, it can be re-educated and shaped in the interests of building socialism, that is, in creating opportunities for the self-emancipation of the working-class.

Labor power, as the capacity or potential to labor, does not have to serve its current master—capital. It serves the master only when it engages in *the act of laboring for a wage*. Because individuals can refuse to labor in the interests of capital accumulation, labor power can therefore serve another cause—the cause of socialism. Socialist education can be used as a means of finding ways of transcending the contradictory aspects of labor-power creation and creating different spaces where a de-reification, de-commodification, and decolonization of subjectivity can occur. Socialist education is an agonistic arena where the development of a discerning political subjectivity can be fashioned (recognizing that there will always be socially-and-self-imposed constraints).

From the perspective of revolutionary critical pedagogy (a term coined by Paula Allman, 1999, 2001, 2008) socialist education is multifaceted in that it brings a Marxist humanist and socialist perspective to a wide range of policy and curriculum issues. The list of topics includes the globalization of capitalism, the marketization of education, neoliberalism and school reform, imperialism and capitalist schooling, and so on.

Revolutionary classrooms are prefigurative of socialism in the sense that they are connected to just social relations in the outside world. Classrooms based on socialist principles try to mirror in organization what students and teachers would collectively like to see in the world outside of schools—respect for everyone's ideas, tolerance of differences, a commitment to creativity and social and educational justice, the importance of working collectively, a willingness and desire to work hard for the betterment of humanity, and a commitment to anti-racist, anti-sexist and anti-homophobic practices.

The core principles for a socialist pedagogy were set out by Karl Marx and Friedrich Engels in their *Communist Manifesto* in 1848: "Free education for all children in public schools. Abolition of children's factory labor in its present form. Combination of education with industrial production, etc." (p. 28) Marx did not write much about education as such, but since his time numerous authors in curriculum and policy-making have, over the years, appropriated from Marxist theory in advancing a critical pedagogy and socialist praxis.

The core idea of socialist education is its emphasis on the unity of human beings, and we are referring here to unity in the positive sense of "unity in diversity" as solidarity between people, or as a common good, and the equality of human beings irrespective of their class, race, gender, sexual orientation, or disabilities. An incipient socialist pedagogy can be seen in the learning tasks described by Stephen Brookfield (2005) in his book, *The Power of Critical Theory* (although Brookfield does not use the term *socialist* but *critical* to describe his pedagogy). The first task that of challenging ideology, is to set people free from the servitude of the repressive ideas. But as Brookfield reminds us, ideologies are hard to catch since they are tightly "embedded in language, social habits, and cultural forms that combine to shape the way we think about the world. Ideologies appear as common sense, as givens, rather than as beliefs that are deliberately skewed to support the interests of a powerful minority" (p. 41). Second, a socialist pedagogy helps students to contest aspects of hegemony that affirms political control in the hands of the rich and powerful. Here Brookfield is using hegemony in the sense of "the way people learnt to accept as natural and in their own best interest an unjust social order" (p. 43). As he aptly points out, "the dark irony, the cruelty of hegemony, is that adults take pride in learning and acting on the beliefs and assumptions that work to enslave them. In learning diligently to live by these assumptions, people become their own jailers" (p. 44).

Third, socialist education is directed at unmasking power. This is accomplished by facilitating people to read the word and the world analytically and critically, and encouraging them to acknowledge and act on the power that they already possess. "Adults learning the possibilities of their own power through sharing knowledge, experiences, tactics, strategies, successes, and failures" (Brookfield, 2005, p. 48) forms an important dimension of what we are called a socialist pedagogy. A socialist pedagogy helps students overcome alienation and creates the context for the struggle for human freedom, which can only exist in a non-alienated world. As Brookfield (2005) notes, "alienation is antithetical to freedom, and the abolition of the former is essential to the realization of the latter" (p. 50). Alienation does not describe only capitalist conditions but all the other forms of social life reducing human beings to commodities in the economical or infrastructure of capitalist society.

Fourth, a socialist pedagogy is learning about liberation. Although socialist education emphasizes collective action, it reserves in its pedagogical agenda a place for reflective distancing. It thus sees momentarily reflective privacy not as retreat from collective solidarity but a true revolutionary act, a deepening step into the real world (Brookfield, 2005, p. 51). The fifth task for socialist education has to do with reclaiming reason (p. 56). An impor-tant element of reasoning is to direct it towards a good cause, to criticize inhuman circumstances, and to construct a better world. Reasoning con-cerns all spheres of life, and can take various forms. In socialist pedagogy it can refer to basic literacy (reading, writing, math) and to economic, health, and media literacy.

And finally, one of the central tasks of a social pedagogy is practicing democracy as part of the overall process of furthering political and eco-nomic transformation. Whatever the final purpose, socialist education is always political in a strict and concrete sense of the term: "it is intended to help people learn how to replace the exchange economy of capitalism with truly democratic socialism" (Brookfield, 2005, p. 351).

Socialist education aims at facilitating human beings as capable of think-ing collectively, co-operatively, and in solidarity with their fellow human beings and often adopts an ecosocialist perspective with respect to the bio-sphere or nature. Socialist education fosters critical and analytical skills to comprehend the world, to read the world, and to act within and upon the world in ways that build the conditions necessary for a socialist soci-ety. In the context of socialist education critical thinking does not refer to isolated cognitive faculties, or new business liturgies found in management textbooks, but to social reality, in that its focus is on "common interests, rejecting the privatized, competitive ethic of capitalism, and preventing the emergence of inherited privilege" (Brookfield, 2005, p. 351). Critical think-ing can thus lead to the radical statements like the following by John Briggs (2005), a retired steel worker, and WWII veteran: "US capitalists, the wealthiest in the world, are at the same time the most savage, brutal, cal-lous bastards since the Nazi regime, actual inheritors of their ideology and racism. Only a conscious working class can end the rationale that greed is good, that war is necessary evil. . . . There is no solution without a revolu-tion by the workers of the world" (p. 4).

A more elaborated view on working class's possibilities to change the world is given by Yates (2004) who states that organized labor needs to meet more consciously its racist bias, conservative, even anti-left past (at least in the United States), and global challenges. The working class needs to edu-cate itself; not only by creating more opportunities for labor education, but also for diverse literacy in economy, media, environment, health, cultural and aesthetics. This will eventually further to a working class and human way of looking at the world and ability to right measures to various socio-political matters. Furthermore workers self-education raises class-consciousness, and overall interest in being-in-the-world, a sense of a leftist and just culture.[3]

Furthermore, the working class needs to co-operate in building "more labor-intensive, smaller-scale, more localized, and energy-conserving production" (ibid.). Other essential tasks for the workers of the world consist of "universal health insurance, meaningful job training, generous leave programs, universal education, and reduced working hours" (ibid.) In addition international solidarity and co-operation are high on the list of urgent tasks as well as environmental issues, for socialist education aims at the balance between human beings, and human beings and nature.

Socialist education assumes after Marx and Engels (1848, p. 28) that "the free development of each is the condition for free development of all." This ruling principle of socialist education and emancipation of all the people is based on the idea that the capitalistic mode of production has long reached its peak: Human beings have become alienated, and transformed into things. Socialization of the means of production is the condition of human freedom, and for the meaningful life at work and elsewhere (see Fromm, 1990, pp. 254–255). Socialist education combines hand and heart, and educates fully developed human beings who possess not only vocational and intellectual skills but also such human qualities, among others, as utilitarianism, solidarity, co-operation, mercy, faith, love, and hopefulness along with a sense of beauty, and respect of others regardless of their race, gender, religion, or age.

Although a plethora of conservative commentators and authors have claimed that socialism is dead, especially given the fall of the Berlin Wall in 1989, and the end of the Soviet Union in 1991, many socialist ideals live inside capitalist schooling and educational practices at the moment. Take for example such teaching and study practices as collaborative learning, study circles, forms of pedagogical constructivism, or action research. Many educational researchers, also mainstreamists, have maintained the virtues of sharing, co-operation, and helping others to learn, and that all students—children and adults alike—should get help, guidance and support according to their needs, and contribute according to their individual abilities (see Bruner, 1996). From the point of the view of socialist pedagogy it is not at all necessary "to make a few individuals into the 'best' and treat the rest as an undifferentiated mass" (Sennett & Cobb, 1972, p. 261). Radical socialist pedagogy restores the original meaning of "not yet," as the sign of the open horizon of the future. It is not a wish in the wind or perpetual optimism but educated hope based on the logic of practice: the practice of educators, factory workers, cleaners, and social workers and so forth.

What is needed more than ever today are pedagogies that connect the language of students' everyday experiences to the larger struggle for autonomy and social justice.[4] And it is imperative that such pedagogies, as they are put into the service of building socialist communities of the future, do so in the spirit of pursuing genuine democracy and freedom outside of capital's law of value. Many of today's socialist educators pursue locally rooted, self-reliant economies, designed to protect society from the corporate globalists. They work to decolonize cultural and political spaces and places of livelihood, to fight for antitrust legislation for the media, to replace indirect social labor (labor mediated by capital) with direct social labor, to live in balance with nature, and replace the dominant culture of materialism with values integrated into a life economy.

Socialist educators develop a vision of the future that transcends the present but is still rooted in it, one that exists in the plane of immanence, and not in some sphere of mystical transcendence. It attempts to "speak the unspeakable" while remaining organically connected to the familiar and the mundane. Socialist educators acknowledge the presence of the possible in the contradictions that human beings live out daily in the messy realm of capital. They seek a concrete utopia where the subjunctive world of the "ought to be" can be wrought within the imperfect, partial, defective and finite world of the "what is" by the dialectical act of absolute negation. Terry Eagleton (2005) makes a similar point when he writes:

> We cannot legislate for the future, not least because it is not ours, but the people's to create. Dreams of the future, as the Frankfurt School reminded us, too often confiscate the very political energies that are necessary for their very realization. Yet there is still something to be said for trying to speak the unspeakable. For the fact is that any authentic future must be to some extent in line with the present as well as discontinuous with it. If it is not—if the future is not somehow inherent in the material forces of the present—then it is just wishful thinking, a vacuous, purely gestural kind of politics. An authentic future must be feasible as well as desirable. Otherwise we will persuade men and women to desire uselessly, and so, like the neurotic, to fall ill of longing. In fact, we could claim that utopia is inherent in the present in at least this sense: that without some dim notion of justice, freedom and equality, we would have no standard by which to judge the present, and so would be incapable of identifying its defects The future is already potentially present in the shape of the blind spots and contradictions of the present—in its silences and exclusions, its conflicts and fragmentations. (pp. 21–22)

Socialist educators work toward a transformation of the social through a form of concrete as opposed to metaphysical transcendence, through entering into the subjunctive mode of "what-could-be." Because they refuse to venture beyond the given, their quest for the transformation of the present into a new social order is not utopian but concrete-utopian. Not only must socialist educators understand the needs and capacities of human beings—with the goal of satisfying the former and fully developing the latter—but they need to express them in ways that will encourage new cultural formations, institutional structures and social relations of production that can best help meet those needs and nurture those capacities to the fullest through democratic participation. Equally important is realizing through their self-activity and subjective self-awareness and formation that socialism is a collective enterprise that recognizes humankind's global interdependence, that respects diversity while at the same time builds unity and solidarity. Socialist educators strive to bring about changes in the economic, social and cultural order not by emptying out subjectivity but by making possible the full development of human capacities for the benefit of all (Gulli, 2005). Labor must cease to be exploitative and compulsory and become "productive at the level of a fundamental and general social ontology" (Gulli, 2005, p. 179). Thus, labor must cease to become a means to an end (as a means for the augmentation of value) and move beyond the realm of socially necessary labor to become, in Marx's terms, "the prime necessity of life" (as cited in Hudis, 2005b).

Revolutionary critical pedagogy is a socialist pedagogy but one that does not seek a predetermined form or blueprint of socialist society. Neither does it endorse the idea of the spontaneous self-organization of the multitude. It's praxiological reaching out is similar to what Michael Steinberg (2005) refers to as a "negative politics":

A negative politics . . . is grounded in the fact that our mutual self-constitution continues regardless of the ways in which we construe our experience. It opposes certainties and assurances of knowledge, but not in the name of either a different certainty or of a human characteristic that is presumed to lie beneath the social. It has hopes, not of a world that it already knows how to think about, but one that will not claim to be the culmination of time and that will not hold to ideas, ideals, or even values that seek to arrest the endless transformation of our lives together. It looks not to the perfection of detached knowledge but to an expanding attentiveness to embodied understanding. It is a path not to the future but to a deeper experience of the present. (p. 180)

Socialist educators seek to move beyond the struggle for a redistribution of value because such a position ignores the social form of value and assumes a priori, the vampire-like inevitability of the market. Value needs to be transcended, not redistributed, since a socialist society cannot be built upon the principle of selling one's labor for a wage. Nor will it suffice to substitute collective capital for private capital. As Hudis (2004a) argues, we are in a struggle to negate the value form of mediation, not produce it in different degrees, scales or registers.

CONCLUSION

Among the most essential and debatable questions in the future is the following: What is the role of economy in developing socialist societies and education? In the debate some have advocated centralized state control of the economy, that is, the state's ownership of the means of production, others have emphasized workers' councils and co-operatives controlling their own economic means as in some experiments in Latin America. Yet some have stressed balanced and politically (and globally) regulated market economy as in current social democracies in Europe where none of the governments lean towards a total state ownership of the means of production.

Socialist educators need also to answer an educational question, who educates whom in the future socialist society? A famous response was given by Paulo Freire (2005) who emphasized critical dialogue—as he puts it "loving, humble, and full of faith"—between student-teachers and teacher-students. In his problem-posing education as a humanist and liberating praxis he maintained that the oppressed and dominated people must fight for their emancipation (p. 86) by educating themselves *and* their educators who can be victims of their own alienated upbringing and consumerist-driven instrumental education. Students of higher education have also approached the former question by maintaining the possibilities of lifelong learning in the societies of postscarcity, largely in the spirit of young Marx:

> For the first time in human history everyone may be able to pursue their own educational ends at any age and for the goal of individual development. When we have freed ourselves from work without end, education isn't required to be only vocational. In the post-work world intellectual and aesthetic interests of students are primary. (Aronowitz, Esposito, DiFazio, & Yard, 1998, pp. 78–79)

In other words, socialist pedagogy stresses—against some populist claims about the socialist *homo economicus*—that people do not live on bread alone. Forms of art become forms of life both in the curriculum of socialist pedagogy, and in the quotidian existence of the population.

Socialist pedagogy defined as revolutionary critical pedagogy works within a socialist imaginary, that is, it operates from an understanding that the basis of education is political and that spaces need to be created where students can imagine a different world outside of capitalism's law of value (i.e., social form of labor), where alternatives to capitalism and capitalist institutions can be discussed and debated, and where dialogue can occur about why so many revolutions in past history turned into regimes of terror. It looks to create a world where social labor is no longer an indirect part of the total social labor but a direct part of it (Hudis, 2005a, 2005b), where a new mode of distribution can prevail not based on socially necessary labor time but on actual labor time, where alienated human relations are subsumed by authentically transparent ones, where freely associated individuals can successfully work towards a permanent revolution, where the division between mental and manual labor can be abolished, where patriarchal relations and other privileging hierarchies of oppression and exploitation can be ended, where we can truly exercise the principle "from each according to his or her ability and to each according to his or her need," where we can traverse the terrain of universal rights unburdened by necessity, moving sensuously and fluidly within that ontological space where subjectivity is exercised as a form of capacity building and creative self-activity within and as a part of the social totality: A space where labor is no longer exploited and becomes a striving that will benefit all human beings, where labor refuses to be instrumentalized and commodified and ceases to be a compulsory activity, and where the full development of human capacity is encouraged.

Socialist pedagogy can help to create a society where real equality exists on an everyday basis by challenging the causes of racism, class oppression, and sexism and their association with the exploitation of labor demands. A socialist pedagogy offers tools for critical teachers and cultural workers to re-examine capitalist schooling in the contextual specificity of global capitalist relations. Critical educators recognize that schools as social sites are linked to wider social and political struggles in society and that such struggles have a global reach. Here the development of a critical consciousness enables students to theorize and critically reflect upon their social experiences, and also to translate critical knowledge into political activism. A socialist pedagogy actively involves students in the construction of working-class social movements. Because we acknowledge that building cross-ethnic/racial alliances among the working class has not been an easy task to undertake in recent years, critical educators encourage the practice of community activism and grassroots organization among students, teachers, and workers. They are committed to the idea that the task of overcoming existing social antagonisms can only be accomplished through class struggle, the road map out of the messy gridlock of historical amnesia. We support a socialist pedagogy that follows Marx's life-long struggle of liberating ordinary people from their commodity-form within relations of exchange, and working towards their valorization as a use value for peoples' self-development and self-realization.

NOTES

This is a significantly expanded and revisited version of Juha Suoranta and Peter McLaren (2006). Socialist Pedagogy in *Public Resistance, 2*(1). Available at: http://web.mac.com/publicresistance/iWeb/publicresistance/Public%20Resistance.html. It also incorporates some sections taken from Peter McLaren. (2007). The Future of the Past: Reflections on the Present State of Empire and Pedagogy. In Peter McLaren and Joe Kincheloe (Eds.), *Critical Pedagogy: Where Are We Now?* (pp. 289–314). New York: Lang.

1. Some of these modern forms of socialism include but are not limited to African socialism, Christian socialism, Communism, democratic socialism, guild socialism, humanist socialism, Islamic socialism, libertarian socialism, social democracy, syndicalism, utopian socialism and their diverse variations in such orientations as Angka, Castroism, Juche, Leninism, Maoism, situationism, Stalinism and Trotskyism.
2. If this "on-job" control was a widely shared dream, and a central aim of modernity throughout the world, since then it has been replaced by "off-job" control

by educating "people into robots in every parts of their lives by inducing a 'philosophy of futility,' focusing people on 'the superficial things of life, like fashionable consumption'" (Chomsky, 2005, p. 21).

3. Working-class education has regained interest both in "new working-class studies," and radical adult education (Russo & Linkon, 2005; Nesbit, 2005). A multidisciplinary field of new working-class studies finds its foundations and inspiration from the early 20th century worker education, Myles Horton's and Don West's popular education and in their fight for economico-social justice in the Highlander School, and Paulo Freire's pedagogy of the oppressed. In radical adult education the very same approaches and figures have long been part of the field's theory and practice, but often in rather domesticated forms. The prolonged aversion of social class has nowadays diminished in adult education discourse, and the concept of class gained new momentum.

4. An expanded version of some of the ideas presented from here on can be found in Peter McLaren. (2005). Fire and dust. *International Journal of Progressive Education, 1*(3). Available at: http://inased.org/mclaren.htm

REFERENCES

Allman, P. (1999). *Revolutionary Social Transformation: Democratic Hopes, Political Possibilities and Critical Education.* Westport, Connecticut: Bergin & Garvey.

Allman, P. (2001). *Critical Education Against Global Capitalism: Karl Marx and Revolutionary Critical Education.* Westport, Connecticut: Bergin & Garvey.

Allman, P. (2008). *On Marx: An Introduction to the Revolutionary Intellect of Karl Marx.* Rotterdam and Tapei: Sense Publishers.

Aronowitz, S., Esposito, D., DiFazio, W., & Yard, M. (1998). The post-work manifesto. In S. Aronowitz & J. Cutler (Eds.), *Post-work: The wages of cybernation.* New York: Routledge.

Bahl, V., & Callahan, M. (1998, Fall). Minorities and mentoring in the postcolonial borderlands. *Radical History Review, 72,* 21–31.

Briggs, J. (2005). Say you want a revolution. *The Progressive Populist, 12*(1), 4. Retrieved January 6, 2006, from www.populist.com/06.1.letters.html

Brookfield, S. (2005). *The power of critical theory.* San Francisco: Jossey-Bass.

Bruner, J. (1996). *Culture of education.* Cambridge, MA: Harvard University Press.

Burawoy, M., & Wright, E. (2000). Sociological Marxism. Retrieved January 5, 2006, from sociology.berkeley.edu/faculty/BURAWOY/burawoy_pdf/sociological.pdf.

Chávez, H. (2005). *Understanding the Venezuelan revolution. Hugo Chávez talks to Marta Harnecker.* New York: Monthly Review Press.

Chavez, R., & Burke, T. (2003). The Bolivarian circles. *Znet.* Retrieved March 1, 2006, from www.zmag.org/content/showarticle.cfm?SectionID=45&ItemID=3971.

Chomsky, N. (2005). *Imperial ambitions. Interviews with David Barsamiam.* New York: Metropolitan Books.

Debray, R. (2007, July/August). Socialism and print. *New Left Review, 46,* 5–28.

Dewey, J. (1929). *Impressions of Soviet Russia and the revolutionary world.* Retrieved January 5, 2006, from geocities.com/deweytextsonline/isr.htm.

Eagleton, T. (2005, June 13). Just my imagination. *The Nation, 280*(23), 20–24.

Ewing, T. E. (2005). Gender equity in a revolutionary strategy: Coeducation in Russian and Soviet schools. In T. E. Ewing (Ed.), *Revolution and pedagogy. Interdisciplinary and transnational perspectives on educational foundations* (pp. 39–59). New York: Palgrave Macmillan.

Flores, R. (2006). *Breaking the ideological hold. Zapatista response to Mexico's bilingual program in Chiapas.* Retrieved January 12, 2006, from www.inmotionmagazine.com/chbilin.html.

Freire, P. (1978). *Pedagogy in process. The letters to Guinea-Bissau.* New York: Seabury.

Freire, P. (2005). *Pedagogy of the oppressed.* New York: Continuum.

Fromm, E. (1990). *The sane society.* New York: Owl Books.

Gadotti, M. (1994). *Reading Paulo Freire.* Albany: State University of New York.

Gotlieb, S. (2006). A letter From Mexico: Happy new year. *Southside Pride, 16*(1), 7. Available at www.southsidepride.com/2006/01/articles/letterfrommexico.html.

Gulli, B. (2005). The folly of utopia. *Situations, 1*(1), 161–191.

Harnecker, M. (2005). Introduction. In H. Chávez (Ed.), *Understanding the Venezuelan revolution. Hugo Chávez Talks to Marta Harnecker* (9–14). New York: Monthly Review.

Herman, E. S. (1997). *Pol Pot and Kissinger. On war criminality and impunity.* Retrieved January 4, 2006, from www.zmag.org/zmag/articles/hermansept97.htm (01/04/2006).

Hilbert. S. (1997). For Whom the Nation? Internationalization, Zapatismo, and the Struggle Over Mexican Modernity. *Antipode* 29 (2) 115-148.

Hudis, P. (2004a). The death of the death of the subject. *Historical Materialism, 12*(3), 147–168.

Hudis, P. (2005a). *Directly and indirectly social labor: What kind of human relations can transcend capitalism?* Presentation at series on "Beyond Capitalism," Chicago. March.

Hudis, P. (2005b, September). *Organizational responsibility for developing a philosophically grounded alternative to capitalism.* Report to National Plenum of News and Letters Committee.

Mäki-Kulmala, H. (2003). *Vastakohdat vai kaksoset. Antipodes or twins: Soviet Marxism and modern western rationality* [In Finnish with an English summary]. University of Tampere, Finland: Acta Universitatis Tamperensis 950.

Marx, K., & Engels, F. (1848). *The Communist Manifesto.* New York: Barnes and Noble Classics. Also at www.marxists.org/archive/marx/works/1848/communist-manifesto/.

McCullum, H. (2005). Education in Africa: Colonialism and the millennium development goals. Retrieved January 4, 2006, from www.newsfromafrica.org/newsfromafrica/articles/art_9909.html.

Meszaros, I. (2007). Bolívar and Chávez: The spirit of radical determination. *Monthly Review, 59*(3), 55–84.

Mission Robinson International, retrieved March 18, 2008, from http://www.venezuelasolidarity.org.uk/ven/web/2006/articles/robinson_international.html.

Nesbit, T. (Ed.). (2005). *Class concerns: Adult education and social class. New directions for adult and continuing education 106.* San Francisco: Jossey-Bass.

Nyerere, J. (1968). Freedom and socialism. A selection from writings & speeches, 1965–1967. Dar-er-Salaam, Tanzania: Oxford University Press. Retrieved January 5, 2006, from www.infed.org/thinkers/et-nye.htm.

Pinter, H. (2005). *Art, truth and politics.* Retrieved March 19, 2008, from http://nobelprize.org/nobel_prizes/literature/laureates/2005/pinter-lecture-e.html.

Rikowski, G. (2005, February 14). *Distillation: Education in Karl Marx's social universe.* Lunchtime Seminar. School of Education, University of East London, Barking Campus.

Russo, J., & Linkon, S. (2005). *New working-class studies.* Ithaca, NY: Cornell University Press.

Sennett, R., & Cobb, J. (1972). *The hidden injuries of class.* New York: Norton.

Steinberg, M. (2005). *The Fiction of a Thinkable World: Body, Meaning and the Culture of Capitalism.* New York: Monthly Review Press.

Vaughan, M. K. (1997). *Cultural politics in revolution: Teachers, peasants, and schools in Mexico, 1930–1940.* Tucson: The University of Arizona Press.

Wagner, S. (2005). *Chavez promises new Venezuelan education model to combat imperialist values.* Retrieved January 5, 2006, from www.venezuelanalysis.com/news.php?newsno=162.

Wilson, E. (2003). *To the Finland station.* New York: New York Review Books. (See also: en.wikipedia.org/wiki/To_the_Finland_Station).

Yates, M. (2004). Can the working class change the world? *Monthly Review.* Retrieved January 6, 2006, from www.monthlyreview.org/0304yates.htm.

Youngman, F. (1986). *Adult education and socialist pedagogy.* London: Croom Helm.

Zinn, H. (2005). Howard Zinn on democratic education. Boulder, CO: Paradigm.

Zinovjev, A. (1986). *Homo Sovieticus.* New York: Grove/Atlantic.

Contributors

Xavier Bonal is associate professor in sociology at the Autonomous University of Barcelona. He is codirector of the Social Policy Research Group (Seminari d'Anàlisi de Polítiques Socials, SAPS) at the Department of Sociology of the same institution. He has worked as external consultant at the General Directorate of the European Commission and has been a visiting fellow in several European and Latin American Universities. He has published widely in national and international journals of education and is author of several books on education policy and sociology of education. He is currently Deputy Ombudsman for Children's Rights in Catalonia. **Correspondence:** xavier.bonal@uab.es

Simon Boxley is a PhD student and lecturer in education studies at the University of Winchester, England. He previously taught for over a decade in early years/primary schools in Hampshire. He has held various officers' positions in the National Union of Teachers at Association and Divisional levels, and he sits on the National Committee of the Alliance for Green Socialism. **Correspondence:** Simon.Boxley@winchester.ac.uk

Mike Cole is research professor in education and equality and head of research at Bishop Grosseteste University College Lincoln, UK. He is the author of *Marxism and Educational Theory: Origins and Issues,* (2008), and the editor of *Professional Attributes and Practice for Student Teachers,* 4th Edition (2008), and *Education, Equality and Human Rights,* (2006) 2nd Edition, all published by Routledge in London and New York. He is the author of *Critical Race Theory and Education: a Marxist Response*, 2009, forthcoming (Routledge). Correspondence: Mike.Cole2@ntlworld.com

Gustavo Fischman teaches in the divisions of Educational Policy and Curriculum and Instruction, at Arizona State University. His research interests are in the areas of comparative and international education, gender studies, and qualitative studies in education. Dr. Fischman is the author of two books and several articles on Latin American education, teacher education, cultural studies and education, and gender issues in education.

He is associate editor for the online journals, *Education Policy Analysis Archives (EPAA)* and *Education Review.* **Correspondence:** fischman@ asu.edu

Luís Armando Gandin is a professor at the Federal University of Rio Grande do Sul in Brazil. He is the editor of the journal *Currículo sem Fronteiras* (http://www.curriculosemfronteiras.org), has published five books and several book chapters and articles in many countries. Professor Gandin's research interests are in the areas of sociology of education, educational policy, and progressive educational reforms. **Correspondence:** gandin@ edu.ufrgs.br

Rich Gibson is professor emeritus in the college of education at San Diego State University and a cofounder of the Rouge Forum. He is the author of *How Do I Keep My Ideals and Still Teach,* now available free online from Heinneman, and co-editor, with Wayne Ross, of *Neo Liberalism and Educational Reform,* from Hampton Press. His, *Education, Labor, and Social Change* is due in 2008. **Correspondence:** rgibson@ pipeline.com

Dave Hill is professor of education policy at the University of Northampton, England, and chief editor of the *Journal for Critical Education Policy Studies* (www.jceps.com). He has (co-) written and edited around a hundred books, chapters and articles on education from a Marxist perspective. He is series editor for the Routledge series on *Education and Neoliberalism,* and also for the series, *Education and Marxism.* He is a long-time political and trade union activist, formerly a Labour Parliamentary candidate and regional higher education chair of the lecturers' union. **Correspondence:** dave.hill@northampton.ac.uk and also dave.hill35@btopenworld.com

John E. Lavin is a teacher in the school district of Philadelphia as well as an adjunct professor of education and English at Saint Joseph's University, Philadelphia. He has written on Latin American workers' rights for *National Catholic Reporter, The Philadelphia Inquirer,* as well as the *Journal of Individual Employment Rights.* He was director of education and communication for United Food & Commercial Workers union in Pennsylvania from 1989 to 1998. **Correspondence:** jlavin@temple.edu

Peter McLaren is professor of education at the Graduate School of Education and Information Studies, University of California, Los Angeles. He is internationally recognized as one of the leading architects of critical pedagogy worldwide. He has developed a reputation for his uncompromising political analysis influenced by a [Marxist humanist] philosophy and a unique literary style of expression. He is the editor and author of over 40 books.

His most recent book, co-authored with Nathalia Jaramillo, is *Pedagogy and Praxis in the Age of Empire* (Sense Publications, 2007). **Correspondence:** mclaren@gseis.ucla.edu

Dalila Andrade Oliveira is Professora do Programa de Pós-Graduação em Educação e da Faculdade de Educação (Professor in the Postgraduate Education Programme in the Education Faculty) da UFMG (Universidade Federal de Minas Gerais), Vice-Presidente da Associação Nacional de Pós-Graduação e Pesquisa em Educação (Vice-President of the National Association for Post-Graduate Research in Education)—ANPEd, Coordenadora do Grupo de Trabalho Educação, Política e Movimentos Sociais do Conselho Latino-americano de Ciências Sociais (Co-ordinator for the Education Work, Politics and Social Movements Latin American Council for Social Sciences)—CLACSO **Correspondence:** dalilaufmg@yahoo.com.br

Greg Queen teaches social studies to high school students in Warren, Michigan. He was an active member in the production of the Rouge Forum newspaper and plays a central role in the Rouge Forum Conference organizing. He has made presentations at local, state and national conferences on high-stakes testing and the role of schools in a capitalist society. **Correspondence:** rumbagarden@ameritech.net

Bernard Regan was the National Union of Teachers National Executive Member representing inner London (1981–2006). He taught in secondary, primary and special schools as well as further and higher education. He is a member of the editorial boards of *Socialist Teacher, Education and Social Justice* and *Socialist Education Journal*. He has written for *The Guardian, Forum* and *Campaign Group News*. He was a founding member of the *Socialist Teachers Alliance* and was the *Cuba Solidarity Campaign National Secretary Latin America Conference 2005, 2006 and 2007* co-organizer. He is *Palestine Solidarity Campaign Executive Committee (Trade Union Officer)*. Currently he is undertaking research into the British Mandate Rule in Palestine. **Correspondence:** bernard.regan@btinternet.com

E. Wayne Ross is professor of education at the University of British Columbia, Vancouver, Canada. He is a cofounder of the Rouge Forum and a general editor of *Workplace: A Journal for Academic Labor* and *Cultural Logic*. His books include, *The Social Studies Curriculum; Purposes, Problems, and Possibilities* (SUNY press), and *Race, Ethnicity, and Education* (Praeger Press), and most recently *Neoliberalism and Education Reform* (Hampton Press) and *Battleground Schools* (Greenwood Press). **Correspondence:** wayne.ross@ubc.ca

Juha Suoranta is professor of adult education in the University of Tampere, Finland. His research interests include radical adult education and critical media education. Recently he has co-edited (with Olli-Pekka Moisio) *Education and the Spirit of Time* (Sense, 2006). Correspondence: juha.suoranta@uta.fi

Antoni Verger was awarded a PhD from the *Universitat Autònoma de Barcelona* (UAB) for his work on WTO/GATS and higher education. Since 2003, he has been a member of the research group "Analysis of Social Policies Seminar" that is part of the Department of Sociology of the UAB. Currently, he is a postdoctoral researcher of the AMIDSt (Amsterdam Institute for Metropolitan and International Development Studies) of the Universiteit van Amsterdam. His principal research topics are globalization and education politics, as well as education and international development. **Correspondence:** a.verger@uva.nl

Kevin D. Vinson is associate professor in the College of Education at the University of Arizona and co-author, with E. Wayne Ross, of *Image and Education: Teaching in the Face of the New Disciplinarity,* from Peter Lang. **Correspondence:** KVinson@u.arizona.edu

Mike Waghorne is the assistant general secretary of Public Services International (PSI), the international federation for public sector trade unions. He is responsible for much of PSI's policy development work, such as: the role of the state; public sector reform and modernization; structural adjustment; privatization and related issues; regulatory reform; (new) public management; and trade policy. **Correspondence:** Mike.Waghorne@world-psi.org

Terry Wrigley has worked in education for over 30 years, and is now a senior lecturer at the University of Edinburgh. His teaching, research and writing spans and connects diverse fields of interest: school development, pedagogy, curriculum studies, social justice. His latest book *Another School is Possible* (Bookmarks/Trentham) is both a sharp critique of a school system damaged by tests, league tables, market competition and privatization, and an exploration of creative, engaged and socially just pedagogies from around the world. **Correspondence:** terry.wrigley@ed.ac.uk

Index